The Railroad Skunk

Copyright © 2022 by Charles D. Caldemeyer
All world rights reserved

Cover design includes facial expressions derived from the photo animation technology at MyHeritage.com.

Cover and book design by Sarah Meiers.

No part of this book may be reproduced, stored in a retrieval system, or transmitted in any form or by any means electronic, mechanical, photocopying, recording or otherwise, without the prior consent of the publisher.

Readers are encouraged to go to www.MissionPointPress.com to contact the author or to find information on how to buy this book in bulk at a discounted rate.

Published by Mission Point Press
2554 Chandler Rd.
Traverse City, MI 49696
(231) 421-9513
www.MissionPointPress.com

ISBN: 978-1-954786-68-4
Library of Congress Control Number 2022900047

Printed in the United States of America

The Railroad Skunk

Lust, Wanderlust, and the Shady Faces of David Wilson Bethel

BY CHARLES CALDEMEYER

MISSION POINT PRESS

This book is dedicated to my father, Everett Samuel Caldemeyer,

who taught me to cherish my family history,

and to my uncle, Harry Drew Fisher,

who began this investigation.

Acknowledgments

This project has benefited from the help and input of many people, especially the ones listed below:

Laura Fisher, for the valuable primary source material she passed along.

Robert Caldemeyer, for his insights and criticisms, especially concerning historical medical practices, and history in general, at all stages of the process.

Drew Cherven and **Mary Beauchamp,** reference librarians at the Petoskey District Library in Petoskey, Michigan, who were ever willing to order microfilm and to assist in the process.

Steve Nielsen, librarian at the Gale Family Library at the Minnesota Historical Society, who provided me with numerous resources about the Minnesota period.

James Sterrett, who gave me a great deal of information about, and eyewitness accounts from, the Ralston branch.

Thomas Trapp, who provided history and photographs of the Rietman branch, as well as investigative assistance in Rincon, New Mexico.

Renee Johnson, whose almost offhand mention of her grandmother's name led to the discovery of the entire Hendricks branch, and reminded me of an important research principle — to turn over every rock, since big discoveries can come from inauspicious beginnings.

Caitlin McGuire Reid and her mother, **Damaris Walsh McGuire,** who provided much valuable material, both anecdotal and documentary, about the Price branch.

Carole Frances Bethel, who provided valuable information about the Reed branch, and who was happy to help her previously unknown cousin despite her increasing disability in the last years of her life. May she rest in peace.

Finally, and most importantly, **Ida Fisher Caldemeyer,** who assisted me with this project much more than I have indicated for the sake of the story, and whose example of persistence, humility, and honest devotion continue to serve as my inspiration. She was a dedicated wife and wonderful mother, and her kind heart and helpfulness were felt by many. May she, also and especially, rest in peace.

Note on Proper Names

The late nineteenth century was a turbulent time in America, and the reader should be aware of some characteristics of proper names of the period. First, men often went by their middle names. For example, David Wilson Bethel was Wilson Bethel on his first marriage license and later, when he went by 'Willis,' it is because he had altered his middle name. This practice often led to the transposition of first and middle names — as in Chapter 15, when Annie's divorce papers call her son "Harry Raymond Bethel," instead of his given name of Raymond Harry Bethel. Men also routinely signed their name with their first two initials (e.g., "D.W. Bethel"), and went by their initials in formal interactions.

Spellings of surnames during this period was not yet standardized, especially among immigrant populations, so the reader will see variations (e.g., McGinnes, MacGinnes, McGinnis, or Reitmann, Reitman, Rietman), sometimes within the same section. Some of this was due to local officials (census takers, for example) attempting to spell foreign surnames that were spoken to them in a heavy accent. It also came about as the immigrants themselves attempted to anglicize the spellings of their surnames in order to blend in with the English-speaking population. It has been my general practice throughout this book to transcribe, not correct, so the reader may see several spellings of the same name, or transpositions of first and middle names, within the same section. I have sometimes added notes to clarify things.

Note on Living People

People who are dead can no longer be victimized, especially by identity thieves and other unscrupulous folks. In writing this book, I sometimes came across the dilemma of how to discuss people who are still alive. Although there were times when their names needed to be mentioned, I have, as much as possible, tried to omit them from the discussion. There are plenty of dead people to write about.

Note: Non-italicized parts of this book are factual (or where speculative, noted as such) and they are documented by footnotes. All sections in italics are fictionalized creations that fit with available evidence, but for which there is no confirmation.

Contents

Introduction: _____ fmxi

On the Trail of the Railroad Skunk _____ fmxi

1. The Upstream Gene Pool _____ 1

2. A Little Help from Uncle Doc _____ 20

3. "If I Had Never Got Medicine into My Head . . ." _____ 30

4. "A Large Stout Well Built, Good Form Woman but Not Purty" ___ 45

5. Meanwhile, Back on the Farm _____ 64

6. "Don't Publish & Oblige Lou Hunnemeyer" _____ 78

7. The Railroad Skunk Goes West _____ 92

8. Mr. Flirt-with-all and Miss Uptodate _____ 107

9. "I Don't Know a Thing to Write You Now" _____ 124

10. Joseph Patterson Steele _____ 143

11. "A Smooth One" _____ 154

12. Dr. George Wilson McGuire _____ 172

13. The Death of Dr. George W. McGuire _____ 187

14. "March 28, 1920" _____ 197

15. The Wives of Willis _____ 213

16. The Downstream Gene Pool _____ 250

Epilogue: Still on the Trail of the Railroad Skunk	306
Bibliography	316
Appendix I: Maps	325
Appendix II: Genealogies	330
Appendix III: Marriage Licenses	340
Appendix IV: Handwriting Samples	347
About the Author	374

Introduction:

On the Trail of the Railroad Skunk

■ THIS INVESTIGATION INTO THE LIFE OF MY GREAT-GRANDFATHER began in the 1980s with my uncle Harry Fisher's curiosity about his grandfather. He had some old documents passed down by his grandmother, Joannetta Fisher, as well as the memory of some references made by his father, Durward Frederick Fisher, about *his* father, whom our family referred to as David Willis Bethel, when they referred to him at all. Harry wrote some letters of inquiry and even made a visit to Flushing, Ohio, accompanied by his sister Ida. The clues were tantalizing, but too disparate to assemble into a cohesive picture. Harry spent some of his retirement time on the project, but research such as this was extremely difficult prior to the electronic age. Many records and documents were on microfilm, which was laborious enough to look through, and many more were still locked in dusty file cabinets in musty storerooms, without indexes. There were no search engines to help the poor researcher out ("what the heck is a search engine?"). Harry received negative answers to his letters, and in 1998 he decided that chestnut farming, gem cutting, and playing Scrabble gave him plenty of ways to spend his remaining time, and he passed everything on to me. Thus, I was lucky enough to begin my research at exactly the moment when the internet was about to revolutionize genealogical study. This story of a misogynistic, sociopathic nineteenth-century con man could not have been assembled without twenty-first-century technology.

In 1998, we didn't know much more about D.W. Bethel than his first and last names, his approximate birth date, the town in Ohio where he grew up, and the fact that he had worked as a railroad telegrapher. Oh, yeah, and that he had married Harry and Ida's grandmother, Joannetta Fisher, bigamously. Early in the process of searching, when I discovered a David *Wilson* Bethel from Flushing, Ohio, Harry didn't even believe he was our guy. 'David Willis Bethel' was the name he had gone by during his time with Joannetta in Clarence, New York, and everyone assumed that Willis was truly his middle name. The Fisher family had no hard evidence of his existence at all after his final letter to Joannetta on September 22, 1897, although Harry seemed to recall that Durward had made a few trips to visit his biological father while the family lived in Wenatchee, Washington, from 1914 through 1931. He thought David lived in southern California, possibly because his letters from 1897 claimed he had a ranch not far from Los Angeles, and he expressed an affection for that part of the country. I began the project with these simple assumptions. But the story, like most true stories, soon became much more complex, and many assumptions proved to be erroneous.

I'm something of a family historian, and that's a role I'm happy to have grown into, but the truth is that while I have always been a student of history, I didn't pay much attention to my family tree when I was growing up. The large movements of culture's great actors seemed to me to be a grand story, only tangentially related to my own uninspiring ancestors. They were just dull, hard-working, (mostly) honest folks, almost all farmers and ministers, who stared severely out of their grainy photographs. When I was young, I thought they were kind of scary — one of my earliest memories is of a feeling of nausea that came over me when I realized that I was descended from the people in the photo below. All the stories of my forebears' challenges and successes seemed irrelevant to me — of course, most of the stories of old people seem irrelevant to young people.

Scary ancestors[1]: Frederick Samuel Caldemeyer II and his wife, Sophia Drees Wellmeyer Caldemeyer, from the *Caldemeyer Family History* (by the author's father), 1941

I remained unappreciative of my genealogy (and most of my older relatives) until the late 1970s, when it became one of the few ways to connect with my declining father, the original Caldemeyer family historian. His example and my fascination with why things came to be

---

[1] From Caldemeyer family papers. This picture dates from around the 1860s. The cameras of the day required sitters to hold still for long periods, which partially explains the expressions. Still . . .

as they are finally merged, and I began to develop an interest in my own family tree. Over time, I have come to view the stories of my ancestors as at least as true a record of their times as anything in the history books. Their experiences signified their eras, and they signed their names, albeit mostly in invisible ink, on the foundations of the life we know today.

They usually followed the rules, dutifully answering the census and other societal obligations. They married for life. Information about them from public records was either already known or easily obtainable. They tended to stay in the same place for years, and when they moved, they took their families with them. The only times their names appeared in the newspapers, if they appeared at all, were at birth, marriage, and death. They didn't indulge in get-rich-quick schemes, crimes, or cons for the sake of dishonesty.

They had little entertainment value. They were nothing like David Wilson Bethel.

At first, this study's purpose was simply to fill in the major blank spot in our tree. D.W. Bethel was never a subject of conversation in our family, but every once in a while, someone would ask my mother or her brothers a question like, "Why isn't your last name Bethel instead of Fisher?" There was the pat story that was trotted out whenever he was mentioned — a private detective sent by his first wife told the Fishers he was already married, and so he was kicked out of the family and divorced and never heard from again. Willis Bethel, the "good-for-nothing,"[2] that goldbricking, adulterous slave to his base instincts, selfish and deceitful — the family disgrace — don't know what ever happened to that guy. My mother, especially, was unaccountably ashamed of the grandfather she had never known, and always changed the question to emphasize the character of her father, who worked hard and advanced from *nothing* to the pinnacle of his profession with no help from his father, *in spite* of his father, mind you, the no-good bigamous skunk.

But wait a minute, Mom. If D.W. Bethel hadn't been a no-good bigamous skunk none of us would exist, including you and your father. How much of your smile, your charm, your intelligence, came to you via the D.W. Bethel bloodline? Where is the curiosity you display about some of your other ancestors? Don't you even want to know where and when he died, and what of? (By the way, her answer was always, "No!")

Since we can't choose our ancestors, I wondered why my mother and some other older relatives always tried to edit the family tree to focus only on the people whose lives met with their approval. Why judge them at all? It created an artificial hierarchy that was illusionary and unnecessary, a selective genealogical view that skewed the truth about who we are and where we came from. There seemed to be an agreed-upon pact among my older relatives on this classification system. Some ancestors were always all right, while others were always questionable, and just the mentioning of a name would trigger the appropriate response, whether it was a fond smile or a disdainful shrug. Relatives on the A list did not screw up or test boundaries — that would indicate otherness — those were the losers in pile B. It was a

---

2 Letter, Anna Fisher Schurr-Eva Katherine Wiley to Alida Fisher, September 27, 1949, from Fisher family papers.

system that saw our genealogy in absolutes and ignored nuance.

David Willis Bethel's memory was certainly its biggest target. But there were other examples, too, like our Dearborn ancestors, who had come back into the U.S. after moving to Canada around the Revolutionary War. We were told that they must have been Tories, and the conversation ended there.³ Walter, Harry and Ida's uncle, was a more contemporary target. He was a free spirit, and though raised on a farm, he was an aspiring writer who despised farm life. Legend has it that he actually planted a Michigan weed (I don't know the species, but it probably wasn't what you are thinking — this was in the 1930s) and cultivated it, even built a fence around it, just to mock the farmers in the area. I'm guessing they probably didn't feel the shame he intended, but that they did think Walter was an odd duck. Later, his indiscretions with an underage girl almost cost him the farm when her father threatened to sue. Whenever his name came up, the room went silent. Maybe that was a good thing in Walter's case (I really didn't want the details), but other relatives also fell, to varying degrees, into the circle of disapproval, and for offenses less egregious than bigamy or treason or acting like a deviant, self-absorbed idiot. Just not living up to your potential or being involved in a pursuit that wasn't viewed as productive would turn on the judgment machine. And while David W. Bethel's memory could at least find peace in family excommunication, Walter's and the rest had to endure the purgatory of family marginalization, forever remaining the scorned relatives in pile B.

My main problem was not that the family did the members of its tree an injustice by failing to extend an understanding hand — people whose selfish actions hurt others deserve all the condemnation (and whatever else) that happens to them. But from a historical point of view, the family did itself an injustice by gold-plating some members and blackballing others. It just wasn't honest. I wanted to know who my ancestors really were, defects and accomplishments together, to understand the truth about my origins, and so to find that truth in myself. That's the beauty of genealogical study, after all. It was unreasonable to assert that we were descended either from a very few unmentionable skunks or from a large crowd of saintly preachers and clod-kickers. But Mom only wanted people of good character in her heritage, and she was willing to rewrite history a little to make things that way. Since we get most of our information about our origins, at least initially, from our parents, I felt that her filtration of events was obstructionist, just as she felt that I was disrespectful.⁴

---

3   My later research has shown that Sherburne Dearborn, my fourth great-grandfather, served in the New Hampshire militia in the Revolution, and that he and his family moved to Canada afterward in search of cheap land, not out of any great loyalty to the British crown.

4   I have studied people (informally, not academically) for years, and one thing I've noticed is that some of us tend to feel, inexplicably, distinction at being descended from a person of significance, no matter what that significance was. Maybe the reasons for this phenomenon stem from the fact that life casts most of us as anonymous actors in a great drama (or comedy, depending on your outlook), and that any distinction, no matter how unsavory, remote, or disconnected from ourselves, makes us feel less abandoned to the unrelenting tides of singular existence and the inevitability of cosmic recycling. Being honest, it may have been a search for escape from that anonymity, unattainable though that goal may be, that also partially drove my interest.

And so, far from discouraging me, my mother's stone-faced omission of David Willis Bethel from the conversation just piqued the interest of her still-somewhat-rebellious son in the lost story. What's lying in the shadows, unnoticed and long ignored? As a result, here I am, writing a whole book about my least-deserving ancestor, partially in rejoinder to my family's shunning of him. Sorry, Mom.

If D.W. Bethel had turned out to be a simple bigamist who abandoned his first family in Ohio for a second one in New York, then disappeared into the mists of late nineteenth-century folklore, his story would not justify a book. But as more families emerged a deeper pattern came with them, the events became more outrageous, and my fascination grew accordingly. I soon discovered that I was not simply looking for my great-grandfather, but also pursuing a unique story.

At every turn, it begged the question of 'why?' What made him take such perverse delight in his marriage-and-abandonment pattern? Why did he think his actions would lead to positive results? Just as he was driven to deceive, he also tended to push things too far and get discovered, having to leave town in a hurry. Was that part of the thrill for him? I'm no psychologist, so I can't comment on his particular clinical issue, but I try to explore some of those patterns in this book.

There was a romance about the wandering me-first lifestyle of D.W. Bethel that made his story compelling. Our culture, unlike some older, more tradition-bound ones around the world, gives a certain respect to those who successfully assert their individuality over the strictures of society. We have built legends around lovable criminals like Butch Cassidy, the Anglin brothers, and D.B. Cooper, largely because our country was founded and populated by rule-breakers, and on some level we view the triumph of individuals over institutions as healthy. In many ways, D.W. Bethel's actions exemplified that entrepreneurial spirit, a restless energy that sought to beat the system.

But those who try and fail become the objects of our ridicule — you have to get away with it. This was a component of my mother's attitude — that D.W. Bethel was a ridiculous failure. From the Fisher family's perspective, since the marriage had been annulled and they had expelled him from Joannetta's and Durward's lives, since his name was erased from the family record, it was an easy stance to hold. But as the number of wives and children kept growing, I began to think that, in many ways, David Wilson Bethel did get away with it. Many of his wives kept the last name of Bethel (or whatever alias he happened to be going by at the time) throughout their lives or until remarriage, and their children had children, all named accordingly. Some of those families maintained a positive view of him, even though they didn't know what became of him. As records of his cross-country marriage-and-impregnation spree piled up, I began to call him Johnny Humanseed. Had he played by the rules and stayed in Flushing with Jennie all his life, none of those people would have inhabited the planet. From a strictly Darwinian perspective, it's possible to view David Wilson Bethel's life as wildly successful.

But if his story explores the uneasy relationship of the individual to his society, it also examines the limits of human conduct. The species certainly wants us to sow our seed, and people who break the rules may gain some admiration for asserting their individuality. But that same species also demands that we nurture our dependents and that we be accountable for our actions. As fascinating as his story was, he lost his connection to the very species he propagated because he systematically abandoned those responsibilities.

It became clear to me that D.W. Bethel was operating under the influence of some pretty serious demons, and in the process abused the people in his life with a manipulative coldness to which most of us simply can't relate. In the detachment that history allows us, he is a captivating character. But in life he was a self-centered fraud who reveled in his deceits, abandoned the obligations he created, and hurt those who trusted and needed him the most. If I had known him, I would have hated the guy. In the end, I had to admit that I have more in common with the preachers and the clod-kickers.

From the beginning, I tried to approach the project in a disciplined manner, but it soon became clear that it would take years, and that complete organization of the process would be elusive, at best. My first step was to transcribe all of the handwritten documents that had been passed down in the family. David's 27 letters to Joannetta Fisher (who was called Nettie, or Net), written between November 1894 and September 1897, were my major source of information. But it was obvious that whatever was mentioned there had to be independently corroborated, since he was a pathological liar and his agenda in writing to her was to reestablish his position in her life, and especially the life of their young son, Durward Frederick Fisher (named Durward Frederick Bethel until 1893). As more records came online, I was able to cross-check some of the assertions in them with actual events. The postmarks on the envelopes, if they were legible, were also a valuable tool for tracking his movements, since he sometimes said or implied that he was in places he was not.

Our family had retained four other letters of great importance to the project. Three were to Nettie — two from Benjamin Franklin Perry, the postmaster in Owingsville, Kentucky, in 1894, and one from John Edwin Seib, her cousin and David's good friend and willing dupe, in 1897. The fourth was a note from the then-81-year-old Anna Fisher Schurr, Nettie's sister, in 1949 (after Durward's sudden death), that provided some eyewitness testimony. In addition, there were his lecture passes at the University of Buffalo Medical Department, a variety of railroad passes that gave his whereabouts at various times during the 1880s, and Nettie's Decree of Annulment from the court in Buffalo. There were also a number of random notes and letters to David, evidently left in their home upon his sudden departure on December 31, 1889.

Finally, invaluably, there was a photograph of David Wilson Bethel, who was using the middle name of Willis at the time, along with one of Nettie, taken in Buffalo around the time of their wedding in 1886.

David Willis Bethel and Joannetta Henrietta Fisher, 1886[5]

The historical records and newspaper websites that began to flourish in the beginning of this century, and which today are behemoth businesses, were my main sources of information for this book. The Family History Centers operated by the Mormon Church, where I could order and view microfilm, were also a great resource, as was the Ohio Genealogical Society facility in Bellville and the Ohio History Center in Columbus.[6] But David was extremely hard to track, and he tried to leave as little evidence of his trail in the official records as possible (although newspapers were a different story). He was an adept census-dodger, and he did not appear in any census (under his given name, anyway) after 1880, when at age 20 he still lived in his father's farmhouse near Flushing.

The census records did, however, produce ample information about his various abandoned families, and they helped establish something of a framework for his movements. Other records, especially the marriage certificates that came online in the early 2000s and the city directories that followed them, provided exponential leaps in my understanding of the

---

5 Photos from Fisher family papers.
6 The first sixteen years of this research was conducted while I lived in Mansfield, Ohio.

true story, as did the DNA matches that came along later. There remain tantalizing clues that may never be resolved, due to incomplete records in certain localities. The 1901 Canadian census in the railroad hub of Innisfil, Ontario, includes a "Mrs. David Bethel," living alone, born about 1860. These are suspicious circumstances, but there is no way to confirm that her husband was our David Bethel. As of this writing, I have been able to positively identify seven wives, and to obtain copies of the marriage licenses for all of them. Another wife is mentioned in the divorce suit of wife #6. All of these marriages, except the first one, of course, were bigamous. All the unions were prior to 1903, and all produced children, eight in all. There were probably more. In addition to the Canadian mystery, we know that he spent some time in Mexico, where the language barrier and incomplete record-keeping complicates research. In 1911, the last year we have official records of him, he was 51 years old, alone, and unlikely to change. You don't just give up a hobby you enjoy.

In addition to the internet searches, I did some traveling to places that were part of the story. Between 2000 and 2011, I went to the courthouses and libraries in Flushing, Ohio, and Owingsville, Kentucky, three times each, along with a trip to the Buffalo and Erie County Library and the Clarence Historical Museum in western New York. Kimball, Ohio, the whistle-stop where his first child Bessie was born in 1885, was only three miles off my route from Mansfield to my mother's place in Michigan, and sometimes I drove through it on my way past, just in case it yielded some inspiration. From 2013 to 2019, I made two research trips to the Newberry Library in Chicago (home of the remaining records of the Illinois Central Railroad), one to the Kansas Historical Society in Topeka (the Atchison, Topeka & Santa Fe) and three to the Gale Family Library at the Minnesota Historical Society at St. Paul (the Great Northern and the Northern Pacific). Following the second visit to St. Paul, I drove out to Sacramento, where I spent some time in the California State Library and the California State Railroad Museum Library, and along the way I stopped at local history centers in Fosston and Ulen, Minnesota, the giant Family History Center in Salt Lake City, and the tiny town of Austin, Nevada (birthplace of Annie Reed, wife #5). Each trip yielded solid information, and I was slowly able to piece together this story about the ghost known as David Wilson Bethel.

Every once in a while, some enticing leads emerged, only to disappear into the void again. On my second trip to Flushing I was in the town's library, in the local family history section. Frustrated and about to leave, I asked the librarian if anyone around there had information about the Bethels or Howells (Jennie Howell was D.W. Bethel's first, and only legal, wife). She said she didn't know, but Robert Howell was doing some genealogical work in his retirement. With the typical helpfulness of both librarians and small-town Americans, she called him up. I could hear him through the phone as she told him who I was and what I wanted. "I have to bring an overdue book back anyways — I'll be there in ten minutes," he said. He was an old country boy who dabbled in photography. He'd known David and Jennie's daughter Bessie, of course, from when she had taught Sunday School, and he thought his cousin might have some information about Bessie's father. He gave her a call and she invited us over. She lived near the library (every home in Flushing is near the library) and as I pulled up the hilly driveway, I was full of excitement. A gentle old lady answered the door. She offered us tea, and when Robert asked whatever had happened to Bessie's father, she said, with a sweet smile in a proud country way, "I know all about it." She left to get some records, coming back in about ten minutes with a stack of papers. "I got the whole story off the internet," she said, and my sky-high hopes began to sink. She then showed me printouts of my own online inquiries in various genealogical forums, where I had told what I knew of the story in hopes of getting more information in return. "He went to New York after he left here," she said with a sweet finality, and that was that. In the case of David Wilson Bethel, the 'whole story' is a very relative term.

Sometimes my trips yielded unexpected findings that clarified his campaigns of deceptions. In 2007, on my way back from Owingsville on I-75, I came across an exit for Sadieville, Kentucky. Remembering that he had listed the town as his birthplace on his and Nettie's marriage license, I pulled off to see the place. It's a railroad stop, and not much more, if there ever was one. As the road climbs into town it curves under a high trestle. There's a storefront row just off the tracks that forms the dominant axis of the town, with some houses dotted around off the high ground. City hall is in the old depot, which also has some memorabilia (I don't know how much business gets done there — it looks more like a tourist stop inside than a government office). The brightly colored sign out front reads, "City of Sadieville, established 1880." It turns out that the place was built strictly as a railway stop for the Cincinnati Southern in 1876 — records show that the post office was established there in 1878.[7] Of course, David Wilson Bethel was born in 1860, when exactly nothing was there. If a long-time railroad telegrapher from Ohio wanted to commit bigamy in New York, and if he had a friend who worked at the depot in Sadieville, this was a good town to list as his birthplace. Telegraphers controlled the flow of information in late nineteenth-century America. Any inquiry about his background as a Kentucky citizen could be misdirected, or at least he could be forewarned of it.

Sadieville City Hall, 2007[8]

---

7 Sadieville City History, cityofsadieville.com; U. S., Appointments of Postmasters, p. 426, Ancestry.com.
8 Photographs by Charles Caldemeyer, 2007.

I hope you enjoy this slice of our family history. I've delayed writing it until now because the search is still not completely successful — I set out to discover where David went and what he did after 1897, which has been only partially answered, and how, when, and where he died, all of which remains unknown.

If more information emerges it may have to be appended, but if I wait much longer, I might not get to write it at all (I am 68, after all). And my mystical side tells me that maybe this is all I'm meant to find, just as Harry found all that he was meant to, and that someone down the line of descent might be destined to find the rest. If they do, I hope they will finish this book. Collaboration across generations — from a genealogist's perspective, that would be the best possible outcome.

1.

The Upstream Gene Pool

■ *ELMER CREPT ALONG TRAIL RUN, his boots sloshing in the water and his head above the small creek's overhanging bank, stalking. He usually enjoyed a good hunt, but this was different. He remembered some of the war stories his uncles had told him, and he tried to control his breathing and keep a clear head, but all he could hear was his heart. He just wanted to get this over with, however it went for him afterward.*

He saw his quarry soon enough, walking down Flushing Road like he owned it. Elmer thought he might even have been whistling a little tune, celebrating the latest assertion of his 'rights.' The sight made his blood rise past all control, and he climbed from the creek, broke from the tree line and headed straight for his target. He was thirty years younger and a lot angrier. This was going to end now.

He was about fifty yards away before the man saw him and began to run himself. The sight of Elmer, holding his Winchester and making for him like an adrenalized deer, allowed for few doubts about what was coming. After another fifty yards, Elmer caught him and knocked him to the ground with the butt of the gun, then covered him as he looked up. Bill Sam decided that bully and bluster were his best bet in a group of bad options.

"You ain't got the guts, boy," he sneered. Elmer let him have another blow with the Winchester's butt, this time to the face, cutting his cheek, but it just brought out the mean in the older man.

"I get her whenever I want, boy. You'd best get used to that and move on off. If you're lucky, I might even forget you done that just now." He started to rise, blood dripping off his chin, but he saw the look on Elmer's face and decided to bow out of the world with one last insult.

"That boy Jesse come outta me, too, you know. You couldn't . . ." Elmer put a bullet in the man's forehead, and he crumpled back earthward. Enraged, Elmer racked the gun and sent a second round into his newly dead genitals.

It was almost sunset, and there was no traffic on the road, but the sound of the commotion and the shots reached the Hambleton farmhouse, and Elmer saw Tom Hambleton step out and look their way, then hurry toward them with a lantern in one hand and his own Winchester in the other. Tom took the scene in with a glance and knelt down to see if his neighbor was still alive. Elmer just stared, breathing hard, in a trance, until the old farmer was finished. Tom looked up grimly.

"He done it again?" he asked.

Elmer nodded. "While I was at work. He beat her somethin' fierce, then he took her right in front of our boy when she couldn't fight back no more."

Tom stood up and looked around. Dusk had mostly given way to evening, but the moonlight was strong enough to see by. "This was a long time comin', Elmer. Can't say as anyone in these parts would find fault with you for doin' it, but let's just make sure Sheriff Foreman don't have to get into it. Help me get him back into them woods." They each took a foot and dragged the body back across Trail Run and into a patch of thick underbrush, throwing some branches on top to keep the buzzards out. Best to have the only scavengers be ground varmints, so folks wouldn't know there was something dead back there.

It's easy for us to forget how hard life used to be. We take for granted things that would have been pure magic for most of human history. If you were born in nineteenth-century rural America, the chances were good that you worked in agriculture, and life was painful, dirty, and difficult. Technology, in the present sense of the word, was non-existent. The patriarchal class structure of the era made women and the poor especially vulnerable. They died routinely from a host of ailments that most of us have never seen. Medicine was a joke. As my brother Rob says, "People were tougher then."

The Bethels were part of the wave of migration across the Appalachians into the Ohio country in the early nineteenth century. They came from northern Virginia — the counties of Loudoun, Fauquier, and Stafford — looking for cheap land and a little more control over their lives. Many people who had no prospects back east proved their worth on the frontier. Some took advantage of the absence of law enforcement to pursue less honest opportunities, and to disappear without consequence. Coming from this 'work, cheat, or die' environment, some of the attitudes developed three generations later by David Wilson Bethel are easier to understand. The desperation a physically lazy and dishonest young man must have felt to escape the torturous grind of hardscrabble farming would have been overpowering.

Most of the Bethels stopped migrating once they got over the mountains. In northern Belmont and southern Harrison counties, just across the Ohio River from Wheeling, they lived in or near the little hilltop towns of St. Clairsville, Uniontown, Moorefield, Cadiz, Holloway, Rock Hill, and Flushing. Surnames such as Pickering, Kirk, Hollingsworth, Holloway, Howell, and Bethel were prominent in the early history of the region, and they are still common today. The topography is mostly steep, rocky hills connected by flat, rich bottom land laced with small streams. It tended to isolate communities and families, compel self-sufficiency, and foster suspicion of outsiders. Large extended families, many of whom stayed in the same area for life, contributed to the insularity. From the censuses, we know that most of the Bethel migration occurred between 1810 and 1820, although some arrived as early as the 1790s.

Norris Bethel, David's grandfather, was born in Virginia in 1807. His father Henry moved the family to Belmont County around 1815. Most of Henry's nine siblings, along with their father Edward, also made the journey. Henry prospered mightily in the Ohio country — at his death in 1846 he had a will of 171 handwritten pages that listed abundant household goods and three different farms.[9] He also had an appetite for more than just goods and land. He married Letitia Hickson in Virginia in 1796, but she died in 1797, probably in childbirth. In 1800, he married Anna Hall, and they had eight children, of whom Norris was the fifth. Anna died in 1815, but Henry married twice more. His third marriage, to Phebe Wilkinson in June 1817, may have been a little rocky. Five months after the happy couple exchanged vows, the following item appeared in a local newspaper:

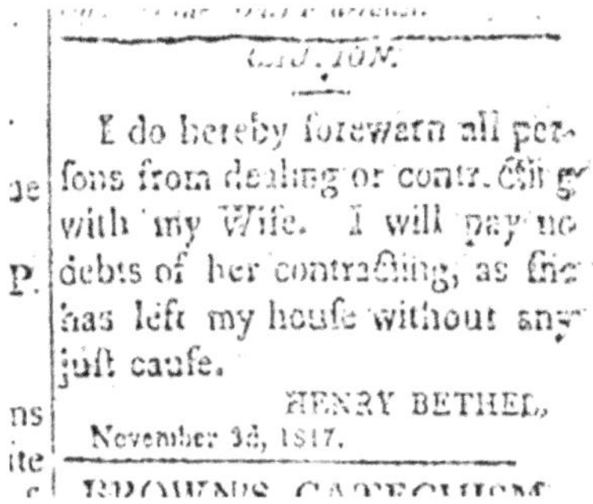
I do hereby forewarn all perfons from dealing or contracting with my Wife. I will pay no debts of her contracting, as she has left my houfe without any juft caufe.

HENRY BETHEL,

November 3d, 1817.

[10]

Transcription: I do hereby forewarn all persons from dealing or contracting with my Wife. I will pay no debts of her contracting, as she has left my house without any just cause.

Henry Bethel

November 3d, 1817.

Phebe was only 17 and Henry was 43, so that alone may be enough explanation.[11] There is scant information about her, but if family histories are to be believed they reconciled long enough to produce a daughter, Mialma, in 1826. Phebe must have been out of Henry's life, whether by death or desertion (divorce was almost unheard of at the time), by 1836, the year of his fourth marriage to Catherine Russell. Henry proved to be devoted to the welfare of his last wife and child above all others.[12]

Nineteenth-century custom recognized a man's will as his last chance to let his descendants know exactly what he thought of them, and unequal divisions of property were common. At Henry's death in 1846, he left the main farm near Rock Hill (a cluster of hilltop houses and a church about two miles west of Flushing) to Norris, provided he let Catherine have almost all the household goods, a milk cow of her choosing, and residence there, and that he see to her needs until her death. Henry included the admonishment that Norris should "keep her cow summer and winter and if her cow should dye [sic] or become useless he is to furnish her with another." If Norris didn't maintain her to her liking, Catherine could apply

9 Last Will and Testament, Henry Bethel, Flushing Township, Belmont County, Ohio, 1846, Ancestry.com.

10 This clipping is from an early Belmont County newspaper, from microfilm at the Ohio History Center, Columbus.

11 Marriage license, Henry Bethel and Phebe Wilkinson, June 1817; John Wilkinson family, Nunziato Family Tree, Ancestry.com

12 Carol and Jim Garde, *The Early Bethells and their Descendants, 1635-1994*, pp. 47-48; Ohio County Marriages, 1774-1993; Ohio Compiled Marriage Index, 1803-1900, Ancestry.com; Find a Grave Memorial 114310733, Findagrave.com.

to the court to have the farm sold and use the proceeds to support herself. At Catherine's death, Norris was to pay Mialma five hundred dollars (about $15,000 today).[13] Another larger farm was to be divided equally between Norris's older brothers, Edward and Braudus, "by runing [sic] a line North and South Edward to have the east half and Braudus the west half." The third farm was to be sold, and the proceeds divvied up according to Henry's specifications. His oldest child, Elizabeth, got five dollars. Five mentioned grandchildren got twenty dollars each. His son Henry Jr. received fifty dollars, and his son Benjamin five. The three children of his deceased oldest son Barnet, age 16 to 23, were awarded one dollar each. Mialma was to receive an additional five hundred dollars (it pays to be the apple of daddy's eye), and the remainder of the proceeds were to be divided equally among all living children. Edward, Braudus, and Norris were co-executors of the estate. There was no mention as to what Elizabeth, Benjamin, and Henry Jr. had done to earn their father's parsimony, but it may have simply been proximity — they had all moved away, whereas the rest of his children still resided in the Flushing area.[14] Maybe Henry Sr. felt that they had abandoned him. Maybe they left to escape him. It seems possible that he was a difficult father.

Many of Henry's relatives also prospered west of the Appalachians. His father Edward was elected the first Flushing Township clerk in 1817. Henry's brother James, who had come to the Ohio country long before most, in the 1790s, was wealthy by his death in 1852.[15] Norris's brother Braudus turned his half-farm inheritance into $7,000 worth of real estate by 1850, and it had grown to $15,500 by 1860.[16] Throughout the 19th and into the 20th centuries, Flushing area residents named Bethel held distinguished positions in the community.[17]

Norris married Lucinda Jones, another Virginia transplant, in 1830, and they had six children, Henry (1834-1910), Elizabeth (1836-1887), William Samuel (1839-19??), Thomas (1840-1864), Virgil (1845-1912), and George Smith (1846-1902). All grew up on their grandfather's farm near Rock Hill. But Norris died only two years after his father, in 1848, at the age of 41. Three years later, Lucinda married respected local farmer and blacksmith David Deselms, who had been one of the witnesses of Henry's will.[18] A member of the large Quaker community in Flushing, he was also from Virginia, also recently widowed.[19] The Deselms and Bethel households comingled at the old Henry Bethel farm through the 1850s, and two Deselms sons, Spencer Brown and Truman Martin, became close friends with Thomas and Virgil Bethel, respectively. Virgil later named his first son Truman. Thomas and Spencer Brown Deselms served together in the 15th Ohio Volunteer Infantry in the Civil War. Thomas

---

13 Inflation calculator, westegg.com.
14 Last Will and Testament, Henry Bethel, Flushing Township, Belmont County, Ohio, 1846, Ancestry.com.
15 Last Will and Testament, James Bethel, Flushing Township, Belmont County, Ohio, 1852, Ancestry.com; *History of the Upper Ohio Valley, vol. 2*, p. 497; *A Centennial History of Belmont County and Representative Citizens*, 1801-1901, p. 273. James Bethel was often acknowledged in early histories as one of the pioneer settlers of the county.
16 Last Will and Testament, Braudus Bethel, Flushing Township, Belmont County, 1870, Ancestry.com. This total amounts to almost $500,000 in today's money (Inflation calculator, westegg.com).
17 J. A. Caldwell, *History of Belmont and Jefferson Counties*, pp. 377-381; *A Centennial History of Belmont County and Representative Citizens, 1801-1901*, pp. 272-278.
18 Marriage license, David Deselms and Lucinda Bethel, Belmont County, Ohio, November 12, 1851. Ohio Marriages, 1803-1900, Ancestry.com.
19 U.S. Census, 1850, David Deselms, Flushing Township, Belmont County, Ohio, Ancestry.com.

mustered in at the rank of Corporal, was promoted to Sergeant in 1862, and was killed in action July 3, 1864, at the Battle of Kennesaw Mountain in northern Georgia.[20]

Headstone of Sergeant Thomas B. Bethel
Marietta National Cemetery, Cobb County, Georgia.

George Smith Bethel, Norris's youngest child, also served in the war. He must have lied about his age to join the 12th Ohio Cavalry on September 2, 1863, about four weeks short of his 17th birthday. Although recruitment offices were open in nearby Harrison County, George traveled west to Guernsey County to sign up, presumably to avoid anyone who might know how old he really was.[21] Morgan's Raid had swept through southeastern Ohio the previous summer, coming near enough to the Bethel farms to cause a panic, and it's likely that those events, along with the desire to follow his older brother to war, played a part in George's decision to enlist. He would become an important player in his nephew's life, and we will revisit him in more detail in the next chapter.

Unlike his single younger brothers, Norris's third child, William Samuel, acquired family responsibilities that kept him from any involvement in the war except for draft registration. He married Mary Clara Wilson on April 5, 1859, when both were twenty.[22] The 1860 census finds them working a small farm in southern Harrison County, just across the line from Flushing. Their first child, David Wilson Bethel, was born on January 23, 1860. His middle name was an obvious tribute to his mother's birth family, and his first name may have been selected to honor William's stepfather. He was followed by three siblings — Luke Voorhies

---

20 *A Centennial History of Belmont County and Representative Citizens, 1801-1901*, pp. 120-121; Register of Ohio Troops - 15th Regiment Ohio Volunteer Infantry, Company K, pp. 502-503.
21 *The 12th Ohio Cavalry, Record of Organization, Services during War, & Roster, 1871*, pp. 26-27.
22 Civil War Draft Registration Roster, Belmont and Harrison Counties, Ohio, June 1863. Ancestry.com. There are two William S. Bethels listed on this page. William Samuel Bethel is at the bottom of the page. The other William S. Bethel was his cousin, William Smith Bethel; Marriage License, William S. Bethel and Mary Wilson, April 5, 1859, Ohio Marriages, 1803-1900, Ancestry.com.

in 1862, Clara Lucinda in 1872, and Franklin Sheets in 1875.[23] The family moved back across the county line early in the 1860s, and in the 1870 census William was listed as a laborer for a man named James Smith on a farm near Rock Hill. The Bethels and their children lived in the same house as James and his wife Dorothy, indicating a closer relationship than was usual for employers and employees. It seems likely that James, who was thirty-three years William's senior, was more of an older friend than a boss.[24]

Young David would have been expected to help his father do the work of the day, and a close connection seems to have developed between them. We know from his later letters that he had a high regard for his birth family, except for his brother Voorhies. And although it's hard to trust the letters for honesty about anything, other evidence indicates that William and David may have shared a special bond.

In 1880, the Bethels still lived in the Rock Hill area, probably in the same house (the Smiths were nearby, running a hotel). David, 20, lived at the farm, but his occupation, 'schoolteacher,' confirms his departure from farm life by this time.[25] He had graduated from the Normal School at Caldwell, Ohio, that year, and he taught, first at a school called Howell's, then at Kirk's.[26] These were local one-room schoolhouses, now long gone, named for the farmers on whose land they were located. Hiram Howell lived southeast of Rock Hill, and Kersey Kirk's place was just north of Flushing.[27]

A list of 'Rules for Teachers' in Belmont County schools from 1872 gives some idea of what his position must have entailed. Besides being required to abstain from drinking, smoking, frequenting pool halls, and getting shaved in a barber shop, teachers were expected to bring a pail of water and a scuttle of coal to school each day, to clean the chimneys as needed, and to whittle the nibs of students' pens, among other tasks. Rule 7 said, "Every teacher should lay aside from each pay a goodly sum of his earnings for his benefit during his declining years so that he will not become a burden on society." Sound advice, but a rule? It was Rule 4 that may have most captured David's attention — "Men teachers may take one evening each week for courting purposes, or two evenings a week if they go to church regularly."[28] In contrast to his later life, David Wilson Bethel probably exhibited a strong interest in religion during this period.

The Bethels attended the Stillwater Baptist Church at Rock Hill, which had been founded

---

23   U.S. Census, 1880, William S. Bethel and family, Flushing Township, Belmont County, Ohio; Birth Record, Clara Lucinda Bethel, May 3, 1872, Flushing Township, Belmont County, Ohio; Birth Record, Franklin Sheets Bethel, September 26, 1875, Flushing Township, Belmont County, Ohio, all Ancestry.com. Only Clara's and Franklin's births are recorded. This may have been due to several factors. It is possible that William and Mary's first two children were born in Harrison County, and that record keeping there lagged behind neighboring Belmont County. It is also possible that record keeping improved during the curious ten-year gap between Luke Voorhies Bethel's birth in 1862 and Clara Lucinda Bethel's in 1872.
24   U.S. Census, 1860, William S. Bethel, James Smith, Moorefield Township, Harrison County, Ohio; U.S. Census, 1870, William S. Bethel, James Smith, Flushing Township, Belmont County, Ohio, Ancestry.com.
25   U.S. Census, 1880, David W. Bethel, Flushing Township, Belmont County, Ohio, Ancestry.com.
26   The Belmont Chronicle, July 29, 1880, Newspapers.com; The St. Clairsville Gazette, April 14, 1881, July 28, 1881, from microfilm at the Ohio History Center, Columbus.
27   Belmont County Atlas, 1888, with land ownership recorded, HistoricMapworks.com.
28   Marguerite Davern, compiler, Rules for Teachers, 1872, from *Yesterday's Schools*, p. 24.

on the hilltop in 1835, although how often they went is, of course, impossible to know.[29] The church is still a going concern, and it stands in the middle of an eight-acre cemetery with many occupants surnamed Bethel. Most of David's relatives, some of whom we will discuss presently, are buried there.[30]

It appears from available records that William Samuel Bethel was never able to afford a farm of his own, but that he rented the acreage on which his family lived throughout his life.[31] None of William and Mary's four children ended up as farmers, possibly an indication of their father's lack of enthusiasm for the job.[32] The country was becoming less agrarian by the late nineteenth century, and other employment opportunities were available. William would certainly have recognized that David was smart enough to pursue work of a more genteel nature, and that his strengths did not involve physical labor. It's easy to believe that he was the favored oldest son who could do no wrong.

He must have moved out of the family home soon after the census. He was married, for the first (and only legal) time, on January 30, 1881.[33] The lucky lady was Eliza Jane Howell, who went by Jennie. Eleven years David's senior, she was the aforementioned Hiram Howell's daughter. It's hard to know what drew them to each other, but it appears that she was a fun-loving country gal with a strong rebellious streak. D.W. Bethel would have success throughout his life with women who were so inclined.

Hiram Howell, like the Bethels a Virginia transplant, was a prominent man in the area. Jennie was the youngest of his three children by his first wife, and she was still a baby when her mother died in 1850. Hiram remarried, and much of his attention was focused on his second wife and their five children.[34]

One of Jennie's two full brothers was killed in the Civil War and the other went on to become a successful local doctor, but she seems to have floundered. In the 1880 census, at age 31, she was listed as a servant in the home of local farmer Simeon Pickering and his wife Mary. The Pickerings were also originally from Virginia, and the Bethel, Howell and Pickering extended families were undoubtedly well known to one another. On the next farm over lived Simeon's 16-year-old cousin, Dillon Pickering, a longtime friend of David Wilson Bethel whose name would become the basis for his first alias.[35]

---

29 J. A. Caldwell, *A History of Belmont and Jefferson Counties*, 1880, p. 378.
30 Esther Weygandt Powell, *Tombstone Inscriptions and Family Records of Belmont County, Ohio*, Closson Press, 1969, pp. 15-18.
31 U.S. Census, 1900, William Bethel family, Flushing Township, Belmont County, Ohio, Ancestry.com.
32 Luke Voorhies Bethel worked as a mail carrier in Harrison County all of his adult life, Clara married a railroad worker, and Franklin Sheets Bethel was a coal miner.
33 Marriage License, D. Wilson Bethel and Jennie E. Howell, Belmont County, Ohio, January 29, 1881, Ohio Marriages, 1803-1900, Ancestry.com.
34 U.S. Census, 1850, Hiram Howell, Flushing Township, Belmont County, Ohio; U.S. Census, 1860, Hiram Howell, Robert Kirk, Flushing Township, Belmont County, Ohio, Ancestry.com. Unlike the rest of her siblings, Jennie lived with her maternal grandparents, Robert and Esther Kirk, in the 1860 census, although she was back with her father and stepmother by 1870. U.S. Census, 1870, Hiram Howell family, Flushing Township, Belmont County, Ohio, Ancestry.com.
35 U.S. Census, 1880, Simeon Pickering family, including Jennie Howell, Flushing Township, Belmont County, Ohio, Ancestry.com.

The wedding happened suddenly. Two notices of the event appeared in the Belmont Chronicle.

Transcriptions:
(Left): Bethel—Howell—Jan. 30, 1881, in Flushing, by D.C. Knowles, Mr. D. Wilson Bethel, of Rock Hill, and Miss Jennie E. Howell, of Flushing — all of Belmont county, Ohio.
(Right): The matrimonial fever is fast becoming an epidemic. On last Sabbath evening, Mr. Wilson Bethel and Miss Jennie Howell, had so violent an attack of the disease, that they hastened to the M.E. Parsonage, where Rev. Knowles made them one flesh. Will Mr. and Mrs. Bethel accept our congratulations?

We can see that he went by his middle name of Wilson at this time. It was common in the late nineteenth century for men to use their middle names in everyday interaction, while on more formal occasions they identified themselves by their initials. Wilson (as we will now call him, until the next chapter) subscribed to both practices. And as we will see, the process of naming and appropriating names would play an important role in his story.

The second of the above blurbs is our first glimpse of his need to be a local celebrity. We can infer from its familiarity that he was already well known to the editor of the Belmont Chronicle. Wilson Bethel was a show-off who loved to read his name in the newpaper. Between 1880 and 1883, when he left Belmont County for good, he was mentioned in personal and local news items of the Belmont Chronicle and the St. Clairsville Gazette at least 25 times.[37] By comparison, no other member of his birth family received any newpaper coverage during the period.

This pattern will be repeated at other stops — D.W. Bethel seduced editors as freely as he seduced wives. Late nineteenth-century newspapers, especially those in rural communities, served many purposes, and one was as local gossip centers. The snippets in the 'Personal Mention' section contained news of peoples' travels, visitors, and other notable,

---

[36] *Marriages*, and mention in the 'Personal Mention' section, the Belmont Chronicle, February 3, 1881, Newspapers.com; Marriage License, D. Wilson Bethel and Jennie E. Howell, dated January 29, 1881, Ohio Marriages, 1803-1900, Ancestry.com. One might think that these circumstances, along with the obvious dislike that he expressed for her in a later letter (D.W. Bethel to Joannetta Fisher #25, August 18, 1897), might mean that the union was a matter of necessity, but no child was born to the couple prior to 1885.

[37] There are no known copies from this period of any Flushing newspaper, where his proximity would have resulted in even greater media exposure than in the Chronicle or the Gazette.

not-quite-everyday doings of those who had established their local prominence through financial success, personal popularity, or because they were friends with the editor. Wilson belonged to the last two groups.

The Stillwater Baptist Church at Rock Hill in 2016. The site has been in continuous use since 1835.

But a career change was in order — the stern environment of the late nineteenth-century classroom was no place for a peacock. He probably started working for the Cleveland, Tuscarawas Valley & Wheeling Railway (known locally as the T. V. Road) in mid-1881. The following year, he became station agent at Bannock, also called Bruce, the two names being used interchangeably.[39] The tiny town is on the road between Flushing and the Belmont County seat of St. Clairsville, about seven miles from the former and five from the latter.[40] A transcription of a telegram from one of the higher-ups at the railroad, passed down in family

---

38 Photo by Charles Caldemeyer, 2016.
39 Emma E. Laughlin, *Place Names of Belmont County*, p. 24. The town was originally given the latter name, after Bruce Caldwell, the son of William Caldwell (the donor of the land and first postmaster), but "the name Bruce became confused with another town" on the railroad line, so it was officially changed to Bannock, because of Bannockburn's association with Robert the Bruce of Scotland.
40 Please refer to Appendix I, Map #1.

papers, reads, "D.W. Bethel Pls go to Bruce and look after it as well as you can until Mr. Rool arrives from Auditors office this telegram will pass you. Wm T. 5/12/82."[41]

There was a crisis at Bruce station, likely involving money (the Auditors office would not have been involved otherwise), and the company called on Wilson as an emergency replacement. He must have already been working as an assistant agent at a nearby station, and he did a good enough job remedying the situation at Bruce that the railroad reassigned him there on a permanent basis. He was 22.

We can only speculate about the skills he possessed to acquire a position of responsibility with so little railroad experience — less than a year earlier he had been a schoolteacher. It's likely that the T.V. had limited options in their employee pool.[42] But the normal process for a young man to arrive at the job of station agent was lengthy — on the Illinois Central Railroad at the time the average age at which a man assumed the reins of the depot was 35.5 years, after first serving as a clerk and then as assistant depot head.[43] It appears that Wilson was in the right place at the right time, and that the small railroad was comfortable assigning him more responsibility. From all reports, he was a natural at telegraphy, one of the foremost aspects of the job, and that, along with his people skills, must have accelerated his advancement. Throughout his career, he seems to have possessed talents that railroads found irresistible, at least initially.

Telegraphy provided many young men and women of the era with opportunities, "an escape route from the small towns to the big cities, and for those who liked to move around, it meant guaranteed work wherever they went."[44] D.W. Bethel would take full advantage of those benefits. Safety demanded that operators be accurate and fast, since this was the only means of communication up and down the line and trains used the same track going both ways. There was a pecking order among telegraphers based on speed and accuracy, and the best ones usually found opportunities in urban settings.[45] It seems likely that, as a good telegrapher who was comfortable remaining in rural assignments, he had value to railroads. Walter Licht writes that agents at small stations "were jacks-of-all-trades. If assistance was wanting, they would attend to switching, pumping, wooding, telegraphing, and to the rough work of hauling baggage and freight."[46] He probably did as little of that last item as possible. Agents also maintained the station, coordinated the schedule, and, of most interest to Wilson, they handled the money. This career sustained him well into middle age, and it gave him the mobility and control of information to mostly escape the consequences of his exploits. He may have even been considered a rising star, for a time, in the various companies that employed him.

---

41 Transcription of telegram assigning D.W. Bethel to Bruce Station, May 12, 1882. This is the earliest item that comes down to us from the papers he left behind.
42 The rural nature of the line, the newness of railroads in the area (Bruce got its station around 1880), and low pay probably all contributed to a lack of quality applicants.
43 Walter Licht, *Working for the Railroad*, p.151.
44 Tom Standage, *The Victorian Internet*, Kindle edition, Loc. 1437.
45 *Ibid.*, Loc. 1453. Commonly used names for the less skilled operators by their more adept colleagues were "plugs" and "hams."
46 Walter Licht, *Working for the Railroad*, p.91.

He must have seen the possibilities in arranging excursion trips, reduced-fare pilgrimages to various places of interest, early in his career. Passengers could go to see a sight for less money than usual, and railroads could guarantee themselves some full cars and good publicity, so they were beneficial to all concerned. The agent who arranged them, of course, was in a position to handle some extra cash, and we'll just leave it at that for now. In late summer 1882, the Chronicle published a long article about an excursion to Niagara Falls collaboratively arranged by the C., T. V. & W. and another railroad, and Jennie was listed as one of the local luminaries who made the trip.[47] Wilson was not mentioned, and we don't know if he was involved in planning the event, but he was certainly exposed to the practice at this time. Arranging excursions would become a hallmark of his later stops on various lines.

The Cleveland, Tuscarawas Valley & Wheeling Railway station at Bruce (also called Bannock). This photo dates from the early twentieth century.

But it was his "aptness for getting along with men," which railroad historian Walter Licht lists as the foremost attribute companies looked for in station agents, that was his greatest strength.[49] By all accounts, he was charming, quick-witted, and entertaining in conversation. This trait is less apparent in his letters — his writing was not nearly as persuasive an instrument as his charisma, although his literacy was likely above average for the time. Also, the purpose of his letters was to work his way back into Joannetta's life, and so they demanded that he address serious issues with more than a shrug and a well-timed joke. In person, he was

---

47 *Niagara Excursion*, The Belmont Chronicle, September 14, 1882, Newspapers.com.
48 Ohio Railroad Stations Past and Present (west2k.com/ohio.htm).
49 Walter Licht, *Working for the Railroad*, p.45.

believable even when he was lying, and he commanded long-standing loyalty from some of his friends even after his transgressions had become apparent.

One of those friends was William A. Hunt, the editor of the Belmont Chronicle. Twenty years Wilson's senior, he spent his early adulthood in Harrison County, and the familiarity of his post about the younger man's marriage suggests that he had known him before that event. The Chronicle began to seriously report on Wilson Bethel's life in fall 1882, soon after his arrival at Bruce. Hunt's little blurbs sometimes bordered on fandom.

Transcription: Mr. D.W. Bethel, the T. V. R. R. agent at Bruce, came near being killed by the engine of a wild train on the morning of the 18th. He was at Barton station when the train came up, and intended boarding it to ride home, but signalled go ahead, intending to jump on the calaboose. He changed his mind, however, intending to ride on the engine, but missed the catch, fell against the wheels, and was thrown, and narrowly escaped being drawn under and crushed. He received some pretty severe bruises, but sustained no serious injury, and continued his business as usual. The same train brought out the miners to the Wheeling creek coal works, and while shifting cars one of them fell between, and had his leg cut off at the ankle.

Transcription: Mr. D.W. Bethel, agent at Bruce station, on Friday, sold all the tickets on hand, and could have sold many more. He is accredited with 76 on that day.

---

50 The Belmont Chronicle, August 24, 1882, Newspapers.com.
51 The Belmont Chronicle, September 21, 1882, Newspapers.com.

> **BANNOCK.**
>
> D. W. Bethel, the agent here on the T. V., has moved to Mr. Wm. Ramage's about a mile east of Bruce. Somewhat inconvenient for cold weather, but there was no house nearer.

Transcription: D.W. Bethel, the agent here on the T.V., has moved to Mr. Wm. Ramage's about a mile east of Bruce. Somewhat inconvenient for cold weather, but there was no house nearer.

It appears that Hunt was trying to make a regional celebrity out of the young man at the train station, no doubt with his subject's encouragement. The fact that Wilson was new to the job may have led the editor to write about him in an effort to introduce his friend to Bruce residents. He may also have been trying to ameliorate an evident undercurrent of mistrust of the new agent.

St. Clairsville's other weekly paper, the Gazette, did not participate in the D.W. Bethel news pageant in fall 1882. It had printed a cursory notification of his marriage to Jennie, a small blurb about an auction in which he was assisting, and the schools to which he had been assigned when he was teaching, but it had left the fascinating details of the life of the man at Bruce station to the Chronicle. That changed in December.

Small-town newspapers of the day tended to be in constant, ostensibly friendly, competition with one another, and the Chronicle and Gazette were no exception. But like insecure artists, each was looking for opportunities to undercut the other's credibility with the public they both served. Business is business, after all. It all began with a local tragedy, and the first, but certainly not the last, controversy of D.W. Bethel's railroad career. On December 7, the Chronicle mentioned him twice. The first was innocent enough, a simple announcement that he was now teaching telegraphy to John A. Downing, the assistant agent at the depot. On the following page, however, this item appeared:

> **Collision on the T. V. Road, Between Maynard and Fairpoint.**
>
> On the T. V. road last Saturday occurred one of those accidents which are peculiar to the carelessness of either trainmen or telegraph operators. Engine No. 9, going north, and running as first section of a freight, collided with train No. 18—engine No. 21, running wild. The accident occurred just outside of the tunnel, about three miles from this place, below the mouth of Pogue's run. Engineer Thos. Wright was caught and fastened in the cab, having a foot crushed, several ribs broken, and a scalp wound, and was not able to extricate himself until assisted by other members of his crew. Mr. Wright is well known here, as having been an engineer on the Northern road, and his speedy recovery is wished for by his many friends. There were two other trainmen considerably injured.
>
> The responsibility of the collision is said to rest upon a telegraph operator who made a mistake in copying an order.

Transcription: On the T.V. road last Saturday occurred one of those accidents which are peculiar to the carelessness of either trainmen or telegraph operators. Engine No. 9, going north, and running as first section of a freight, collided with train No. 18 — engine No. 21, running wild. The accident occurred just outside of the tunnel, about three miles from this place, below the mouth of Pogue's run. Engineer Thos. Wright

---

52 The Belmont Chronicle, November 9, 1882, Newspapers.com.
53 *Collision on the T.V. Road, Between Maynard and Fairpoint,* The Belmont Chronicle, December 7, 1882, Newpapers.com.

was caught and fastened in the cab, having a foot crushed, several ribs broken, and a scalp wound, and was not able to extricate himself until assisted by other members of his crew. Mr. Wright is well known here, as having been an engineer on the Northern road, and his speedy recovery is wished for by his many friends.

There were two other trainmen considerably injured.

The responsibility of the collision is said to rest upon a telegraph operator who made a mistake in copying an order.

Wilson was the telegraph operator who was blamed. It was serious business, and it also turned out to be one of the few times in his life he was falsely accused. The Gazette, in reporting the same accident, simply stated, "The cause of the wreck was misunderstood orders."[54] But they were quick to point out the errors of their rival paper when the railroad's investigation exonerated Wilson. The following week, they opined,

> Very great injustice was done in charging upon D.W. Bethel, the telegraph operator at Bruce Station, the responsibility for the recent railroad accident near Fairpoint. The officials of the road have investigated the matter thoroughly and find that Mr. Bethel was not to blame in any manner whatever. The papers that published the item reflecting on Mr. Bethel ought now to correct it.[55]

Hunt was forced to agree, and the Chronicle stammered out a retraction:

> LAST week in our report of the collision on the T. V. road, reference was made to the responsibility being placed upon an operator along the line. An investigation has resulted, we understand, in exonerating from blame Mr. D. W. Bethel, the operator at Bruce.[56]

Transcription: Last week in our report of the collision on the T. V. road, reference was made to the responsibility being placed upon an operator along the line. An investigation has resulted, we understand, in exonerating [sic] from blame Mr. D.W. Bethel, the operator at Bruce.

These items tell us more than they say, and demand some reflection, since they are our only glimpse of the events. First, there was clearly at least a rumor in the community that Wilson was to blame for the crash, or Hunt would not have put it in his initial story.[57] But

---

54   *Fairpoint*, The St. Clairsville Gazette, December 7, 1882. From microfilm at the Ohio History Center, Columbus.
55   The St. Clairsville Gazette, December 14, 1882. From microfilm at the Ohio History Center, Columbus.
56   The Belmont Chronicle, December 14, 1882, Newspapers.com.
57   We don't know which other local papers, if any, published a similar story, but the account in the Gazette indicates that there was at least one other.

why would anyone accuse him groundlessly? It seems likely that there was a segment of the hardworking farming/mining community that disliked D.W. Bethel. They probably regarded him as just a young clown, not to be taken seriously. They tolerated him if he handled his job well, but were out for blood if he made a mistake. It also appears that a more familiar local man, possibly Downing, had been passed over for his job, and was undercutting him (baseless rumors have to get started somehow). If his carelessness caused a maiming injury to one their neighbors, well, no more local celebrity for you, pal.

The next week, the Gazette moved to calm the divided community, and also to jump into the void created by Hunt's initial siding with Wilson's detractors. They wrote, innocuously enough, "D.W. Bethel, with the assistance of Jno. A. Downing, is as ever ready to attend to the wants of the patrons of the T. V."[58] Why, Mr. Gazette, you have never noticed me before! As sensitive as a middle schooler to the possibility that his friend was being stolen, Hunt started falling all over himself to make amends, reiterating his retraction and implying that Wilson's accusers should shut up:

> Mr. D. W. Bethel, the T. V. agent, has, after a thorough investigation by the company, been exonerated from all blame in regard to the late collision at Henderson. It is but just to him to have public notice, as the odds were fearfully against him, but he has proven himself entirely clear of all errors in delivering his orders. [59]

Transcription: Mr. D.W. Bethel, the T. V. agent, has, after a thorough investigation by the company, been exonerated from all blame in regard to the late collision at Henderson. It is but just to him to have public notice, as the odds were fearfully against him, but he has proven himself entirely clear of all errors in delivering his orders.

That "the odds were fearfully against him" indicates the strength of the anti-D.W. Bethel crowd in the community. Some loud voices were determined to make him into a scapegoat, and both papers were letting them know that Wilson had the high ground, and that he deserved better.

But the mood shifted again about a month later, on January 25, 1883, when the Chronicle published the following unusual item:

---

58 The St. Clairsville Gazette, December 21, 1882. From microfilm at the Ohio History Center, Columbus.
59 *Personal Mention*, The Belmont Chronicle, December 28, 1882, Newspapers.com.

> D. W. Bethel, the T. V. agent here, lost his pocket book on Friday, containing near $100 of the company's money. A general search at the office, also at Bentley & Coffland's store, failed to find it, but on going to his home in the evening, he discovered he had not taken it to the office at all. So much for being absent-minded.

Transcription: D.W. Bethel, the T. V. agent here, lost his pocket book on Friday, containing near $100 of the company's money. A general search at the office, also at Bentley & Coffland's store, failed to find it, but on going to his home in the evening, he discovered he had not taken it to the office at all. So much for being absent-minded.

Agents of the day were entrusted with personally safeguarding the company's cash, accounting for it at various intervals. Hunt implied that it was just an innocent mistake, but why put it in the paper at all, especially so soon after the controversy about the accident? Maybe it was just more harmless reporting of the mundane events in the life of Wilson Bethel, the scatter-headed local funny-boy with his own way of doing things, but this item had an edge to it.

A skeptical view appears to be justified by later events, as it turned out to be a prelude to him leaving the T. V. A month later, in two consecutive issues, the Chronicle bowed its erstwhile hero out the door:

> THE PEOPLE —Mr. D. W. Bethel, the agent and operator for the T. V. R'y Co., at Bruce, resigned his position last week. Mr. Bethel kept the station in a manner that would reflect credit and honor on any agent. It was characterized by quiet, civility, order and decency, and the best wishes of his friends will follow him wherever he may locate.......

Transcription: Mr. D.W. Bethel, the agent and operator for the T.V. R'y Co., at Bruce, resigned his position last week. Mr. Bethel kept the station in a manner that would reflect credit and honor on any agent. It was characterized by quiet, civility, order and decency, and the best wishes of his friends will follow him wherever he may locate.

---

60 *Bannock*, The Belmont Chronicle, January 25, 1883, Newspapers.com.
61 *Uniontown* column, The Belmont Chronicle, February 15, 1883, Newspapers.com.

Transcription: Mr. D. W. Bethel, agent and operator at Bruce has resigned his position, and been offered a position on the U., St. L. and P. R.R. in Michigan, to which place he will soon go. He is now in charge of the office at Butler.

J.A. Downing who has been learning telegraphy this winter, is now in charge of the office at Bruce.

The Gazette reported the same event, but with different details.

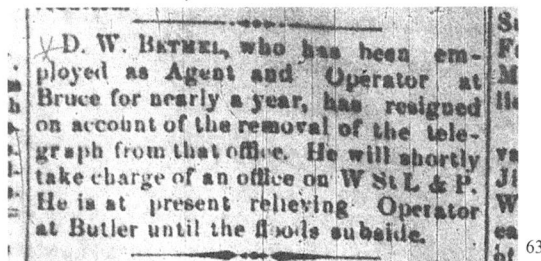

Transcription: D. W. Bethel, who has been employed as Agent and Operator at Bruce for nearly a year, has resigned on account of the removal of the telegraph from that office. He will shortly take charge of an office on W. St. L. & P. He is at present relieving Operator at Butler until the floods subside.

These accounts contradict one another — obviously, if the telegraph had been removed from the office at Bruce, there would be no need for Mr. Downing to have those skills going forward, although the Chronicle also reported that "hopes are entertained that it will soon be restored again," probably if Downing ever got up to speed.[64] Also, while Hunt reported that Wilson was "now in charge" of the office at Butler, Indiana, the Gazette correctly said that he was a "relieving Operator," which was just a temporary position. It seems that both papers were trying to give him some cover for leaving, the Gazette by implying that his main skills were no longer needed, and the Chronicle by reporting that he now had a more important job. Or maybe Wilson just fed a different set of information to each newsman, as he so often did throughout his career.

Had the railroad become suspicious that he was skimming, and asked him to resign because they couldn't prove it, and/or because it was easier and better for public relations?

---

62 *Bannock*, The Belmont Chronicle, February 22, 1883, Newspapers.com. The "U" in the railroad's name was a typo — Wilson's new position was with the Wabash, St. Louis & Pacific Railroad.
63 The St. Clairsville Gazette, February 22, 1883. From microfilm at the Ohio History Center.
64 *Bannock*, The Belmont Chronicle, February 22, 1883, Newspapers.com.

It's impossible to know, but the "lost pocketbook" episode hints at the possibility of financial shenanigans, similar to his "unconventional practices" that would come to light at later venues.

It's almost certain that he got the temporary position with the Wabash, St. Louis & Pacific Railroad, which operated from Detroit to St. Louis at the time, by calling in a favor from his favorite uncle, George Smith Bethel. But a relieving operator, whose job was to fill in for agents when they were sick or on vacation, or during times of high volume (as was the case here, due to flooding of the rivers in northern Indiana), was a less secure, lower paying job than a regular station agent. It was generally a step down, even though the Wabash was a more substantial railroad. Whatever was going on behind the scenes at the C., T. V. & W., it's possible that Wilson just got tired of the politics and negative attention at Bruce, decided he would do better in a new place, and worked his only important connection to leave with his head held high.

Two months later, the final whisper of D.W. Bethel (at least until the early 1890's when Jennie was suing him for divorce) appeared in the Chronicle:

D. W. BETHEL, ESQ., of Newcomb, Mich., is on the sick list, and has returned home for a week or two. He will in future occupy a position on the S. L. & P. railway, as agent and operator with a good salary. He is worthy of a good position, and has the esteem and best wishes of many friends.[65]

Transcription: D.W. Bethel, Esq., of Newcomb, Mich., is on the sick list, and has returned home for a week or two. He will in the future occupy a position on the S.L.& P. railway, as agent and operator with a good salary. He is worthy of a good position, and has the esteem and best wishes of many friends.

The suffix, "Esq." was a final gesture of respect from Mr. Hunt to his unemployed friend. Wilson had escaped from the farm and was now a member of the society of gentlemen. Hunt had already given him a heartfelt, complimentary goodbye two months earlier, but he again felt the need defend his friend's character in the last sentence. He believed that Wilson had been wronged, he was sorry for the role he had played in it, and by God he wanted everyone to know it. But there must have been people in the area, and in the railroad's front office, who were happy their fast-talking young agent was gone.

The Indiana floods had subsided, the full time position hadn't materialized, and he was temporarily without a job. But just as Wilson Bethel was becoming acquainted with the complexities and cross currents in the world of business, he was also familiarizing himself with how to conduct business of his own, to operate a disinformation campaign, giving pieces of his story to different people so that the whole picture could never quite be assembled. This would not be the last time he would exaggerate his employment situation to

65 *Uniontown*, The Belmont Chronicle, April 19, 1883, Newspapers.com.

aggrandize himself and soften the embarrassment of his failures, and then get sick when his hopes failed to bear fruit. The sequence would be repeated, variously, in future escapades in different locales: 1.) D.W. Bethel is asked to resign his job; 2.) He tells everyone he quit and now has a new (better) job somewhere else that is difficult to verify; and 3.) He gets sick for a while. *"I didn't screw up, I'm moving up! Oh, and (cough, cough, cough) pity me if you don't believe me."*

2.

A Little Help from Uncle Doc

■ AFTER THE CIVIL WAR, PRIVATE GEORGE SMITH BETHEL must have been a local hero. His regiment, the 12th Ohio Cavalry, had played an important role in the conflict, beginning with a decisive victory over John Hunt Morgan's forces, who were hated by the people of southeastern Ohio for their 1863 raid, at the Battle of Cynthiana, Kentucky.[66] The 12th was one of the units involved in General George Stoneman's forays into western Virginia, Tennessee, and the Carolinas in 1865, and they ended the conflict as part of the pursuit of Confederate President Jefferson Davis and his cabinet across Georgia, capturing Vice President Alexander Stephens.[67] George's underage enlistment, along with his unit's record, must have inspired admiration when he came back to civilian life. Add in his older brother Thomas's death in action, and the folks of Flushing/Rock Hill would certainly have been proud of the part that Norris Bethel's children had played in squelching the rebellion. George was only 19 at the war's end, and opportunities of all sorts must have come his way in numbers.

But while he was proud of his service to his country, regularly attending his unit's G.A.R. meetings and maintaining his friendships from the war, he was not one to seek the limelight. The only two mentions of him in the Belmont Chronicle in the late 1860's were the call for participation in the Soldiers Mass Convention in September 1866, in which all the veterans of the county were listed, and his wedding announcement:

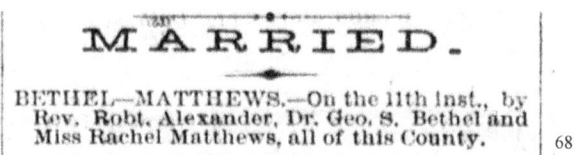
[68]

Transcription: On the 11th inst., by Rev. Robt. Alexander, Dr. Geo. S. Bethel and Miss Rachel Matthews, all of this County.

He must have known his wife since childhood. Five years his junior, Rachel Regina

---

66 F. H. Mason, *The Twelfth Ohio Cavalry: A Record of Its Organization and Services in the War of the Rebellion*, pp. 43-49.
67 *Ibid*. pp. 95-115. Stephens surrendered without fleeing, but the 12th still claimed credit for his capture.
68 The Belmont Chronicle, July 18, 1867, Newspapers.com.

Matthews, known as 'Ret' by family and friends, also grew up on a farm not far from Rock Hill. Their union was not the only connection between the two families — Ret's sister Lacy married another of Henry Bethel's grandchildren, Edward Bethel's son, Isaac. It's hard to know how many other unions there were between the large extended families, since matrilineal descents are difficult to trace prior to 1850.[69]

David Wilson Bethel was five years old when the war ended, and we can only imagine how much larger than life his uncle appeared to him, a member of the cavalry of the triumphant Grand Army of the Republic, with his consummate riding skills and confident bearing. They seem to have enjoyed a special bond, at least for a time, and it's likely that Wilson began calling him 'Uncle Doc' early in life. George was the closest thing the Bethel family had to a famous person, and that was a status to which his nephew aspired.

George must have acquired his medical credentials soon after the war, and he made a living from them for a time. The 1870 census finds the young family living near Rock Hill, but by 1880 he and Ret had moved to Lucas County, Ohio, just southwest of Toledo.[70] The couple had five children — Addie (born 1869), Alice (1870), Bessie (1873), Emma (1876), and Ralph (1878). George's occupation was listed as 'physician' in 1880, but soon after the census he must have decided that doctoring no longer fit him. The medical profession in America was changing rapidly — physicians were increasingly expected to know what they were doing. In the 1860s, Louis Pasteur and other French scientists began to actively promote the revolutionary idea that microorganisms caused many diseases, and the ramifications of those discoveries were slowly winding their way through the American medical community, where many esteemed professionals still believed that ailments were the product of an imbalance of the four humors.[71] The mysticism that lay at the root of those beliefs went back to the ancient Greeks, and it gave ground to the new science as grudgingly as Lee had to the Federal armies in Virginia. Purging with laxatives, blistering with hot irons, and bloodletting were still accepted treatments for a variety of disorders in the 1880s, as doctors mistrusted the new discoveries almost as much as the American public mistrusted doctors.[72] George's education would have come from the old system (two four-month terms of lecture with no admittance requirements and a perfunctory oral exam at the end) and even though he knew how to set a broken bone and dress a wound (the majority of a country doctor's practice), he would have increasingly seen his profession running away from his training.[73] This probably factored into his decision, in 1881, to accept a position as the first station agent at Newcomb (Willis), Michigan, a new stop on a subsidiary of the Wabash, St. Louis & Pacific.[74]

---

69 Marriage license, George Smith Bethel and Rachel Regina Matthews, Belmont County, Ohio, July 11, 1867; Isaac Bethel and Lacy Smith Matthews, November 7, 1877, Ohio Marriages, 1803-1900, Ancestry.com. Before 1850, census records only listed the male head of household by name. Other family members were simply enumerated.
70 U.S. Census, 1880, Neapolis Providence Township, Lucas County, Ohio, George Smith Bethel and family, Ancestry.com. His location is further evidence of George's adventurous spirit — none of his siblings ever moved farther away from Flushing than St. Clairsville.
71 Kenneth M. Ludmerer, *Learning to Heal*, pp. 76-77.
72 Harvard University Library, *Contagion: Historical Views of Diseases and Epidemics*.
73 Kenneth M. Ludmerer, *Learning to Heal*, pp. 10-11.
74 Donald J. Heimburger, *Wabash*, p. 20, p. 29.

Located about 30 miles across the Ohio/Michigan line in Washtenaw County, and about the same distance southwest of Detroit, Newcomb was specifically founded as a railroad stop. The town was originally named Potter, after Willis L. Potter, the farmer who had donated the land to increase the area's (and his own) commerce. In 1881, when a post office was established, the name was changed to Newcomb, Mrs. Potter's maiden name. But evidently nobody except Ohio newspaper editors called it that. Residents continued to refer to the place by Mr. Potter's first name, and in 1889 'Willis' became the official name of the town.[75] In the late nineteenth century it was a vital rural center. It's no longer that, but it's still there — just take exit 31 east off U.S. 23 in southern Michigan.

Willis, Michigan, in the late nineteenth century.

Willis, Michigan, in 2016, also looking west, from near the railroad tracks.

---

75 Walter Romig, *Michigan Place Names*, L.H.D., p. 606; *Stations On Line*, The Ann Arbor Argus, April, 1881, GenealogyBank.com; *Augusta Township History* (augustatownship.org/history/).
76 Photo from *Augusta Township History* (augustatownship.org/history/).
77 Photo by Charles Caldemeyer, 2016.

Road signs in Willis, 2016. This may be the only remaining vestige of the town's founder and namesake.

We don't know when George acquired expertise in telegraphy, but it likely dated from the Civil War. Three of his children, Addie, Alice, and Ralph, became proficient enough to find employment as operators in adulthood.[79] He probably also taught the skill set to his doting nephew.

George Smith Bethel lived the remainder of his years in Willis, idolized by his children and respected by the community. He proved to be a model employee for the Wabash, aside from a six-month period during the tumultuous 1890s when he was relieved of his duties because of union involvement.[80] He remained at the depot nine more years after his reinstatement in 1893, probably even more locally admired for his principles.

His obituary in the Ann Arbor Argus-Democrat on April 18, 1902, communicates his importance in the area, the esteem in which he was held, and the shock of his loss:

SUDDEN DEATH OF GEORGE S. BETHELL

> Willis, Mich., April 8 — Miss [sic] Alice Campbell of Detroit, who came out home last Wednesday to attend the funeral of her father, George S. Bethell, was taken sick with the measles and could not attend the funeral. Her youngest sister, Emma, was so overcome with grief that she could not attend.
>
> Died, at this place last Tuesday, of heart failure, George S. Bethell. He had not been well for several days and there was a man working in his place at the depot, but the Wabash railroad auditor came out that morning and Bethell went

---

78 Photo by Charles Caldemeyer, 2016.
79 The Ypsilanti Commercial, April 25, 1890, Addie Bethel; The Ann Arbor Argus-Democrat, March 22, 1889, August 9, 1889, Alice Bethel, GenealogyBank.com; U.S. Census, 1900, Mills Creek, Williams County, Ohio, Ralph Bethel, Ancestry.com.
80 The Ypsilanti Commercial, January 27, 1893 and July 7, 1893, GenealogyBank.com.

over to the station to settle up with him. They had got through and he attended to some other business, after which he started for home, which is about 40 rods from the station. When within about 10 rods of his home he fell down. Several saw him fall but when they got to him he was dead. Dr. Post was called in and he pronounced him past all help. He had been station agent at this place ever since the Wabash railroad was built through here, about 22 years. He was a man well liked by all who had business to transact with him, in fact by all who knew him. His health had not been good for the past eight years or more. He was a veteran of the war of the rebellion, having served in the 12th Ohio cavalry. He has a fine war record, enlisting when only 15 years of age, served three years, and saw some very hard service. He was 55 years of age the 28th day of last September. He had a pleasant little home here in this place. He was a member of Carpenter Post, No. 180, G. A. R., of Ypsilanti; also a member of the 12th Ohio Veteran Cavalry Association. It will be a hard matter to find another man that will fill his place at this station. He leaves a wife and five children to mourn his loss, four daughters and one son. The funeral was held at the M. E. church last Friday at 2:30. The services were conducted by the Rev. H. J. B. Marsh, assisted by the Rev. Mr. Brown of the Friend church. The text was Job 15: 11. The Willis choir sang two pieces, "Nearer my God, to Thee," and "Pass under the Rod." The coffin was draped with the national colors and there were many beautiful flowers. The remains were laid to rest in the Udell cemetery. The pall bearers were ex-soldiers, Wm. A. Russell, Reuben Morrill, E. S. Butts, James A. Blackmer, Jos. Bird and Mr. Vanderpool.[81]

Eldest daughter Addie died six months later, the grief of her father's loss being at least a contributing factor.[82]

We don't know if D.W. Bethel attended the funeral, but since he was going by an alias about a thousand miles away in 1902, it's doubtful. But he had evidently bragged to Joannetta about his uncle's exploits while he was in Clarence, because in his first letter to her, from November 1894, he asked, "Would you like to see a photo of Uncle Doc, Aunt Ret and cousin Alice? If so I will send them to you to see."[83] He was trying to cement his status with his second wife by associating himself with George's impeccable character, although by 1894 the days of the honest Uncle Doc being a shining example for his nephew to emulate were long over.

---

81 *Sudden Death of George S. Bethell*, The Ann Arbor Argus-Democrat, April 18, 1902, GenealogyBank.com.
82 Death certificate, Addie Bethel Reick, October 28, 1902, Ancestry.com.
83 Letter, D.W. Bethel to Joannetta Fisher #1, November 1, 1894, from Fisher family papers.

In April 1883, however, Uncle Doc had convinced the Wabash to hire his struggling relative and protégé. He may have even believed that his influence could put Wilson's feet on the right path again after his dubious departure from Belmont County. Wilson probably lived at George's house while he commuted to Butler, in northern Indiana, for his temporary job with the Wabash. He may have gotten some other work with the company as a relieving agent off and on that summer, but it appears that he never received a steady job, despite the assertion in Hunt's paper that he would soon "occupy a position" on the road.[84] And while he may have behaved honestly while under his uncle's roof, we know that George Smith Bethel's impact on the young man was not lasting.

But the early 1880s was a time of great rail expansion, and a new position with another railroad opened up soon enough. A set of passes dated November 14, 1883, shows that by that date Wilson was employed by the New York, Chicago & St. Louis Railway, commonly and famously known as the Nickel Plate Road. He was the station agent/operator at Kimball, also called Higbee, Ohio.[85]

It's a small place in the middle of the north-central Ohio plains, about sixty miles west of Cleveland. Now there is just a small cluster of houses there, running along the track, and it probably was not much different then, except that there used to be a depot. And while it was not an important station, the central hub of the Nickel Plate was just one stop away, at Bellevue, providing an opportunity for building the kinds of relationships necessary for advancement. In 1883, the Nickel Plate was still a fledgling railroad, and Wilson was probably the first agent at Kimball.[86] He was certainly the first postmaster for the small town, serving from January 11, 1884, until February 5, 1886.[87]

[88]

The station house at Kimball, also called Higbee, just prior to its removal in 1960. This frame structure may well have been the one in place 75 years earlier, when D. W. Bethel was agent there. The building was larger than it appears in this picture, with a warehouse extending some distance behind, but Kimball was still a small stop.

---

84 *Uniontown*, The Belmont Chronicle, April 19, 1883, Newspapers.com.
85 Rail passes, New York, Chicago & St. Louis Railway, November 14, 1883, from the Fisher family papers.
86 Preserving the History of the Nickel Plate Road (nkphts.org); information included in an email from Bill Godby to Charles Caldemeyer, April 5, 2002.
87 Appointments of U.S. Postmasters, Kimball, Erie County, Ohio, 1884; Roster of postmasters, Kimball, Ohio, 1885, Ancestry.com.
88 Photo provenance unknown. From an email from Bill Godby to Charles Caldemeyer, April 5, 2002.

It was at Kimball, on January 7, 1885, that Jennie gave birth to Bessie Ota Bethel. His first, and only legitimate, child evidently did not inspire the 25-year-old father with much of a sense of responsibility, and soon afterward he began to act upon the "restlessness" he mentioned in his later letters to Joannetta. A pass from Buffalo to Cleveland, debited from the account of the agent at Wickliffe (a stop just northeast of Cleveland) indicates that he may have been employed there as early as August 8, 1885.[89] It's unknown whether Jennie and Bessie lived with him there, but he clearly had abandoned his first family by August 6, 1886. He was agent for the West Shore Railroad at Clarence, New York. We have two letters to him from management on that date congratulating him on the success of a recent excursion trip he had put together.[90]

It seems likely that he began to go by the adopted name of 'Willis' around the time of his move to western New York.[91] Interestingly, Willis L. Potter and his wife, Calista, had a son named David Willis Potter, and the two Davids may have known each other during Wilson's brief residence in Michigan in 1883. He may have adopted the moniker as some kind of tribute, but I think it's more likely that he renamed himself after the popular name for the town. It would not be the last time he would name a person after a place. He would use Willis as his middle name, and go by it in everyday interactions for about eleven years, until 1897, when he abandoned his name entirely.

The West Shore was a lessee of The New York Central, which also ran the Nickel Plate, and he may have used some of his recently developed connections to land the job. There was a lot of cronyism in the hiring processes of railroad companies of the era, and a letter from a prominent man (a stockholder, former employer, high official in the company, or other person of influence) went a long way.[92] It's likely that he held one or more such letters and used them to full effect throughout his career.

He represented himself to the Clarence community as a single man from the outset. We don't know whether anyone at the station knew about his Ohio wife and daughter, but abandoning one's family was a fireable offense on nineteenth-century railroads, so management certainly didn't.[93] It's also unknown whether Jennie availed herself of the Nickel Plate's assistance to track her man down in 1886. The railroads were related to one another, but Willis lived in Clarence for over three years without being discovered, so he was able to cover his tracks somehow.

There are a number of possibilities. Jennie may have been only too happy to be rid of him. They may have had an irreparable disagreement. As we will see later, Jennie was a strong and independent woman. If he was sending her money now and then, she would not have wanted him to lose his job. It's also possible that she was caught in a tryst with another man, and so was in no position to protest his desertion, since the offense of adultery was much more

---

89 Rail pass, New York, Chicago & St. Louis Railway, August 8, 1885, from Fisher family papers.
90 Letters from The West Shore Railroad to D.W. Bethel, August 6,1886, from Fisher family papers.
91 His marriage license to Joannetta listed his middle name as 'Willison,' but he was known as Willis in everyday interaction from 1886 until 1897.
92 Charles Stephenson and Robert Asher, *Life & Labor*, p. 100.
93 Walter Licht, *Working for the Railroad*, p. 172, pp. 225-226.

serious at the time if the woman was the one committing it. It seems most likely, though, that he just disappeared one day, and she did not know where, or how, to look for him.

Jennie's laugh could sound a little like a witch's cackle. When he was younger, Wilson had found it endearing. It was as if she was making fun of the world both of them found so difficult and ridiculous. The same was true of her directness — at first, it was a refreshing change from the demure young women of the age, but after a while her unvarnished honesty, along with her chortle, became irritating. By the time the couple arrived at Kimball, he was roundly sick of his marriage, and he did everything he could to damage her reputation. No lie was too low for him to tell if it would inspire sympathy for him and loathing of Jennie. When he finally did leave her, he thought, the fewer people who would help her find him, the better.

Jennie always had trouble reading those around her, and she sometimes went too far with her comments for the stolid folk in the small village. After she caught him with Sarah Gillette, a floozy from nearby Norwalk, Jennie advertised her husband's deficiencies whenever an opportunity presented itself, thinking people must now surely see him for the skunk he was. But the residents reserved their sympathy for their genial station agent, who maintained his good humor in the face of her onslaughts. When she wasn't around, he would quietly tell anyone who asked that Jennie was a little unbalanced and made things up, but that she was his wife and by God, he loved her. The men in the yard admired Wilson's devotion, and they avoided his wife if they could. It was just no way for a woman to behave, talking that way to, and about, the man who provided for her.

Wilson traveled the six miles down the line to Bellevue as often as he could find a good excuse, and he also periodically visited the corporate offices in Cleveland, just to schmooze with some of the more important officials on the line. In the process, he made friends with some of the supervisors, notably Alfred Farrell, who oversaw station assignments for the road.

Farrell admired Wilson's telegraphy skills, his easygoing ability to run the depot and meet the public with unfailing good cheer, and his sense of humor. His aptitude for telling a funny story and delivering a scorching one-liner became legendary soon after his arrival at Kimball. The two men often went to the racetrack together. They talked horseflesh, placed bets, and complained to each about their marriages. Farrell's wife, Katherine, consumed too much laudanum, he confided. She was always walking around in a daze, half asleep. "I look forward to the times my wife is asleep," said Wilson. "She doesn't talk as much." Farrell chuckled, and based on the things he'd heard, he couldn't disagree. Both men referred to Jennie as "the shrew."

"Why ever did you marry her?" he once asked Wilson, and his friend rolled his eyes. He went on to spin a tale about how the older Jennie, hating domestic work and despairing of ever finding a husband to support her, had manipulated the young man into a fast marriage. "She said she was pregnant back in '81, but she never got big until just this year," he said sarcastically. He looked out the window. "Four years is the longest pregnancy on record, I'll

wager." Farrell was horrified by the story, and he determined to help his friend however he could.

When Wilson mentioned that he would like to captain a station closer to his hometown of Reading, Pennsylvania, his obliging supervisor had him reassigned to Wickliffe. Jennie wasn't happy about it, saying he only asked for the move to find new dalliances. "He run outta whores on the west end of the line," she said one day, not caring who heard her. Bessie had been born at Kimball the previous January, and Wilson was disappointed that his first child was a girl. "Now, she will grow up to be exactly like her mother," he ruefully told to his friend.

About six months later, over a round of drinks, Wilson told Farrell that he had finally had enough of his wife. He was going to pursue opportunities in western New York, since it was the only way he saw to escape her. Anyway, his widowed sister lived in Buffalo, and she needed his help. Instead of acting like a supervisor and requesting that the young man reconsider, work things out at home, and remain with the company, Farrell responded as a friend, asking how he could be of service. Wilson asked for a letter of introduction, and Farrell was accommodating, even accepting the suggestion that the plan would work better if his middle name was changed to Willison. The letter was effusive in its praise of both his character and his abilities.

When a distraught Jennie came to Farrell's office one day in early 1886, he told her with a straight face that he had no idea where her husband might have gotten to, and he thought it odd that he was not at his post. He promised to launch a thorough investigation and to keep her informed of the results, but all he did was hire a replacement at the station. "There, my friend," he thought with a touch of satisfaction. "You are finally free of her." Jennie wasn't one to give up, though, and she reached out to other members of the Nickel Plate management team, and to anyone else who might help her locate her husband. Farrell soon had his supervisors, along with some important stockholders on the road, asking him some uncomfortable questions.

Alfred Farrell died suddenly about a week after Wilson left, when Katherine put some arsenic his soup. The drugs had made her delusional, and several times that evening she thought she heard her husband mutter, "that stinking shrew!" as he sat in his chair. Assuming he was referring to her, she imagined that he intended to kill her, and she decided to not bother playing defense. She lived out her days in the Newburgh State Hospital, a mental health facility near Cleveland.

At some point, Jennie moved back to Flushing, taking her young daughter with her. Thus began, for them, a partnership that would last 54 years. Bessie lived with her mother until Jennie's death in 1939 at the age of 90, first raised by her and then supporting her with a longtime job at a local bank. In her later years, Bessie became something of a local celebrity. Two newspaper articles from the early 1960s detailed her contributions to her church and community, her well known sense of humor and longstanding friendships, her selflessness, and her strong moral fiber.[94] In so many ways, except for that sense of humor thing, she was not her father's daughter. She never married, although photos reveal a pretty young lady who must have generated interest among the local male population. One can only imagine the diatribes of mistrust of men heaped upon her by her mother, whose early 1890s attempts at divorce failed and who, consequently, could never remarry, even if she had been so inclined. Jennie listed herself as widowed in the 1900 census, married in 1910, divorced in 1920, and widowed again in 1930. This is probably the first, but certainly not the last, example of the confusion that D.W. Bethel inspired in the women in his life.[95]

Eliza Jane (Jennie) Howell Bethel, probably about 1925.

Bessie Ota Bethel, High School senior class picture, 1903.

---

94 *Veteran Flushing Bible Teacher Is Remembered by 'Her Boys,'* The Ohio Valley News, April 9, 1961; *Friendship of Four From 1903 Flushing Class Kept Intact*, The Flushing Times-Leader, September 21, 1960. Copies of these articles shared via email, Dan Smith to Charles Caldemeyer, April 17, 2001.
95 U.S. Census, 1900, 1910, 1920, 1930, Jennie Bethel, Flushing, Belmont County, Ohio, Ancestry.com.
96 Photo originally shared by LynnGoodman245 on Ancestry.com.
97 Photo edited from *Friendship of Four From 1903 Flushing Class Kept Intact*, The Flushing Times-Leader, September 21, 1960, shared via email, Dan Smith to Charles Caldemeyer, April 17, 2001.

3.

"If I Had Never Got Medicine into My Head..."

■ **WHEN BUFFALO CREEK,** a small trading village on the eastern shores of Lake Erie, won the right to be the western terminus of the Erie Canal, a population boom ensued. After the canal was completed in 1825, the area became a destination for waves of immigrants trying to escape war, poverty, religious persecution, and the general oppressiveness of European societies. German and Irish settlers flooded into the area, which was ideal for the kind of northern temperate zone farming to which they were accustomed.[98] An old British settlement about nine miles east of the city, named after the House of Clarence, an English dukedom, became a popular German enclave.[99]

Two of the newcomers, Frederick Fisher, from Kindenheim, and Eva Catherine Speith of Bunzwangen, arrived around mid-century. Frederick left home in 1843 to avoid compulsory conscription into the Prussian army at eighteen, emigrating under an assumed name, Hans Schwartz, and sailing from outside the country. According to family lore, there was a trunk in the attic of the old farmhouse near Clarence with the initials H.S. still on it.[100] Eva Catherine was an unwanted child who had a difficult time at home, and she sailed for America alone, at age seventeen, in 1850. Her mother's letters reveal a severe and judgmental woman who was especially hard on her daughter, and young Eva Catherine was evidently only too happy to get away.[101]

These were tough, self-disciplined, no-nonsense people. They arrived with little money, but worked long, hard days at whatever jobs were available to save enough to exert some control over their lives. Initially, Frederick was mostly a farm laborer, and he also worked at a local hotel. He was on the crew that built the first railroad through Clarence. Eva Catherine was a domestic servant in Buffalo for a time, but she soon found her way to Clarence, where she waited tables at a tavern. They were married on March 6, 1853, while Frederick was

---

98   J. Henry Priebe, Jr., *Beginnings — The Village of Buffalo*, The Buffalonian, 1997.
99   *A History of the Town of Clarence*, published by the Buffalo and Erie County Historical Society, 1971.
100 Daniel C. Fisher and Irene A. Fisher, *A History of the Family and Descendants of Frederick and Catherine Speith Fisher, 1825 - 1978*, p.1.
101 Letters, Katerina Roos to Eva Catherine Speith; Last Will and Testament of Katerina Roos, from Fisher family papers.

still on the workforce for the railroad. Children came soon after, like a parade: Mary (1854), Catherine (1856), Jacob (1858), Joannetta (1860), George (1862), Frederick, Jr. (1865), Anna (1867), Katherine (1870), and Charles (1873). Around 1856, they were able to buy a small farm, which they worked, profitably enough, for over 20 years.[102]

In the late 1870s, Frederick was able to trade up to a larger farm of over 100 acres. His parents and all six of his siblings had immigrated after him, largely on his advice and with his financial assistance. Most of them lived in the area, and the Fisher farmhouse was the center of a close familial community. When his younger sister, Gertrude Fisher Meyer, died of typhoid fever at the age of 40, a year after her husband, relatives in the area took over the raising of their four young children, and young Bertha Meyer became part of Frederick and Eva Catherine's household. Frederick was one of the first trustees of the German Reformed Church in Clarence, selling one of his cows to help finance its construction. But he developed some health problems, and on August 17, 1887, after building a new life in the American wilderness with only work and willpower, Frederick Fisher, Sr. died of a kidney ailment. He was 62.[103]

He knew the man called David Willis Bethel toward the end of his life, and he wasn't very impressed. Willis's courtship of Joannetta, the Fishers' fourth child, must have begun in earnest soon after his arrival as the West Shore Railroad station agent in 1886. Family accounts indicate that in her younger days Nettie was more free-spirited than was normal for the family, and an object of worry by her parents. "Her life would make quite a book if one knew it all," her sister Anna wrote in 1949.[104] Nettie had left the family farm, although not the family, by the 1880 census, living in the home of Theron and Alathera Whipple, farming neighbors and good friends of Frederick and Eva Catherine. She was listed as a domestic, but it's likely that the fun-loving young woman had a closer relationship with Mrs. Whipple than with her own mother, who had little patience for her rebelliousness.[105] The Whipples may have been doing their longtime friends a favor by taking in their daughter, but Nettie, like her beau, was looking for answers that could not be found in the regimentation and daily grind of late nineteenth-century farm life.

In addition to finding refuge with the Whipples, Nettie stayed for a time with older sister Mary and her husband, Adam Hoeman. The Hoemans lived in Kansas until Mary's death from tuberculosis in 1882, making her the second of Frederick and Eva Catherine's children to die before them (Catherine, their second child, had passed away from scarlet fever as a toddler).[106] Interestingly, our only glimpse of this chapter of Nettie's life comes from one of Willis's letters. On May 2, 1897, he wrote, "I was near McPherson Kans. — thought of you. Thought of the night you & Adam were going home & you got scared of robbers & threw the pocket book in the bayou."[107] The story sounds like an interesting one, and the fact that

---

102 Daniel C. Fisher and Irene A. Fisher, *A History of the Family and Descendants of Frederick and Catherine Speith Fisher, 1825 - 1978*, pp. 4-6.
103 Daniel C. Fisher and Irene A. Fisher, *A History of the Family and Descendants of Frederick and Catherine Speith Fisher, 1825 - 1978*, pp. 4-7.
104 Letter, Anna Fisher Schurr to Eva Katherine Wiley, September 27, 1949, from Fisher family papers.
105 U.S. Census, 1880, Clarence, Erie County, New York, Theron and Alatheara Whipple, Nettie Fisher, Ancestry.com.
106 Daniel C. Fisher and Irene A. Fisher, *A History of the Family and Descendants of Frederick and Catherine Speith Fisher, 1825 - 1978*, p. 9.
107 Letter, D.W. Bethel to Joannetta Fisher #14, May 2, 1897, from Fisher family papers.

it included her sister's husband, but not her sister, makes one wonder if it was even more complex. It also hints at the nature of the bond Willis and Nettie enjoyed — shared experiences and swapped stories, love of laughter and raucous times, the joys of being young, and a mutual disdain for hard work.

Nettie could not reconcile her feelings with the strictures of her upbringing, and Willis played on these insecurities to cement himself further into her life. He represented to her the white/dark knight, the bright prospect of escape from the mundane life of hard, routine work combined with the romantic rogue. He was charming, well-traveled, funny, and more intelligent than the average farm boy. He liked to socialize, and he actually listened to her, laughed at her jokes, and enjoyed it when she laughed at his. He acted more knowledgeable than he really was, able to expound a little on a lot of subjects, just enough to impress the naïve young woman. Nettie was 26 in 1886, and except for her time in Kansas she had lived her whole life in Clarence, surrounded by family. She was pretty, curious, devoted by nature, and bored. Joannetta Henrietta Fisher was, in short, just what the 'doctor' ordered.

Frederick and Eva Catherine's hard worldly experiences had certainly introduced them to a few Willis Bethels, and they knew that any marriage to such a man was doomed, that the cheating would start as soon as vows had ended, that the big deals would always fall apart, and that the creditors, and possibly the law, would always be hovering nearby. But their disapproval of him made Nettie all the more defiant, and she doubled down on the relationship, not only to vindicate Willis but also her own romanticism. Nettie's sister Anna, in the 1949 letter referenced above, wrote that Willis "was a good for nothing and our folks did every thing to prevent the wedding but Net would not give in and had to suffer for her dissibedience [sic]." The 89-year-old Anna's letter also gives us our only eyewitness account of the wedding ceremony, which took place on November 16, 1886:

> Aunt Net was married to Bethel by a M.E. minister named Swift much to our folks dissapointment [sic]. Mr. Schaad was here at the time and he too felt badly about it as he always came to my father if in trouble. I can remember the wedding very well. It took place in the parlor at home and Aunt Sarah & I stood at the door leading to the hall. Mother was on the other side of the room dress [sic] in black.[108]

Aunt Sarah was Sarah Lester, who would marry Nettie's older brother Jake a year and a half later but was probably already considered part of the family. Long friendships that became courtships were preferable in the slow seasonal rhythms of farm life at the time — you wouldn't want to have to get an annulment or something, after all. Mr. Schaad was Frederick Schaad, a minister and old friend of the Fishers, who was visiting from his home in Ohio. He made the trip specifically to try to talk Nettie out of the marriage.[109]

---

108 Letter, Anna Fisher Schurr to Eva Katherine Wiley, September 27, 1949, from Fisher family papers.
109 This information was related to me by my mother, Ida Fisher Caldemeyer.

This photograph from 1886 shows the Fisher children, along with some unidentified members of the extended family, standing in front of the house where they grew up on the family farm near Clarence, New York. Frederick and Eva Catherine raised their nine children, along with other relatives, in this home. Written on the back of the photo, probably by Joannetta: "The dear old log house our childhood home and memories never to be forgotten." The house was torn down soon after this photo was taken. D.W. Bethel is not in this picture, but he and Joannetta would marry a few months later, in November 1886.

Cropped from the previous photograph. (L-R): Katherine Fisher, unknown, unknown, Joannetta Fisher, unknown, Bertha Meyer, George Fisher.

Anna Fisher, Charles Fisher, Jacob Fisher, unknown (possibly Frederick Fisher, Jr.), unknown (possibly Frederick Fisher, Sr.).

The state of New York asked for more information than did Ohio on marriage licenses, and Willis must have been a little bemused when he filled out the form. This was his first excursion into bigamy, as far as we know, and his answers to the questions not only give us valuable information, but they also offer insights into his developing processes of deception. While on later licenses he lied about his age, he listed it correctly on this one. But he said his middle name was Willison and that his birthplace was Sadieville, Kentucky. He had clearly established some Kentucky connections by this time, and he may have been envisioning a move there, even at this early date. His father's name was recorded as William S. Beethel. Oddly, his own surname was spelled correctly, meaning that this was probably a misdirection decision he made in the moment, and did not fully consider. His mother's maiden name was Mary Williamson. According to the license, it was his first marriage.[111]

Bigamy was a serious offense that could have resulted in prison time had the authorities discovered it. At the same time, bigamy by geographic relocation was not uncommon in late nineteenth-century America, given the restrictiveness of divorce laws and the increasing mobility of the population.[112] The 1880s were a bustling time, and Willis knew that records were usually just filed away and forgotten. He must have believed that he was far enough

---

110 Photo from Fisher family papers. Included in *A History of the Family and Descendants of Frederick and Catherine Speith Fisher, 1825 — 1978*, by Daniel C. Fisher and Irene A. Fisher.
111 Marriage license, David Willison Bethel and Joannetta Fisher, Erie County, New York, November 16, 1886, Ancestry.com.
112 Beverly Schwartzberg, *"Lots of Them Did That": Desertion, Bigamy, and Marital Fluidity in Late-Nineteenth-Century America*, Project Muse, Journal of Social *History* 37.3 (2004): 573-600.

away from Ohio to pull it off, at least for a while, as long as he remained quiet about it. In support of this view is perhaps the most curious of the miscellaneous papers left to us by Nettie: a diagrammed sentence (ask an older relative if you don't know what it is) in her handwriting that reads, when written out, "One of his favorite maxims was that the only way to keep a secret is never to let any one suspect that you have one."[113] This statement is an apt description of D.W. Bethel's philosophy — he operated in several different circles at once and tried to never let any of them intersect. He also seemed to view all of his marriages as temporary arrangements. He interpreted "till death do us part" as "until I get bored."

It should be noted that Willis never owned up to bigamy in any of his 27 letters trying to reattach himself to Joannetta's life. He was certainly apologetic, mostly for his passions, and he offered many excuses for his conduct, but he always maintained that his past contained mistakes (like filling out an illegal marriage application or something?), not intentional wrongs, and that he was now a changed man. He was never specific about his exact transgressions, and he cast himself as a victim whenever his version of events allowed. As with any con man, his constant shift of focus talked around the issues. Since these letters are our primary records of events until 1897, this tendency frustrates our attempts to determine exactly what happened. But I'm sure Nettie found it even more irritating than I do.

Durward Frederick Bethel was born August 17, 1888, exactly one year after the death of his grandfather. The choice of middle names was an obvious tribute, but why the young couple chose the first name of Durward is unknown. From a Middle English occupational surname that meant "Door Guard," it was not as unheard of at the time as it is today, but it was still extremely uncommon.[114] The customs of the time generally called for the oldest son's first name to be chosen by the father.

Willis left his position as station agent on the West Shore Railroad sometime between March and August 1888. We don't know if he quit or was fired, but in his two years there he seems to have been an entrepreneurial employee, planning profitable excursion trips to Niagara Falls and Coney Island. We have two letters from his superiors commending his ingenuity and dedication to the company. On the other hand, there is another letter, dated August 22, 1888, after he had left the railroad, to Willis via the agent who had succeeded him in the office. It was from the auditor, wondering where the proceeds from 46 trip commutation tickets (tickets for multiple trips sold at reduced rates) were. It's unknown how, or if, the matter was resolved, but it was not the last time one of his employers would ask him what had happened to their money.[115]

He was an active member of the men's social community in the Clarence area. He belonged to the Independent Order of Odd Fellows in Lancaster, about 10 miles southwest of Clarence. He paid his dues continuously from July 1887 to October 1888, with a partial

---

113 Diagrammed sentence and transcription, from Fisher family papers.
114 BehindtheName.com.
115 Passes from the West Shore Railroad; Letters, *Officers at the West Shore Railroad to D.W. Bethel*, dated August 6, 1886 (2), August 22, 1888, from Fisher family papers. The last rail pass is dated March 19, 1888, and the letter from the Auditor's Office was dated August 22, so we know he left between these dates. It is likely that his departure was closer to the latter date than the former, since railroad auditors were usually prompt in their examination of the books, especially those of departed employees.

payment in April 1889, after which he evidently allowed his membership to lapse. It had probably served its purpose by this time, introducing him to some of the important men in the area and allowing him to establish relationships with them.[116]

He also owned a mare, named Kitty, that he bred actively in 1888 and 1889 at the Village Farm, a well-known breeding establishment for high-end racehorses in East Aurora, about 15 miles away. The farm, owned by Cicero J. Hamlin, "the most prominent and successful horse breeder" of his day, specialized in the development of elite Standardbred trotters.[117] Trotter racing was extremely popular in the late 1800s, and competition was especially fierce between New York and Kentucky stables. Some of the most famous horses of the day, including the great Mambrino King, were in Hamlin's possession. Willis was trying to establish his credentials in the highly competitive arena of harness racer breeding, and Kitty was fixed up with another of Hamlin's well-known trotters, Blackwood Chief, in 1888, a service which cost Willis twelve dollars.[118] We don't know what became of Kitty, or any foals she may have borne, after December 31, 1889, but Hamlin and his stallion will play a role in the next chapter.

In fall 1888, Willis enrolled in the University of Buffalo Medical Department. How much influence his uncle Doc's example had on this decision is unclear, as is how he financed his training. We know from his letters that he owed money to several people in the Clarence area, and maybe these were loans for his education. He was enrolled for the 1888-1889 and 1889-1890 sessions. We have his Practical Anatomy passes, which allowed him into lectures, and a 'perpetual ticket,' which meant he had paid his tuition and could attend whatever sessions were necessary for his program.[119] We don't know if the already-skeptical Fishers knew that he maintained his horse breeding activities and Odd Fellows membership while going into debt for his schooling, but if they did, it would only have fueled their negative opinions of him.

As mentioned in the preceding chapter, medical training in 1888 was not what it was to become in the twentieth century. It should not be considered bizarre that Willis, with only a high school diploma and some Normal school training, would set out on this path, even if the timing, with a newborn at home to support, seems strange. Doctors were often respected members of their communities, and they could make decent incomes. But their level of knowledge, along with the public's expectations and opinions of them, was substantially less than today, to be polite about it. A four-year undergraduate degree was not a requirement for matriculation until later — in fact, "in the immediate post-Civil War years . . . the most stringent entrance requirement was the ability to read and write, and many schools accepted less if the students could afford the fees."[120] In 1870, a prominent member of the Harvard medical faculty (generally considered the top medical school in the country at the time)

---

116 IOOF receipts. From Fisher family papers.
117 Ed Keller, *Cicero J. Hamlin *Village Farm* Among Trotting's Greatest*, from *Harness Horse*, included in *Pictorial and Historical Review, East Aurora and Vicinity*.
118 Receipt from the Village Farm, "for service Blackwood Chief 1888." From the Fisher family papers.
119 University of Buffalo Medical School passes, 1888-1890. From the Fisher family papers.
120 Kenneth Ludmerer, *Learning to Heal*, p. 43.

estimated "that over half of Harvard's medical students could barely write," and so could not be expected to pass written exams.[121] That professor, Henry Jacob Bigelow, along with many other of that institution's most distinguished professors, also saw the education of doctors and scientists as "mutually incompatible goals," and so eschewed laboratory experience from their instruction.[122] Charles W. Eliot, Harvard's president, wrote in 1880, "an American physician or surgeon may be, and often is, a coarse and uncultivated person, devoid of intellectual interests outside of his calling, and quite unable to either speak or write his mother tongue with accuracy."[123] The curriculum at most medical schools was taught for profit, 'on the side' by practicing doctors who divided the proceeds from student fees.[124] By 1888, several of the top medical schools in the U.S. (Harvard among them, at Eliot's insistence) were undergoing drastic and positive reforms to become the forerunners of today's world-class institutions. Matriculation requirements were stiffened to require bachelor's degrees, and the program was lengthened first to three years, and finally to four. Hands-on laboratory and clinical experiences, along with a gradated curriculum, became standard. But it's unknown how many of these changes had made their way to the University of Buffalo. There was probably an ongoing movement to strengthen the coursework when Willis enrolled, and there were some perfunctory nods toward laboratory instruction in their catalog, along with alliances with three local hospitals that allowed students to get some clinical understanding, but the place still adhered to the old philosophy of "practical" medicine, which emphasized lecture and demonstration.[125]

Doctors needed to know how to fix mechanical body failures and diagnose major illnesses, and to be comforting and sympathetic presences in their patients' lives. Willis was probably good at the last item. Unlike the present, there were few public expectations that they know how to cure diseases, even if they might know what caused them, especially the big killers such as typhus, tuberculosis, typhoid fever, scarlet fever, diphtheria, and influenza.[126] The newspapers were full of ads for tonics that promised relief from everything Pandora had let out of the box. Almost all were worthless concoctions whose major ingredient was either alcohol or opiates.[127] People were tougher then.

We have a small scrap of paper from Nettie's collection, in Willis's handwriting, that provides an interesting illustration of his powers of compartmentalization as well as a brief glimpse of the young family's life in Clarence.

---

121 Ibid., p. 12.
122 Ibid., p. 49.
123 Ibid., p. 13.
124 Ibid., p. 48.
125 University of Buffalo Medical School catalog, 1888-1889 fragments. From Fisher family papers.
126 Kenneth Ludmerer, *Learning to Heal*, p. 77.
127 Stewart H. Holbrook, *The Golden Age of Quackery*, pp. 5-9.

The top half of the slip lists medical courses followed by numbers. The bottom half reads, "Thanks Giving Nov 28th 1889 Kitchen Table Nettie preparing dinner & Durward coughing badly Not very hard Cough Bethel"

They are the idle scratchings of a nineteenth-century family man waiting for dinner. It appears that he sat down to make a budget and then began a reverie punctuated by random observations from his new profession. Part of Willis's complex personality may have truly enjoyed his home life with Nettie and being the head of his small New York household. But just over a month after this note was written, that family would be destroyed by the other part.

We know that the events that propelled him from Clarence occurred on December 31, 1889, but the exact circumstances remain unspecified in both the documents and in family

---

128 Scratch note, from Fisher family papers.

lore. The old story my mother told about a private investigator informing Nettie and her family about his still-binding Ohio marriage certainly may have been true, but it's unlikely that it happened on that date, or that it precipitated his exit from town. Eva Katherine Wiley, Nettie's niece, wrote to Alida Fisher in 1949, ". . . you said he (Willis) was married to someone else when he married Aunt Net. I had never heard that and I wonder if it was really true, now that I think of it." If her extended family did not even know of his bigamy, how could that have been the reason they chased her husband from his home? In the same letter Eva Wiley also wrote, "I have always heard that Durward's father ran around with other women — that was his weakness."[129] Oh, yeah. That rings true.

I believe that a private investigator or some other informant did contact the Fishers, but at a later date, and that the events of December 31, 1889, most likely flowed from the discovery of adultery, not bigamy. I think that he was found with another woman in a compromising situation, probably in the very act, by more than one person. Only overt infidelity would have turned the faithful Nettie against him and enabled her birth family to finally win her over — a passing flirtation was probably something she had come to expect. I believe that the other woman was Matilda Ralston Gilmour, that the family's informant was a man named Frank L. Carpenter, and that these events occurred at or near the University of Buffalo Medical Department building at the corner of Main and Virginia Streets.

Willis made references, some only in passing, to the events of that New Year's Eve in at least seven of his letters to Nettie. In the first one, on November 1, 1894, he wrote, "No body ever had any influence over me but you & if I had never got medicine into my head I'd always been true to you for when with you I was all right — when away I lost my head."[130] A letter from Nettie's cousin, Ed Seib, who was also a friend of Willis's, confirms the location of the transgression — "I do not approve of all he had done especially the trouble in Buffalo."[131] Both lines suggest that Willis's difficulties with the Fishers were related to his medical training.

In light of subsequent events, we can also speculate about the identity of the woman with whom he was caught. On November 22, 1894, also early in his correspondence and still full of apology, he wrote, "My application of passion for Mary's mother was so strong that it seemed I never could control it. She was a good woman but like me had such strong passions."[132]

We know that "Mary's mother" was Matilda Gilmour, whose maiden name was Ralston. She was born in Ireland around 1859, and she immigrated along with six of her siblings, settling in western Pennsylvania and working as a domestic. At some point in the 1880s, Matilda married a man named Gilmour, but he died in 1888. It seems likely that she arrived in the Buffalo area with her husband, then went back to working as a domestic servant to support herself following his death. And while it's pure conjecture, my suspicion is that she was employed as a housekeeper by the University of Buffalo Medical Department.

---

129 Letter, Eva Katherine Wiley to Alida Fisher, October 4, 1949, from Fisher family papers.
130 Letter, D.W. Bethel to Joannetta Fisher #1, November 1, 1894, from Fisher family papers.
131 Letter, Ed Seib to Joannetta Fisher, March 21, 1897, from Fisher family papers.
132 Letter, D.W. Bethel to Joannetta Fisher #6, November 22, 1894, from Fisher family papers.

Another major character in the drama that unfolded that New Year's Eve was Frank Carpenter. Willis's letters cast him in the role of Chief Scapegoat.

> No I never have seen Carpenter neither do I want to. If I ever do I am going to kill him in cold blood right where I meet him. Ever since you left me on his account I have carried a large revolver & always loaded purposely to kill him. Once I started to Buffalo when you told me he was practicing on William St. with the full determination of killing him. I got as far as Marietta, Ohio & told Dillon Pickering where & what I was going for. He persuaded me to not go further that day. He kept me visiting him there until my leave of absence had expired & I had to go back to my work but do you think I will not get his life some time? I took him in my house & kept him & then to have him step between the object I loved better than life. Had it not been for his acct. you never would have gone away.[133]

Willis was just proving his love with a little harmless trash talking. Later that year, he wrote, ominously, "No I don't think I am railing at fate. Fate has nothing to do with my case. It was Frank Carpenter the beggar I took in & not fate. I wish you would learn his exact location & give it to me. I want to go & see him when I go back to Calif. this fall. I will make a side trip to see him."[134]

What we know about Frank Lossing Carpenter fits nicely into the sequence of events. Born in central New York state in 1868, he received his medical degree from the University of Buffalo in the early 1890s. After graduation, he practiced for a while in the city, but he soon moved to California, eventually landing in Berkeley, where he maintained a lucrative private practice and a teaching position at the University of California. He became a prominent citizen, and by 1930 he lived in a prosperous area of Berkeley with his wife, son, and daughter-in-law.[135]

His introduction allows us to construct a plausible scenario for how events unfolded. Willis either lost or quit his railroad job in summer 1888, and he decided to begin training to become a doctor. That would allow him to support his family, and depending on his acumen, it might have provided a step up in pay from his job as station agent. It may even have been seen as a positive move by some of the Fisher family and their close-knit community of friends, since doctors were of more use to them than telegraphers, and he probably borrowed

---

[133] Letter, D.W. Bethel to Joannetta Fisher #16, May 16, 1897, from Fisher family papers. The reader may initially interpret Willis's rantings as an accusation that Nettie was somehow involved with Frank Carpenter, but there is nothing that supports that scenario. Had this been the case, even in Willis's suspicions, the tone and content of all of his correspondence would have been much different. He was simply blaming Frank Carpenter for informing the Fishers of his indiscretions in these passages. Willis always claimed that his misdeeds were not as bad as they were represented, and so Dr. Carpenter became the object of his fury.

[134] Letter, D.W. Bethel to Joannetta Fisher #20, July 3, 1897, from Fisher family papers.

[135] New York State Census, 1892, Buffalo, Erie, New York, Dr. F. L. Carpenter; Directories, Berkeley, California, Frank L. Carpenter, 1904 (p.602), 1909 (p. 1014), 1917 (p. 300); U.S. Census, 1920, 1930, Berkeley, Alameda County, California, Frank L. Carpenter; California Voter Registration, Frank Lossing Carpenter, Vacaville, Solano County, California, 1896, all Ancestry.com.

money from some of them to pay his tuition and expenses while he was in school. Frank Carpenter was a friend of the Fishers who shared Willis's medical aspirations. He roomed with the Bethels, and the two men probably rode the train together to classes each day. When he somehow witnessed Willis's indiscretions with Matilda Ralston Gilmour, Carpenter felt compelled to tell the Fishers. The evidence must have been so incontrovertible that even the fast-talking Willis Bethel couldn't find a way around it — that's why I think the lovebirds may have been discovered at the medical school, *in flagrante delicto*, by a group of people. It was an intolerable embarrassment for the Fisher family, who disliked Willis anyway, and there must have been a formidable array of angry relatives assembled when he returned to Clarence that evening. It seems that they removed Nettie and Durward from the Bethel home to the family farm, and that is what Willis meant when he wrote, "What feelings came over me that Dec. 31st when I came home & found you gone your things too & all without a single word of warning,"[136] and, "I can hardly allow my self to think of those days & the days that have elapsed since on that Dec. 31 I left your front door & your yard — you standing there face wet with tears and our darling boy in your arms."[137]

It must have been clear to him that none of his misdirection plays would work, and he just packed his trunk and left. In his haste, he neglected to take some articles, which Nettie saved and passed down to us. It's probably fair to say that Durward's farm-hardened uncles strongly encouraged Willis to leave as soon as possible, and that they made some convincing arguments, both verbal and physical.

The year 1890 dawned without D.W. Bethel in his home in Clarence. Ida Fisher Caldemeyer reported that after the initial hurt had subsided, Nettie wanted to follow her man. Hearing this, Eva Catherine Speith Fisher had finally had enough. For the previous four years, through the grief of her husband's death and the worry her daughter's decisions had caused her family, she had put up with the situation, waiting for the inevitable, but hoping that Joannetta would come to see the world more realistically, that her 29-year-old child would finally grow up. She now told her that it was time to choose between her fantasy world and the real one. Should she go, she was no longer a member of the family and could never return. Nettie, forced to choose between the man she loved and the network of kinship that loved and protected her and her sixteen-month-old son, finally made a wise decision. She would pay a psychological and emotional price for it for the rest of her life.

It was probably sometime later that Nettie was informed of Willis's still-binding marriage to Jennie Howell Bethel of Flushing, Ohio, which only escalated and confirmed her mother's negative opinion of him, and so bigamy became the reason for the separation in the family story that was handed down to Durward's children. We don't know whether this was via a private investigator hired by Jennie or by some other means. In 1892, Jennie gave written testimony that her marriage was still binding to a referee of the New York courts as part of Nettie's annulment proceedings. She also initiated divorce proceedings against Willis in November of that year, and it may have been the discovery of his marriage to Nettie that

---

136 Letter, D.W. Bethel to Joannetta Fisher #16, May 16, 1897, from Fisher family papers.
137 Letter, D.W. Bethel to Joannetta Fisher #13, March 19, 1897, from Fisher family papers.

convinced her to pursue that action. But prior to the 1920s detective agencies, whose services were expensive, were almost exclusively retained by governments or corporations, so it seems unlikely that Jennie, who cleaned houses for a living, hired one.[138] It's possible that a railroad company or a bonding agency employed a P.I. to dig into Willis's background, and that they informed the Fishers of his marriage to Jennie, and Jennie of his bigamous marriage to Nettie.

A bizarre twist in the story comes to us via the previously quoted letter to Nettie from her cousin, Ed Seib. In 1897, he lived in Missouri with his wife Millie and their young daughter when Willis paid them a visit. Both men openly admitted that his purpose was to get Ed to put in a good word for him with Nettie, which he was happy to do in a long, imploring letter. A single line, delivered almost offhandedly, deserves mention here. Seib wrote, "He told me all about Jennie & that you knew of that before you married."[139] At first glance, this is a family history hand grenade, indicating that Nettie had married a man she knew to already be married.

Although difficult to believe for a number of reasons, it certainly deserves exploration. The young Joannetta Fisher seems to have been liberal in her views, especially for her era. Ben Perry (the Owingsville, Kentucky postmaster who will come into prominence in the next chapter) observed that from her letters Nettie didn't seem to be too indignant about Willis's bigamy with Matilda. As Perry put it, "it's a Penitentiary Offence to have two Wifes without Being divorced from One. but from the way you write I take it that you would not Interrupt Dr. Bethel with the law. . ."[140] Young Nettie held a contemptuous attitude toward social mores and retained a naïve belief in the power of love over social contracts. But it's hard to believe that she would have knowingly entered into a sham marriage, no matter what her beliefs, or that she would have brought a child into the world that she knew to be illegitimate, no matter how smitten she was.

But the main argument against Ed Seib knowing the truth about Willis's first marriage comes from the contents of his own letter. He was clearly a devoted family man who would never treat an offense such as bigamy so lightly, and make just a passing, almost casual, reference to it. If, as he had already said, he didn't approve of the "trouble in Buffalo," meaning adultery, then he would have been aghast to find that his old friend was a bigamist who had purposely made a fool of his cousin. In his next letter to Nettie, Willis revealed, "I never told Ed's wife any thing but he did. She told him she pitied me and blamed me but she felt sure that had I another chance she believed I would be all right."[141] Adultery might deserve pity, blame, and maybe forgiveness, but bigamy and family abandonment would not be something that Millie Seib, or any other nineteenth-century wife, would view as anything but a fatal character flaw. Women of that era were simply at too much risk if their man left them. Abandonment violated the most basic aspects of the marital contract — a wife's submissiveness was purchased by the promise of male protection and financial support. Ed's

---

138 *History of Private Investigations*, asginvestigations.com.
139 Letter, Ed Seib to Joannetta Fisher, March 21, 1897, from Fisher family papers.
140 Letter, Ben Perry to Joannetta Fisher #2, June 4, 1894, from Fisher family papers.
141 Letter, D.W. Bethel to Joannetta Fisher #14, May 2, 1897, from Fisher family papers.

words and actions show that he subscribed to this view. If he had known the whole truth, as Willis claimed he did, Ed would never have sent Nettie a letter on his behalf. So, regardless of how it might first appear when we read it now, it's almost certain that Ed Seib was not referring to bigamy when he wrote the words, "all about Jennie." The most likely explanation is that Willis told both Ed and Nettie (prior to their marriage) that he had had an affair with Jennie, whom he likely portrayed as a seductive older woman, when he was a young man in Flushing. He probably also admitted that a child had resulted from the union. That was scandalous enough in that era.

By the time Ed wrote his letter to her in 1897, of course, Nettie did indeed know 'all about Jennie,' and she must have read his words with the consternation of the falsely accused. Willis's next letter, on May 2, 1897, seems to confirm this view, although it requires that we read between the lines. "I desire to thank you cordially for waiting to write Ed Seib until you should hear from me further. You know Ed & I were always good friends & he being your cousin I thought I would go & see him & see if he could help me in some way." Obviously, there were some things Nettie knew that Willis did not want her to tell his honest, gullible friend Ed. We don't know how, or even if, she answered Ed's letter, but Willis's pleadings, promises and excuses, along with her own intentions to possibly reunite with him, would have prevented her from telling Ed the whole truth, anyway. That, of course, fit neatly into Willis's plans.

Over three years after his exit, on April 14, 1893, the Supreme Court in and for the County of Erie, New York, granted Joannetta Bethel's petition to annul her marriage to David W. Bethel,

> upon the ground that the former wife of the defendant was living and that the marriage with the former wife was then in force; and it appearing to the Court that the marriage between plaintiff and defendant was contracted by the plaintiff in good faith and without any knowledge on the part of the plaintiff of such former marriage which fact the Court hereby determines.

The most persuasive pieces of evidence were, "written interrogatories of Jennie Bethel a material witness in this action."[142] Unsurprisingly, Willis was a no-show.

With that decision, Nettie's and Durward's surname officially became Fisher.[143] It appears that Joannetta kept the annulment proceedings secret from some members of her family. Her sister Anna, to whom she was not close, did not know the particulars, as evidenced by her 1949 note to her daughter Eva Katherine Wiley, "I never knew if she had a divorce but must have or she could not have married again."[144] Nettie must have had financial help to hire the legal assistance she needed, and it seems likely that Eva Catherine Speith Fisher, the matriarch who most wanted to press the 'undo' button on her daughter's ill-conceived

---
142 Bethel vs. Bethel Annulment, Supreme Court of Erie County, New York, April 14, 1893, from Fisher family papers.
143 Ibid.
144 Letter, Anna Fisher Schurr to Eva Katherine Wiley, September 27, 1949, from Fisher family papers.

marriage, was the one who paid the cost to legally erase David Willis Bethel from her family. Nettie probably undertook the suit unenthusiastically, at her mother's insistence, after Eva Catherine learned the truth about the bigamy. In fact, the naïve and faithful Nettie remained in secret communication with her skunk of a husband.

Eva Catherine Speith Fisher, around 1913, twenty years after the annulment of Nettie's marriage to Willis Bethel.

---

145 Photo from Fisher family papers.

4.

"A Large Stout Well Built, Good Form Woman but Not Purty"

■ WE DON'T KNOW WHERE WILLIS SPENT EARLY 1890, but he was probably in Bowling Green, Kentucky for a while.[146] He probably also visited Cincinnati from time to time. He needed to rebuild a career of some kind, whether on a railroad or via some new option. Matilda may have remained in western New York, or she may have moved back to her sister's place in Pennsylvania while he secured a new home for them in the south. There is no way to know how much she knew about his marital situation. It seems unlikely that she knew about Jennie or Nettie, although one would think that the "trouble in Buffalo" might have made her ask some questions. Was she like Nettie, smitten to the point of forgiveness of almost all his shortcomings, or did he have her convinced that he was single? We'll probably never know the answers to these questions. Matilda was over 30 by this time, widowed, childless, and perhaps possessed of limited options, as we will see. She may have known a good deal of the truth, but still saw David Willis Bethel as the best in a group of rapidly diminishing possibilities.

On September 3, 1890, eight months after Willis left Clarence, the two lovers were married in Venango County, Pennsylvania, at the farmhouse of Thompson McGinnes.[147] McGinnes was married to Matilda's older sister, Sarah Jane. The farm was near the small town of Emlenton, about 70 miles north of Pittsburgh and 180 miles south of Buffalo.

The marriage license recorded Willis's age as 29 (he was 30) and his father's name as Daniel W. Bethel, but the most interesting item was his occupation — 'Physician.'[148] We don't know how much of his medical education he had completed. The only lecture/demonstration passes left in Nettie's possession were from the 1888 — 1889 academic year, although there is a matriculation receipt for the 1889 — 1890 year, which he would have received

---

146 The only evidence of his residence there is his own declaration on the marriage license, hence it is unreliable information, although he had no real reason to lie. That sometimes didn't prevent him from doing so, however.
147 The spelling of this surname has become standardized as "McGinnis" since the early twentieth century, but all records of Thompson McGinnes use this spelling.
148 Marriage License, David W. Bethel and Matilda R. Gilmour, Venango County, Pennsylvania, September 3, 1890, Ancestry.com.

after payment of his fall tuition. But he seems to have decided, probably correctly, that the completion of his training was unnecessary to the actual practice of medicine in rural areas, given the low expectations of patients there. This calculation may also have influenced his choice of states.

The first part of his Kentucky period, from 1890 through 1892, contains some of the more bizarre incidents of his story. We can trace the origins of his schemes at his previous stops, but it was in Kentucky that he put them all into action, in a crescendo of spectacular failure. It's also a period that was generally well documented, and thanks to the letters Nettie kept, newspaper accounts, and, especially, a surviving issue of Wallace's Monthly, a periodical dedicated to the trotter racing industry, we have a good idea of what happened at Owingsville, and later at Lexington, in 1892.

He began in the familiar position of station agent, this time for the Chesapeake & Ohio at Preston (the place was also known, appropriately enough, as Crooks) in Bath County, about 40 miles east of Lexington. In a pattern that he would repeat at other stops, Willis hired an assistant and trained the young man in the necessities of the agent/operator's position. His name was Leslie B. Wilson, and he was from Stanford, just south of Lexington. He was about 21 years old, and he may have been related on his mother's side — he certainly bore the same surname, and we know that Willis had extended family from both the Bethel and Wilson clans in the region. After his apprenticeship, when he got a job with the Kentucky Union Railroad, the Owingsville Outlook reported that, "Mr. Wilson learned railroading under Dr. D.W. Bethel, and is therefore amply qualified for the responsible place he is now filling,"[149] an indication of the esteem with which Willis was regarded in the community in early 1892. In addition to his station agent duties, he was also in the horse breeding business. He maintained a pedigreed stallion at a farm southeast of Cincinnati.

Matilda gave birth to Mary R. Bethel (her middle name was almost certainly Ralston, her mother's maiden name), at Preston on September 30, 1891. It was probably in early 1892 that the family moved to nearby Owingsville, the Bath County seat.

Benjamin Franklin Perry was a lifelong resident of Bath County, amiably inclined, trusted by all who knew him, and just a bit of a busybody. He had been an important member of Owingsville society for years, working in a variety of retail capacities, and serving as treasurer of the local masonic lodge and as a deacon in his church. Perry began his tenure as postmaster of Owingsville in 1893.[150] He was 65 when he exchanged two letters with Nettie in spring 1894, some two years after the events in question, in response to her inquiries about her bigamous former husband. Notwithstanding the annulment of her marriage in April 1893, she yet remained curious about his whereabouts and marital situation. It seems likely that she was secretly corresponding with Willis before he was forced to leave Owingsville in summer 1892, and that she wrote to the postmaster trying to find his new location. From our point of view, except for his vagueness on timelines and specifics, she could not have picked a better correspondent. Like most postmasters of the era, Perry was one who kept close watch on the

---

149 The Owingsville Outlook, March 22, 1892, reprinted in the (Stanford) Interior Journal, Newspapers.com.
150 James Adair Richards, *A History of Bath County, Kentucky*, pp. 534-535.

doings of his small town, and he appears to have also been a member of Willis's general, although not inner, circle of friends. His first letter was just a warm-up for the revelations that were to come in the second one.

> May 24th 1894
> Mrs. Nettie Fisher
> Clarence
> N.Y.
>
> Yours of the 21st inst. to hand, asking about D.W. Bethel. I was well acquainted with him, he lived in my town, for some time.
>
> Passed as Dr. D.W. Bethel, had for a while considerable practice. I have not heard from him for some time. He had a wife while here and one child or at least passed her for his wife. I have a friend that I think knows whare [sic] he is.
>
> Are you any kind to him and how long since you heard from him. I received yours as asked by you Strictly Confidential. You asked me to tell you if married. He told me he was. His wife was a large likely woman had one child. Any further information will be thankfully given and held Strictly Confidential. Let me hear from you.
>
> Very Respectfully,
> Ben F. Perry, P.M.[151]

Notice that he addressed her as "Mrs. Nettie Fisher," which must have been how she had signed her letter to him. It was, of course, self-contradictory, since Fisher was her maiden name, and this gives us some indication of her internal conflict. Nettie still considered herself to be married, no matter what the law or her mother said. Her most pressing question seems to have concerned Matilda, whether Willis was married to her and what she looked like. She must have written right back, because on June 4 Perry described Willis's time in his town in some detail.

> June 4th 1894
> Mrs. Nettie Fisher
> Clarence
> N.Y.
>
> Yours of the 30th May to hand in reply will say that Dr. D.W. Bethel lived

---

151 Letter, Benjamin F. Perry to Joannetta Fisher #1, May 24, 1894, from Fisher family papers.

> Some time at Preston Station, Ky. 5 miles South of this place. He was Rail Road Agent at that Station, and the nearest Station to this town, and whare all the goods are Shipped for the town. He was very well acquainted with all the business men of this town and his Standing was very good. He went into Partnership with Dr. J.T. Catlett of this town to Practice Medicine. Dr. Catlett is a very Prominent Physician. Dr. Bethel then moved to this town. Seemed to me to have a good practice, and I thought was doing very well.[152]

Willis's brief medical career came into focus first. Kentucky had established its State Board of Health in 1878, at which time it was discovered that 20% of the doctors in the state had never attended medical school, and it set out to remedy the situation.[153] By 1892 it had established statewide licensing requirements, although verification was left to local communities. As the garrulous local station agent, Willis must have talked up his medical training, saying he had his diploma, and probably experience, and was looking to go back into practice. John Thruston Catlett was descended from a prominent old Virginia family from Gloucester County. Catlett was 52 in 1892, twenty years Willis's senior. He was a Confederate Civil War veteran who had moved to Owingsville afterward, where he married the daughter of a local judge. The couple had three children, and the family was frequently included in the Personal Mention section of the local papers. Like Perry, Catlett merited a brief biography in J. A. Richards's *A History of Bath County, Kentucky*.

> Dr. Catlett ranked high in his profession and enjoyed a large practice. Socially he enjoyed the highest popularity and was always a welcome member of the most cultivated circles. He was a man of striking physique, of splendid form, handsome and distinguished in appearance and possessing the cultured manners of a dignified gentleman of the politest society.[154]

He was also a colorful character, which was probably not unusual for a gentleman in the lawless Kentucky countryside of the late nineteenth century. He was involved in at least three lawsuits (one as a plaintiff and two as a defendant) in the 1880s, and in August 1891 a warrant had been issued for his arrest, probably for gambling.[155] Catlett was a good old boy who saw the rules as advisory, and his friends were probably similarly inclined. It was exactly the kind of group where Willis was comfortable working his magic, although Catlett and his crowd certainly possessed boundaries that Willis didn't. It appears that, initially, at least, they welcomed him warmly.

We know that the partnership began in spring 1892. Willis's Kentucky medical license

---

152 Letter, Benjamin F. Perry to Joannetta Fisher #2, June 4, 1894, from Fisher family papers.
153 Hamilton Tapp and James C. Klotter, *Kentucky: Decades of Discord, 1865-1900*, p.85.
154 James Adair Richards, *A History of Bath County, Kentucky*, p.307.
155 Summons Orders, Bath County Circuit Court, Farmers National Bank vs. J.T. Catlett, February 16 and April 1, 1887; Summons Orders, Bath County Circuit Court, J. M. Richart vs. J.T. Catlett, September 22, 1885; Bath County Circuit Court Index to Suits, J.T. Catlett vs. S.E. Fratman; Bath County Circuit Court Bench Warrant, J.T. Catlett, August 1891, all photographed from the Bath County Courthouse records, Owingsville, Kentucky.

was dated April 29, but a blurb from an Owingsville newspaper dated March 31, 1892, referenced the formation of the partnership.[156] Although the license was voided as of April 30, the County Clerk must have done that after Willis left town that summer, as his frauds became evident. We know that he practiced medicine for "a few months,"[157] (from his own account) and "for a while" (from Perry's).[158] The information on the license lists his age as 27 (he was 32), and he said he had been born in Buffalo, New York. He even listed the date of his graduation as March 24, 1889, although since he was still enrolled at the University of Buffalo for the 1889 — 1890 academic year, that was obviously impossible. So how was he able to obtain a license without a diploma? He may have had a falsified one, but it seems more likely that he just promised the County Clerk, W. W. Perry (who was probably related to Ben Perry in some way) that his diploma was on the way. Maybe he said he had left it in New York, and it was being sent to him, or he may have used some other combination of excuse and promise, along with his powers of persuasion, to extract what he wanted without producing the evidence.

Dr. Bethel seemed to have everything a man could want in early 1892 — a profession, a family, and even a lucrative side business. But it was that business and his involvement in the vibrant Kentucky horse racing culture that created the scandal that would blow everything up and reveal his other deceptions. At the time, the Bluegrass State was competing with New York to be the center of the industry, and the discussion of horses was "the one subject always in order."[159] The Bath County Stock & Trotting Association was the local organization that supported these activities, sponsoring the annual races at the nearby Sharpsburg Fair each August. Gambling was illegal, but it was still the pastime of many men of means, and it was generally tolerated as long as it remained discreet. But discretion was sometimes difficult for a Kentucky gentleman of the era to maintain, and in early 1892 the Association had been convicted of not so secretly running a variety of betting machines and games at the 1891 fair. They ended up paying a fine of $250.[160] The charges against Catlett were probably related to those events.

In western New York, Willis had bred Kitty at least twice at the Village Farm. As the owner of the mare, he had been responsible for all the cost and risk of the breeding process. But the stallion simply donated his semen and left, and that course of action must have appealed strongly to Willis's own inclinations. As a bonus, the studding process also yielded fees to the stallion's owner.

---

156 *Yesterdays*, Bath County News-Outlook, March 24, 1938, clipping photocopied from the files of the Bath County Historical Association in the Bath County Memorial Library, Owingsville, Kentucky.
157 Letter, D.W. Bethel to Joannetta Fisher #3, November 4, 1894, from Fisher family papers.
158 Letter, Benjamin F. Perry to Joannetta Fisher #1, May 24, 1894, from Fisher family papers.
159 Hamilton Tapp and James C. Klotter, *Kentucky: Decades of Discord, 1865-1900*, p. 103.
160 *Big To Dos*, The Bath County News-Outlook, September 2, 2004. This story looks back at some of the more memorable fairs in Bath County history, including the one in 1891, clipping photocopied from the genealogy section of the Bath County Memorial Library, Owingsville, Kentucky; Bath County Circuit Court Bench Warrant, The Bath County Stock and Trotting Association, August 1891, photographed from the Bath County Courthouse records, Owingsville, Kentucky.

161 Medical License, Dr. David W. Bethel, Bath County, Kentucky, 1892. Image from microfilm on file with Family History Library, Salt Lake City, Utah.

Blackwood Chief 7670 was the Village Farm stallion that Willis had bred with Kitty.[162] The horse was well known and hailed from a distinguished trotting pedigree, including the legendary Dictator, who was the father of his dam, Dictator Maid. It should be noted here that there was another, older horse that also bore the name of Blackwood Chief, numbered 6360. In those early days of Standardbred breeding, registrations under the same name were allowed by the Trotting Association, with the number establishing the difference. Willis would use the confusion caused by this duplication, along with a change in naming requirements by the Trotting Association in 1891, as part of his smokescreen to disguise the schemes that were to follow.

On February 2, 1892, J. H. Steiner, registrar for the Trotting Association, received a request to register a Standardbred stallion named Dictawood, son of Dictator. The request came from a man named E. H. Smith, who lived in New Jersey and was acting on behalf of H. P. Brown, a telegraph operator living at Crooks, Bath County, Kentucky.[163] Brown had supplied Smith with all the necessary paperwork, including a certificate dated March 4, 1880, signed by H. C. McDowell, Dictator's owner, that read,

> Sold to-day to H. P. Brown, Cincinnati, brown colt Dictawood, four white ankles, star, strip and snip, foaled May 3, 1879. Sired by Dictator, 113. First dam Rosewood, by Blackwood, 75; second dam Rose Edwards, by Frazier's Mambrino, for $400, and I hereby release all claim to said colt, in consideration of the purchase money having all been paid.[164]

The horses mentioned were well known in racing circles, and Dictawood appeared to be a valuable property. Steiner issued the registration in March, but two months later he had cause to regret it. Information from multiple informants in southern Ohio and northern Kentucky attested that the horse in question was, in fact, owned by Dr. D.W. Bethel, now living in Owingsville, and that he had been studded out the previous year under the name of Blackwood Chief 7670. Dr. Bethel kept the horse in a stable owned by Zeno F. Barker, near Carthage, Kentucky, about 80 miles from Owingsville. The gentlemen were wondering why the horse's name and lineage seemed to have inexplicably changed over the winter. Steiner contacted McDowell, a well-known horse breeder who lived near Lexington. McDowell declared that the certificate was a forgery and that no such colt had ever been foaled at his establishment. In his letter back to Steiner, he called the fraud "just the slip an unprincipled scamp would make."[165] Steiner then revoked Dictawood's registration and wrote letters to both H. P. Brown and Dr. Bethel, demanding that the registration certificate be returned.[166]

---

162 The number following a horse's name was a consecutive designation assigned by the trotting registry at the time of registration, meaning that this Blackwood Chief was the 7670th stallion registered. Of course, registration of a Standardbred, as with any pedigreed horse, required evidence of its lineage.

163 Crooks was the name of the U.S. Post Office and Preston was the name of the station (Robert M. Rennick, *Kentucky Place Names*).

164 *A Big Fraud*, Wallace's Monthly, August 1892, p. 448.

165 Ibid. This quote is a great description of Willis Bethel in the language of the day.

166 Ibid., pp. 447-448.

His letter to Dr. Bethel concluded,

> We propose to thoroughly ventilate this fraud through *Wallace's Monthly*, and hope you will be able to show that you are in no way connected with it, and give you this opportunity to make your statement in the case.

For some strange reason, Brown never responded to the registrar, but Willis wrote back promptly:

> Owingsville, Ky., June 15, 1892
> J. H. Steiner, Esq.,
>
> Dear Sir: Yours is just before me. In reply will say that I bought the horse from Brown on March 4, 1891. At the time he gave me written statement of his breeding, giving me a note of hand to have him registered. This he neglected to do until I forced him to do it. He then had it done and had the certificate sent to himself at Crooks and gave me an order to get it. I would send you the certificate, but when I got sufficient evidence that the horse was a fraud, I burned it because I wanted no horse that was in controversy, more especially where I could see that it had been done so fraudulently.
>
> His address was Montgomery, W. Va., but you will see by the returned letter enclosed that he is not there now.
>
> I hope you will expose this and let it be a lesson to him. I would not again suffer the humiliation for the horse were his pedigree straight. If there is anything I can do to help you in any way let me know, of if anything remains unanswered I will take pleasure in answering it.
>
> Yours very truly,
> D.W. Bethel[167]

Doggone that H. P. Brown fellow, anyhow! He had humiliated, even swindled, our long-suffering hero, after all. Unfortunately for Willis, Steiner already had numerous accounts that contradicted his letter, including signed affidavits by at least three owners of mares who

---

[167] Ibid., p. 449. Note that Willis had planned ahead somewhat in case accusations of dishonesty were directed against him. He had sent a letter to the apocryphal H. P. Brown in West Virginia, knowing that it would be returned to him, and he then sent the returned letter on to Steiner as evidence that Brown was the true fraudster. Were it not for all the other evidence that came to light, this dodge might have been effective.

had bred their stock to the stallion they believed was Blackwood Chief 7670 in 1891. They questioned the existence of anyone named H. P. Brown. One of these men, James A. Burke, wrote, ". . . it will do you no good to write to H. P. Brown. He is known as a railroad telegraph operator, and you are just as liable to find him in Oklahoma as Crooks, Bath county, Ky. You write the postmaster there and you will find he is unknown." In rural America in 1892, if the postmaster didn't know you, then you didn't live there.

Burke, clearly incensed, had done some detective work of his own. His letter to Steiner continued,

> Mr. Bethel bought this horse from M. M. Marks, No. 111 Court St., Cincinnati, Ohio. Mr. Marks bought him from a man at Warsaw, Ky., name unknown but he was proprietor of a hotel at that place. The horse is supposed to be a saddle-horse. I sent a gentleman to see Mr. Marks yesterday and charged him how he should approach him, which is how I got this information. He says the horse is a high-bred saddle-horse. My agent didn't tell him how Bethel had the horse represented, and he is ignorant of the facts of the case.[168]

So, Brown was fictional, and Marks was ignorant of the scam and off the hook, but Willis now had it firmly embedded in his jaw.[169] Burke recommended that Steiner confirm his accusations by writing to two other horse breeders in northern Kentucky, Jacob Anderson and Edward Treaver, who had bred mares to Willis's stallion in 1891. Both men were "very sore about the matter," as rumors spread that the horse was a fake. These gentlemen swore affidavits under oath that the horse Willis had represented as Blackwood Chief 7670 and Dictawood were the same animal. Anderson's contribution read, in part, that in 1891 he had,

> bred to a horse standing for service, owned or controlled by D.W. Bethel . . ., advertised as Blackwood Chief 7670. The affiant further swears that he has seen the horse now standing at the barn of Z. F. Barker, Carthage, Ky., owned by D.W. Bethel, and advertised as Dictawood, 18652.
>
> The affiant further swears that the horse Dictawood, and Blackwood Chief as above mentioned, are one and the same horse.[170]

---

168 Ibid.
169 For readers who are wondering, E. H. Smith was also ignorant of the scam. Smith simply ran a registration service for pedigreed horses, and Willis, under the pseudonym H. P. Brown, responded to his advertisement.
170 *A Big Fraud,* Wallace's Monthly, August 1892, p. 449-450.

Wallace's Monthly went on,

> Mr. Treaver also enclosed a letter from Dr. Bethel evidently in reply to the one calling attention to the fact that the horse Blackwood Chief was not what he was represented to be. In this letter Dr. Bethel says, "Probably you are not aware that prior to May 19, 1891, two different stallions could be registered under the same name. Such was our unfortunate predicament, hence the change in the name, because the other Blackwood Chief, 7670, was an older horse. Mr. Hamlin never owned the horse that Mr. Barker has, hence of course the difference," etc.[171]

The games were in full swing now, and Willis was losing badly. His lies upon lies were being discovered, and his answers to every inquiry just buried him deeper. The statements in his letter to Treaver were, of course, contrary to all known facts, not to mention self-contradictory. He now claimed that the horse he studded out in 1891 was another Blackwood Chief, not 7670. Not only was this an obvious fabrication (Blackwood Chief 6360 was in St. Louis at the time, and was older, not younger, than Blackwood Chief 7670), it was the opposite of what he had told the breeders the previous year. And then there was the question of lineage. Blackwood Chief 6360, Blackwood Chief 7670, and Dictawood all had different lineages, and (unsurprisingly) Dictawood's was the most impressive of the three. One would think that having to re-register a stallion under a different name would not affect his ancestry, but in this case, Dictawood's family stock had miraculously improved.

To further muddy the waters, Willis traveled back to Buffalo in March 1892 and leased the real Blackwood Chief 7670 from Hamlin, bringing him to Kentucky. Presumably, his intention was to add him to, or switch him with, Dictawood at Barker's stable. Then he could point to the similarity in the horses' appearances and say that the breeders who were accusing him of fraud were simply mistaken. But the attempt fell apart once Steiner revoked the registration and sent a letter to Hamlin inquiring about Blackwood Chief 7670. Hamlin's response was to send his superintendent to Kentucky, ". . . and (take) Blackwood Chief away from Dr. Bethel, Mr. Hamlin not caring to have any further dealing with the man."[172]

Ben Perry chimed in with his own account, as his letter continued:

> Claimed to have a very fine Stallion, or Stable horse thorough bred, had him registered at Lexington, Ky., name and all. And it was all fictitious and was so Denounced by the Stock farm at Lexington, Ky. And Just about that time a party Come from the east that owned the horse. he had no intrest in the horse. And Dr. Bethel promised the man that he would go with him next morning to the Country, whare he had the horse but Dr. Bethel Left that night and never Come back to town any more. but before the man Come for the horse, I Showed

---

171 Ibid., p. 450.
172 Ibid.

Dr. Bethel what was published in the Paper about him and that what he Said about the horse was a lie. He Said to me that it was not a lie and Claimed that he had bought the horse from a Party and that the Party had given him a bill of Sale of the horse. I then Said to Dr. Bethel that you are all wright if you have the bill of Sale of the horse. And he replyd to me that when it Come out in the Paper, that he tore up the bill of Sale. I Saw then he had never had any bill of Sale. And I further Said to him that was I in his place that I would go among the People whare I was raised and Show my Standing. he Said to me that he would do that but he left in a hurry and never Come back and he left owing Considerable.[173]

The stories in the papers and the arrival of Hamlin's superintendent shattered all of Willis's pretenses, as well as what was left of his reputation. Without the real Blackwood Chief 7670 in his possession, and with the disavowals of McDowell and the Trotting Register, the whole house of cards came down. If we look past the double-talk, it seems clear what really happened. Willis visited Moses M. Marks, a horse dealer in Cincinnati, where he noticed a horse that he thought could pass for Blackwood Chief 7670, with whom he was familiar from his time in western New York. He bought the stallion (relatively cheaply, no doubt), housed him at Barker's stables, and bred him as Blackwood Chief 7670 during the 1891 season.[174] According to Burke, the horse was studded to "some fifty or sixty mares," which must have yielded some good returns.[175]

But for some reason he had to push the fraud further, and early in 1892 he decided to have the horse registered under a false pedigree. He invented the fictional railroad telegrapher, H.P. Brown, and forged the bill of sale from McDowell along with whatever other paperwork was needed. In February, under Brown's name, he sent his 'evidence' to E. H. Smith in New Jersey, who was in the business of securing registrations for horses of pedigree who remained undocumented. Smith sent in the application and Steiner issued the papers in March. To confuse the situation, Willis leased the real Blackwood Chief from Hamlin the same month. But by June, McDowell's disavowal of the bill of sale and the outcry by the owners of the mares, who had been suspicious before the name change but certain of wrongdoing afterward, made Steiner reconsider. Once Hamlin's superintendent arrived to take Blackwood Chief home, Willis finally realized that the scam wasn't going to work, and he decided it was time to disappear. Being diplomatic, as nineteenth-century custom demanded, Wallace's Monthly concluded:

> The Monthly leaves its readers to judge for themselves as to Dr. Bethel's

---

173 Letter, Ben Perry to Joannetta Fisher #2, June 4, 1894, from Fisher family papers.
174 Barker may have been related somehow to Willis. Records indicate that another descendant of Henry Bethel, Benjamin Bethel's granddaughter Ella Jane, had married a man named Barker, and that he had connections to northern Kentucky. Although a direct connection to Zeno F. Barker of Carthage, Kentucky, cannot be established at this time, it seems likely that Zeno was one of Willis's many friends from his broad extended family.
175 *A Big Fraud*, Wallace's Monthly, August 1892, p. 448.

position in the matter. It may be said that the American Trotting Register Association will accept no pedigrees which depend in any degree upon statements made by Dr. Bethel until this transaction is cleared up, and under no circumstances from H. P. Brown.[176]

Of course, shenanigans such as these were a serious matter, especially in horse-crazy Kentucky, and Willis was right to leave town quickly. And although his scam was probably one of the most ambitious ones, it appears that he was not alone. The following blurb appeared in many Kentucky newspapers during this period:

Transcription: The practice of buying cheap stallions, reporting them as having cost fabulous sums, and then filling their books at fees four times larger than either their breeding or performances warrant, has become entirely too common. – Kentucky Stock Farm.[177]

Willis had taken the practice a few steps further, passing off his unexceptional stallion as a well-known one, and the next year attempting to register it under a different name, with a false pedigree and forged papers. What forces drove this urge to push all limits, blind to moderation and common sense, is unknown. It pains me to be descended from such a dumbass.

Perry's letter continued, waxing poetic in places, and finally touching on the subject of most interest to Nettie, a description of Matilda:

> I never saw a man have a nicer Start than he did when he first Come to town. The People Seemed to have Confidence in him and he Seemed to be a nice gentleman, and I have thought for So little he ruined himself. At first I felt So Sorry for him and advised him to Clear it up but the further a long the More of his Crookedness come out. His wife Sold out their house hold goods, and left here, and I think he owed for nearly all of them. O I felt So Sorry for her. My very heart went out for her, and With all of this I feel Sorry for him, to think he had So little Sense to ruin himself for So little. After this I heard of him being in business in the railroad office at Lexington, Ky., and the books was found to be Crooked. And he left thare, and I have not heard from him Since. his wife

---

176 Ibid., p. 450.
177 The Mt. Sterling Advocate, Mount Sterling, Kentucky, May 17, 1892, Chronicling America.

was a large Stout well built, good form woman but not purty. Had a young "Baby." Did not dress much.[178]

We will get into the Lexington mess, which was also well documented, presently. But Nettie was writing to Perry in large part to ascertain the practicality of reuniting with Willis. She must have had some guilt about being such a failure as a wife that her man had strayed, and great curiosity about the woman who had replaced her. Perry's description in his first letter of "a large likely woman" is expanded upon here in succinct but devastating detail, and it must have hit Nettie hard to read Matilda's description. Whether it was accurate or not is another question that will come up later, although Perry appears to be a reliable source with no reason to lie.

The events subsequent to the horse scheme, and Willis's sudden departure, were catastrophic for Matilda and little Mary. Leaving them abruptly, without funds, in fact, owing money, showed a complete disregard for their well-being. Matilda moved her young daughter back to the safety of her sister Sarah Jane's home in Pennsylvania. We don't know how much communication they had, but he was at least aware of their location. The entire experience must have taken a terrible toll on Matilda, and she died at the farmhouse, either in August 1892 or, more likely, 1893, still in her early thirties. Our only eyewitness was William McGinnis, Thompson and Sarah Jane's son.[179] Reminiscing to a relative in 1965, at the age of 83, he wrote,

> As my mother Sarah Jane Ralston married Thompson McGinnis in 1881, Mar. 28, and Matilda Bethel her sister married D.W. Bethel, General Agent for Kentucky Union Railroad, had one daughter Mary Bethel who came to our house to live when she was only a few months old and her mother passed away at our home. Bethel was let out from RR and never seen his wife after.[180]

The familiar pattern, 'don't know what ever happened to that guy,' repeats itself. Willis's Owingsville scam disintegrated in late June or early July 1892, which means that Mary was nine or ten months old when she and Matilda arrived at the McGinnes farm. We have very little other information about Mary's childhood, and none about her mother's illness and death.

Willis's letters to Nettie also give us only scant information about Matilda and Mary, and the Owingsville period. He wrote about his third wife as little as possible, of course, but he had to tell Nettie something, since his behavior with Matilda was central to her concerns in resuming a relationship with him. Out of his 27 letters, the quotations that follow were his only references to Matilda and Mary, ordered chronologically.

---

178 Letter, Ben Perry to Joannetta Fisher #2, June 4, 1894, from Fisher family papers.
179 William McGinnis changed the spelling of his surname to include the more conventional 'i' in adulthood.
180 Excerpt of letter from William McGinnis to James Sterrett, April 28, 1965. Quoted by Jim Sterrett in an email to Charles Caldemeyer, January 22, 2007.

> . . . not because I have a woman living with me as my wife for I have not. Two years ago in August ended all with her — a baby girl she left. It's with her people in Penna — Mary her name — Now Nettie believe me ask P.M. or any God & you will find that I tell you only <u>truth</u>.[181]
>
> My application of passion for Mary's mother was so strong that it seemed I never could control it. She was a good woman but like me had such strong passions. Now I take the blame all on myself let the cost be what it will for I think the dead should be allowed to rest in peace.[182]
>
> I can never forget the long weary tramp nor the months that passed with so little sleep, of the desperation that finally seized me & finally such actions as I was driven to through desperation. Death however ended that unhappy act. It is well that it did. Hence I am now where I was when we separated except that I've seen nearly all the U.S. & Mexico.[183]

The first two were from November 1894, in his first flurry of correspondence. "P.M." refers to "postmaster," that is, Ben Perry. Even though he calls her "a good woman," Willis's general coldness toward both Matilda's memory and Mary's existence, and his dismissiveness of their relevance, is striking throughout. He never mentioned Matilda by name, calling her only "Mary's mother."

The third passage, from 1897 (late in the letter sequence), reflected his ongoing attempts to edit history into a more favorable view of his actions. He blamed his failures at Owingsville on Matilda. He implied that she made him sleepless and desperate, and that the actions he was "driven to through desperation" (the horse fraud scheme?) were to meet her needs. But Perry said that Matilda "did not dress much," and it seems much more likely that the family member with the expensive habits was Willis, not Matilda. He was the one trying to insert himself into the genteel society of the town. It was in Willis's interest to distance himself from Matilda in his correspondence with Nettie, but she must have noticed his cynicism.

The final paragraph of Perry's letter hinted at where the next three years would lead Nettie, and if we read between the lines, we see that Mr. Perry had a few agendas of his own. He was clearly digging for some dirt on Dr. Bethel, who must have still been a topic of conversation in his town some two years after the events that drove him away. Postmasters were often notorious gossips who were expected to know things, and Perry probably didn't want to disappoint his constituents. It also appears that he was slyly playing matchmaker.

> I hope you will pardon me for asking you, you Say the reason of your Separation was other parties being mixed up in it. You Seem to be so pleasant about it that I ask you how was others mixed in it. I take all you write in Strict Confidence,

---

181 Letter, D.W. Bethel to Joannetta Fisher #1, November 1, 1894, from Fisher family papers.
182 Letter, D.W. Bethel to Joannetta Fisher #6, November 22, 1894, from Fisher family papers.
183 Letter, D.W. Bethel to Joannetta Fisher #16, May 22, 1897, from Fisher family papers.

that No Eye will See it or ear heare it. please give me all why you Separated from him and whare You married him at and what mister [sic] of the Gospel married you. you Seem So Kind about the Whole Matter is the reason why I ask you this. And I feel So Sorry for you to think how badly you have been treated and how Christian like you take it. Was Dr. Bethel Divorced from you or did he take the chances and marry this lady. it's a Penitentiary Offence to have two Wifes without Being divorced from One. but from the way you write I take it that you would not Interrupt Dr. Bethel with the law, and I ask the question would you live with him if he was to Come back and Offer to live with you. I had a talk with my friend. he has not heard from him Since he left Lexington, Ky. I never let him Know why I wanted to hear about him. I have another friend that was mixed up with him that I think Knows whare he is. I will do all I Can to find out and let you Know. Answer this as Soon as Recd. and give me all the Particulars and will be received Strictly Confidential.

Very Respectfully,
Ben F. Perry[184]

    This is all of their correspondence that we have, although it's possible there were other letters. It's also possible that Perry, knowing of Matilda's death the previous August and still in contact with Willis, was passing all this information on to him. Perry may have held the mistaken belief that Willis was an eligible bachelor again. He wasn't, and not just because of Jennie, but that's a story for a later chapter. About four months after Nettie received this letter, she and Willis renewed their correspondence.
    He landed on his feet in Lexington, but not for long. He began working as General Freight Agent for the Kentucky Union Railroad in fall 1892. How he got this position, a step up from the station agent jobs he had held previously, with all the questions about his character that must have been hanging in the air from the regional papers, is unknown. It seems likely that he again presented one or more letters of recommendation from well-known railroad men. I'm betting that the subjects of horse frauds and doctor scams never came up in the interview.
    The Kentucky Union was a failing company, having gone into receivership the previous year. A freight outfit that carried coal and timber from the eastern hill country to markets via Lexington, it was on its way under for good by 1892.[185] If the situation was already chaotic, Willis's presence didn't improve matters. He was only a few months into his employment when his escapades again surfaced in the news. Papers from as far away as Dallas carried stories about the events, but as usual with D.W. Bethel, there were varying accounts. The first salvo was launched on December 17, by The Lexington Morning Transcript.

---

184 Letter, Ben Perry to Joannetta Fisher #2, June 4, 1894, from Fisher family papers.
185 From Abandoned (abandonedonline.net). This website includes a brief history of the Kentucky Union Railroad.

This photograph, already marked with names, is in the files of the Bath County Historical Society at the public library in Owingsville. It is roughly contemporary with Willis's time there and shows many of the town's important officials. Two of the central characters in this chapter, Benjamin Franklin Perry (Postmaster) and W. W. Perry (County Clerk) stand in the back row, framed by the doorway.

Mr. W.D. Bethel, General Freight Agent of the Kentucky Union railroad, has been requested to resign his position. Captain Phillips, Superintendent of the road, said last evening to a Transcript reporter, when asked the cause of the change in office: "Yes, it is true that Mr. Bethel has been requested to resign, but through no misdemeanor of any kind, as his books are all right. He simply got too careless with his duties, and I thought best to remove him from the responsibilities of the office. He will be succeeded by Mr. W. B. Slack, of Dallas, Texas, who is well up in the railroad business, having been connected with some of the largest roads in the South."[187]

The next day, The Louisville Courier Journal took up the story:

Lexington, Ky., Dec. 17 — (Special) — W.D. Bethel, local agent of the Kentucky Union railway here, has resigned that position in favor of W.B.

---

[186] Photocopied from the files of the Bath County Historical Association in the Bath County Memorial Library, Owingsville, Kentucky.

[187] *Will Resign*, The Lexington Morning Transcript, December 17, 1892, from microfilm in the collection of the University of Kentucky Libraries.

> Stack, of Dallas, Tex. Capt. Phillips, Superintendent of the Kentucky Union road, has given orders to the agents of the other roads here not to make any settlement with Mr. Bethel, and await the arrival of Mr. Stack before settlement is made. Bethel was asked to resign. Mr. Bethel is a man of about thirty-eight, and addicted to no bad habits. Capt. Phillips, however, states that looseness in the management of the business was the cause of Bethel's dismissal.[188]

So far, not much news had been made. A reader might only question why he was asked to resign from the company and not reassigned to another position, and why he was not trusted to handle the settlement of open accounts. But better was yet to come. On the same day as the Courier Journal story, The Cincinnati Enquirer published a more detailed account.

> Special Dispatch to the Enquirer. Lexington, Ky., December 17 — Local railroad circles were thrown into an unusual state of excitement this afternoon when it became known that D.W. Bethel, General Agent of the Kentucky Union Road, had been relieved. Yesterday General Manager Phillips, accompanied by a Traveling Auditor, made an examination of Bethel's accounts with the road. No shortage was then discovered, but Bethel's methods were such that Phillips discharged him, assigning as his reason that Bethel was too careless about his work. Subsequent investigation, however, proved that there was a shortage. As to the exact amount it has not yet been determined, but it is not believed to be over $2,000. Bethel displayed an unusual amount of interest in the manner in which the investigation was conducted, and this is what caused Manager Phillips to become suspicious. Bethel was formerly agent for the C. and O. Road at Preston, but was discharged for some irregularities. He was not a man given to the grosser vices, nor was he regarded as sportively inclined. In domestic life his relations have been as unfortunate as were those which characterized his career in railroad circles. He is now living apart from his wife, who is a beautiful woman. The cause of Bethel's shortage is claimed by his friends to be due to his inability to master the details of business. While another story in circulation implicates a young man at the other end of the road. The road holds a bond sufficient to cover the shortage signed by the North American Company, and if Bethel experiences trouble from his shortage, it will originate from that source. W.D. Stack, of Dallas, Texas, has been appointed to fill Bethel's berth.[189]

The Kentucky Leader chimed in that the "young man at the other end of the road" may have been "in cahoots with Bethel."[190]

---

188 *A Bad Manager*, The Louisville Courier Journal, December 18, 1892, Newspapers.com.
189 *Relieved From His Post of Duty*, The Cincinnati Enquirer, December 18, 1892, Newspapers.com.
190 *Bethel's Bad Box*, The Kentucky Leader (Lexington Herald-Leader), December 18, 1892, Newspapers.com.

Willis had evidently again triggered his own apprehension, this time by displaying "an unusual amount of interest in the manner in which the investigation was conducted." In so doing, he betrayed his own maxim that "the only way to keep a secret is never to let any one suspect that you have one." As with the Dictawood scheme, he was not able to live up to the standards of dishonesty required to be a con man. But that didn't keep him from trying. His only admirable trait appears to have been his perseverance.

The newsmen weren't finished. On December 20, a follow-up article in the Morning Transcript defended Willis, and by implication, their own reporting:

> There was nothing really sensational in the item published in a Sunday paper regarding the dismissal of D.W. Bethell from the service of the Kentucky Union Railroad company, as will be seen from the following conversation with Captain Phillips: "Captain, is it true that Mr. Bethell was short to the amount of $800 in his books?" "No, sir, it is not true. I was never more surprised in my life when I picked up the morning paper and saw those large "flash" head lines. Bethell may be short to the amount of a few dollars, but all railroad employes are more or less that way, as it is very hard to keep a straight account until the books are posted, but whatever he may be short it will be made good. I never saw a reporter from any paper after you left me on Friday afternoon, and where the information came from I can not say, but I will say that the report is groundless, and did Mr. Bethell a great wrong. He was simply requested to resign his position because he was too careless, not because he was a robber."[191]

Bad call by the editors on that one. The same day, the Maysville Daily Public Ledger ran a small blurb that read, "It is reported that W.D. Bethell, agent of the Kentucky Union at Lexington, is nearly $1,000 short."[192] The following week, the Kentucky Leader reported more information about "the young man at the other end of the road." He was Leslie B. Wilson, Willis's protégé from his time at Preston.[193] By late 1892, he was the agent at Elkatawa, about 85 miles southeast of Lexington. Willis must have trained him well. Under the headline "Another Man Gone," the story read:

> The trouble among the agents of the K.U.R.R. which resulted in the summary removal of the agent at Lexington, has also resulted in the dismissal of the agent at Elkatawa, the station four miles from Jackson. The cause assigned for the removal of the agent at the latter point, whose name is Wilson, was the same as given out for the removal of Bethel at Lexington; namely: Gross carelessness.

---

191 *Bethell Not Short; On the Other Hand His Books Are Square,* The Lexington Morning Transcript, December 20, 1892, from microfilm in the collection of the University of Kentucky Libraries.
192 The Maysville Daily Public Ledger, December 20, 1892. One thousand dollars in 1892 is the equivalent of about $29,000 in 2020 (The Inflation Calculator, westegg.com).
193 The Owingsville Outlook, via the Interior Journal, Stanford, Kentucky, March 22, 1892, Newspapers.com.

> Whether there is a shortage in their accounts and, if so, how much cannot be learned at present. It is clear, however, that there is something wrong. The Auditor of the road is now engaged in making a thorough examination of these offices.[194]

Willis may have guessed that the disorganized financial affairs of the company would allow him some leeway to skim, which turned out to be false, and that Superintendent Phillips was likely inclined to downplay the seriousness of the matter to protect the railroad (and himself) as the bankruptcy process was being negotiated, which was true. It was never mentioned exactly how much the shortage ended up being, or if Willis ever "made good" on it, but I doubt it. A judge ordered The Kentucky Union to the auction block just three days later.[195]

The most revealing of the accounts are from The Cincinnati Enquirer and the Kentucky Leader. They appear to be from sources that knew the details of the investigation but were unofficial, and so were likely the most accurate. These articles give us more information than we have previously had about his methods of stealing from his employer, as well as other aspects of his story. We don't know exactly how the scam worked, but he seems to have acted the part of the lovable airhead, with loose recording of accounts and amounts, while behind it all he knew exactly what he was doing.

We also learn from the Cincinnati Enquirer that Willis had been discharged from his job with the C. & O. at Preston for "some irregularities," although not before training another con man in Mr. Wilson. If anyone is keeping score, the loss of his Kentucky Union position makes at least four railroad jobs where his bookkeeping methods, and honesty, were at least questioned.[196] In a letter to Nettie in 1897 he wrote, "I never in my life misapplied a cent." Yeah, well. . . The Enquirer also mentioned that the wife from whom he was separated was "a beautiful woman." Which one? Was Perry's description of Matilda purposely inaccurate? Was the paper referring to Joannetta? To Jennie? Someone else? At least one Cincinnati resident must have read all of it with great interest.

---

194 *Another Man Gone,* The Kentucky Leader (Lexington Herald-Leader), December 25, 1892, Newspapers.com. Leslie Wilson was employed at several locations in the state after serving his apprenticeship under Willis at Preston, ending up in Elkatawa. He apparently returned home to Stanford, Kentucky, after his firing by the K.U., and he did not get another railroad job. He died suddenly in his hometown nine months after his dismissal, in September 1893, of typhoid fever at the age of 22 (*Death's Doings,* The Interior Journal, September 29, 1893, Newspapers.com).

195 *Kentucky Union to Be Sold,* The Lexington Morning Transcript, December 21, 1892, from microfilm in the collection of the University of Kentucky Libraries.

196 Willis left his employments at Bruce (the C., T. V. & W.), Clarence (the West Shore), Preston (the C. & O.), and Lexington (the Kentucky Union) under a cloud of suspicion.

5.

Meanwhile, Back on the Farm

■ **WHILE HIS SON WAS EXCITING COMMENT IN NEWSPAPERS** throughout the upper Ohio valley and lower Great Lakes, William Samuel Bethel was evidently engaged in a darker form of excitement. William and his wife, Mary Clara, were still raising their two youngest children, Clara Lucinda (b. 1872) and Franklin Sheets (1876), at the farm at Rock Hill, and in July 1889 another child came along. But Mary, who had turned 50 the previous April, was not the mother of Charles William Bethel, who was born on July 4th or 5th (records vary) to 17-year-old Clara.[197]

In fact, between the ages of 17 and 24 Clara gave birth to three illegitimate children — Durward Otha came along in 1893 and Francis Allen in 1896. While Francis's birth was recorded as required, Charles's and Durward's were not, although there is an erroneous birth record for Durward Otha Bethel which we will discuss later in this chapter. The stigma of illegitimacy, along with a worse stigma, seems to have hung over all three children, and throughout their lives they were reluctant to acknowledge their true parentage, giving false and contradictory information on many official documents.[198] We will get to the question of who sired them later, but first, since the records disagree, we will establish that Clara Lucinda Bethel was, in fact, their mother.

On most of the official forms that Charles, Durward Otha, and Francis filled out during their lives, and also in their obituaries, William and Mary Bethel were named as their parents. When they did not list William and Mary, if they did not answer 'unknown,' or 'not available' to the question about their parentage, they listed Clara Lucinda Bethel as their mother with an unknown father. All three children were raised to adulthood by William and Mary and bore

---

197 Death certificate, Charles William Bethel, Cleveland, Cuyahoga County, Ohio, May 19, 1953, Ancestry.com; Find a Grave Memorial 147626168, Findagrave.com. While his birth was unrecorded, Charles William Bethel's death certificate correctly listed "Clara Bethel" as his mother. The year of his birth is listed in some records as 1890, but most of the earliest records say 1889. The difference of a year is more pronounced for a child than an adult, and 1889 is also the most commonly cited birth year.

198 Application to correct Birth Record, Durward Otha Bethel, January 29, 1946, records request from the Belmont County, Ohio Probate Court; Application to correct Birth Record, Francis Allen Bethel, September 14, 1942, records request from the Belmont County, Ohio Probate Court; Birth Record, Francis Allen Bethel, Flushing Township, Belmont County, Ohio, November 10, 1896, from microfilm at the Ohio Genealogical Society, Bellville; Birth Record, Archibald Bethel, Wheeling Township, Belmont County, Ohio, August 11, 1892, from microfilm at the Ohio Genealogical Society, Bellville; Durward O. Bethel Social Security Application, May 24, 1937, records request from Social Security Administration; Francis A. Bethel Social Security Application, November 30, 1936, records request from Social Security Administration.

the surname of Bethel throughout their lives. But Mary Bethel never claimed them as hers. In both 1900 and 1910, she told the census taker that they were her grandchildren, and she steadfastly listed the number of her own children as 'four' (David Wilson, Luke Voorhies, Clara Lucinda, and Franklin Sheets).[199] Most mothers at least claim their kids for the census, even if, like my own mother, they might be tempted to disown them at other times.

If William and Mary had really been their parents, one would think that Charles, Durward, and Francis might have referred to David, Luke, Clara, and Franklin as their siblings, but they never did. But all records make it clear that they regarded each other as brothers. The best illustration of this, and how it relates to Clara Lucinda Bethel, is found in Francis's and Durward's answers to questions on forms they each filled out in the 1940s. Francis's original birth record, in 1896, the only one of the three recorded at the time of birth, correctly listed him as illegitimate, with Clara L. Bethel as his mother, father unknown. The record, however, incorrectly listed him as a female with the first name of "Frances," a common enough error. In his application to correct it, filed in 1942, he listed 'Clara L. Bethel' as his mother, and as usual, he left the section about his father blank. But his answers in Section 21 on the form also demonstrate Clara's motherhood of Charles and Durward Otha. This section was entitled "Children born to this mother before this birth." To the question, "How many other children of this mother were living?" as of the date of his birth, Francis answered, "2," referring, of course, to Charles and Durward.[200] When Durward Otha filled out the same form three years later he answered, "1," referring to Charles.[201] Charles's death certificate in 1953, filled out by his daughter Rita, owned up to Clara being his birth mother, even though he had unfailingly listed William and Mary as his parents throughout his life.[202] All of these facts, along with other items in the record, make it undeniable that Clara Lucinda Bethel was the mother of all three children.

So, who was their father? Young Clara may have been generous with her affections, and with men she could not, or would not, identify, but under the circumstances it's highly unlikely. Three illegitimate children over the span of eight years prior to the age of 25 is a lot, especially given late nineteenth-century mores and considering that she lived with her parents the entire time. The Bethels were hardscrabble farmers struggling to make ends meet on rented acreage, and extra children brought extra expenses. Many families of the day, when confronted by similar circumstances, pursued the baby's father for both financial help and legal responsibility. But the Bethels filed no bastardy suits on Clara's behalf for any of the

---

199 U.S. Census, 1900, 1910, Flushing Township, Belmont County, Ohio, William and Mary Bethel and family, Ancestry.com.
200 Application to correct Birth Record, Francis Allen Bethel, September 14, 1942, records request from the Belmont County, Ohio Probate Court.
201 Application to correct Birth Record, Durward Otha Bethel, January 29, 1946, records request from the Belmont County, Ohio Probate Court.
202 Death Certificate, Charles William Bethel, Cleveland, Cuyahoga County, Ohio, May 19, 1953, Ancestry.com. This record also listed a "Joseph" as Charles's father, almost certainly a reference to Joseph Schrank, Clara Lucinda Bethel's second husband. But Joseph Schrank was born in Germany in 1879 and was ten years old at the time of Charles's birth. He immigrated with his birth family in 1890, and did not even meet Clara prior to 1900, at the earliest. This listing was almost certainly an attempt by Charles's daughter, who was the informant on the death certificate, to maintain a family tradition by obscuring the identity of Charles's father.

three births, and in fact did not even report the first two to the authorities. Either William Samuel and Mary Clara Bethel were the most indulgent parents a promiscuous late nineteenth-century young woman ever had, or the children were the products of ongoing incest, most likely father-daughter rape.

For obvious reasons, births that were incestuous were even less likely to be documented than other illegitimate births, and the failure to record Clara Lucinda's first two contributions to the species is more evidence of sexual abuse by a family member. None of Clara's brothers seem to be a viable candidate, despite her oldest brother's obvious preoccupation with sex and sirehood. The approximate dates of conception for each of Clara's children were, respectively, October 4, 1888, October 18, 1892, and February 10, 1896. In late 1888, Willis lived in Clarence and attended medical school in Buffalo, and in late 1892 he was with the Kentucky Union in Lexington. It's unlikely that he made the trip home and had a heartfelt reunion with his younger sister at those times, although it's possible. But in early 1896 he was in Perris, California, and the local newspaper documented his continuous presence there throughout January, February, and March. With his close ties to the editor, any trip he had made to Ohio would have been well covered. It's also clear from his letters that once he left Belmont County for good in 1883 he did not return very often. He never wrote about visiting his birth family. Willis's sights were always set on the horizon.

Luke Voorhies is also an unlikely candidate. He seems to have wanted nothing to do with his birth family. He was actually counted twice in the 1880 census, when he was 18, once on the family farm and once as a resident in the home of nearby farmer Lycurgus Dunlap, son of his great-aunt Elizabeth, where he worked as a laborer.[203] By 1894, at the time of his first marriage (which is the next available record of him), he lived in southern Harrison County, and it seems likely that he had absented himself from his parents' farmhouse many years before.[204] Willis and Voorhies were both gone, and most importantly, neither possessed the authority within the family to perpetrate ongoing sexual abuse over a span of eight years. Franklin Sheets Bethel, the only other male living at the farm in the late 1880s and 1890s, was only 13 at the time of his sister's first pregnancy, and brother-sister incest "almost always involves an abuse of power in which an older brother sexually abuses a younger sister," and is "significantly less likely . . . to occur over a period of more than a year."[205] All of these factors point to William Samuel Bethel as the sire of Charles, Durward Otha, and Francis. He was living in the home continuously during the years in question, and his position as head of the household allowed him to command both the silence and acquiescence of his family.

The laws of the late nineteenth century provided stiff penalties, even death in some states, for fathers who violated their daughters, and if that were not deterrent enough, the practice was social kryptonite.[206] Stories in the papers of the day told of fathers being lynched before they could be arrested when community members heard the news, with ostracism being the

---

203 U.S. Census, 1880, Flushing Township, Belmont County, Ohio, Luke Voorhies Bethel in the houses of William Bethel and Lycurgus Dunlap, Ancestry.com.
204 Marriage Record, L. Vorhies Bethel and Laura L. Tipton, Harrison County, Ohio, January 24, 1894, Ancestry.com.
205 Diana E. H. Russell, *The Secret Trauma*, p. 272, 273.
206 Lynn Sacco, *Unspeakable*, p. 34.

norm.[207] William Samuel Bethel probably knew his risks were low, living as he did in the hill country of eastern Ohio, where neighbors distrusted authorities and tended to mind their own business. But they still would have disapproved of what was going on, and one wonders about his interactions with them. His efforts to hide Clara Lucinda's pregnancies must have been a family operation, with Mary and Franklin helping out under William's direction and control. The picture that emerges is a dark one of a tyrannical father imposing his will on all aspects of his household and insulating it from the prying eyes of outsiders. According to the 1940 census, when the question was first asked, Clara Lucinda Bethel's education ended after her second year of high school (more, by the way, than was normal in rural America at the time, although less than her older brothers).[208] This would have been about the time her first pregnancy began to show.

We know from his letters that Willis had a high regard for his father, and one wonders if his attitudes toward women, which form much of the subject of this book, came to him from that source.[209] Did William teach his sons that females were only there to be toyed with, manipulated, and exploited? The scant evidence provided by the lives of William and Mary's other two boys, Luke Voorhies and Franklin Sheets, is not supportive of this idea — both were evidently good family men — but they probably sympathized with their mother and sister while remaining powerless to stop their father. Voorhies was estranged from his birth family, and while Franklin stayed at the farm at least until age 24, he may have been in the role of the youngest child outside the center of the storm who just wanted to smooth things over. It seems likely that both brothers were in fear of their father.

A final tantalizing item provides us with further evidence of William Samuel Bethel's authority in the house, and it also gives us some insight into the relationship between father and oldest son. It is the naming of Clara's second child. The reader must have remarked on the coincidence of two children from the same gene pool being given the unusual first name of 'Durward.' Almost unknown today, the name was only extremely uncommon in 1893, given to .006 percent of newborn boys that year, or less than 50 nationwide.[210] It was not a family tradition — no other known members of the Bethel or Wilson families bore that first name. But Joannetta's annulment of her New York marriage to Willis was finalized on April 14, 1893, and with that action Durward Frederick Bethel became Durward Frederick Fisher. Durward Otha Bethel was born in Flushing on July 18. I believe that William named his and Clara's second child 'Durward' to honor his oldest son and to compensate for the consequences of the annulment — there may no longer have been a Durward Bethel in Clarence, New York, but there now was one in Flushing, Ohio. It was a defiant act that demonstrated William's full knowledge and endorsement of his bigamous son's actions.

We know little more about William Samuel Bethel than what the records tell us, but it seems clear that he had some angry aspects to his personality that he may have masked, as Willis did, with a bright and clever countenance. We find the symbolic use of naming by both

---

207 Ibid., pp. 28-31.
208 U.S. Census, 1940, Cleveland, Cuyahoga County, Ohio, Clara Bethel Schrank, Ancestry.com.
209 Letter, D.W. Bethel to Joannetta Fisher #17, May 30, 1897, from Fisher family papers.
210 These statistics were originally published on Behindthename.com.

men, and we can safely say that both regarded women as playthings. We might go so far as to say that Willis was his father's protégé, and that his migrations across the country, impregnating and abandoning women as he went, were his way of fulfilling his father's dream.

It almost defies belief, but Clara Lucinda Bethel was not the only Clara L. Bethel having illegitimate children in the Flushing area at the time. That fact, along with a strange sleight-of-hand in 1945-1946 by one of our characters, makes the confusing morass of misinformation concerning Charles, Durward, and Francis even harder to decipher. Clara *Leona* Bethel was born in 1874 (two years after Clara Lucinda) to Thomas and Mary Jane Bethel, who lived in tiny hamlet of Uniontown, about four miles from Flushing and six from Rock Hill. Although the communities are close together and there has always been a lot of interaction between them, Flushing is in Flushing Township and Uniontown is in Wheeling Township. Thomas Smith Bethel was likely a cousin of William's to some degree, but the exact connection is unknown.

In 1886, the Belmont Chronicle announced that William A. Sharp, along with Thomas S. Bethel a Democrat, had been appointed postmaster at Uniontown by the first Grover Cleveland administration, but since he lived so far from town he would be conducting his postmaster's affairs from the "business room" of Thomas S. Bethel's blacksmith shop. At the time, Thomas was 35, and he and Mary Jane had three children, of whom Clara Leona was the second. Sharp was a 29-year-old bachelor, and since the two men were business associates, there were certainly interactions between William Sharp and members of Thomas Bethel's family.[211] You can probably see where this is going.

On August 11, 1892, eighteen-year-old Clara Leona Bethel gave birth to an illegitimate son named Archibald Ivoy Bethel, and the family promptly sued William A. Sharp for bastardy.[212] The case was a local sensation, with jurors failing to reach a verdict twice before finally finding for the plaintiff on the third try. Sharp was ordered to pay $300 over two years, and that was the extent of his obligation.[213] Little Archie was raised by Thomas and Mary Jane, while Clara Leona (who now went by her middle name) married a local laborer and started another family. Thomas and Mary Jane had moved their family to Flushing by the 1900 census, and Archie is found living with them.[214] They were still there in 1910, but seventeen-year-old Archie had left town by that time.[215]

It was not easy being a bastard in late nineteenth-century America. If people knew, the

---

211 *Uniontown*, The Belmont Chronicle, April 1, 1886, Newspapers.com; Postmaster Appointment, Thomas S. Bethel, March 6, 1886, Ancestry.com.
212 Birth Record, Archibald Bethel, Wheeling Township, Belmont County, Ohio, August 11, 1892, from microfilm at the Ohio Genealogical Society, Bellville.
213 *Courts*, The Belmont Chronicle, June 15, 1893, Newspapers.com; Belmont County, Ohio, Court records, p. 125, record of Clara Leona Bethel vs. William A. Sharp, suit for Bastardy, photographed from Belmont County Courthouse records, St. Clairsville, Ohio.
214 U.S. Census, 1900, Flushing Township, Belmont County, Ohio, Thomas S. Bethel and family, Ancestry.com.
215 U.S. Census, 1910, Flushing Township, Belmont County, Ohio, T. Smith Bethel, Ancestry.com.

child was often treated like it was his or her own fault. When Clara Leona Bethel abandoned Archie to her parents, he essentially became an orphan, and he seems to have been unwanted by his grandparents, too. We find him in the town of Cambridge, in nearby Guernsey County, in 1910-1911, working as a chair finisher.[216] He joined the Army in 1911, but was dishonorably discharged seven months later, and he had a reckless, angry young adulthood.[217] His first marriage collapsed, but his second one settled him down, and he raised six children and worked at a variety of semi-skilled jobs before starting his own contracting business. We have records of him in several places across the Midwest before he moved to southern California, where he died in 1969.[218] None of this would matter to us at all were it not for something that happened in 1945.

In that year, Archie's birth record was stolen by Clara Lucinda Bethel's second child, Durward Otha Bethel. He petitioned the Belmont County Probate Court, complaining that his original birth record had "not been properly and accurately recorded" (actually, it had not been recorded at all). He asked the court for four remedies: 1) that the name of Archibald be changed to Durward Otha, 2) that the date of birth be revised from August 11, 1892 to July 18, 1893, 3) that the place be "corrected" from Uniontown, Wheeling Township to Flushing Township, and 4) that his mother's name be "corrected" from Clara L. Bethel to Clara Bethel. The last item is especially puzzling, since both Clara Lucinda and Clara Leona obviously had the same middle initial, but it may give us some hint of Durward Otha Bethel's motive in this bizarre quest — to normalize his records as much as possible by having Mary Clara's middle name listed as his mother's only given name. He was trying to mitigate both his illegitimacy and his incestuous origins — he wanted to be known as William and Mary's legitimate child — but the records would only cooperate so far. The notation that he was, in fact, born out of wedlock and that his father was "Unknown" did not change. Durward had two friends sign affidavits testifying to the truthfulness of his application, Judge Harry L. Albright found the whole sham credible, and on January 29, 1946, Durward Otha Bethel officially and legally pilfered the birth record of Archibald Ivoy Bethel.[219]

Judge Albright probably just took the affidavits at face value, because if he had examined things a little more closely some red flags might have emerged. First, there was the over-eleven-month discrepancy between the two birth dates — how drunk did the recorder have to be to miss by that much? Also, there was the name of the person who reported Archie's birth, Daniel M. Brewer, a local businessman who had been Wheeling Township Assessor in 1892. He reported another birth at the same time as Archibald's, and that baby was, of course, also born in Wheeling Township. Why would the Wheeling Township Assessor report a birth from Flushing Township? The Flushing Township Assessor at the time was a man named 'S.

---

216 Cambridge, Guernsey County, Ohio, directory, 1910-1911, Archie Bethel, p. 49, Ancestry.com.
217 U.S. Army Register of Enlistments, Archie I. Bethel, 1911-1912, Ancestry.com.
218 U.S. Census, 1920, 1930, 1940, Archibald Ivoy Bethel; World War I (June 5, 1917) and World War II (April 27, 1942) Draft Registration Cards, Archie I. Bethel; Inglewood, California directory, 1964, p. 18, Archie I. Bethel; California Death Index, Archie I. Bethel, November 12, 1969, all Ancestry.com.
219 Birth Record, Archibald Bethel, Wheeling Township, Belmont County, Ohio, August 11, 1892, from microfilm at the Ohio Genealogical Society, Bellville; Application to correct Birth Record, Durward Otha Bethel, January 29, 1946, records request from the Belmont County, Ohio Probate Court.

Williams,' and the births he reported during that period are recorded in a different section on the same page as Archie's birth, grouped by township, as was customary.[220]

Ohio law before 1908 required births to be reported by a family member, the doctor, or the township assessor, but "sometimes none of these individuals did so."[221] Applications to correct birth records were common because record-keeping was haphazard, and mistakes were common. These corrections became especially prevalent in the 1930s and 1940s as applicants sought to prove their births to enroll in, or collect from, the nation's new system of social safety nets. Willis and Jennie's daughter Bessie, as well as Durward Otha's brother Francis Allen, had both petitioned to have theirs corrected. So, with a volume of applications coming through his office it's not surprising that Judge Albright would sign off without too much research. When Bessie applied to correct her record, it was because her first name had been recorded as 'Jessie' and her mother's maiden name was listed as 'Huell' rather than Howell, and we have covered Francis Allen's reasons. But why did Durward Otha Bethel undertake such a quest? After seeing all the discrepancies between Archibald's record and his own circumstances he must have known that the entry referred to the birth of someone else and was not a botched attempt at recording his. Moreover, the two Bethel families (William and Mary's and Thomas and Mary Jane's) were listed only four pages away from one another in the 1900 census, and they were likely related. It is impossible that Durward Otha Bethel and Archibald Ivoy Bethel, growing up in close proximity in the same rural community, almost the same age and possibly even attending the same schools, did not know each other. Durward Otha Bethel certainly knew that his application was fraudulent. Maybe he figured he could get away with it because he knew that Archie had left the area long before, and so was unknown to the local authorities in 1945. But poor Archie — abandoned first by both mother and father, disregarded by the grandparents who raised him, now had his identity stolen by a childhood classmate. He was smart to leave town. Some folks just can't get no respect.

Durward Otha Bethel worked for the W. P. A. in the 1940s, and it's possible that he needed a birth record to apply for some form of government program. Maybe the application to change Archie's records was an easier, or less embarrassing, course of action than admitting that his own incestuous birth was never recorded. Maybe Archie had bullied him in his youth, and this was his payback. But still, what did it gain him? Sure, his birth was now recorded, but it was still illegitimate, and people in the area would have known that he was the product of incest, anyway. It appears to be a pathetic attempt to make his very abnormal birth circumstances appear more typical, without success. Of all the head-scratching, shrug-your-shoulders moments in the history of the Bethel family, this one is right up near the top.

---

220 Report of Births in Belmont County, Ohio, 1892-1893, from microfilm at the Ohio Genealogical Society, Bellville.
221 Ohio History Connection, ohiohistory.org.

William Samuel Bethel was present in the 1900 census, at age 61 living with Mary, Franklin, and his three children/grandchildren at the Rock Hill farm. But by 1910 he was deceased, and Mary lived at the farm with just her two youngest grandchildren. What happened to William Samuel Bethel is a mystery. No death record was ever filed for him — he simply disappeared sometime between 1900 and 1910. His burial spot is unknown — his name is missing from existing rosters of the Rock Hill Cemetery, although he may well be buried there, since those records are incomplete.[222]

Mary Clara Wilson Bethel passed away in 1917 at age 78, her death certificate listing exhaustion and old age as the primary causes, with "Myocardial Insufficiency" as a contributing factor. Her death certificate lists her burial spot as Rock Hill.[223] Franklin, ever her attentive youngest son, filled out the paperwork, and one gets the feeling that he was the member of the family trying, as best he could, to assuage conflicts — to fix the unfixable. A coal miner all his adult life, Frank married Mary Celeste Addudle in 1903, but they had no children. He died less than two years after his mother, at the age of 43, of kidney disease. According to his death certificate, he too was buried at Rock Hill.[224]

Luke Voorhies Bethel, William and Mary's second son, lived most of his life in nearby Harrison County, serving as a rural mail carrier in the Cadiz area. He and his first wife, Laura Lillian Tipton, had three children, Hazel Caroline, Joseph, and Lloyd Raymond, who died while still a toddler. Laura died in 1908, and Voorhies married a local widow, Mary Hendershott Steele, with whom he spent the remainder of his days. He retired from the postal service in 1920 and he died in 1935, at the age of 72. Unlike most of his birth relatives, he and his wife were buried in Cadiz Union Cemetery in Harrison County.[225]

Clara Lucinda Bethel escaped at least the physical confines of the Rock Hill farm on April 4, 1899, when she married Elmer Nelson Van Fossen, although the effects of her sexualized childhood appear to have pursued her well into adulthood. Elmer was a farmer's son from nearby Holloway. The marriage license also lists Clara's residence as Holloway, so it's possible she had moved away from the Rock Hill farm sometime after November 10, 1896, Francis Allen's birth date.[226] Francis, along with her other sons by her father, Charles William (age 10) and Durward Otha (6), remained at Rock Hill with William and Mary. Her marriage to Elmer seems to have had an urgency behind it — five months later she gave birth to Jesse

---

222 U.S. Census, 1900, 1910, Flushing Township, Belmont County, Ohio, William and Mary Bethel, Ancestry.com.
223 Death Certificate, Mary Wilson Bethel, Flushing Township, Belmont County, Ohio, September 20, 1917, Ancestry.com.
224 Marriage License, Frank S. Bethel and Mary C. Aduddle, Belmont County, Ohio, September 7, 1904; Death Certificate, Frank Sheets Bethel, Wheeling, Ohio County, West Virginia, March 16, 1919, Ancestry.com.
225 Marriage License, L. Vorhies Bethel and Laura L. Tipton, Harrison County, Ohio, January 25, 1894; Marriage License, Luke V. Bethel and Mary E. Steele, Belmont County, Ohio, September 13, 1910; Death Certificate, Luke Voorhies Bethel, Cadiz, Harrison County, Ohio, February 26, 1935, all Ancestry.com; Interment Records, Luke Voorhies Bethel and Laura Tipton Bethel, Cadiz Union Cemetery, Harrison County, Ohio, November 2, 1908, Find a Grave Memorials 160605233 and 160605149, Findagrave.com.
226 Birth Record, Francis Allen Bethel, November 10, 1896, Flushing, Belmont County, Ohio, from microfilm at the Ohio Genealogical Society, Bellville.

Earl Van Fossen. Whether he was sired by William or Elmer remains unknown.[227]

The 1900 census finds the Van Fossens living in Holloway, with Elmer working as a laborer on the railroad.[228] Naturally enough under the circumstances, Clara identified herself as the mother of only one child — her marriage to Elmer represented a 'reset' for her as she worked to escape her past.[229] In 1910, Elmer and Clara still resided in Holloway, but Jesse was no longer with them, having died in the interim. The couple had a new addition, however, Harry Eldon, born the previous November. A 31-year-old German immigrant, Joseph Schrank, also boarded with the family. Both Elmer and Joseph worked for the railroad — Elmer as a track repairer and Joseph as a car inspector.[230]

Evidently there was more between Joseph Schrank and Clara Bethel Van Fossen than just rent and housekeeping. By 1918, they were both living in Cleveland. On September 24, Elmer and Clara were divorced, and less than three weeks later, on October 10, Joseph and Clara were married.[231] The divorce documents themselves are unavailable — the only indication of their existence comes to us from Joseph and Clara's marriage license, and from Elmer's second marriage license.[232] Joseph had registered for the World War I draft just a month prior, and the urgency of those events may have driven the couple, then 39 (Joseph) and 46 (Clara), to solemnize what had been going on for years. The Schranks were found living together in Cleveland in the 1920, 1930, and 1940 censuses. They must have moved back to Flushing soon after the 1940 census, because Clara died there in 1941, and Joseph followed her in 1943. They were buried side by side in the Rock Hill Cemetery, a stone's throw from the old farm where Clara had endured such a traumatic youth.[233]

Evidently Harry Eldon (who, like so many men of the era, went by his middle name) experienced some confusion about his father's identity. In both the 1920 census (when he was a child of 10 in Joseph and Clara's home in Cleveland) and 1930 (when he was living with his new wife) his surname was listed as Schrank, but by the time of his enlistment in the Army for World War II he had adopted the last name of Van Fossen, and that is the name he thereafter lived under, and was buried under in 1961.[234] Presumably, this means that he discovered later in adulthood that Elmer was his true father. Elmer married a widow named

---

227 Marriage Record, Elmer N. Vanfossen and Clara L. Bethel, Belmont County, Ohio, April 4, 1899, Ancestry.com; Report of Births in Belmont County, Ohio, Jesse Earl Van Fossen, September 11, 1899, from microfilm at the Ohio Genealogical Society, Bellville.
228 U.S. Census, 1900, Flushing Township, Belmont County, Ohio, Elmer Vanfossen family, Ancestry.com.
229 Clara never claimed motherhood of any of her illegitimate sons on any census, possibly indicative of the shame she felt.
230 U.S. Census, 1910, Flushing Township, Belmont County, Ohio, Elmer Van Fossen family, Joseph Schrank, Ancestry.com.
231 Marriage License, Joseph Schrank and Clara Bethel Van Fossen, Cleveland, Cuyahoga County, Ohio, October 10, 1918, Ancestry.com. This license is also the only source we have for the date of Elmer's and Clara's divorce.
232 Marriage License, Elmer N. Vanfossen and Sarah Fields, St. Clairsville, Belmont County, Ohio, April 1, 1919, Ancestry.com.
233 U.S. Census, 1920, 1930, 1940, Cleveland, Cuyahoga County, Ohio, Joseph Schrank family; Death Certificate, Clara Bethel Van Fossen Schrank, Flushing Township, Belmont County, Ohio, October 17, 1941; Death Certificate, Joseph Schrank, Flushing Township, Belmont County, Ohio, July 20, 1943, all Ancestry.com.
234 U.S. Census, 1920, 1930, Cleveland, Cuyahoga County, Ohio, Eldon H. Schrank; World War II Army Enlistment Records, Harry Eldon Van Fossen, April 15, 1942; California Death Index, 1940-1997, Harry E. Van Fossen, May 31, 1961, all Ancestry.com.

Sarah Fields in 1920, and the couple had at least one child. They lived in Holloway in both the 1920 and 1930 censuses. It seems likely that Elmer never moved away but watched helplessly as his boarder ran off to the big city with his wife and son. He died in 1931, and he is also buried at Rock Hill Cemetery.[235]

Elmer Nelson Van Fossen's birth family portrait, Holloway, Ohio, about 1895. Elmer is the mustachioed young man in the back row.

Clara's three children by her father, William Samuel Bethel, all remained in eastern Ohio, and all lived seemingly normal lives in which the circumstances of their birth were not obvious detriments, although we can infer that at least one (Durward Otha Bethel) suffered emotional trauma over his ancestry. None received education past the eighth grade, but that was common in rural America at the time. Charles William Bethel began like so many others in the region, working as a coal miner. He served in the Army in World War I and was severely wounded in the Meuse-Argonne offensive, earning the Purple Heart. After the war, he married Bertha Garrett, and they had four children. His war injuries affected his ability to earn a living, and there were times when he could not work at all. The family moved back

---
235 U.S. Census, 1920, 1930, Flushing Township, Belmont County, Ohio, Elmer Van Fossen; Marriage License, Elmer N. Van Fossen and Sarah Fields, Belmont County, Ohio, April 1, 1920; State of Ohio Death Index, Elmer Van Fossen, February 13, 1931, all Ancestry.com; Burial Record, Elmer N. Van Fossen, Rock Hill Baptist Church Cemetery, 1931, Find a Grave Memorial 33509602, Findagrave.com.
236 Originally shared on August 12, 2010, on Ancestry.com by mrwest072107.

and forth between Flushing and the Cleveland area throughout his life. It's unknown if he had any contact with his birth mother while living in and around Cleveland. He died there in 1953 and was buried back at Rock Hill with a military veteran's headstone. He was 63.[237]

Headstone, Charles William Bethel, Rock Hill Baptist Church Cemetery, Flushing Township, Belmont County, Ohio.

Durward Otha Bethel also started out as a coal miner, a job he periodically went back to throughout his life. In 1916, he married Edna Rebecca Huff in West Virginia, and they had five children. Although he registered for the World War I draft, he was not called. In 1930, he was farming rented acreage in Kirkwood Township, just south and west of Flushing. By 1940 he owned the home, but was working as a road laborer, probably for the W. P. A., where he still worked at the time of his World War II draft registration in 1942. In later years, he served as an elder in the Rock Hill Baptist church. While he used the name of Durward for official business, in everyday interactions he went by 'Jack.' Both he and Edna died in 1975, and they are buried at Rock Hill.[239]

---

237 U.S. Census, 1920, Flushing Township, Belmont County, Ohio, Charles W. Bethel; U.S. Census, 1930, Cleveland, Cuyahoga County, Ohio, Charles W. Bethel; U.S. Census, 1940, Flushing Township, Belmont County, Ohio, Charles William Bethel; Ohio Soldiers in World War I, Charles William Bethel; World War I and World War II Draft registration cards, Charles William Bethel; Death Certificate, Charles William Bethel, Cleveland, Cuyahoga County, Ohio, May 19, 1953; Application for Military Headstone, Charles William Bethel, 1953, all Ancestry.com.
238 Find a Grave Memorial 147626168, Charles W. Bethel, Photograph by potterc, Findagrave.com.
239 U.S. Census, 1920, 1930, 1940, Kirkwood Township, Belmont County, Ohio, Durward Otha Bethel; Marriage License, Durward Otha Bethel and Edna Rebecca Huff, Wellsburg, West Virginia, June 3, 1916; World War I and World War II Draft registration cards, Durward Otha Bethel; Death Certificate, Durward Otha Bethel, Flushing, Belmont County, Ohio, March 19, 1975; Obituary, probably in the Flushing News, Durward Otha Bethel, Find a Grave Memorials 41636795 and 41636962, Findagrave.com.

Durward Otha "Jack" Bethel and his wife Edna's portrait on their headstone, Rock Hill Baptist Church Cemetery, Flushing Township, Ohio.

The youngest of William and Clara's children, Francis Allen Bethel (nicknamed 'Shorty'), served, like his brother Charles, in World War I, although it appears that he escaped physical harm. Early in his adult life he moved from the Flushing area to Newcomerstown, in Tuscarawas County, where he married Ethel Holder in 1924. Francis worked as a clerk for the railroad for 18 years, and by 1940 he was a foreman at a tool factory, a job he maintained until his retirement in 1961. He was a member of the American Legion and a Sunday School teacher at the First Baptist Church at Newcomerstown. He and Ethel had three children. He

---
240 Photos by Charles Caldemeyer, 2002.

died in 1979 and was buried at West Lawn Cemetery at Shady Bend, Coshocton County, Ohio. Ethel lived until 1998, when she was laid to rest alongside her husband.[241]

Francis Allen "Shorty" Bethel, about 1918.

---

241 U.S. Census, 1920, 1930, 1940, Newcomerstown, Tuscarawas County, Ohio, Francis Allen Bethel; Ohio Soldiers in World War I, Francis Allen Bethel; World War I and World War II Draft Registration Cards, Francis Allen Bethel; Ohio Deaths, 1908-1932, 1938-2007, Francis Allen Bethel, all Ancestry.com; Obituary, Francis Allen Bethel, The Times Reporter, Dover/New Philadelphia, Ohio, January 5, 1979, Newspapers.com.
242 photo shared on Ancestry.com by Brandon Lyons, July 16, 2018.

Headstones, Francis Allen Bethel and his wife, Ethel Holder Bethel, West Lawn Cemetery, Shady Bend, Ohio.

---

243 Find a Grave Memorials 59555219 and 59555218, Findagrave.com. Photography credit: Nancy Ankrum.

6.

"Don't Publish & Oblige Lou Hunnemeyer"

■ **LOUIS HUNNEMEYER HAD A PROBLEM.** *The longtime Cincinnati civil servant, a clerk for the Probate Court, didn't like the situation, but he knew it came with the territory. Lou was a quiet worker who went scrupulously by the book, and he hated to ask anyone, especially the man he worked for, to bend the rules. Rules were the basis for order, after all — that's how Lou had always seen it — and everyone, everyone with ties to the old country at least, appreciated the clarity they provided. But Lou, who had risen to a prominent position in the Cincinnati bureaucracy despite the fact that his father had been an immigrant laborer, also liked to think of himself as one of the leaders of the German American community in Cincinnati, a man who could help his countrymen get things done. So, when an old friend asked for a favor, Lou didn't hesitate. George Rietman had come over with his parents in 1851, when he was only ten, and Lou had known him all his life. George was jovial, hard-working, and honest, a good man who supported his family by painting houses and streetcars. His children were all go-getters, too, but some of these kids these days, well, the rules just don't mean so much to them.*

George and Elizabeth Rietman's daughter, Minnie, was the source of Lou's problem. She was 24 and had begun her working life when she was just sixteen, as a telegrapher for Western Union at the Grand Hotel. Minnie was a real live wire, no mistake about that, but she had done things just about arse-backwards to get in a scrape like this, Lou thought. These kids don't understand that once you start breaking the rules, it just never stops. Minnie had broken the rules, and now Lou had to bend them if he wanted to help his friend. Schnickety.

She was about to be married, the marriage license had just been filled out, and it was now on Judge Howard Ferris's desk for his approval. Part of the job of the Clerk of Court's office was to advertise marriage licenses in the local papers, so the public knew about the doings at the office, and Judge Ferris was usually a stickler about adhering to it. They were public servants, after all, and the public had a right to know what was going on. Lou knew Ferris well, respected him greatly, and he hated to make himself the center of attention before the judge. He also hated Minnie's choice of a husband, but that was a different story, and it was not exactly the problem at hand. The problem was that everyone in town thought that

Minnie Rietman and David Willis Bethel were already married, because they had a one-year-old daughter, Elsie, living with Minnie under George and Elizabeth's roof. Minnie had been going around calling herself Mrs. David Bethel for almost two years now. When Elsie had come along in July 1892, the Rietmans had told everyone that Willis had a job in Kentucky, that he and Minnie had been married down there in 1891, and that he couldn't yet be here for his family. This man, David W. Bethel, was right there with Lou in Judge Ferris's chambers, and both he and Lou were asking for the same favor — to keep the marriage unpublished.

But this dummkopf had already given Lou a headache, and it had nothing to do with the Rietmans. He hadn't stopped talking since they had first met in the office about thirty long minutes earlier, and by now Lou hated to agree with him about anything. Willis had started off by making jokes about the intelligence of people who work with their hands for a living, then bragged about all the places he had seen on his travels, dropping salacious little tidbits along the way and referring to Lou as "a fellow man of the world." By the time Ferris saw them in his chambers, Lou was nursing a serious dislike for David Willis Bethel.

". . . please don't publish this marriage license, please, Judge Ferris. It will ruin the family's reputation. Minnie and I, we got a little ahead of ourselves because I worked down in Kentucky, don't you know? And we did not get to see each other very often, and we could not get married before this because my former wife was still alive, but she was so sick for such a long time, Your Honor, and you know I am a man who has my needs, but Matilda, she was just in no condition to do her wifely duties." He finally took a breath, "But she finally died just last month, oh thank God she is finally at peace, and now I'm here to make things right with the love of my life, my dear little Minnie and our darling little daughter, Elsie, oh what a little angel she is . . ."

"That will be enough, Mr. Bethel." The normally genial judge spoke in his usual controlled tones, but Lou could see that he wasn't very happy.

"If I were Mr. Rietman," Ferris said, "I would be more inclined to fill up your hindquarters with rock salt from a scattergun than to let you see my daughter, child or no child. This woman is not some adventuress you can toy with, sir — she is the daughter of a good Cincinnati family! You must know that is not the way things are to be done, Mr. Bethel." He stared at Willis like a cat stares at a church mouse. Willis dropped his eyes, adding to the effect, and mumbled, "Yes, Your Honor." He looked genuinely contrite.

"I have had some trouble in my life, and I'm sorry for it all. When Matilda got sick, it hit me hard, and I lost my self-control, I'm afraid." Lou couldn't believe how quickly his demeanor changed, how sincere he now seemed. Just a few minutes earlier he had been making suggestive jokes about Mexican women. Willis raised his eyes, breathed deeply, and continued, "I am a man full and free now, though, and I am here to claim my family and do my duty as a husband and a father." He looked at Ferris with solemn determination on his face, his eyes slightly teary.

Ferris remained unconvinced. "Say, are not you the same D.W. Bethel who was fired from the Kentucky Union down in Lexington last December? For cooking the books?"

"Your Honor, I was not fired, I was asked to resign. And I did not cook the books. I never in my life misapplied a cent. The job was just too big, Your Honor. Captain Phillips himself

The Railroad Skunk | 79

said he never had a better man, but the accounts, there were so many, and I got behind with my record keeping, and you must know that I have my own way of doing things." Willis gazed straight into Ferris's eyes. "I am now rebuilding my career on the rails, down in west Kentucky. I just got an operator's position with the Ohio Valley Railway. I hope to come back to Ohio soon, and to get a steady position with a bigger road, and then I will be able to give my darling Minnie and Elsie the home they deserve." Ach, this man is a bauernfanger, thought Lou. Surely the judge will see through all this braunschweiger.

Instead, Ferris sighed. He gestured to Willis to take a chair and leaned back in his own. "It is a fascinating occupation. No other industry has had as positive an effect on American life as the railroads. Tell me about your rail experiences, Mr. Bethel."

Willis's face brightened. His voice grew lively as he told how he had been born in central New York state, the son of a minister, and had begun working at a young age as a station hand, then a clerk, at a small, rural stop on the Delaware, Lackawanna & Western. Ferris showed an interest in this, asking him about his time there, because his own family had ties to Essex County, New Jersey, which was Lackawanna territory. Willis continued that he had heard that there were opportunities in the south, and in the early '80s, when he was still young, he had been hired as a clerk on the Richmond & Danville at Ruffin, North Carolina. From there, he had worked his way up to station agent at Opelika, Alabama, before landing a job with the C&O at Preston, Kentucky. The Kentucky Union had come calling soon afterwards, but Willis declared that he would never again accept a position higher than that of station agent. He disliked the bookkeeping obligations and dealing with commercial customers. He liked the public and helping everyday people with the transactions of their lives. He regaled Ferris with some stories of the practical jokes the employees of the station would play on one another, all in good fun, of course. Like the summer the station hands at Opelika had brought a goat into his office after hours the night before his birthday, hung a card around its neck with their best wishes, and tied it so that it stared out the window at passersby, and when he came into work the next morning his 'birthday present' was chewing on the previous day's receipts. ". . . and do you know we had a devil of a time getting him out of the office so that we could conduct the business of the day? He was just as glad to stay. The happiest goat I ever did see." Both Willis and Ferris laughed while Lou grimaced through gritted teeth. Finally, he interrupted the party to remind the judge of his appointments.

"Thank you, Hunnemeyer." said Ferris, still chuckling. "Mr. Bethel, I am glad to sign your license, and I hope your life with Miss Rietman will be a happy one. And I will instruct Dumont not to send a notice to the papers, just as you and Mr. Hunnemeyer wish. That is correct, is it not, Hunnemeyer? Dumont may direct any questions to you?"

"Yes, Your Honor. It will save the family a lot of embarrassment, and since this man is now here to make things right . . ." He sent a dubious look in Willis's direction that escaped Ferris's notice. Ferris pulled the marriage license over and signed it, then scrawled "Don't Publish & oblige Lou Hunnemeyer" at the top and sent it back across the desk to Willis.

"You are obviously a man of ability, Mr. Bethel, and I hope you find your way back to a good line soon. I have enjoyed our visit today." Willis thanked the judge, took the license, and bowed out the door.

Lou was about to leave, too, but Ferris stopped him, "A minute, Hunnemeyer." After the door closed, the judge said, "Hunnemeyer, that man is a good-for-nothing. He appears to be an amiable fellow, but he is a liar. He was never on the Lackawanna, I know that for sure, and the rest was probably balderdash, too. Who knows what his real story is? I am afraid your friend's daughter may have a difficult time."

"Yes, sir," said Lou, with newfound faith in his boss's abilities.

"Keep me apprised of how he handles himself from here on out. It is possible that he has turned his life around, and I want him to have every chance. I will even try to help him get back on his feet again, if an opportunity presents itself, for the sake of Miss Rietman and the child. But I suspect there will be problems, and if there are, I want to know about them. If he works as a station agent, then he must be bonded, and I have some friends at the railroad bonding agencies."

"Yes, Your Honor. Thank you, sir." Lou stepped out, relieved. He was even more relieved when he saw that David Willis Bethel had already seen Charles T. Dumont, the Deputy Clerk, gotten his signature, and had left the building in search of a preacher.

Marriage License, D.W. Bethel and Minnie Rietman.

---

244 Marriage license, David W. Bethel and Minnie Rietman, Hamilton County, Ohio, September 13, 1893, Ancestry.com.

Probate Judge John Howard Ferris, about 1896.

It may or may not have gone something like that in Judge John Howard Ferris's chambers on September 13, 1893, but the license does have those words, in Ferris's distinctive script, at the top of the page. Ohio still did not require nearly the amount of information asked for on New York and Pennsylvania licenses, and all Willis had to do was swear that he had no legal wife living and that he and his prospective spouse were not nearer relatives than second cousins. So, he was able to answer fifty percent of the questions honestly.[246]

Of course, while the intentions of the Rietmans and Lou Hunnemeyer in keeping notice of the marriage out of the papers was to spare Minnie and her family embarrassment, Willis had a different agenda. Cincinnati was all the way across the state from Flushing, but news can travel fast if the wrong person happens to read it. The one thing he didn't need in 1893 was more publicity.

Both of his first two wives were in court that year to rid themselves of his name. On November 26, 1892, Jennie had filed for divorce, citing "Absconce" as the cause. It seems to us like an easy enough case to make, but it was continued in February 1893, and in October 1893 it was "dismissed at costs to Plaintiff," the most likely reason being that no one could find him to serve him with the summons.[247] Two notices of unclaimed letters for "D.W. Bethel" in newspapers in 1893, one at Lexington in July and one at Nashville in October,

---

245 Photo from Ohio Legal News, Volume IV, October 17, 1896 to October 9, 1897, p. 172, Google Books.
246 Marriage License, David W. Bethel and Minnie Rietman, Cincinnati, Hamilton County, Ohio, September 13, 1893, Ancestry.com.
247 Bethel vs. Bethel, Belmont County Circuit Court records, fall term, 1893, court records photographed at the Belmont County, Ohio, courthouse. No explanation for the dismissal is given in the record.

may have been attempts by the court, or by one of his early wives, to locate him.[248] Of course, if anyone had suspected that he was in Cincinnati in September to marry Minnie, the Belmont County Circuit Court would have been able to serve him with more than just a summons, and prison time for bigamy would also have been in the offing. The other lawsuit, Nettie's annulment case in April 1893, succeeded, primarily because there was evidence — an affidavit signed by Jennie — that his first marriage was still in force. If all this didn't make his life interesting enough, an investigator may also have been poking around into his business. Even with the agreement to keep his fourth marriage quiet, he was taking a big risk.

He had been carrying on his affair with Minnie for at least two years, and possibly since before his marriage to Matilda. Elsie Ruth Bethel was born July 30, 1892, just after Willis's life in Owingsville disintegrated. We know that he bought the horse he called Dictawood in Cincinnati the early 1890s, and Minnie's presence there makes it seem likely that it was a regular destination for him. He would have had access to free passes while he worked for the C. & O. and the Kentucky Union, and as a doctor he could have arranged his schedule to suit his needs. He must have excused himself from time to time for a rendezvous.

Minnie was born May 28, 1869, making her nine years Willis's junior. She is first found in the Cincinnati directory in 1886, living with her parents, George and Elizabeth, working as a Western Union operator. She was not exceptional in her employment — unlike many nineteenth-century jobs, the telegraph industry, even the jobs in the notoriously male-centric railroads, employed a lot of women.[249] It was, to an extent unheard of in other professions of the day, largely a meritocracy. There was a strong bond between telegraphers, a camaraderie born of mastery of the technology. This community "had their own customs and vocabulary."[250] Operators were even able to distinguish their distant friends by "the style of their Morse code — something that was, apparently, as recognizable as an individual human voice."[251] Whatever news came over the wires was always seen first by a telegrapher, so it was also a community that considered itself 'in the know.' We know that Willis had an extensive circle of friends in stations across the country, and Minnie must have maintained a similar group of contacts. She probably considered herself to be one of his cronies, at least initially.

Since this was a networked community that gossiped, Minnie could easily have received word of Matilda's passing, and so asserted her 'rights' to the man who had fathered her daughter.[252] We know from William McGinnis that Matilda died at his parents' home in Pennsylvania. In November 1894 Willis wrote to Nettie, ". . . two years ago in August ended all with her . . ." in reference to Matilda's death. As usual, unspecific. At first, it seems to mean August 1892, but it could also be 1893. No death record or headstone lets us know the true date, but a couple of circumstances argue for the later year. First, it was to Willis's

---

248 The Kentucky Herald-Leader, July 3, 1893; The Nashville Banner, October 28, 1893, Newspapers.com.
249 Tom Standage, *The Victorian Internet*, Kindle edition, Loc. 1387. The reader will remember that George Smith Bethel's two oldest daughters, Addie and Alice, also worked as telegraph operators.
250 Ibid., Loc. 1350.
251 Ibid., Loc. 1354.
252 Ibid., Loc. 979.

advantage that Nettie believe that Matilda was as far out of the picture as possible, since she was the only competition of which Nettie was aware. He was packaging himself as a lonely, single man who had learned his lesson, and the more time he could say had passed, the more sympathy he might inspire. But it's the timing of his marriage to Minnie, on September 13, 1893, that is most convincing. If, as I suspect, Minnie had heard of Matilda's death, she may have pressured Willis to quickly do the right thing by her and their one-year-old daughter. The mere mention of a bastardy suit would have been persuasive, especially with the problems he must have had finding work at the time.

The debacles at Owingsville and Lexington the previous year had left him in danger of losing his career on the rails entirely, and the mobility it provided him was essential to his romantic aura — the Railroad Skunk without a railroad was just an easy-to-find cheating husband. He probably went to Indianapolis soon after his dismissal from the Kentucky Union. He was listed in the 1893 directory, living in a boarding house on Belmont Avenue that catered to manual laborers and railroad yard and engine workers.[253] If the listing is correct, it appears that he truly had to start over — his occupation was 'brakeman.' This may have been a recording error, and he was really doing low-level office work while living in a house with a working-class clientele, but it's clear that he was not in control of a station. If he was a brakeman, it must have been a challenge for him, as well as a big comedown. In 1893, hand brakes were still applied from the roofs of the cars as they came into each station. It was a dangerous job, requiring each man to set the brakes on multiple cars at each stop. Accidents and deaths were common. It's kind of comical to envision Willis Bethel, the 'good for nothing' who so abhorred physical labor, jumping between the rooftops of the swaying cars in bad weather to turn the braking cranks. Brakemen also did a variety of cleaning and signaling tasks on the train.[254] It may have been his only way of reentering the business, and he probably served his penance time as obsequiously as possible until he gained office work again.

The only other information about his whereabouts in 1893-1894 comes to us from his letters, which referenced multiple people and incidents in western Kentucky and Tennessee. The Hart family, from Dyersburg, notably Milton Hart's daughter, Madge, made some appearances, as did the Baker family, near Fredonia, Kentucky. Peter Payne Baker had an Ohio Valley Railroad station on his land, and it's possible that Willis was an early, perhaps the first, agent there. One of Baker's sons, probably Edward, was a friend, and Ed's sister Mattie will have a role in a future chapter. The letters also mention a Mr. Tichenor, most likely Joseph McHenry Tichenor, a fellow station agent who worked at Morganfield. Willis also established relationships with other western Kentucky residents who will come into his story later.[255]

It's likely that he was hired by either the Ohio Valley Railroad or the Newport News &

---

253 Indianapolis, Indiana, directory, 1893, 97 Belmont Avenue, p. 188, Ancestry.com. Since directories compile their information early in the year, we can assume he was there in late December/early January.
254 Walter Licht, *Working for the Railroad*, pp. 90-91, pp. 182-183.
255 Letters, D.W. Bethel to Joannetta Fisher. Letters #1 (November 1, 1894), #3 (November 4, 1894), and #7 (November 23, 1894) refer to Madge Hart. Letter #8 (February 15, 1895) mentions the Baker family in passing. Letter #6 (November 22, 1894) mentions Mr. Tichenor, and from the context, it appears that he was a railroad man. The other people from the region will be covered in Chapters 12 and 13. All from Fisher family papers.

Mississippi Valley Railroad sometime in 1893. These were small, regional lines about which little is known today. The Ohio Valley, later absorbed by the Illinois Central, had the modest purpose of connecting Evansville, Indiana, with the coal-producing regions of western Kentucky. The N. N. & M. V., running through western Tennessee to Paducah, then east, was affiliated with both the C. & O. and the Kentucky Union. Willis may have called on some old connections for his appointment.[256]

We might wonder how, with his troubles at Lexington being so well publicized, he managed to get work at all. While the public stance of the company might have been to exonerate him from blame, railroad men would have understood that he had not just been promoted past his level of competence, that he must have been skimming. The same suspicions had, seemingly, also accompanied his departures from Bruce, Clarence, and Preston, although it's unclear how widely known they were. It's clear that he had not yet made an official railroad blacklist, which would have been cause for immediate rejection of any application for employment.[257] Stealing, if discovered, was never tolerated in the late nineteenth-century railroad world, and employers went after employees and former employees for even small amounts if it became known.[258] But pilferage and embezzlement were still common.[259] In 1862, Allan Pinkerton's detectives estimated that the Philadelphia and Reading Railroad's conductors pocketed 32 percent of their fares, and station, ticket, and freight agents also "frequently absconded with company funds."[260] Companies fought back the best they could, with traveling auditors and centrally located accountants, but in an age when the books were kept by the man taking in the money, strict accounting was impossible. Companies frequently circulated flyers amongst themselves describing the appearances of former employees found to be guilty of stealing.[261] I'll bet that worked well. I wonder if there was ever such a document issued for D.W. Bethel.

But an understanding of industry processes and the ability to do the job were invaluable, especially in rural stations where agents with a full range of skills were difficult to find. We have some testimonial evidence that Willis was good at all aspects of the day-to-day doings of the office. He was fast and precise on the wire, and it appears that he was also good with other office equipment — when the station at Perris, California, got its first typewriter in 1895 an observer wrote, "Mr. Bethel is quite an expert at the machine and can manipulate the keys at a lively rate."[262] An account from a newspaper editor at a later stop speaks of his "genial disposition and thorough knowledge of the railroad business."[263] A company may have extended an offer to an agent whose talent they felt they could harness, especially if

---

256 Abandonedonline.net. As usual, Willis had his defenders, and one of them may have vouched for him.
257 Walter Licht, *Working for the Railroad*, p. 44.
258 Letter exchanges from Illinois Central Railroad management over amount owed the company by former agent D. S. Wilson, May 12, May 15, and June 2, 1897. The three letters went into great detail and finally arrived at the conclusion that Wilson owed the company $1.00, and his pay was deducted accordingly. From the records of the Illinois Central Railroad Company held at the Newberry Library, Chicago, Illinois.
259 Charles Stephenson and Robert Asher, *Life & Labor*, p. 102.
260 Walter Licht, *Working for the Railroad*, pp. 96-97.
261 Ibid.
262 The Perris New Era, July 4, 1895, microfilm from the California State Library, Sacramento.
263 The Thirteen Towns, Fosston, Minnesota, July 9, 1897, microfilm from the Minnesota Historical Society, St. Paul.

he produced a letter of introduction from a prominent man, even if they had knowledge of some black marks on his record. And then they would put him out in some rural depot where nobody else wanted to be stationed, and where little money passed through, and hope for the best.

By late 1894, Willis was once again working for a major railroad, although not at a particular location. He was back with the Nickel Plate, headquartered in Chicago, as Division Relief Agent between that city and their hub at Bellevue, Ohio.[264] It was neither the first nor last time he would find himself in the position of a temporary agent, and it was one that was well suited to both his temperament and the interests of the company. For his part, he got to move around and satisfy some of his wanderlust. The Nickel Plate got to take advantage of his skill set while at the same time minimizing the risk that would come from giving him full control of a depot. It appears that he never lived in Cincinnati with Minnie. She is found in the directory with her parents throughout this period.[265] He must have visited occasionally, and he probably sent money for Elsie's care. He may also have had demands from Thompson and Sarah Jane McGinnes for the support of young Mary. His salary could not have provided much extra.

Notwithstanding these obligations, on November 1, with Minnie close to term with their second child, Willis renewed his correspondence with Nettie. Ben Perry must have let him know that his second wife was still interested in the fugitive man of her dreams, even with charges of fraud and embezzlement now added to adultery and bigamy. We will cover the first eight of his 27 letters, dating from November 1, 1894, to February 15, 1895, in this chapter. Seven were written in November, as he made a strong initial push to impress upon her that he was a changed man, living single, and that he deserved her forgiveness. One of his comments on November 4 makes it clear that there were also previous letters while he was at Owingsville. He confessed, "I used to be afraid to get a letter from you & yet what joy they always brought me . . ."[266]

The November 1 letter set his agenda, and more of the same would follow. The first two paragraphs are worth quoting in their entirety:

> Dear Good Nettie — I have just returned from my annual vacation — & do you know that the first thing I got was your letter — When I wrote you I then expected to go away Oct 1st but I waited until Saturday the 6th before I went hoping to hear from you but as I did not I feared that you would not answer me & so faint at heart I left. I went to Cleveland, Buffalo, Rochester & NY City. Again I hunted up Tobius I wanted to be where you had once been. I tried to go over the same ground & tried to think some happy thoughts but they were

---

264 Letter, D.W. Bethel to Joannetta Fisher #1, November 1, 1894, from Fisher family papers.
265 In 1895 and 1897 she was listed as "Mrs. D.W. Bethel" and "Mrs. Minnie R. Bethel," respectively. The earliest she lived on her own was 1899, and that is also the first year she was listed as Willis's widow rather than his wife. Either she heard gossip that he had died, or she assumed it because he had been gone for so long (Cincinnati, Ohio, directories, Minnie Rietman, 1886 {p. 1129}, 1892 {p. 1251}, Mrs. D.W. Bethel, 1895 {p. 186}, Mrs. Minnie R. Bethel, 1897 {p. 179}, Minnie Bethel, widow, David W., 1899 {p. 184}), all Ancestry.com.
266 Letter, D.W. Bethel to Joannetta Fisher #3, November 4, 1894, from Fisher family papers.

> choked back by the very bitter recollection that we are -------------
>
> I could not long stay there because I have a friend away in the City of Mexico Old Mexico whom I had promised to visit & he was expecting me — I looked longingly at Clarence as I passed thro I could see the top of Auntie Sadler's house & Mrs. Whipple's old domicile but the train hurried me along & I was soon on my way into the Sunny South. I got to El Passo [sic] Tex at 5 PM. I took a sleeper & when I woke up I was away South among the Mexicans — Of all the pretty women I ever saw the Spanish women are the finest. You will be surprised to know that Don Martinez wanted me to marry his daughter Inez. He is very wealthy & a widower & she his only child. I saved both their lives once two years ago in a wreck — that is how we knew each other. It was at West Point, Ky. She is indeed beautiful but I had to decline — not because I have a woman living with me as my wife for I have not. Two years ago in August ended all with her — a baby girl she left. It's with her people in Penna — Mary her name — Now Nettie believe me ask P.M or any God & you will find that I tell you only <u>truth</u>. No Nettie <u>no</u> — <u>no</u> <u>no</u> <u>no</u> I suppose that my fate is sealed but God knows how bitter are my recollections to know that you are lost to me — I have tried to be a Christian but I can't. When I try to do right everything goes wrong. But Nettie there is one thing I have quit viz "<u>women</u>." I brot a few relics home with me from Mexico. I will give you and Durward some. Mexico is called The Land of the Aztecs from the Latin Azecates. Messy greasy — I have knocked around & done no good. Doubt if I ever do. Suppose I will die in the infirmary. No body ever had any influence over me but you & if I had never got medicine into my head I'd always been true to you for when with you I was all right — when away I lost my head — but I'm 34. Age has taught me a few things & experience more so that today I am worse off than I was at 21 I think.
>
> I would be glad to have you write me. You are the only one whom I ever <u>loved</u> . . .[267]

I wonder how many times he used that line.

Willis pulled out every trick in the con man's handbook trying to convince her to reunite with him. He gave her a taste of his exotic lifestyle with tales of his travels, knowing it would contrast starkly with her own mundane existence. He admitted his past wrongs while simultaneously minimizing their severity (a delicate balancing act), and he emphasized that only she could heal him. He mentioned his friendships with other women to make her jealous, but insisted he was living a chaste life without her. And he threw in an ethnic slur or two here and there to remind her of his late nineteenth-century white sense of humor and their common

---

[267] Letter, D.W. Bethel to Joannetta Fisher #1, November 1, 1894, from Fisher family papers. As was the case with most of his letters, this one was handwritten. The long line that Willis drew at the end of the first paragraph of this quotation was his way of indicating that his and Nettie's relationship was broken.

bonds.

When he felt that her interest was waning, or when he was trying to pressure her into doing something, he was not above going into the good old 'Poor me, I'm so sick and lonely' routine. In letter #7:

> I am not at all well. Indeed I am almost laid up with a cold. By the way, are you going to give me your photo? Don't think because I write often that I want to bore you for I don't. I am so lonesome & your letters are practically all the comfort I have.[268]

And in letter #8:

> How do you stand this severe weather? My it was awful on me after spending some south [sic] then to come here where it is so cold. I have had trouble with my right arm. Threatened with paralysis I can now hardly hold the pen. Mr. Jones relieves me of all the work he can & I may get better soon. I think it's better gradually now for past few days.[269]

Better take him back quick, honey, before he strokes out.

He even went so far as to invoke some cosmic symbolism. In his fifth letter, on November 20, he wrote,

> I remember our wedding day? Do you? First early morn clear — then cloudy & rain a while & cleared again. I remember what thought's [sic] went through my mind. They were the first of our life sunshine — the middle clouded with trouble — the old age clear & happy. God grant it may be so.[270]

Two and a half years later, in letter #14, he repeated the same story. Willis Bethel had his finger on the pulse of the universe, don't you know.

We see evolution of all these strategies in subsequent letters, as he pursued his con-by-mail, which was so much less natural for him than using the force of his personality. As it became clear that the jealousy angle wasn't working, for example, he replaced it with statements of devotion to their son, a change that seemed to resonate with Nettie. Madge Hart, whom he mentioned several times in the first few letters, disappeared after letter #7, and he never again mentioned an unmarried female friend by name. In later letters, as he gained Nettie's trust, he increasingly switched the blame for his actions from himself to Nettie, but in these early stages it was his contrition that gained him the most points. His apologies were many and piteous as he pushed his reunification agenda throughout November. He asked for

---

268 Letter, D.W. Bethel to Joannetta Fisher #7, November 23, 1894, from Fisher family papers.
269 Letter, D.W. Bethel to Joannetta Fisher #8, February 15, 1895, from Fisher family papers.
270 Letter, D.W. Bethel to Joannetta Fisher #5; November 20, 1894, from Fisher family papers.

updates about Nettie's relatives and their mutual friends in the Clarence area. He said he was a changed man, unattached and lonely.

For a full appreciation of the duplicity of his actions, consider the timing. In November 1894, the pregnant Minnie was raising two-year-old Elsie in her parents' Cincinnati home. Mary Ralston Bethel, an orphaned and abandoned toddler, was being raised by Matilda's sister Sarah Jane on the McGinnes farm in Pennsylvania. Jennie still lived in Flushing, where she supported nine-year-old Bessie by cleaning houses, almost certainly with no assistance from Willis. And yet, his third letter, on November 4, ended with the postscript, "If I keep employment I will help both you & Durward all I can if you will allow it — There is no other strings to my coat tail."[271]

His time in Chicago allowed him to regale her with descriptions of the World's Fair, as well as other big city doings he knew would impress her. Sometime between November 4 and November 15 the opportunity for a full-time position arrived, and he was named train dispatcher (a step up in responsibility) for the Toledo & Ohio Central Railway at Columbus. The superintendent of the western division of the railroad (which included Columbus), was a man named Henry Carr Ferris, whose father was the road's general manager. I've found no evidence that this family was related to Cincinnati judge John Howard Ferris, but it's possible they were cousins of some degree, and that Willis had some help getting the job. On November 4, he had written, "I may go to Columbus O as train dispr. For T&OC RR. Can't tell but we are negotiating now & I think there's a possibility."[272] That makes the matter sound undecided, but in his next letter he wrote, "I wrote you nearly two weeks ago. At the time I told you I was expecting an appointment here as Train Disp'r & I got it."[273] If Judge Ferris had arranged things behind the scenes, the timing, with Minnie only weeks away from delivering their second child, could not have been better. Strangely enough, Henry Carr Ferris will come back into the speculative part of our story seventeen years later, when D.W. Bethel wore another name in a different country.

This period of Nettie Fisher's life, from all accounts, was difficult. She was 34 and unmarried, with a six-year-old son. They lived with Alathera Whipple in her home (Theron Whipple had died by 1894) and Nettie did the housework and took care of her 81-year-old friend, who was likely her only confidant. Nettie did not dare to share with her family members that she was corresponding with Willis, but we know that she consulted with Alathera Whipple. Willis hated Nettie's entire support group, and he let her know it in his later correspondence, but he made nice in his first letter, writing, "Poor Mrs. Whipple I hope she don't suffer so much with her rheumatism."[274] It went downhill from there. On November 20, "I think you better not counsel Mrs. Whipple to [sic] much."[275] On November 22 he advised his second wife "Not to tell her all for I think she is prejudiced against me."[276] Really? Now,

---

271 Letter, D.W. Bethel to Joannetta Fisher #3; November 4, 1894, from Fisher family papers.
272 Ibid.
273 Letter, D.W. Bethel to Joannetta Fisher #4; November 15, 1894, from Fisher family papers.
274 Letter, D.W. Bethel to Joannetta Fisher #1; November 1, 1894, from Fisher family papers.
275 Letter, D.W. Bethel to Joannetta Fisher #5; November 20, 1894, from Fisher family papers.
276 Letter, D.W. Bethel to Joannetta Fisher #6; November 22, 1894, from Fisher family papers.

why would that be? The next day he wrote, "My ears are burning & I suppose you are saying good and Mrs. Whipple giving me Old Billy Ned."[277]

On November 22 he wrote,

> Now dear Nettie can I ask you to forgive me? Can you not allow me to go on probation? You may put any time on me you like & see how well I will behave. Now for Durward's sake if not for my own I should turn around. That is the conclusion I came to nearly 3 years ago & I have tried to be steadfast to it ever since. I find that I can be happier by curbing my passions than by letting them go head long.[278]

Lies, of course, all lies. After the first seven letters, all written in November 1894, things cooled off some, as Nettie evidently paused their correspondence, a practice she would repeat several times over the next three years as doubts overtook her thoughts. That they were not certainties gives us some idea of her desperation.

On January 17, 1895, Minnie gave birth to Clarence Aubrey Bethel in Cincinnati. In Willis's next letter to Nettie, on February 15, which is also the last one in the first group, he wrote:

> Dear Little Nettie:
>
> I have looked & looked to hear from you but it seems you have quit. What's the trouble? I have been very busy & then lost 3 weeks sick just now back at work. I wish you would write. I sent you stamps in plenty to cover your correspondence with me. I wrote you the last letter & I don't understand why.[279]

He loves her so much, after all. His postscript: "I am living a good respectable life sure as you live."[280]

The 'three weeks sick' was probably leave he took from his job in Columbus to be with his Cincinnati family for Clarence's birth. All the double-dealing seems to have come naturally to him by this point, in fact, he relished the excitement of the con. But his biggest deception may have come from the choice of the first name of Clarence, which the reader will remember was also the name of Nettie's hometown. It was relatively popular in 1895, and it may have come from another source. Minnie's great-grandson writes that, "Grandma Bethel named Clarence because it could not be contracted, i.e., Robert to Bob. Seems like a silly thing, but who knows?"[281] But nineteenth-century custom acknowledged the authority

---

277 Letter, D.W. Bethel to Joannetta Fisher #7; November 23, 1894, from Fisher family papers. Note: 'Old Billy Ned' was a nineteenth-century euphemism for 'the Devil.'
278 Letter, D.W. Bethel to Joannetta Fisher #6; November 22, 1894, from Fisher family papers.
279 Letter, D.W. Bethel to Joannetta Fisher #8, February 15, 1895, from Fisher family papers.
280 Ibid.
281 Email correspondence, Thomas Trapp to Charles Caldemeyer, October 25, 2016

of fathers in all aspects of family life, especially the naming of offspring, while the mother often chose the middle name. Willis had certainly been the one who chose to call his New York son Durward, with Nettie choosing the middle name of Frederick to honor her father. It's also likely that he chose to honor his own mother by naming his second daughter Mary, with the middle name of Ralston coming from Matilda. It seems likely that he would have insisted on the naming rights for Clarence as well. He had renamed himself after a town, but if he named his new son after the hometown of the former wife he was slyly trying to reunite with (a move he would have thought was clever), it was a secret betrayal and mockery of the woman who had given birth to two of his children. She was also a woman he would soon abandon forever.

7.

The Railroad Skunk Goes West

■ SOMETIME BETWEEN FEBRUARY AND JUNE 1895, David Willis Bethel ditched his Cincinnati family.

According to his and Minnie's great-grandson, "The legend of David W. was he was a doctor, & for undisclosed reasons left the family. Not much was said about him to my Mom and Uncle, except they kept up a good opinion of him, despite his disappearing act. I guess everyone filled in the missing info with positive assessments."[282] Whatever those reasons were, it seems that Minnie knew about them and, to her family anyway, deemed them legitimate.

They may have stemmed from his presence at the Columbus depot. Belmont County was only about 120 miles to the east. If he was recognized by someone who knew his past, it would have triggered a swift movement toward greener pastures. Did Minnie know about Jennie, believe Willis's predictable claim that he was a victim, and accept his decision to leave Ohio to avoid being caught? Did he spin her some other yarn? Or were the "undisclosed reasons" just a story she told her children and grandchildren to avoid talking about the most painful incident of her life? Minnie never sought a divorce and lived the rest of her long life as David Willis Bethel's wife, then his widow.[283] Like Nettie, she was smitten.

He may have corresponded with her for a time, telling her how much he missed them all, here's a little money, please be patient, soon all our dreams will come true, etc. But once he had gotten away, with only himself as the protagonist in his own play, he probably cut all ties. It seems likely that the undisclosed reasons were just a smokescreen, and that abandonment was his plan all along, but as with many of his stories, there may have been a grain of truth to them.

Perris is in Riverside County, about 50 miles east of Los Angeles and 25 miles south of San Bernardino. It's basically desert country, although farming, particularly of grains and fruit trees, is excellent if there is a water source. In 1895, there was also a good amount of

---

282 Email correspondence, Thomas Trapp and Charles Caldemeyer, October 25, 2016. It is doubtful that he tried to practice medicine during this period, although he may have packaged himself as a non-practicing doctor. Letter #7 to Nettie, written November 23, 1894, mentions that he had practiced for only "a few months" in the previous five years, the approximate amount of time he had been in partnership with Catlett at Owingsville.

283 The first directory that listed Minnie as his widow was in 1899 (Cincinnati, Ohio, directory, 1899, p. 184), and she was so listed continuously until 1958. U.S. City Directories, Ancestry.com.

precious metal mining going on nearby.²⁸⁴ The weather is great if you like sunshine — as a Riverside paper reported, "During nine months of the year Perris valley stands second to no section in California for desirability of climate. The heat of July, August and September makes a trip to the sea coast or mountains a welcome change."²⁸⁵ Willis marveled at the southern California climate. He wrote to Nettie, "I think you will be surprised to know that I have only seen two small showers since I came to this state. I am in sight of snow the year around but never snows here can see it on the mountain but don't come with us."²⁸⁶ In early 1895, Perris had about 1,000 residents, mostly a diverse group of transplants from other places. "Almost every state of the Union was represented . . . and they had nothing but good words for the youthful city and its bright future," read an article in the Riverside Enterprise.²⁸⁷ With so large a non-native population, there were probably many residents who, like Willis Bethel, were running from something in their pasts.

Since 1891, the ranches and farms had thrived due to the water supplied from the San Bernardino mountains, about 30 miles to the north, by the Bear Valley Water Company irrigation system, a large network of "dams, ditches, canals, pipe lines, [and] reservoirs."²⁸⁸ By 1895, however, the company had become overextended, and since "other places having prior rights must be supplied," there was a growing water shortage which would ultimately undercut the positive outlook of the residents.²⁸⁹

Perris was also a railroad town, although just barely. The Southern California Railway had been built through the place (then known as Pinacate, which roughly translates as "stink bug") in the 1880s, to connect San Bernardino and points east with San Diego via an overland route. By the early 1890s, it operated as a subsidiary of the giant Atchison, Topeka & Santa Fe Railroad, forming the last western link in a line that stretched all the way to Chicago. But washouts in the steep canyons through which the track had to run, along with the completion of a coastal route, had pushed the section through Perris off the main line, and by 1895 it ran only two trains a day.²⁹⁰

William Seaburn Wise was a lawyer, born in Indiana in 1855, who had migrated to southern California sometime after 1880. Like many western gentlemen, his business interests catered to multiple demands in the small town, and he ran a real estate and insurance enterprise and was a notary public. But he must have spent most of his time in his favorite role, as owner and editor a local newspaper, the Perris New Era.²⁹¹ On June 13, 1895, the paper ran the following item:

---

284 *Prosperous, Progressive Perris*, The Riverside Independent Enterprise, April 28, 1895, GenealogyBank.com.
285 Ibid.
286 Letter, D.W. Bethel to Joannetta Fisher #10, January 7, 1896, from Fisher family papers.
287 *Thriving Perris*, The Riverside Independent Enterprise, April 25, 1895, GenealogyBank.com.
288 Elmer Wallace Holmes, *The History of Perris Valley (Part 2)*, p. 3.
289 Ibid., p. 8.
290 Richard V. Dodge, *Perris and its Railroad*.
291 *The Editors: How Riverside's Visitors Were Entertained*, Riverside Independent Enterprise, February 5, 1895, GenealogyBank.com.

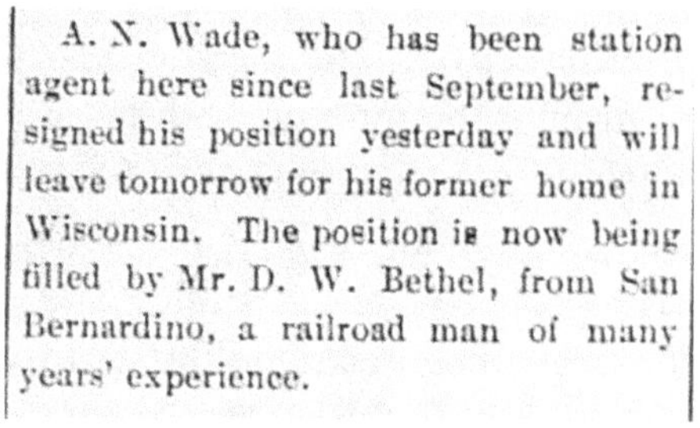

A. N. Wade, who has been station agent here since last September, resigned his position yesterday and will leave tomorrow for his former home in Wisconsin. The position is now being filled by Mr. D. W. Bethel, from San Bernardino, a railroad man of many years' experience. [292]

Transcription: A.N. Wade, who has been station agent here since last September, resigned his position yesterday and will leave tomorrow for his former home in Wisconsin. The position is now being filled by Mr. D.W. Bethel, from San Bernardino, a railroad man of many years' experience.

San Bernardino? He was probably staying with Hubert McCray Baty, one of his many friends among railroad telegraphers, while he looked for work. Baty was twelve years his junior, from Elmira, New York. Whether Willis knew him from his days in Clarence or through the wires is unknown, but he was certainly one of the contacts he used to establish himself in California. We don't know whether Baty helped his friend get the job at Perris.

Willis made friends with W.S. Wise almost immediately upon his arrival in Perris, and he quickly became part of the editor's inner circle. In less than sixteen months, the paper, which was a weekly, mentioned the doings of D.W. Bethel no less than 48 times, giving us excellent eyewitness commentary of his time there. He enjoyed "unrivaled popularity" in the small town and was the local celebrity he had always aspired to be, but had not been, since his brief ascendancy in Owingsville three years earlier.[293] The wide-open attitudes of the West in 1895, which valued colorfulness and eschewed judgment, no doubt contributed to his fame.

[294]

W.S. Wise in his passport application photo in 1919, at age 63, some twenty-four years after he knew Willis in Perris, California.

292 The Perris New Era, June 13, 1895, microfilm from the California State Library, Sacramento.
293 *What Perris Saw*, The Perris New Era, May 14, 1896, microfilm from CSL.
294 Passport Application, William Seaburn Wise, April 7, 1919, Ancestry.com.

He was a dynamic and creative presence from the day he took command of the depot. He improved the commerce of the railroad, and he also made the station a place of increased social activity. From all appearances, he was enthusiastic in his new surroundings, probably glad that he had put some distance between himself and all his midwestern entanglements. For the first time in three years he could read his name in the papers and marvel at what a clever, wonderful, and popular person he was.

Perris station, circa 1892.

On June 20, Wise's paper reported, "Station Agent Bethel is making numerous changes in the arrangement of affairs in his various offices, looking to neatness as well as convenience in the dispatch of business."[296] The following week: "If any accident or sickness overtakes you in the vicinity of the station just call Dr. Bethel, the station agent. He is a graduate of Buffalo Medical college of Buffalo, N.Y., and know's [sic] just exactly how, even if he's not practicing."[297] On at least one occasion that summer, Willis got an opportunity to show off his skills by helping a local doctor, W.B. Payton, set a broken bone in a boy's leg.[298]

To endear himself to his new employer, he immediately trotted out one of his favorite tricks — excursion trips. The first was for San Diego, advertised one week after his appointment was announced, on the same day as the station changes. Others, for Santa Monica and Redondo Beach, soon followed, as the residents of Perris looked to get some relief from the inland summer heat.[299] The new station agent was an industrious employee who wanted to

---
295 Photo from Railswest.com.
296 The Perris New Era, June 20, 1895, microfilm from CSL.
297 The Perris New Era, June 27, 1895, microfilm from CSL.
298 The Perris New Era, August 8, 1895, microfilm from CSL.
299 The Perris New Era, June 20, July 25, August 29, September 26, 1895, microfilm from CSL.

impress his supervisors and accommodate the residents of his new town. A cynic might also note that, well, you know.

On July 25, less than six weeks after assuming his new duties, a strange juxtaposition of items appeared in the New Era. First,

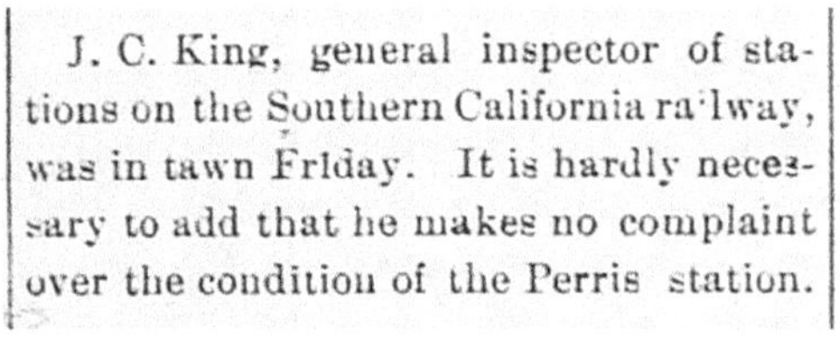
J. C. King, general inspector of stations on the Southern California ra'lway, was in tawn Friday. It is hardly necessary to add that he makes no complaint over the condition of the Perris station. [300]

Transcription: J.C. King, general inspector of stations on the Southern California railway, was in tawn [sic] Friday. It is hardly necessary to add that he makes no complaint over the condition of the Perris station.

But Willis didn't like anyone checking up on him. In the next column was an item that will ring false to anyone who has been paying attention:

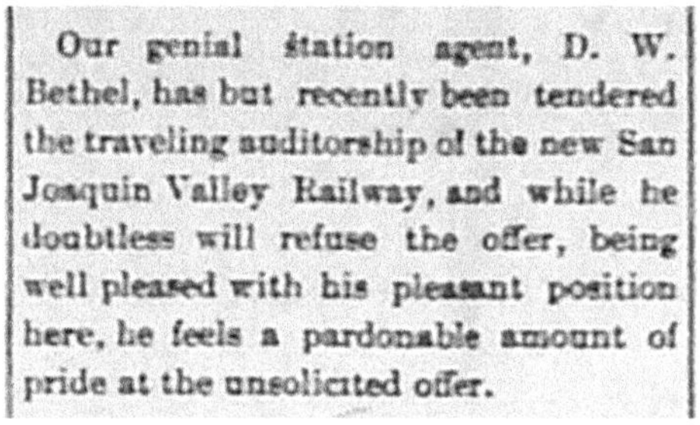
Our genial station agent, D. W. Bethel, has but recently been tendered the traveling auditorship of the new San Joaquin Valley Railway, and while he doubtless will refuse the offer, being well pleased with his pleasant position here, he feels a pardonable amount of pride at the unsolicited offer. [301]

Transcription: Our genial station agent, D.W. Bethel, has but recently been tendered the traveling auditorship of the new San Joaquin Valley Railway, and while he doubtless will refuse the offer, being well pleased with his pleasant position here, he feels a pardonable amount of pride at the unsolicited offer.

Yeah, right. Why would any railroad company offer the position of traveling auditor to someone who didn't apply for it, and who had never served in even a bookkeeping capacity for any company, and who in fact . . . oh, never mind, you get the idea. Willis had begun to play his new friend W.S. Wise like a violin. It would be in character for him to mention something like this while the station inspector went about his duties ("hey, you know I don't need this job. I was just offered this traveling auditor gig . . ."). Just some harmless chest-thumping between friends, after all, but Wise swallowed it.

---

300 The Perris New Era, July 25, 1895, microfilm from CSL.
301 Ibid.

July 25 was a busy day, as the following unusual item also appeared:

> **Watermelon-Eating Contest.**
>
> A novel contest took place at the depot here last Friday afternoon. It was a watermelon-eating match, and the contestants were Will Newerf and Lou Barrow. The first heat consisted of a large watermelon, which was divided and half given to each contestant. This disappeared quicker than it takes to tell it, with Barrow in the lead. Then they each tackled a whole melon, discarding their knives and burying their faces in the juicy melons. Barrow had set the pace thus far, but when they struck the home stretch Newerf spurted ahead and won the race by nearly a half a melon, having gotten away with 10½ pounds of melon in 3 minutes flat. This is the first of a series of three contests, and we would advise our farmer friends to guard well their melon patches until the championship question is settled.
>
> Doctor Bethel acted as referee and had on hand a supply of paregoric and stomach pumps. Allan Mackenzie acted as bottle-holder for Barrow and Bert Moulton filled a similar position on behalf of Newerf.
>
> Newerf left on Sunday for Santa Barbara to train for the next match, and Barrow is trying to locate a melon orchard in this vicinity so that he can rehearse nearer home. The prize to be given the winner is a coffin, donated by J. H. McSquire of Perriside.[302]

Let the good times roll. Who wouldn't eat themselves sick for the chance to get a free coffin? There was no word on whether the inspector was put off by all the non-train-related activity, but the company had to like the uptick in business that Willis's energy created.

Throughout summer and fall 1895, he thrived in this environment, updating the depot and running excursions. On September 26, Wise's paper applauded him as "a close observer of the people here" who "knows just about what it takes to catch a crowd."[303] He became friends with the entire town, and not surprisingly, his focus was on the young, fun-loving, single crowd.

---

302 Ibid.
303 The Perris New Era, September 26, 1895, microfilm from CSL.

Three of them would have important parts to play in the tale to come. The first was Joseph P. Steele, Willis's protégé at the station in summer 1895. A Missouri transplant born in 1870, he had moved west with his widowed father sometime in the early 1890s. He evidently began his unpaid apprenticeship at the station soon after Willis's arrival. We will develop Steele's story more fully in the chapters to come.

The second was Noah Huston Greer, who went by Hugh. A pipe maker and plumber, originally from Tennessee, Greer was about four years younger than Willis, and he was known in the area for his work on pumps and irrigation systems, his general ability to fix things, and his interest in applications for the newly developed gasoline engine. Like everyone else in town, he also liked to have a good time. He and Willis became friends sometime during the summer of 1895, and they would become business partners early the following year.

The third was Annie M. Reed. Annie was only 15 in 1895, and that summer the paper announced her as a member of the seventh grade for the upcoming school year.[304] This may or may not have been a commentary on her intelligence — school was often less important in the rural west than in other parts of the country, and it was common for students' grade levels to lag their ages. Annie lived with her mother Martha and three brothers and a sister. They had moved from Austin, Nevada, where Martha's husband William H. Reed had been a silver miner. They must have been an interesting couple — William was born in 1833 in Alabama and Martha about 1844 in New York state. He seems to have gone west prior to the Civil War, and she just after, and they both ended up in the silver town of Austin, where they had married in 1870. The silver ran out, William died in 1891, and Martha moved the family to Perris, likely so her older sons could pursue the good mining opportunities there. In 1895, she wove rag carpets for a living, oldest son John William (1873-1934) was a miner, and Guy Bertram (1876-1952), Bessie Dalton (1878-1968), Annie (1880-19??), and George Bernice (1882-1916) helped out as they could.[305]

Annie may not have helped out very much. Although the Reeds were a family that all enjoyed their leisure time, she seems to have been even more dedicated to those activities than the other members. She was mentioned many times in Wise's paper, sometimes because she was "on the sick list," but mostly as a participant in recreational outings. In a town like Perris in 1895, young people must not have had a lot of places to spend their free time. Camping and hunting trips to the mountains were common, along with almost any other imaginable strategy to break the boredom (watermelon eating contests, for example). Annie's brother Guy, among others in town, was an enthusiastic practitioner of the new sport of bicycle riding. With the depot now providing a welcoming atmosphere and the promise of some excitement, it's not surprising that Annie, who had lost her father some four years earlier, should gravitate toward the funny, fast-talking, well-traveled older man who projected

---

304 The Perris New Era, July 11, 1895, microfilm from CSL.
305 *History and Directory of Riverside County, 1893-1894*, p. 131; Marriage License, William H. Reed and Mattie Frasier, Lander County, Nevada, July 16, 1870; U.S. Census, 1880, Austin, Lander County, Nevada, William H. Reed family, both Ancestry.com; According to LadyLittle, who manages the *Seeley Family Tree* on Ancestry.com and who is a descendant of William and Mattie Reed through their daughter Bessie, William H. Reed died September 2, 1891, of stomach cancer.

such an aura of self-confidence. In a way, she was in the same mold as Nettie Fisher had been some nine years earlier, although her youth made her even more vulnerable.

We know that Annie and Willis went on at least one of the coastal excursion trips together, to Redondo Beach in August. Wise wrote that on the trip she had "obtained her first glimpse of the shimmering sea."[306]

On September 5, W.S. Wise and his wife hosted a going-away party for a member of their group of friends, Lou Barrow, the loser of the melon eating contest, and we can get a glimpse of the players and relationships that were being formed.

Transcription: Farewell Party. One of the pleasantest events of the season was the social given at the home of Mr. and Mrs. Wise on Saturday evening by a number of the friends of L. R. Barrow, in whose honor it was given. Ten couples were present and enjoyed an elegant collation provided for the occasion consisting of good things not necessary to mention. The tables were handsomely decorated with roses and vines and all enjoyed themselves to the uttermost.

The party consisted of Misses Lizzie and Emma Peters, Clara Timmons, Lou Thomas, Annie Reed, Maude Conwell, Nellie Wise and Clara Johnston, and Messrs. D. W. Bethel, J.P. Steele, Chas. Timmons, David Whiting, Henry Dickman, L. R. Barrow, John Pell, Will Hunter, and Hugh Greer.

Although this article references "ten couples," it does not say who was with whom, and there may have been no set relationships among the group at that time. Willis and Annie may have just been part of a circle of friends who recreated together, although there was certainly flirting, and maybe more, between them. But that was true to some degree with every female who crossed his path. We get our first solid indication of the bonds that were forming between them about a month later, not from the New Era but from the Riverside Daily Press, which ran the following item in its Perris section, referencing a touring theatrical production headed by singer/actress Pauline Hall:

---

306 The Perris New Era, August 22, 1895, microfilm from CSL.
307 The Perris New Era, September 5, 1895, microfilm from CSL.

> D. W. Bethel, Miss Anna Reed, Hugh Greese and Miss Lizzie Peters of Perris were in to the performance and drove back by moonlight last evening.[308]

Transcription: D.W. Bethel, Miss Anna Reed, Hugh Greese [sic] and Miss Lizzie Peters of Perris were in to the performance and drove back by moonlight last evening.

Sounds like a double date to me, but who knows? The New Era also mentioned the event, although it did not include names, calling the group "several of Perris' leading young people."[309] Maybe Wise didn't want to make the single women in town jealous.

On November 26, the Daily Press ran the following item in its Perris section. Modesty must have prevented Wise from mentioning it in his own paper.

> Saturday evening W. S. Wise and wife entertained a company of young people in honor of D. W. Bethel, station agent of the Santa Fe line at this place. A very pleasant evening was spent in converse, music and games, and a bountiful supper had been prepared for the refreshment of the guests.[310]

Transcription: Saturday evening W.S. Wise and wife entertained a company of young people in honor of D.W. Bethel, station agent of the Santa Fe line at this place. A very pleasant evening was spent in converse, music and games, and a bountiful supper had been prepared for the refreshment of the guests.

Willis had shot to the top of the list of cool kids after only a few months. Being the object of admiration by young and free hearts was just a burden that came with the territory of being David Willis Bethel.

In early August, less than two months after his arrival, the Perris New Era reported the following item:

---

308 The Riverside Daily Press, October 6, 1895, GenealogyBank.com. Although his name is misspelled, it is clear that Hugh Greer was the other gentleman mentioned.
309 The Perris New Era, October 10, 1895, microfilm from CSL.
310 The Riverside Daily Press, November 26, 1895, GenealogyBank.com.

> James M. Blair of Frederickstown. Ohio, an old friend of Dr. D. W. Bethel, will arrive in Perris in a few days and make his future home among us. Mr. Blair is an excellent attorney and will most probably practice his profession in our midst.[311]

Transcription: James M. Blair of Frederickstown [sic], Ohio, an old friend of Dr. D. W. Bethel, will arrive in Perris in a few days and make his future home among us. Mr. Blair is an excellent attorney and will most probably practice his profession in our midst.

This is our first sighting of James Martin Blair, a Civil War veteran from Uncle Doc's generation. Blair's name will weave in and out on the edges of D.W. Bethel's story in the years to come. As far as moving to Perris was concerned, though, he turned out to be a no-show. As long as we're foreshadowing, we should mention that the following month Joe Steele was transferred to a salaried position at nearby Hemet. "Agent Bethel feels quite proud of the part he has taken in the matter," the paper reported.[312] The friendship between Willis and Steele would claim a central role in the Railroad Skunk's story over the next six years.

The new station agent was a star in Perris, but the place was teetering on the edge of hard financial times in late 1895, with a looming water crisis and a generally lackluster economy. On September 23, the situation got worse when a major fire swept through town. Many of Perris's bone-dry structures, mostly businesses, were destroyed or damaged, and few had enough insurance. A bucket brigade brought it under control after a couple of hours, and the New Era singled out fourteen citizens, including Joe Steele and Will Newerf (the winner of the watermelon eating contest) for their heroism. Willis was not among those mentioned, although he was "threatened with an attack of pneumonia as a result of his untimely rising and perigrinations [sic]."[313] He got sick? Go figure. Among the buildings damaged was the hotel where he lived, and two weeks later the paper reported, "Dr. Bethel has a trophy of the late fire in the way of his fine shaving mug. Its appearance indicates that it had a close shave."[314] Probably smoke damage. In a letter to Nettie almost two years later, Willis lamented, "I lost every thing I had in the way of mementoes & keepsakes" in the fire, including Durward's photograph.[315] Not all of the citizenry's efforts were related to dousing the blaze. "They say Joe Steele made an effort to swipe Newerf's bicycle suit and made a failure of it.," Wise's paper reported.[316] It's easy to see what Willis saw in his opportunistic protégé.

---

311 The Perris New Era, August 8, 1895, microfilm from CSL.
312 The Perris New Era, September 5, 1895, microfilm from CSL.
313 The Perris New Era, September 26, 1895, microfilm from CSL.
314 The Perris New Era, October 10, 1895, microfilm from CSL.
315 Letter, D.W. Bethel to Joannetta Fisher #16, May 16, 1897, from Fisher family papers.
316 The Perris New Era, September 26, 1895, microfilm from CSL.

If the population did not have had much admiration for his willingness to help out when physical prowess was demanded, they did appreciate his efforts in the fire's aftermath, and so did officials at the Southern California Railway. On October 17, the paper reported that, "Station Agent Bethel has secured 100 feet of good large hose and reel complete, for the protection of the depot."[317] The same issue ran the following two items:

> **Good.**
>
> Station Agent Bethel is not happy unless he's accomplishing some improvement in and about the station building or grounds. His latest and best effort in this line is the granting by the company of the necessary material, expenses and shrubbery for a depot park. It will be located between the two tracks, north of and adjoining the depot building, and will be about thirty by fifty feet in size, will be surrounded with an iron railing and gilded chains, and will contain plants of the very choicest varieties suitable to this locality. Chief Engineer Fred T. Perris, in whose honor this town was named, has been solicited in the matter by Agent Bethel and has become interested to such an extent that the people of Perris may rely upon having a first-class "Beauty spot," for the greater portion of which they will gladly feel themselves under obligations to our genial agent.[318]

Transcription: Good. Station Agent Bethel is not happy unless he's accomplishing some improvement in and about the station building or grounds. His latest and best effort in this line is the granting by the company of the necessary material, expenses and shrubbery for a depot park. It will be located between the two tracks, north of and adjoining the depot building, and will be about thirty by fifty feet in size, will be surrounded with an iron railing and gilded chains, and will contain plants of the very choicest varieties suitable to this locality. Chief Engineer Fred T. Perris, in whose honor this town was named, has been solicited in the matter by Agent Bethel and has become interested to such an extent that the people of Perris may rely upon having a first-class "Beauty spot," for the greater portion of which they will gladly feel themselves under obligations to our genial agent.

---

317 The Perris New Era, October 17, 1895, microfilm from the CSL.
318 Ibid.

> Our new depot park is fenced in in good shape and Agent Bethel is justly proud of it, and says that while it is small, that fact will be more than balanced by the quality of it.
>
> Ground for the depot park was broken Tuesday morning. It will receive a dressing of manure and then thoroughly soaked with water. After which the ground will be turned over to a depth of 18 to 20 inches and then laid off in beds of artictic designs. The Santa Fe company will furnish plants, etc., but not enough to fill the plot, and those residents here wishing to supply plants, etc. the same will be thankfully received by Agent Bethel who has taken great interest in the park.[319]

Transcription: Our new depot park is fenced in in good shape and Agent Bethel is justly proud of it, and says that while it is small, that fact will be more than balanced by the quality of it.

Ground for the depot park was broken Tuesday morning. It will receive a dressing of manure and then thoroughly soaked with water. After which the ground will be turned over to a depth of 18 to 20 inches and then laid off in beds of artictic [sic] designs. The Santa Fe company will furnish plants, etc., but not enough to fill the plot, and those residents here wishing to supply plants, etc. the same will be thankfully received by Agent Bethel who has taken great interest in the park.

The little park by the depot was not a significant item in the big picture, but it was an important symbol as Perris tried to recover from the various troubles it faced. Wise was right, Willis was a close observer of the residents, and his positive attitude during the town's hard times was certainly welcomed.

In early December, The New Era reported that "Station agent Bethel has completed his mastery of the bicycle."[320] He referenced his interest in cycling in one of his later letters to Durward, calling himself "a great bike rider." When I first read it I laughed because it seems bizarre for him, but there is evidence that he actually did master 'the wheel,' as early bikes were called.[321] At one of his stops a few years later, a local newspaper reported that he "can be seen almost every day, spinning around on his new wheel. Although a heavyweight, he can hold his own with our best riders."[322] This article was written in northwestern Minnesota in early March, not exactly a bike rider's paradise, so we can infer that he truly became proficient at the sport. There were several local riders among his friends in Perris, and it was

---
319 Ibid.
320 The Perris New Era, December 5, 1895, microfilm from CSL.
321 Letter, D.W. Bethel to Joannetta Fisher #17, May 30, 1897, from Fisher family papers.
322 *Gary,* The Twin Valley Times, March 9, 1898, p. 1, microfilm from the Minnesota Historical Society, St. Paul.

probably a humorous sidelight for the teenagers and twenty-somethings to watch the fleshy middle-aged man, still pretending to be young, learning how to ride. But he became good at it.

He maintained his correspondence with Nettie and Durward, although sporadically, during this period. This is the second group of letters in our possession. While there are only four, some of them refer to packages exchanged, in which there were almost certainly notes included, and there may also have been others, now lost. Willis seemed confident and successful, at least through early 1896, and while he continued to apply pressure on Nettie to reunite with him, the tone of this group was mostly newsy, friendly, and conversational.

The first one was a short note addressed to Durward on August 14, 1895:

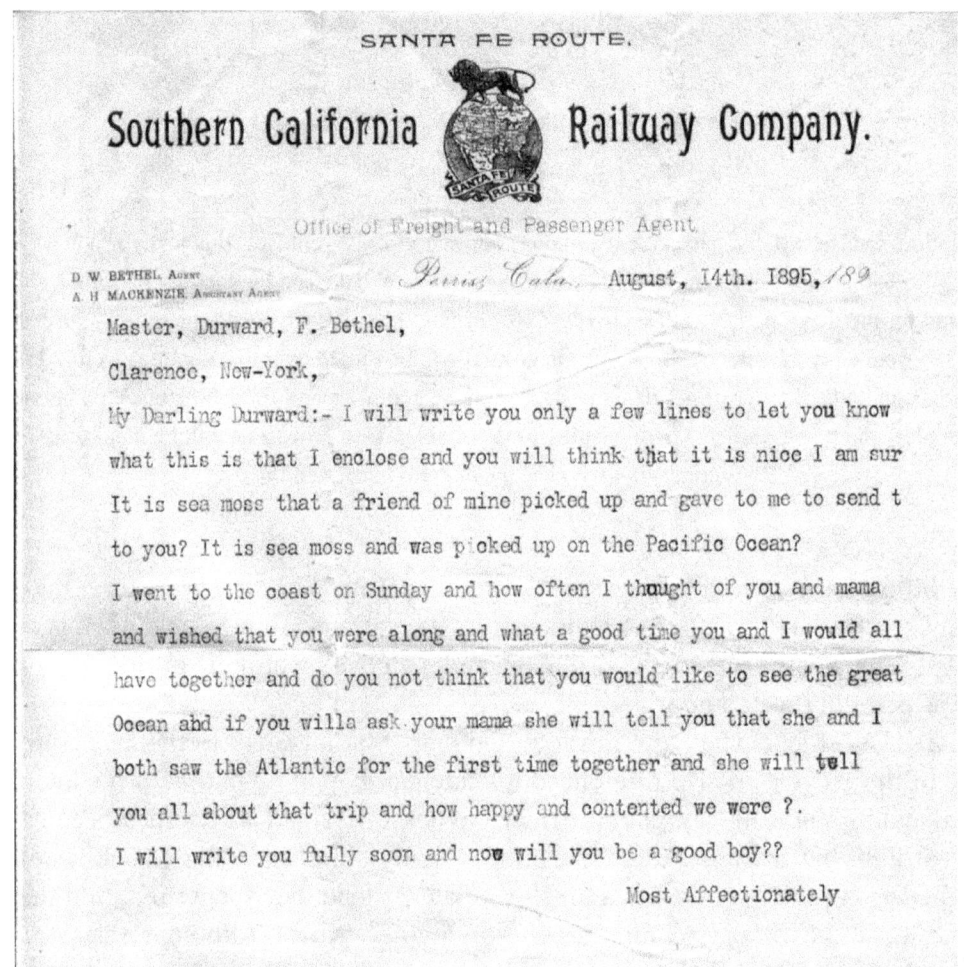

[323]

Transcription: Master, Durward, F. Bethel, Clarence, New-York, My Darling Durward:- I will write you only a few lines to let you know what this is that I enclose and you will think it is nice I am sur [sic] It is sea moss that a friend of mine picked up and gave to me to send t [sic] to you? It is sea moss and was picked up on the Pacific Ocean?

---

323 Letter, D.W. Bethel to Joannetta Fisher #9, August 14, 1895, from Fisher family papers.

I went to the coast on Sunday and how often I thought of you and mama and wished that you were along and what a good time you and I would all have together and do you not think that you would like to see the great ocean and if you willa [sic] ask your mama she will tell you that she and I both saw the Atlantic for the first time together and she will tell you all about that trip and how happy and contented we were?

I will write you fully soon and now will you be a good boy??

Most Affectionately

Typewritten on Southern California Railway letterhead, with "D.W. Bethel, Agent" on the header, it must have impressed both Nettie and her seven-year-old son. It referred to the previously mentioned excursion trip to Redondo Beach on August 11, on which Annie also went, and one wonders if she was the friend who picked up the sea moss for Durward. Willis would have found that amusing. And the fact that he would only send such a small curiosity as sea moss is one of the reasons I think there may have been more communications during this period than those which are in our possession. If you're only going to write to your son once or twice a year you've got to do better than sea moss, don't you?

On December 9, the most severe blow yet came to the town in the form of the failure of the Perris Valley Bank, the only one to service the region. Depositors were promised the return of all their money, but the event still caused panic and financial hardship, and it cast a pall over the entire valley. As the New Era wrote, "with the Irrigation district in trouble; the late disastrous conflagration; the losses by robbery and other drawbacks, there has been nothing that has affected the whole community as much as the closing of the bank."[324]

Willis's letter on January 7, 1896, also typewritten on letterhead, referenced both the fire and the bank failure, and used them as excuses. "I would have sent you some money before now but the hotel burning and then our bank breaking so that I was the looser [sic] in both so you will see that I have had some losses."[325] This letter also marked the beginning of a change in his assessment of his departure from Clarence. In the first group of letters, he was full of contrition and apparent self-loathing, "I am doing fairly well. As well or better I suppose than I deserve,"[326] and "I've been a very very wicked man & done indeed very very wrong,"[327] typified this 'oh-I'm-so-sorry' attitude. But as time went along and he gained a measure of Nettie's confidence, he began to portray himself as a victim. In the January 7 letter he remarked, "I regard N. Y. as the scene of the only happiness that I ever seen and also the place that I suffered all that any man could suffer and on your account. I idolized you and you know that your word was law and if I had you today I would make you as happy as any woman in the world."[328] As usual, plenty of double-talk, but we can see that the affectation of apology was retreating. This turnabout will only accelerate as we go forward.

He spent Christmas day 1895 in San Bernardino with the Batys, according to both his

---

324 The Perris New Era, December 12, 1895, microfilm from CSL.
325 Letter, D.W. Bethel to Joannetta Fisher #10, January 7, 1896, from Fisher family papers.
326 Letter, D.W. Bethel to Joannetta Fisher #3, November 4, 1894, from Fisher family papers.
327 Letter, D.W. Bethel to Joannetta Fisher #5, November 20, 1894, from Fisher family papers.
328 Letter, D.W. Bethel to Joannetta Fisher #10, January 7, 1896, from Fisher family papers.

letter and a small item in the New Era, and he closed the year free of commitment, still employed, and with his past as yet undiscovered. He had begun 1895 in his home state with the birth of his fifth child to his fourth wife. He ended it with his complete reestablishment in a new town over 2,000 miles away, revered by its citizenry, and seemingly in control of who knew his whereabouts and his secrets. To the devious, cynical, self-centered mind of D.W. Bethel, the world must have looked pretty good. But the dance he was doing was one he could not sustain, and he was about to trip himself up again, with a little help from his past transgressions.

8.

Mr. Flirt-with-all and Miss Uptodate

▰ WILLIS WAS WELL-LIKED BY MOST OF THE MEN WHO WORKED WITH HIM. We can conclude this from the various letters and notes left in Nettie's possession, which show a strong sense of camaraderie, from his large network of friends in various places, and from newspaper accounts like the one below. His colleagues must have appreciated his competence, his sense of humor, and his easygoing attitude.

> Station Agent Bethel celebrated his 32nd birthday last Thursday and the various trainmen made things pretty lively for him. [329]

Transcription: Station Agent Bethel celebrated his 32nd birthday last Thursday and the various trainmen made things pretty lively for him.

Except that he was really 36. But who's counting, right?

The same day, under the headline *Butter, Cheese, Hogs Etc.*, subtitled *The Future of our Valley has at Last Been Definitely Settled*, Wise's paper published the following, partially tongue-in-cheek, account:

> Friday last Messrs. D.W. Bethel, capitalist, and Hugh Greer, expert rancher and ex-professor of hogology, closed a contract between themselves and Mr. See, whereby these gentlemen have become the possessors of 20 acres of Mr. See's alfalfa ranch north-east of town. They have secured a team, and by the way, one of the horses is a white one, and we advise the red headed girls in the valley (if there are any) to look a little out.
>
> These gentlemen are now negotiating with the leading commission houses of Los Angeles with a view to have them handle their dairy products and it is

---

329 The Perris New Era, January 30, 1896, microfilm from the California State Library, Sacramento.

given out as a fact that Messrs. Cudahy & Co. will tackle their pork product single handed.

These gentlemen will seed the entire tract to alfalfa as soon as the weather will permit. They have a never failing well of water and will put in a private pumping plant.[330]

D.W. Bethel, capitalist? It must have been onetime railroad money, or he went into debt, as he was known to do. The use of private wells with pumps was the last hope of establishing large scale agriculture in the Perris Valley, since the deal with the Bear Valley Land and Water Company to pipe in water had collapsed. This issue had divided the valley's residents — there were many who were convinced that wells could never supply enough water to support large farms or ranches, and they were already leaving. Dr. William B. Payton was generally credited with putting down the first successful wells in 1895.[331] Willis and Greer knew Payton and were likely following his lead and advice. Residents who remained hopeful that their region would still become prosperous agricultural country, and not revert to the stinking desert it had been before 1889, would have read the above article with interest.

Not surprisingly, we see that if there was actual, physical work to be done, Mr. Greer would be the one to do it. This was also indicated by a blurb in early March, over a month into the venture, when the paper offhandedly reported,

> Hugh Greer is satisfied with the assistance he has had in irrigating.[332]

Transcription: Hugh Greer is satisfied with the assistance he has had in irrigating.

Well now, why was it even a question?

Willis kept his social life humming, finding time to visit the hot springs at nearby Elsinore to relax a little in January, and of course maintaining his vibrant circle of friends. We can assume that his relationship with Annie continued to blossom. The age difference did not seem to bother either of them, or anyone else in the small town. But on February 27, a complication arrived in the form of a visitor from Willis's past.

---

330 Ibid.
331 Elmer Wallace Holmes, *The History of Perris Valley (Part 2)*.
332 The Perris New Era, March 5, 1896, microfilm from CSL.

> Dr. D. W. Bethel drove over to Riverside Monday evening in response to a telegram and brought with him on his return Miss Mattie Baker, an old time acquaintance from Freedonia, Ky., who comes to this mild climate in search of health.[333]

Transcription: Dr. D.W. Bethel drove over to Riverside Monday evening in response to a telegram and brought with him on his return Miss Mattie Baker, an old time acquaintance from Freedonia [sic], Ky., who comes to this mild climate in search of health.

He had made a passing reference to the Bakers in Kentucky in one of his letters about a year earlier.[334] Peter and Louisa Baker were farmers who owned about 400 acres near Fredonia, in Caldwell County. When the Ohio Valley Railroad wanted to build across his land, Peter had said sure, but you have to build a station there, too. The early depot was nothing more than a boxcar on a siding, and Willis may have been the agent at some point during his penance period in 1893-1894. Later iterations of the company constructed passenger and freight buildings, as well as a tobacco receiving house. At least one enterprising local merchant built a store, and a small collection of buildings resulted, named, appropriately enough, Baker Station, or simply Baker's.[335] It seems likely that Willis met the family either in early 1890, when he was between Nettie and Matilda, or more likely in 1893, when he was rebounding from the Lexington fiasco.

Peter had a total of ten children, five from each of his two wives.[336] Mattie was number eight. Born in December 1864, she was educated, appropriately enough, at Bethel College in Hopkinsville, Kentucky.[337] She evidently possessed a fun-loving spirit, a southern belle's demeanor, and an interest in Willis Bethel. The paper said she came to Perris in search of health, but she was probably, ill-advisedly, also looking for a husband. There is evidence that Annie was not pleased by Mattie's presence.

But the main story of the day was the irrigation experiment. Throughout February 1896, the Perris New Era, its competition, the Perris Record, and the Riverside papers kept their readers informed of Bethel and Greer's progress at developing and maintaining good, tillable, well-watered land. In mid-February, in hopeful answer to the concerns that were circulating, the Riverside Daily Press reported that "the amount of water existing there [underground] is without limit."[338]

---

333 The Perris New Era, February 27, 1896, microfilm from CSL.
334 Letter, D.W. Bethel to Joannetta Fisher, February 15, 1895, from Fisher family papers.
335 Samuel W. Steger, *Caldwell County, Kentucky, History*, p. 78.
336 His first wife, Nancy E. Mansfield, died around 1856, and he married Louisa Ann Slaughter Baker, a first cousin. She was Ed and Mattie's mother.
337 Samuel W. Steger, *Caldwell County, Kentucky, History*, pp. 205-206.
338 The Riverside Daily Press, February 18, 1896, GenealogyBank.com.

The writer was clearly an optimist, but by the middle of March, the enterprise showed real promise. The New Era gushed:

> The alfalfa ranch of Messrs. Bethel and Greer is a sight to behold. It is only about two months since the land was leveled, plowed and seeded, and at this date the alfalfa is nearly two inches high, and one of the prettiest patches to be seen in this section. "Not one seed has failed to germinate," said a gentleman yesterday, as he was looking over the ground. [339]

Transcription: The alfalfa ranch of Messrs. Bethel and Greer is a sight to behold. It is only about two months since the land was leveled, plowed and seeded, and at this date the alfalfa is nearly two inches high, and one of the prettiest patches to be seen in this section. "Not one seed has failed to germinate," said a gentleman yesterday, as he was looking over the ground.

Willis and Hugh appeared to be on the cutting edge of agricultural production in the Perris Valley, with the possibility of realizing good profits. It would take some time and hard work, but, oh wait, that's right . . .

At the Perris station, Willis's usual issues had finally begun to overshadow the initial positives. On January 6, he had received a letter from the Auditor of the railroad asking him to account for his waybills.[340] It was not really damning — it simply stressed procedures, and everyone knew he had his own way of doing things, right? In mid-February, all the officers of the A.T.S.F. came through Perris, but the paper reported that they were just doing "an inspection tour of the road."[341] Possibly routine. But the following week, the paper reported the following enigmatic item:

> S. C. King, inspector of the S. C. Ry. was in town last Friday. He was not here to investigate as to the truth or falsity of any charges this time however. [342]

Transcription: S.C. King, inspector of the S.C. Ry. was in town last Friday. He was not here to investigate as to the truth or falsity of any charges this time however.

---

339 The Perris New Era, March 19, 1896, microfilm from CSL.
340 Letter from Southern California Railway Auditor Office to D.W. Bethel, January 6, 1896, from Fisher family papers. How this letter came into our possession is a mystery. It is possible that a bonding agency sent Nettie a copy, but for what reason? Or, Durward may have recovered it from his father's possessions after his death, but why would Willis have even kept it that long? For that matter, why would Durward have saved it? The letter is not a smoking gun, just an implication of shady practices. All scenarios as to why we still have it seem unlikely.
341 The Perris New Era, February 13, 1896, microfilm from CSL. The Atchison, Topeka & Santa Fe Railroad leased the Southern California Railway lines.
342 The Perris New Era, February 20, 1896, microfilm from CSL.

What charges had previously brought Inspector King to the station? It appears that something was going on behind the scenes, and W.S. Wise was not giving his subscribers all the information available. By March 19, it was evident. The same day that his paper raved about the quality of the alfalfa patch, the following item also appeared:

> Theo. Nauright, our new station agent, together with his wife and child, arrived in Perris on Friday last. Mr. Nauright held an important position for many years in New Jersey. Upon his arrival in California he was assigned the station at El Torro, near Santa Ana. [343]

Transcription: Theo. Nauright, our new station agent, together with his wife and child, arrived in Perris on Friday last. Mr. Nauright held an important position for many years in New Jersey. Upon his arrival in California he was assigned the station at El Torro, near Santa Ana.

How's that again? Wise withheld some pertinent information — namely, that for Mr. Nauright to take over the station, D.W. Bethel had to be fired first. There was no mention of it, but two columns over was the following item:

> D. W. Bethel is on the sick list, threatened with an attack of pneumonia. [344]

Transcription: D.W. Bethel is on the sick list, threatened with an attack of pneumonia.

Shocking.

We do have a news source of his firing from the Riverside Independent Enterprise, in its 'Perris section' on March 17. It was unspecific as to cause, and they also misspelled his name, but it's clear who they meant.

> S. W. Brethel has been removed as Santa Fe agent at this point and the affairs of the office are now being conducted by Theo. Nanright, late of El Kora. Mr. Nanright was accompanied here by his family. [345]

Transcription: S.W. Brethel [sic] has been removed as Santa Fe agent at this point and the affairs of the office are now being conducted by Theo. Nanright [sic], late of El Kora. Mr. Nanright was accompanied her by his family.

---

343 The Perris New Era, March 19, 1896, microfilm from CSL.
344 Ibid.
345 *Perris,* The Riverside Independent Enterprise, March 17, 1896, GenealogyBank.com.

Mattie Baker and her brother Edward, as pictured in Samuel Steger's *Caldwell County, Kentucky, History*. The occasion for this photograph was Mattie's graduation from Bethel College in Hopkinsville, Kentucky in 1884 (she seems to have narrowly escaped a real-world education from 'D.W. Bethel college' about twelve years later). Ed, like his father a farmer near Fredonia, was about Willis's age and likely also a friend of his.

W.S. Wise was probably just trying to spare his friend some public embarrassment. Word of a local star like Willis getting canned must have gotten around quickly anyway, so why advertise it?

In a couple of letters the following year, he told Nettie that the National Surety Company of Kansas City "having declined to bond me" was the reason he had lost his job at Perris.[347] We don't know if this action was in response to some precipitating event or the result of a standard review, but since Inspector King had visited Perris to "investigate the truth or falsity" of charges, it seems likely that something out of the ordinary had set things in motion. The most obvious explanation is that he was caught exercising his magic on the books,

---

346 Ibid., p. 78.
347 Letters, D.W. Bethel to Joannetta Fisher #14, May 2, 1897 and #16, May 16, 1897, from Fisher family papers.

but it's also possible that his adventures at other stations, his adulteries, the multiple wives without divorce and the unsupported children, were coming into focus, although the extent of those transgressions was clearly unknown at this point. Unfortunately, all National Surety Company records are gone. The folder on David Wilson Bethel would be interesting reading.

It was a big fall from grace. Perris was the high-water mark of his career to this point. Less than six months earlier, his employer had taken his recommendation to hire his protégé at another station and had committed resources to upgrade the depot, all because of Willis's enthusiasm and apparent dedication to the job.

He must have appealed the decision, both to the A.T.S.F. and to the National Surety Company, and as we will see, the final resolution of his case took some time. On March 26, one week after he was "threatened with an attack of pneumonia," the New Era reported that he had visited both Hemet and Los Angeles. In all likelihood, he was looking for contacts who could help him out of his situation, just as he had in the past. The former trip was probably to see his old friend, Joe Steele, who was still in charge of the station there. As for the L.A. trip, it seems likely that he was calling at the offices of the A.T.S.F. to see if there was any chance of being reinstated.

His efforts must have met with limited success, and his disinformation campaign on the pages of the New Era emerged soon thereafter. In early April, an old story resurfaced:

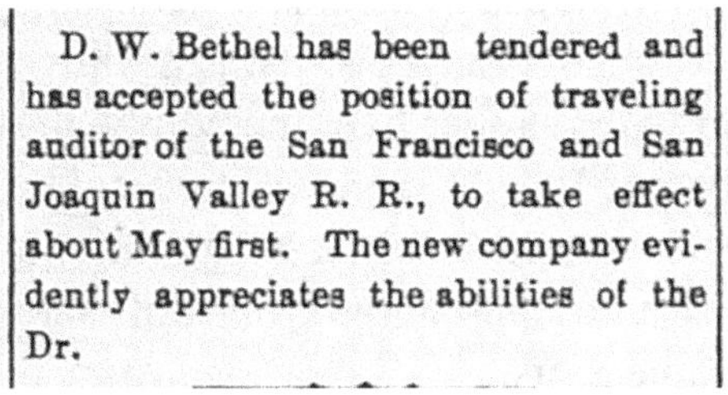
D. W. Bethel has been tendered and has accepted the position of traveling auditor of the San Francisco and San Joaquin Valley R. R., to take effect about May first. The new company evidently appreciates the abilities of the Dr.

[348]

Transcription: D.W. Bethel has been tendered and has accepted the position of traveling auditor of the San Francisco and San Joaquin Valley R.R., to take effect about May first. The new company evidently appreciates the abilities of the Dr.

Why this obvious fabrication kept coming up is a mystery. Willis had no background as an auditor — in fact, auditors were the people who kept getting him fired. He may have had a letter that alluded to the possibility of a position with the San Joaquin Valley Railroad which, like the Southern California, was a subsidiary of the A.T.S.F. Or, more likely, he just made the story up. In any case, unsurprisingly, May 1 came and went without the job materializing.

One might think that he could have just shrugged off his dismissal and discarded his railroad career. He was engaged in farming now, he and Greer had had some important successes, and for a brief time it looked as if he would follow that direction. In early April, a Riverside paper reported that the pair had planted olive trees, and that they "still have the

348 The Perris New Era, April 9, 1896, microfilm from CSL.

improvement fever."[349] But things seem to have fallen apart after that. Hugh Greer, with his mechanical skills and good work ethic, was content to work for the Sieberts and Vernon See, but to let them handle the finances and take the risk. And Willis was looking for office work. The Railroad Skunk needed a railroad.

The party in Perris was breaking up, anyway. In mid-April, the New Era ran the following item:

> Miss Mattie Baker, who has been visiting friends here for the past two months, departed for her home in Fredonia, Kentucky, yesterday morning. Quite a number of friends presented her with handsome bouquets of flowers as they wished her good bye at the depot.[350]

Transcription: Miss Mattie Baker, who has been visiting friends here for the past two months, departed for her home in Fredonia, Kentucky, yesterday morning. Quite a number of friends presented her with handsome bouquets of flowers as they wished her good bye at the depot.

There may have just been too much drama surrounding Willis Bethel for Miss Baker. His murky job situation probably added to the tension caused by her competition with Annie Reed, and she decided to bow out. Or maybe she was healthy again.[351] Her departure set the stage for Willis's union with wife number five. Incredibly, his proposal to the then-sixteen-year-old girl was actually recorded on the pages of the New Era.

Every spring, Los Angeles hosted a festival spanning multiple days called La Fiesta. Parades with floats, vendors, and community groups all showed up to celebrate southern California life, with its Hispanic roots. People traveled from all over for the celebration, and railroads ran specials to accommodate residents of nearby communities. On April 23, the New Era published a list of local attendees:

---

349 The Riverside Independent Enterprise, April 7, 1896, GenealogyBank.com.
350 The Perris New Era, April 16, 1896, microfilm from CSL.
351 Mattie went back to Caldwell County, and she remained on her father's farm for most of the rest of her life. He died in 1909, and she ran the place with her younger brother William, while their older brother Ed farmed the next plot over. Their brief mentions in Samuel Steger's Caldwell County, Kentucky History relate that Ed and his sister, who was called "Aunt Mattie" or "Miss Mattie," "cast a lasting influence on all who came their way." In the 1900, 1910, and 1920 censuses she was still single, and at 55 in 1920, she seemed destined to remain that way. But around 1922 she married Samuel Cornelius Booth, a 72-year-old farmer from nearby Webster County. It didn't last, and the pair divorced in 1927. In the 1930 and 1940 censuses she again is found farming the family acreage with William. Mattie was eventually committed to the Kentucky State Hospital near Danville, a mental health facility, in late 1951, suffering from dementia, and she died there the following year at the age of 87. The Baker family had evidently suffered some reversals of fortune after Ed's death in 1929, and Mattie's obviously homemade headstone now marks her grave back in Fredonia. (1900, 1910, 1920, 1930, 1940 U.S. censuses, Mattie Baker, Caldwell County, Kentucky; Death certificate, Mattie Baker Booth, Kentucky State Hospital, Boyle County, Kentucky, all Ancestry.com; Memorial 157725692, Martha Louisa "Mattie" Baker Booth, Hill Cemetery, Fredonia, Caldwell County, Kentucky, Findagrave.com).

> **For the Fiesta.**
>
> From the following list of residents it will be seen that Perris was well represented at the Fiesta in Los Angeles. Every train since Tuesday has been literally packed. Tuesday morning's train as well as the afternoon train were crowded to their utmost capacity:
>
> James Patterson and wife,
> C. R. Johnson and wife,
> J. Nolan and wife,
> W. S. Wise and wife,
> Mrs. Orman Oak,
> Mrs. G. A. Helmstadter,
> Mrs. S. N. Reppert and son,
> Mrs. R. Reynolds,
> Mrs. J. J. Nance and daughter,
> Mrs. S. L. Rowley,
> Mrs. J. J. Preston,
> Mrs. May Elder and child,
> Mrs. A. S. Gardner,
> Mrs. S. E. Walker of Menifee,
> Miss Dora Austin,
> Miss Tracy Preston,
> Miss Ida Blount,
> Miss Annie Reed,
> L. E. Leeman and daughter Jessie,
> C. S. Willis,
> Frank Deutsch,
> John Nolan,
> M. A. Gruwell of Elsinore,
> George Burrill,
> John D. Maxfield,
> Claus Burfend of Menifee.
> George A. Doyle,
> S. A. Stewart of Elsinore,
> B. D. Gardner,
> D. W. Bethel,
> D. W. Wickerd of Menifee.

Transcription: *For the Fiesta.* From the following list of residents it will be seen that Perris was well represented at the Fiesta in Los Angeles. Every train since Tuesday has been literally packed. Tuesday morning's train as well as the afternoon train were crowded to their utmost capacity: James Patterson and wife, C.R. Johnson and wife, J. Nolan and wife, **W.S. Wise and wife,** Mrs. Orman Oak, Mrs G.A. Helmstader, Mrs. S.N. Reppert and son, Mrs. R. Reynolds, Mrs. J.J. Nance and daughter, Mrs. S.L. Rowley, Mrs. J.J. Preston, Mrs. May Elder and child, Mrs. A.S. Gardner, Mrs. S.E. Walker of Menifee, Miss Dora Austin, Miss Tracy Preston, Miss Ida Blount, **Miss Annie Reed,** L.E. Leeman and daughter Jessie, C.S. Willis, Frank Deutsch, John Nolan, M.A. Gruwell of Elsinore, George Burrill, John D. Maxfield, Claus Burfend of Menifee, George A. Doyle, S.A. Stewart of Elsinore, B.D. Gardner, **D.W. Bethel,** D.W. Wickerd of Menifee. (Names in bold face added to aid in identification).

As we can see, Annie, Willis, and W.S. Wise and his wife were among the partygoers. Mrs. Wise must have harbored some literary pretensions, which she revealed in a long, sardonic account of the trip, entitled *What Perris Saw*, under the charming pen name of Miss Sooty Smutt. The point seems to have been to poke fun at herself and some of her friends and neighbors, and to generally wax philosophical about the vicissitudes of life in Perris, California. After waiting over three weeks, her husband evidently decided it would be entertaining for everyone to see it, and he published the story in his paper on May 14. Real names were never mentioned, but the characters are surprisingly identifiable.

'Miss Smutt' began her account with the train ride from Perris to Los Angeles. She wrote that she sat behind a man,

> with a head not unlike the well-preserved heads of the Caesars. This head belong [sic] to one of the few men who, minus the crown of olives, enjoys

---

352 *For the Fiesta,* The Perris New Era, April 23, 1896, microfilm from CSL.

unrivaled popularity in the town we are rapidly leaving. This gentleman has for some considerable time past been suffering the consequences of his declared intentions with one of Perris' fairest and sweetest daughters.

One digressive paragraph later, she continued:

> I am about to get myself comfortably settled in my easy reclining chair, when I recognize the sound of two voices near me, very much unlike each other in gender. Now, I have often times wondered why lovers always act on trains as though they were forever going through a tunnel.
>
> As the train dashes along I hear the low impassioned tones of Mr. Flirt-with-all,—taking the advantage of the low rumble and hum of the train—to pop the question to Miss Uptodate. He tells her how he was struck with her beauty the first time he saw her at the ice-cream social, and how he never cared a cent for Miss Downsouth, and that he never was engaged to any girl before, etc., etc.
>
> It begins to dawn on my mind, like an X ray through a defunct bank, that Miss Uptodate is jealous of Miss Downsouth, as my traveling companion nudged my elbow and suppressed a giggle.
>
> "What an uninteresting creature Miss Downsouth was, any way." said Miss Uptodate, as she turned and twisted uncomfortably in her seat and tried to look solemn.
>
> "Ugly as a mud fence," remarked her companion, as he carelessly stroked his moustache.
>
> "You did'nt seem to think so, once."
>
> "Oh, yes I did."
>
> "Now, my own dearest little girl, I earnestly assure you that Miss Downsouth is nothing whatever to me, and never was, nor never will be, I promise you."
>
> At this juncture the peanut boy comes along and interrupts the conversation.
>
> Later on I learned that the little difficulty which had passed between this couple had been amicably settled, and that when the fiesta was over there would be a wedding uniting two loving hearts that have an intense longing to beat as one.

[353]

---

353 *What Perris Saw*, The Perris New Era, May 14, 1896, microfilm from CSL.

> "Oh, yes I did."
>
> "Now, my own dearest little girl, I earnestly assure you that Miss Downsouth is nothing whatever to me, and never was, nor never will be, I promise you."
>
> At this juncture the peanut boy comes along and interrupts the conversation.
>
> Later on I learned that the little difficulty which had passed between this couple had been amicably settled, and that when the fiesta was over there would be a wedding uniting two loving hearts that have an intense longing to beat as one.

"Miss Uptodate" was a revealing characterization of Annie. The teenager must have prided herself on being in tune with the latest trends. "Miss Downsouth" was, clearly, Willis's old Kentucky friend, Mattie Baker. The most unmistakable pseudonym, though, is "Mr. Flirt-with-all." A better description of Willis Bethel would be hard to devise.

Although the pseudonyms and circumstances fit our characters and story well, a little more analysis is required to say with confidence that the lovers described by Miss Smutt were Willis and Annie. Thanks to the nineteenth-century formality of referring to unmarried females as 'Miss,' we know that there were three other single women, besides Annie, on the list of people who took the train from Perris: Dora Austin, Tracy Preston, and Ida Blount. Dora Austin, the Perris postmaster in 1896 (a post that came to her after the death of her brother-in-law), was born in Missouri in 1872. While she was well-known around town, and she was mentioned occasionally in the New Era, it was always in the most respectful terms, and she was clearly revered for her competence, not as "one of Perris' fairest and sweetest daughters."[354] She is found, still single, in the 1900 census, living in Perris with her widowed sister. She married John Henry Pell (a member of Willis's and Wise's circle) in 1901, but no one before, and Pell was not a passenger on the train. Tracy M. Preston, age 19 in 1896, was another friend of Annie's and Willis's and a part of their group of fun-loving young folks.[355] She was likewise found, still single, in the 1900 census, living with her parents. The reader will notice that she was accompanied on the train by her mother, Mrs. J.J. Preston, hardly making her a tempting target for a proposal. Tracy married a man named John Holme in 1905.[356] Of Ida Blount, there is no record whatsoever, anywhere — the only thing we know about her is what the list of passengers tells us — that she was single in April 1896. There was no one with the surname of Blount living in Perris in the 1893-94 directory (the only one that survives), or the 1900 census. Ida Blount is a ghost, and her name did not appear at all in the personals of the New Era in 1895-96.

It's clear from the writing that the two lovers were well known to the Wises, and probably members of their inner circle. W.S. Wise "nudged my elbow and suppressed a giggle," something he would likely not do if overhearing two strangers. It's also clear that the specifics

---

354 1900, 1910 U.S. Census, Perris, California, Dora A. Austin, Ancestry.com; *Unjustifiable*, The Perris New Era, February 6, 1896, microfilm from CSL. This opinion piece, while more about the grudge between W.S. Wise and J.W. Nance, is an example of the tone taken toward Dora Austin in the New Era.
355 The Perris New Era, July 9, 1896, microfilm from CSL.
356 1900, 1910 U.S. Census, Perris, California, Tracy M. Preston, Ancestry.com.

of their situation were well known in the town of Perris, or Miss Sooty Smutt would not have taken up so much of her column with a description of their dialogue. She wanted to be entertaining to the paper's readers, and this would only be the case if the people mentioned enjoyed "unrivaled popularity."

If we take all this evidence together and combine it with the appropriateness of the descriptions of the characters, the overwhelming likelihood is that Miss Sooty Smutt gave us a first-hand account of David Willis Bethel proposing to Annie M. Reed.

But he needed to be in better professional circumstances before he could act on her acceptance. On May 14, it looked as if those might come soon enough, as another of his red herrings swam into view on the pages of the New Era:

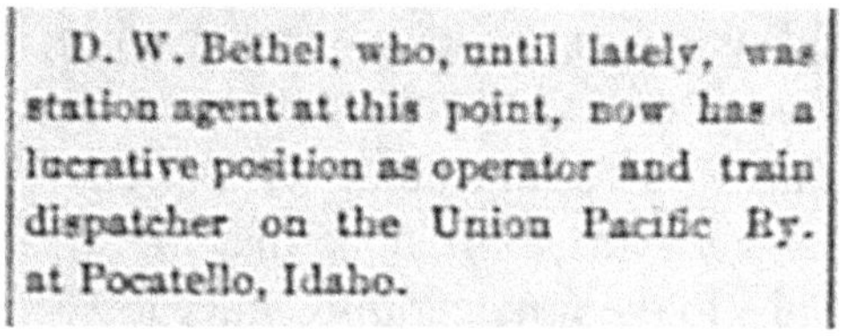
D. W. Bethel, who, until lately, was station agent at this point, now has a lucrative position as operator and train dispatcher on the Union Pacific Ry. at Pocatello, Idaho.

357

Transcription: D.W. Bethel, who, until lately, was station agent at this point, now has a lucrative position as operator and train dispatcher on the Union Pacific Ry. at Pocatello, Idaho.

He may have worked for a short time at Pocatello in May of 1896, but it was no better than a temporary job, and probably not lucrative. We know he was in the northwestern U.S. during that time, though, because on May 24 he sent a desperate and hurried missive to Nettie. At first glance, it appears that he was writing from Perris (the letter is on his stationery from the Southern California Railway), but the envelope had a Cheyenne & Huntington Railway Post Office postmark.[358] Cheyenne was the Union Pacific hub for that section of the country, and on the route a letter from Pocatello to western New York would take.

> Dear Nettie:
>
> You will get a letter in a few days asking you about your trouble and mine. The letter will be from The National Surety Co. of Kansas City, Mo. If you will tell them whether or not I was kind to you & provided for you that will I think be all that you need tell. Can tell them that there was a good reason for separation but that I was honest & paid my debts & provided for you & was kind to you. These are all facts I think. Don't tell them why you left me please? I've not been well. Indeed been very sick.[359]

357 The Perris New Era, May 14, 1896, microfilm from CSL.

358 R.P.O. postmark 932-P-1, Cheyenne and Huntington (Oregon), from the R.P.O. catalog, published by the Mobile Post Office Society, p. 209 (219 of 1398); postmark of letter, D.W. Bethel to Joannetta Fisher #11, May 24, 1896, from Fisher family papers.

359 Letter, D.W. Bethel to Joannetta Fisher #11, May 25, 1896, from Fisher family papers.

This guy sure got sick a lot.

He must have underestimated how deeply into his past the investigators had dug, and now they had discovered that Nettie was on his list of wives, and they might also discover his adultery with Matilda. Did they know about Jennie and Minnie? The bonding agency investigation now threatened his career like nothing before.

About three weeks later, on June 17, he sent along another short note, a sigh of relief in print, thanking her "with all my heart" for her reply to the National Surety Company. Evidently, she had acquiesced to his requests for omissions from her testimony, at least for the time being, and he had escaped again. He gave her a brief non-explanation: "The National Surety Co. go my bond. No I've done no wrong thing & I'm not going to do any. Rest easy on that. This is simply an inquiry from them and you answered them just right."[360] The postmark is almost obliterated — the only legible letter is a 'Q' at the end of the space for the Railway Post Office. This was likely part of the abbreviation for Albuquerque, New Mexico.[361] We know that Willis was re-hired by the A.T.S.F. while he was appealing to the bonding company, and that he was agent/operator at Rincon, New Mexico, at a significant cut in pay from the salary he had received in California (from $110/month to $70/month, according to his letters).

Rincon, in the desert about eighty miles north of El Paso, was evidently not the most desirable of assignments. The pay drop-off is evidence — Perris was a backwater, but Rincon was about as far down the ladder as you could go on the Atchison, Topeka & Santa Fe. Each station on the line was associated with a restaurant near the depot run by Fred Harvey and staffed by young women, called Harvey Girls. The girls were expected to be single and stay that way, with all the chastity and forbearance of temptation that Victorian mores imposed on their gender. Many of the Harvey Girls met their husbands and resigned their positions to marry while working in these restaurants, but nothing except a "high moral tone" was tolerated while they were employed.[362] Rincon was one of the two stops nationally (the other was Needles, California) to which "bad girls" who were not fired were reassigned.[363] There is no word as to whether station assignments served the same punitive purpose for A.T.S.F. telegraphers, but given Willis's circumstances, the location, and the close association between the railroad and the restaurants, it seems likely. Although meant as a punishment, he may have enjoyed his brief time there.

We don't know how he knew the contents of the letter Nettie had written to the National Surety Company — they may have communicated to him that all was well with his bonding, or maybe she sent him a copy. He might have begun to feel safe again, but as we will see, the Surety Company followed up, and she wrote a second letter. It seems likely that other ghosts from D.W. Bethel's past were also finding their way to the bonding agency's offices in Kansas City about this time. It was probably in August or September (Willis wrote that he worked at Rincon for "three or four months"), that his bond was revoked permanently, and

---

360 Letter, D.W. Bethel to Joannetta Fisher #12, June 17, 1896, from Fisher family papers.
361 Ibid.
362 Keith L. Bryant, Jr., *History of the Atchison, Topeka & Santa Fe Railway*, p. 114.
363 Ibid., p. 116.

the A.T.S.F. fired him for good.[364] The Railroad Skunk's railroad career was hanging by a thread. All he had left were his friends up and down the line.

Early in September 1896, the Perris New Era announced that George A. Doyle, a local notary and insurance man, was now the agent for the absent D.W. Bethel, "under a power of attorney." In an adjacent column, the following item appeared:

> D. W. Bethel has sold to Geo. Seibert, quit claim deed, to the n. ½ of the n. e. ¼ of the s. e. ¼ section 29, township 4 south, range 3 west, S. B. M., containing 20 acres more or less. Consideration $1.

[365]

Transcription: D.W. Bethel has sold to Geo. Seibert, quit claim deed, to the n. ½ of the n.e. ¼ of the s.e. ¼ section 29, township 4 south, range 3 west, S. B. M., containing 20 acres more or less. Consideration: $1.

He must have owed money, hence the nominal consideration. Willis's farming/ranching experiment, on life support for months, was officially dead.

While he had been away from Perris, Annie had been playing. The New Era reported three events on her social calendar from May through July. One, on June 18, was a birthday party for L. E. Best, "the gentlemanly assistant at the Railway Station" which Annie hosted at her mother's home.[366] Maybe she just liked those railroad types. If she was trying to make Willis jealous, it seems to have worked. He returned to Perris on September 30, and the New Era made certain to proclaim, "D.W. Bethel dropped in town yesterday to renew acquaintances with his large circle of friends."[367]

David W. Bethel and Annie M. Reed were married the next day, on October 1, 1896. The ceremony took place in Perris, with Reverend W. N. Burr doing the honors. Willis's residence was still listed as Rincon, New Mexico, even though it's clear that he was no longer employed there. And although he had "celebrated his 32nd birthday" the previous January, his age was recorded on the license as 33. He was really 36. No matter — Annie, who was sixteen, was listed as seventeen. Age is just a number, right? Neither party had ever been married before.[368] Hmm.

W.S. Wise, who would leave Perris for good two months later, ran a more detailed series of announcements about the wedding than usual. Willis was an old friend by now, and despite his difficulties with his employer, sentiment in town remained firmly behind him, and he was still a local star. The following items appeared in the October 8 issue:

---

364 Letter, D.W. Bethel to Joannetta Fisher #16, May 16, 1897, from Fisher family papers.
365 The Perris New Era, September 3, 1896, microfilm from CSL.
366 The Perris New Era, June 18, 1896, microfilm from CSL.
367 The Perris New Era, October 1, 1896, microfilm from CSL.
368 Marriage license, David W. Bethel and Annie M. Reed, Riverside County, California, October 1, 1896, Ancestry.com.

> Bethel—Reed.
>
> D. W. Bethel, our former station agent, and Miss Annie Reed, a young lady well known in Perris, were married last Thursday evening, Rev. W. N. Burr performing the ceremony which was witnessed by only a few friends.
>
> Mr. and Mrs. Bethel have the best wishes of a host of friends in and around Perris, and the New Era joins them in wishing the couple a long and happy married life. They will remain In Perris for a few days, after which they will go to Los Angeles, intending to make that city their future home.

Transcription: Bethel-Reed. D.W. Bethel, our former station agent, and Miss Annie Reed, a young lady well known in Perris, were married last Thursday evening, Rev. W.N. Burr performing the ceremony which was witnessed by only a few friends.

Mr. and Mrs. Bethel have the best wishes of a host of friends in and around Perris, and New Era joins them in wishing the couple a long and happy married life. They will remain in Perris for a few days, after which they will go to Los Angeles, intending to make that city their future home.

> Joe Steele came up from Orange on Tuesday to see old acquaintances.

Transcription: Joe Steele came up from Orange on Tuesday to see old acquaintances.

> A number of the friends of Mr. and Mrs. D. W. Bethel serenaded them last Saturday night.[369]

Transcription: A number of the friends of Mr. and Mrs. D.W. Bethel serenaded them last Saturday night.

The wedding was also announced in the Riverside papers, and the Independent Enterprise added solemnly that "the application was accompanied by the consent of the young lady's parents."[370] No parental consent is indicated on the license, but there may have been an application, now lost, that included Annie's mother's permission. Martha Reed would die soon

---

369 The Perris New Era, October 8, 1896, microfilm from CSL.
370 Riverside Independent Enterprise, October 2, 1896, GenealogyBank.com.

afterward, reportedly at a church camp meeting in the nearby mountains.[371]

In the same issue of the paper was the following item:

Rev. W. N. Burr has resigned his position here as pastor of the Congregational church and will remove to Ventura. [372]

Transcription: Rev. W.N. Burr has resigned his position here as pastor of the Congregational church and will remove to Ventura.

Maybe Reverend Burr was so ashamed of what he had just done he felt he had to get out of town. But the town of Perris was fading anyway, the water issues and the bank failure making it a good place to leave. It would rebound, but only years later, when reliable sources of water, mostly acquired by drilling wells, turned the arid country into some of the best farmland, especially for fruits and cereal grains, in the country.[373] Willis and Greer had been on to something, but they just didn't see things through.

His promising start had blown up again. He had been a respected man in town, and he had built a network of friends quickly. He always did so wherever he landed, but there was something about the wide-open attitudes of the West, combined with Willis's carefree ways, that harmonized.

What was less harmonious, unsurprisingly, was married life for the newlyweds. The couple stayed in Perris until October 10, when they left for Los Angeles.[374] Willis was still without a job, and he must have gone on the road to look for work, likely in Mexico, soon afterward. Annie came back to Perris to visit friends on October 30, staying until November 3.[375] According to the divorce papers she filed in 1902, Willis left her side for good on November 7, 1896, only five weeks into their marriage. Annie, up to date though she may have been, was still just a naïve teenager, unaccustomed to the ways of the world, and especially the ways of some men. She must have anxiously read his letters, which would have been full of promise and hope if she could just wait a little longer, having no idea that he never intended to come back to her. He seems to have corresponded with her for over a year, but "on or about the 7th day of December 1897, [defendant] abandoned the plaintiff with the intention to desert her."[376] That was probably the date of his last letter. The seventeen-year-old girl saw her dreams come crashing down.

---

371 The following note about Martha Frasier's death was shared by LadyLittle, who manages the Seeley Family Tree on Ancestry.com and is a direct descendant of Martha Frasier. This information came down to her from Bessie Dalton Reed, Annie's sister: "Died at a campmeeting. Her children were turned against that church because some of the people who had been at the meeting told the kids that their mother wouldn't have died if they had attended with her. (oral story from Marjorie Kendall, grandaughter of Martha Frazier)."

372 The Perris New Era, October 8, 1896, microfilm from CSL.

373 Elmer Wallace Holmes, *History of Perris Valley, California, Part 2*, p. 8.

374 The Perris New Era, October 15, 1896, microfilm from CSL.

375 The Perris New Era, November 5, 1896, microfilm from CSL.

376 Divorce documents, Bethel vs. Bethel, filed April 10, 1902, dismissed June 7, 1902, case #38621, records request from the Superior Court, Los Angeles County, California.

As an added reminder that the real world is not always exactly like the one our fantasies create, their month together made her pregnant. Willis was nowhere to be found when Raymond Harry Bethel was born in summer 1897. There is no birth record for Raymond, and other of his many life records variously list his place of birth as Perris, Illinois, Nevada, and Michigan. Of these, Michigan is mentioned most often. Annie's mother Martha, who died in early 1897, had family in Shiawassee County. A desperate and pregnant Annie, with her husband absent, her mother dead, and her sister and brothers working to establish their own lives, may have traveled to Michigan to give birth there before heading back to southern California with her son. The Nevada listing was likely an error — that was Annie's birthplace, but it was a state to which the Reed family was no longer connected. The Illinois listing, found in only one record, may have derived from the fact that Willis had last written to her from Chicago. Wherever Raymond was born, his early life was a challenging one, spent in at least two orphanages in the Los Angeles area. As for Annie, she disappeared from all records in 1902.

9.

"I Don't Know a Thing to Write You Now"

■ "JUST WAIT UNTIL SUMMER, SEÑOR," SAID JULIO, *the young man who was helping them with their trunks. Julio was the son of the local section chief and he worked at the station doing odd jobs, mostly the heavy work that his elders didn't want to do. He was a scrawny fourteen-year-old, but surprisingly strong. His father was American, his mother Mexican, and he had lived his entire life in this small village in the middle of a high-country desert. Joe had remarked that the heat was not as bad in Yermo as he had feared it would be, and Julio had delivered a broad smile along with his reply.*

If Joe Steele was favorably impressed by the climate, at least for the season, he was less enthusiastic about the location. Yermo was isolated, a small island of rudimentary culture in the middle of a sea of sand and rocks, in Durango just across the state line from Chihuahua, connected to north and south only by the railroad. It had its own peace, but that was about all.

Their arrival in the remote outpost in January was the first time Joe had wondered about the wisdom of this move, but not the last. Three months later, he was looking forward to going back to the States as soon as his finances would allow. By contrast, Willis seemed to thrive in the small village. Of course, he knew some Spanish, which Joe did not, at least no more than he needed to conduct business at the station. And Willis had other ways to relieve the boredom in a place like Yermo.

When they had first met at Perris, Joe, 25, was directionless, still recovering from the shock of the deaths of his mother and brother. Willis had taught him telegraphy and the tricks of the station agent's trade (including how to discreetly supplement one's salary), and it had given Joe a profession, for which he would ever be grateful. That was two years ago. Joe was only too happy to go to Mexico to work with Willis again after the Santa Fe let both of them go in late '96. Thanks to the older man's connections, they found station agent positions on the Mexican Central at Yermo, Willis taking the first shift and Joe the second.

But ever since the train had pulled out of Perris, Joe had seen a different side of Willis, and he didn't like it. It was one thing to skim a little from the railroads — hell, they could afford it, and everyone knew they underpaid their agents, anyway. And flirting and practical jokes are fine, as long as nobody gets hurt too much and it's all in good fun. But Joe had always felt a strong sense of loyalty to the people closest to him, and four months with Willis had revealed that was a value he did not share. Annie was a good kid — she was a bright and funny presence, not too smart, but a nice girl, and Joe had been happy for both of them. He knew that she was full of hope for their marriage, and that she was looking forward to Willis getting a steady job somewhere and sending for her and the baby that was coming.

But D.W. Bethel had been on the make ever since they left California. Just south of Juarez, while they were still on the train, he had found a likely target, a 26-year-old widow named Gertrude Mossmeyer, who was returning home after visiting a cousin in El Paso. It turned out that Gertrude lived with her young daughter in Torreon, about fifty miles south of Yermo, perfect for his designs. Willis pitched the woo in torrents, and after a couple of months, convinced that she was his one and only, she gave in and married him. It left Joe shaking his head — another marriage in less than four months, and not even a whisper about Annie. When Joe had asked about her, Willis had said, "Oh, yes, I need to write her a letter." Two nights later, when he brought the subject up again, Willis told his friend to mind his own business, that he was done with Annie.

That was bad enough, but while Gertrude was at her house down the tracks, Willis was working on a new project. She was Angela Morello, the sixteen-year-old daughter of one of the conductors at Yermo, Oscar Morello. Willis had remarked about her beauty when they had first pulled into Yermo station, and for the past few weeks he had been chasing her with that look in his eye. Oscar wasn't very happy about it — he didn't like Willis, in fact, he didn't like Americans, period. But he put up with it. He had to marry his daughter off sometime, and gringos are all rich, no? Neither Angela nor Oscar had any idea about Gertrude, of course. But that evening in early March, they somehow found out.

Joe was almost on the back side of his shift and Willis, who had stuck around to do some paperwork, was about to leave for the night. The 7:15 was steaming up and about to leave. The station was empty of passengers, it being dinner hour in the village. Looking up from his desk, Joe saw Oscar striding their way in the dusk, his expression grim. He held a revolver in his right hand.

"I don't think he's coming after me with that thing," he said to Willis, who looked up just in time to see Oscar level the barrel while saying, "¡Sucio gringo! ¿Qué le decimos a su esposa que haya grabado en su lápida?"[377] *The first shot plowed into the floor near Willis's feet. It inspired more physical activity than he was accustomed to, and he ducked into the freight storeroom, with Oscar about 30 feet behind him. As Willis ran out the loading dock sliders, Oscar's second shot hit the door above his head, caromed off a bracket and whistled out into Yermo's early evening. A third bullet hit the granary across the street, Oscar letting loose with a smorgasbord of epithets in Spanish the entire time.*

Joe was still at his desk when he saw that Willis had doubled back on the freight platform and pulled out that pocket .32 he always carried. Without even looking back, he let loose three wild shots in rapid succession behind him. One knocked out a lantern, one put a hole in the roof of the awning, and the other wandered off into the desert air. It was enough to make

---

377 *"Dirty gringo! What should we tell your wife to put on your tombstone?"*

Joe duck under his desk.

Oscar, undeterred and still looking for a clean shot, followed Willis across the freight platform. Both men fired again, at almost the same time, Willis again sending his lead away without looking where the gun was pointed as he ducked around a warehouse. The bullet shattered a window and dug into the wall of the empty passenger waiting room. Oscar's shot also missed its mark, but as he let it loose the blinding smoke and blinding rage combined to make him lose his vision and his bearings, and he hit his head hard on the handle of the loading dock jack. It knocked him silly. He went down in a corpulent heap on the dusty planks, bleeding from his forehead, out cold.

Joe saw Oscar go down, and realizing that the danger had passed, he went out to check on him. As he knelt by the unconscious conductor Willis, wondering why things had suddenly gotten so quiet, peeped around a corner and saw his attacker lying on the ground, blood coming from his head.

"I-Is he dead?" he stammered.

Joe sensed an opportunity. He looked up at his old friend with as grave an expression as he could muster under the circumstances.

"That was one hell of a shot, Willis," he marveled.

Never one to say 'aw shucks' to credit when it was offered, Willis puffed up a little. "I thought I had him," he said.

"You need to get out of here," Joe said firmly. "The coppers will be here any second." The barracks were at the other end of the village, but people were already milling around, looking their way. "Grab a pass and hop on. And let me have your hotel key. I'll send your trunk to Torreon. Willis, you hear me? You need to get north."

"It was self-defense . . ." Willis objected weakly.

"Willis! The judge and jury will be Mexican. Angie and her mother will testify. And so will Trudy . . ." Joe had to bite down hard on his inner cheek to keep from laughing at the expression that slowly crawled across his friend's slack-jawed face.

Willis looked down at Oscar's motionless body one more time in disbelief, then nodded, in a daze. He handed over the key, went into the station and scribbled himself a pass, and boarded through the caboose, still numb. At Torreon, he told Gertrude a slightly modified version of events, instructed her to have his trunk sent to Laredo when it got there, and then he jumped right back on a train. He didn't relax until 22 hours later, at the Hotel Hamilton. How he had managed to outpace the telegrams that must have been sent after him was a mystery to him. Maybe Joe just sat on the message or told the rurales that he was headed for El Paso. Joe was a good friend.

Oscar started groaning and coming to right after the train pulled out. He was nauseous and had a headache, and at first he was disappointed that his target was too far away to take one last shot, but he calmed down once he heard that Willis was gone for good. The railroad officials who came to investigate the incident the next day were none too pleased with Oscar. On the other hand, they were all fathers of daughters, and good conductors were hard to *find, so they decided to leave the bulk of his punishment to law enforcement.*[378] *The local constabulary, having absolutely no tolerance for gunfire within the limits of their small village, menaced Oscar severely until the Americans all left, then they lauded his defense of Angela's virtue and laughed at his marksmanship.*

The events of that evening settled some things in Joe Steele's mind. The next day, he wrote a long letter to Ida, his Los Angeles girl, and in it he proposed. They were married in El Paso the following month.

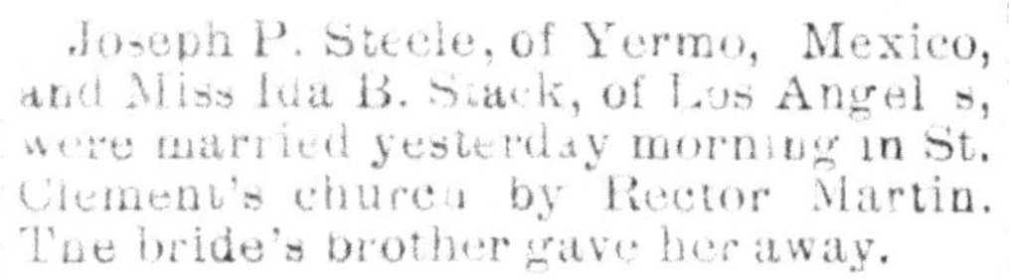
Joseph P. Steele, of Yermo, Mexico, and Miss Ida B. Stack, of Los Angel s, were married yesterday morning in St. Clement's church by Rector Martin. The bride's brother gave her away.

[379]

Transcription: Joseph P. Steele, of Yermo, Mexico, and Miss Ida B. Stack, of Los Angeles, were married yesterday morning in St. Clement's church by Rector Martin. The bride's brother gave her away.

My uncle, Harry Fisher, was a great guy. A C.P.A. and longtime comptroller for the University of Maryland, he retired in his mid-fifties and spent his remaining years building, from nothing, a chestnut farm on the old family land in northern Michigan. Uncle Harry was born in 1922, and he always said that during his youth his father, Durward Frederick Fisher, would make periodic trips to see *his* father, David Willis Bethel. Harry thought David was living in southern California, farming or ranching.

Harry was also the first family researcher into the life of David Willis Bethel. He had read all of Willis's letters to Nettie, and I've always wondered if they colored his memories. Willis wrote only four letters (that were passed down to us) during the time he was in southern California. Two of them were very short, begging or thanking Nettie for her help with his bonding issues. While there were probably others, this period seems to have been a general lull in their correspondence. In none of them did he mention his farming experiment with Greer.

But less than a year later, in May 1897, Willis insisted that he owned "a little property 40 acres just got it all paid for not far from Los Angeles," that "will be worth $5,000 or $6,000 . . . to Durward in two or three years."[380] He went on to mention his ranch no less than ten times in seven of the 15 letters that comprise the final group of correspondence with Nettie and Durward. It was one of his central arguments for reuniting with them, an unmistakable assertion of maturity and parental responsibility:

> Of course in buying the ranch in California I had one thought above all else. Namely, to secure a place for Durward that he might have a home for himself

378 *Oscar Morello received a thirty-day suspension from the Mexican Central Railroad, of which only five were actually imposed.*

379 El Paso Herald, April 5, 1897, Newspapers.com.

380 Letter, D.W. Bethel to Joannetta Fisher # 14, May 2, 1897, from Fisher family papers.

some time. I thought too that if you change your mind that you too might like to come there.[381]

Uncle Harry always wondered what had become of this property, but after studying the letters and going through newspaper accounts and other records of the time I question whether it ever existed. Willis had sold his interest in the 20 acres he held with Greer, and received no proceeds from it, the previous September. We know that he was without steady work in 1897, traveling around the continent living hand-to-mouth off temporary jobs. His estimated valuation of the ranch was over three times as much as his annual salary had been at Perris when he was at the height of his earning power. He had a new wife who certainly needed his support (although he gave little, if any). How in the world could he have bought an additional 40 acres, and paid it off so quickly, under such circumstances?

I think the ranch was just a fiction, a lure to bring Nettie, and with her their son, to his side. With her farming background, she must have been intrigued — in fact, one can see him answer her interest in his letters. She also expressed skepticism about the property's existence, and he responded to that, too. On August 18, he wrote, "My 40 acre ranch is in the Canengo (it might also be "Cassengo") Valley . . . I just lifted the mortgage in January," and "I will be pleased to give you the land location if you want it."[382] But no future letter gave that location, and I can find neither the Canengo nor Cassengo Valley on any map, anywhere, from 1897 to the present.[383]

Willis's 27 letters to Nettie form much of the basis of this book. We only came to find the information we have because of the letters, but the letters revolve around manipulation, misdirection, and hidden agendas, and as I've said before, they can't be trusted for anything. The 15 missives in Group 3, some of which were quite long, were written between March 19 and September 22, 1897. They were Willis's final arguments to Nettie.

A number of strategies which had been emerging in his previous correspondence flower fully in this group, where he made his most strident pleas. He still adopted a tone of apology when necessary, but he increasingly lashed out, blaming her and her family for their separation. And there is a lot of the by-now-familiar double-talk.

The first of the group, which came after a lull of nine months, began much like the first letter in Group 1 — again returning from Mexico, again trying to rebuild his railroad career after a catastrophe. But Willis's situation in March 1897 was much more desperate than it had been in November 1894. He was "temporarily out of work" and on his way to Kansas City to plead with the National Surety Company to reestablish his bond. Without bonding, he could land no better than temporary relief jobs, at reduced pay, with inconsistent hours, of unknown duration, at different places.

---

381 Letter, D.W. Bethel to Joannetta Fisher # 16, May 16, 1897, from Fisher family papers.
382 Letter, D.W. Bethel to Joannetta Fisher #25, August 18, 1897, from Fisher family papers.
383 There is, of course, the Cahuenga Pass in Los Angeles. I believe that as Willis developed this fictional property in his letters, he just appropriated a similar name to make the story more believable. As usual, he just made this stuff up as he went along.

He wrote from the home of Ed Seib, Nettie's cousin and Willis's good friend.[384] Seib resided in western Missouri with his wife and young daughter in 1897, and he worked as a clerk in a telegraph office. Willis began by apologizing for taking so long to write, made the first mention of his phantom ranch in California soon after, then launched into multiple, piteous pleadings for Nettie to reunite with him. He compared their situation to the Seib's happy home life.

> Mrs. Seib is a most delightful lady, a good musician and agreeable. She is a splendid housekeeper. I have told Ed that she makes him as good a wife as you did me & that no woman ever lived who was such a good wife as you. This is correct — I have told him that you were all that any woman could be for a wife — I am going to work one or two more years on the road & then I am going on my ranch where I hope to pass the remainder of my days in California — I hope as soon as I get settled on my place to have yourself & Durward with me. I have always said that when you were ready to come to me I would be ready to give you a home. Then Durward can go to school & we can educate him properly. I hope you will see your way clear to rejoin me. When I see the good home the pleasant family & the way Seibs live I can't but make one more plea to you to come & live with me. Surely I will try to live correctly and make you a good home.[385]

He sounded more mature than he ever had, and Nettie must have been tempted, especially when he wrote later, "I would be willing to quit the road & go on the ranch & work there." She also must have been suspicious, since Willis wasn't known to be the working type. His responses to her subsequent letters indicate that she asked him some hard questions about his itinerant lifestyle, his relationships with women, and his claim to own the ranch. If this long-distance flirtation was going to advance to the next level, the time was at hand, and Nettie wanted to be sure she wasn't being duped again. Her prospects for a union in Clarence must have looked especially bleak in 1897. She was 37 and working as a domestic with an eight-year-old son in tow. A ranch in California must have sounded pretty good in her fantasies, and that was exactly what Willis was counting on.

The second letter is dated May 2, and he again began with an apology for his slowness in writing and thanked her, as noted in Chapter 3, for "waiting to write Ed Seib until you should hear from me further." He was in Kenner, Louisiana, at a temporary job with the Illinois Central Railroad. After pleading with her again for a reconsideration, he disclosed the final outcome of his appeal to have his bond reinstated.

> I went to Kansas City to see the National Surety Co. about my bond there they having declined to bond me was the reason I left Perris. I saw the two letters

---

384 John Edwin Seib's aunt, Maria Barbara Seib, was Nettie's paternal grandmother.
385 Letter, D.W. Bethel to Joannetta Fisher #13, March 19, 1897, from Fisher family papers.

you wrote them. The first one was all right but I think you might have let the second one go. I don't think however you meant to do me as much injury as your second letter really done. I was sorry to see it but let it go. All is right now. You wanted to be fair but could have left things unsaid in that & still have done as well.[386]

Willis was a forgiving guy, after all. Actually, he was seething with anger at his second wife. He would continue to reference his loss of bond as the reason he could not send any money for Durward throughout the next four months, and it reads like a sideways swipe at Nettie every time.

This long letter, the fourteenth in the series, along with the next two, are where Willis made his strongest pitches to reunite. He laid it on thick, trotting out some of the finest of his neck-twisting array of apology, accusation, excuse, martyrdom, and misdirection strategies, along with the usual sprinkling of outright lies. Some samples:

> "When I went to Seibs I told him all that actually I was to blame for. I swear I did not in any way shield myself. While I know I done wrong I never did do as wrong as you seemed to think I had."

> "I'm sorry so sorry. No one will never know what I have suffered what I still suffer."

> "What do you want me to do to prove to you that I am doing all right. No man living could think more of you than I. If I had you & Durward I would try to be what a true devoted husband should be. I think you know that I was kind to you and the fault I had then I know is gone from me now."

> "You score me in your letter about not staying in one place. Well I know it but to save my life I can't be contented. If however I can hope for a reconsideration from you on any terms under the sun I will settle down."

He closed with, "God bless you my darling sweet wife sweet Nettie sweet & only life I have."[387]

The next letter, from May 11, began, "Wife of My Heart Darling — I should have written to you some two or three days ago but a violent cold & bilious attack got the better of me. Feeling some better now though not at all well."[388] Oops! I forgot to say I was sick the last time! In the next paragraph,

---

386 Letter, D.W. Bethel to Joannetta Fisher #14, May 2, 1897, from Fisher family papers.
387 Ibid.
388 Letter, D.W. Bethel to Joannetta Fisher #15, May 11, 1897, from Fisher family papers.

I am sure that if I can be assured of getting a reconsideration from you of our affairs that I would do better. No matter however what comes of your decision I can never think but one thing of you. No one else ever has had a little corner even of it. True I have been led astray, rather I voluntarily <u>went</u> astray why I can't say but that is past. Could I have it to do over again I would I know do very differently. If you will from now on put me on probation or if you will promise me that you will review the matter without prejudice I will surely have a much lighter heart. I think that I would feel differently & would I'm sure be different. I should like very much to have an expression from you how you feel as regards reconsidering the matter.[389]

Letter #16, written on May 16, began:

My own Dear Nettie:

Yours of 9th came to hand yesterday. I will write you now and you will get it Tuesday Eve I think. Your letter found me quite well & still at work though I guess I will loose out because they want bond and "<u>The National Surety Co.</u>" will hardly grant it. I went to see them in Kansas City but fraid they won't grant it. This looks pretty hard when a man has always handled all the money honestly ever entrusted to him. I never in my life misapplied a cent & to be bobbed about this way hurts. At Perris I was making my $100 to $110 a month & that went up on this account. Then I went over in New Mex. & was getting $70 there & for the same reason lost that after 3 or 4 months served. Rail Road Co. said they never had a better man in their service but could not use unless I could give bond with The National Surety Co. Lost that. Came here expecting to secure a place where no bond would be required or get to give in another Co. <u>but</u> I find I'm handicapped & disappointed. Goodness what a trial it is — I have no money. Every cent I got I put into the California property. Luckily I've got that safely & well paid for. If I have to tramp I will do it but have the property paid out.[390]

Then he excoriated her:

What feelings came over me that Dec. 31st when I came home & found you gone your things too & all without a single word of warning. I've tried to put a charitable construction on your conduct in that trouble but it will still hang to me like an ugly night mare. I've always thought that you with your Christian

---

[389] Ibid.
[390] Letter, D.W. Bethel to Joannetta Fisher #16, May 16, 1897, from Fisher family papers. This long letter is reproduced in its entirety in Appendix IV.

> religion might have waited until I came home or in case you could not do that have sent for me where we could have talked the matter over in our own home without being molested & threatened with the battering ram. I can never forget the long weary tramp nor the months that passed with so little sleep, of the desperation that finally seized me & finally such actions as I was driven to through desperation. Death however ended that unhappy act. It is well that it did. Hence I am now where I was when we separated except that I've seen nearly all the U.S. & Mexico.[391]

His vitriol was just getting started. He went on, "I'm sorry you are going out to clean house. I don't think you ever would have done this had you not left me as you did. Surely no man living could have thought more of you or provided for you more ungrudgingly than I did. I done all I could." This was followed by the long paragraph quoted in Chapter 3 in which he threatened Frank Carpenter's life. He then lapsed into self-pity, "I looked at & repeatedly kissed your photo at Seib's. Seib & wife felt so sorry for me that they gave me your photo. I had none you know & you always refused to send me one." Nettie's support group was his next target: "It seems Mrs. Whipple didn't remember you in her will as she said she would. Instead of living with me in your own house you chose to live with her as her servant & the letter that her brother had the impudence to write to me demanding money for you. Surely I wish the whole gang in hell."[392]

Actually, the Whipples, who loved Nettie like a daughter, had left her their house on Main Street in Clarence in their will.[393]

Willis was working every angle he could think of in the sixteenth letter, which was his longest and most insistent. He knew that some elements of Nettie's personality truly didn't care about the legalities — she only wanted some assurance that he would be a good husband and father, that she wouldn't be abandoning her own family for a man who would leave her completely alone. Even at age 37, part of her remained the naïve, trusting farm girl who had fallen so hard for the smooth-talking station agent. But she didn't know about Minnie, Elsie, and Clarence, or Annie and Raymond, or . . .

When he wasn't criticizing or threatening, his groaning self-pity showed up. "I don't think I ever felt so bitter over my fate as I do tonight. I see other men who are no smarter than I going to church with their wives on their arms." Which wives were those again? Toward the end, he wrote, "If I do well I will hold you to your promise to see me prior to cold weather." It was understandable enough, given the amount of emotion they had expended on each other, although as we will see, she still had her doubts, which only grew stronger as the time approached. And in the final paragraph, in the middle of his usual barrage of closing questions, the beast peeked out from behind the mask, "When will Kate be back? What wages does she get teaching? Does Durward go to school to Miss Rittersbaugh? How tall is

---

391 Ibid. The last part of this passage has been quoted before in reference to Matilda's death.
392 Ibid.
393 Daniel C. Fisher and Irene A. Fisher, *A History of the Family and Descendants of Frederick and Catherine Speith Fisher (1825-1978)*, from Fisher family papers.

Durward? What room is your bed room?"[394] What was that again? Ick, the creep factor . . .

May 30 found him in Chicago, either trying to work out a way to remain with the Illinois Central or looking to latch on to another company. He wrote a long letter that day, not to Nettie but to Durward, evidently in response to one his son had written him. His approach was typical Willis, with lots of self-exoneration along with the kinds of embellishments that only a long-distance relationship, especially one with an eight-year-old, will allow.

> Mr. Durward F. Bethel,
> Clarence, NY
>
> My Darling Son — Your letter of the 20th came to me some days ago. I dropped you a postal card telling you I got the letter. I will now try to answer it — You don't know how proud I am to know that you are able to write to me. The last time & moment I saw you you were a little baby in your dear mama's arms. You held in your little hands a rubber rattle upon which you were testing your little & new teeth. When I kissed you good bye and my heart though bursting with anguish & sorrow I little thought it would be more than a few days at least until I should again see you. Instead of a few days long years have come & gone. My darling baby has grown to be large enough & wise enough to write to me. How long Oh God how long until I can once more see you & love you as you should be loved & cared for?[395]

Addressing his son as Durward F. Bethel, which had not been his legal name for 4½ years, was a clear assertion of parental rights, as well as a shot at the Fishers and the New York court that had granted the annulment. For some reason, he didn't go into detail about why it had been so long since they had seen each other. In the next paragraph, incredibly enough, he wrote,

> I have in a manner provided for you my dear boy. I have a nice ranch of 40 acres but absolutely no money. The ranch in Calif. will in one more year be abundant to keep you & your mama. It's all paid for and deed in my trunk — also your & your mama's name & address so that in case of death to me you can get it. There is also a $5,000 Life Insurance policy to you & your sister Bessie Bethel of Flushing Ohio. Now Durward should papa die or be killed you won't forget that deed, will, Life Insurance, etc. will all be found in the small tray inside the large tray in my trunk. Remember one half of the $5,000 is for your sister Bessie will you? Durward you write a good & sensible letter. I wish you would write to your sister & also to Grandpa & Grandma Bethel at Kennon Belmont Co. Ohio. Grandpa will be so glad to hear from you. Don't

---
394 Letter, D.W. Bethel to Joannetta Fisher #16, May 16, 1897, from Fisher family papers.
395 Letter, D.W. Bethel to Joannetta Fisher #17, May 30, 1897, from Fisher family papers.

do this unless you like & also if your mama is unwilling.[396]

In a later letter to Nettie, Willis told her of his instructions to their son in this letter. "Durward has instructions to give Bessie $2,500 if I should die. I hope you will see that these requests are complied with. I don't want Bessie's mother to have anything."[397]

We all know that lying to children isn't nice, but wasn't it wonderful that Willis wanted Durward to finally get to know his older sister, Bessie? But wait, what about Mary and Elsie? Or his brothers Clarence and Ray? Never mind. Telling his son where to find his life insurance policy, which was likely as fictitious as the deed to his ranch, and how to divide the proceeds should he die, was a burden most parents would not lay on an eight-year-old. How must young Durward have reacted to thoughts about his absent father's possible death, and the strange responsibilities entrusted to him? And asking him to write to William Samuel Bethel was just a stroke of genius. What was William going to write back? Something like, "Hey, I love you so much I named my son/grandson after you . . ."

His honesty didn't improve as he went along:

> Papa would have sent you some money about the 20th of this month but I lost my position account the National Surety Co. failed to go my bond. I don't know when or where I will get work but I must have work to live. I have always been honest & to find myself unable to give bond hurts me. I hardly know how I will live for awhile. I think I will be elected Superintendent of the Union Schools at San Diego Calif. to begin in Sept. at a salary of $1,600 a year. I'm not sure. I am also trying to secure a chair as Professor in Language in a College in Kentucky. I'm not sure of either. One thing I can never get work on a rail road to last any length of time while I cannot get bond.[398]

Oh, and by the way, Durward, be a good boy and always tell the truth. Willis went on to boast about his bike riding skills and what a good student he had been at Durward's age, to discuss his love of bullfights and the theatre, and to reminisce a little about his and Nettie's wedding trip to New York City.

At the end he told his son to write back to Kenner, Louisiana, so he must have retained some hopes that he would remain with the Illinois Central. But less than three weeks later he wrote from Fosston, Minnesota. He was now working for the Great Northern Railway in the familiar role of relieving agent. In late June, he wrote:

> My Dear Son — I will write you a few lines today. Trust these few lines will find you well. They leave me quite well and in fair spirits. I have written your mama twice and you once & no reply yet.

---

396 Ibid.
397 Letter, D.W. Bethel to Joannetta Fisher #25, August 18, 1897, from Fisher family papers.
398 Letter, D.W. Bethel to Joannetta Fisher #17, May 30, 1897, from Fisher family papers.

I am at work for a while. How long I can't say. I will enclose you a dollar for the 4th of July. I wish I could send you more but I can't. If I can get in two or three months work I can send you some things or rather send you the money to get them. How much would you have to pay for a wheel, the kind of one you would want? Let me know. I may be able to scrape up enough before long to get it for you. I'm not sure I can, however, but I will try.[399]

A little later, he decided to give his child a little scare:

It grows very cold here in the winter. The snow gets 4 or 5 feet deep. A great many people freeze to death. I am told — last winter a postal clerk got out of his car to go get some lunch. The lunch house was only 10 rods away, but the snow was blowing so badly & it was so cold that he missed his way in going that short distance and was found several weeks after this time frozen to death close by.[400]

Willis was working his magic. Implying that he was in danger of freezing to death by staying in Fosston through the winter (and by the way, it was his mother's fault he lost his bond) was his way of trying to stir up a commotion in Nettie's house. Willis was looking for an ally in his son.

What he didn't tell either Nettie or Durward was that he had gotten the job with the Great Northern by abandoning his own name and he now was sporting the alias 'Dillon Bechtel.' As he had at previous stops, he befriended the local newspaper editor almost immediately, and he became a well-known local fixture in Fosston in summer 1897. The paper was named The Thirteen Towns, named after the thirteen original neighboring townships, the hardy settlements peopled mostly by Scandinavian immigrant farmers in the eastern part of what is now Polk County.[401] The first mention of Willis came on June 11.

[402]

Transcription: D. Bechtel, division relieving agent for the Great Northern, will take charge of the depot at this point while Agent Lynch makes a visit to his former home. Mr. Lynch will leave tomorrow. Mr. Bechtel arrived on Wednesday and finds Mr. Lynch's books in excellent form.

---

399 Letter, D.W. Bethel to Joannetta Fisher #19, June 23, 1897, from Fisher family papers.
400 Ibid.
401 Email from Ed Lavelle, editor of the Thirteen Towns, to Charles Caldemeyer, February 19, 2021.
402 The Thirteen Towns, Fosston, Minnesota, June 11, 1897, microfilm from the Minnesota Historical Society, St. Paul.

Two weeks later, a familiar opportunity for summer recreation was offered to the area's residents:

Transcription: Grand Excursion Next Sunday from Fosston, McIntosh and Erskine to this Popular Summer Resort

75 Cents for Round Trip

Excursions from the West Also. Don't Miss this Chance for a fine Outing and Picnic.

Through the efforts of our temporary local agent, Mr. Bechtel, a special excursion train has been secured which will be run from here to Maple Lake next Sunday, leaving Fosston at 8 o'clock in the morning.

Returning, it will leave Maple Lake at 7 in the evening.

This train will be provided with an ample number of coaches to accommodate large crowds from Fosston, McIntosh and Erskine and a pleasant day's outing can be had at small cost as a fare of 75 cents for the round trip has been fixed upon.

To add to the day's enjoyment the Fosston Cornet Band has been persuaded to accompany the excursion and enliven the hours at the lake with some of their best music.

Don't forget that the train will leave at 8 o'clock, or as soon after as possible.

At Maple Lake they have a fine hotel where excellent meals can be had by those who do not care to take their baskets, there are a large number of row boats to be had on the beach and the steamboat and a large new sailboat will be on hand to carry passengers about the lake.

As far as we know, aside from the invented H.P. Brown in the Dictawood horse caper, this was his first use of an alias. Dillon Bechtel was employee number 14990 on the Great Northern company roster, but no other information about him remains.[404] Dillon Wilson Pickering, of course, was Willis's childhood friend and neighbor, and he probably arrived at his new name by appropriating his buddy's first name, then altering his own last name on one of the letters of recommendation/introduction that he used to gain employment. The switch from 'Bethel' to 'Bechtel' would not have been a difficult one to forge.[405] The man known as David Wilson (Willis) Bethel was out of other options for railroad work in the U.S. by

---
403 The Thirteen Towns, Fosston, Minnesota, June 25, 1897, microfilm from MNHS.
404 Great Northern Railway Employment records, from microfilm on file at the Gale Family Library, Minnesota Historical Society, St. Paul, Minnesota.
405 In the formal traditions of the day, the letter would have called him 'Mr. D.W. Bechtel,' so all his alias's first name had to have in common with his was the first letter.

mid-1897. The practice of adopting all or part of a friend's name will only escalate as we go forward.

Agent Bechtel proved to be a popular replacement for Agent Lynch that summer, as the paper made clear. The following item appeared on July 9:

> Agent D. Bechtel informs the reporter that he will soon leave for Neche, N. D., where he goes to relieve the local agent in the same manner as he came to Fosston. Mr. Bechtel has been here only a few weeks, but during that time has made friends with everyone. His genial disposition and thorough knowledge of the railroad business enables him to conduct the affairs of this important depot without friction and to the satisfaction of all patrons of the road. While extremely accommodating, he is "business" through and through, and when he goes he will take with him the highest regards of our citizens.[406]

Transcription: Agent D. Bechtel informs the reporter that he will soon leave for Neche, N. D., where he goes to relieve the local agent in the same manner as he came to Fosston. Mr. Bechtel has been here only a few weeks, but during that time has made friends with everyone. His genial disposition and thorough knowledge of the railroad business enables him to conduct the affairs of this important depot without friction and to the satisfaction of all patrons of the road. While extremely accommodating, he is "business" through and through, and when he goes he will take with him the highest regards of our citizens.

No matter what name he went by, he was one hell of a guy. On the same day this item appeared, Annie Reed Bethel was giving birth to Willis's sixth child in Michigan. He was not there to see Raymond Harry Bethel brought into the world. He was busy being "extremely accommodating" to the townsfolk of Fosston some 900 miles away.

Annie likely had no idea where he was, and she seems to have escaped his mind entirely, although he probably continued to correspond with his California girl until December.[407] It's doubtful that he was still writing to Minnie in Cincinnati. He was certainly still writing to Nettie and Durward, but not for long.

---

406 The Thirteen Towns, Fosston, Minnesota, July 9, 1897, microfilm from MNHS.
407 Since Willis had contacts at many stations, and since the trains carried the mails, he would have had many ways to disguise his location. My guess is that he sent his letters in an outer envelope to an associate in Chicago, who mailed them from there. According to Raymond's orphanage records, that was where Willis died.

Fosston, Minnesota, in 1902, some five years after Willis was temporary agent there.

In mid-July, he wrote, "I expect to see you & Durward in August. Can Durward go to New York City with me for a visit of a few days, week, or ten days perhaps? . . . It will do Durward good to get away for a trip like that."[409] Nettie must have been filled with fear when she read those words. The prospect of sending her son off to places unknown with Willis Bethel would have done something her own mother's diatribes never could — arouse her protective maternal instincts against an imminent threat. I believe that it was at this point that she realized that her fantasy world of reuniting with Willis could never co-exist with the very real responsibilities of motherhood. She began to shut it down, to see the harsh world clearly, and to eventually mutate into the pathetically dependent and cloying creature we find in her later letters to Durward and Alida.

But for nearly three years she had been indulging herself in those notions. They were at the core of Willis's agenda in writing her — he knew her weaknesses were her idealism and her stubbornness, what her family would call her immaturity, and she was still trying to hold onto the dreams they had once talked about. She still loved her smart-mouthed railroad man who had seen so many strange and wonderful places.

While it's easy to believe that Nettie carried on her correspondence with Willis just to keep her childish dreams alive, his motivation is harder to discern, and like so much with

---

408 Fosston, Minnesota in 1902. Photograph from Wikipedia Commons.
409 Letter, D.W. Bethel to Joannetta Fisher #21, July 14, 1897, from Fisher family papers.

him, darker. He wrote that he regarded his time with Nettie in Clarence as "the scene of the only happiness"[410] he had ever seen, but it's hard to see it as anything but sweet talk. His actions and his lies about, well, everything, make it likely that his real motive was more sinister. I believe that he wanted to reunite with Nettie just so he could ditch her, and so pay her back for ditching him and changing his son's last name to Fisher so many years before. But I think it's likely that he gave up on that idea sometime in mid-1897, when she wouldn't swallow the fiction about his ranch, and he devised the 'New York City vacation' with his son as a strategy to steal Durward away from her. Willis may have thought that Nettie owed him a debt that would only be paid when he dumped her in a distant location and/or took their son away from her. For her part, she seemed to have sensed the agenda and realized that if she sent Durward off with him she would never get him back.

Ironically, it was Ed Seib, Nettie's cousin and Willis's naïve friend, who may have tipped her off that such a caper might be in the works. In his long letter the previous spring, Seib had written, "Actually Nettie I cried for you both when I heard the sad story. I said to him "at that leaving why did you not say come baby you are mine & must go with me" He said for your sake he left it . . ."[411] Sure, parental rights were much less evenly divided in the nineteenth century, and males were dominant in the most important areas, but the thought of the adulterous Willis Bethel 'tramping' out of Clarence with a sixteen-month-old toddler in tow is ludicrous. Now that Durward was almost nine, though, it was a threat Nettie took seriously.

Eight days later, he wrote again. His tone was accusatory.

> Dear Nettie — Three weeks ago I wrote & sent Durward a dollar for the 4th. Twice since then I have written. Seems strange to me you won't answer me. I also sent Durward a watch & chain. Seems to me that there is little appreciation in you or you would at least answer the letter. I will put in some stamps this time & I hope to have you signify at least that my child got the watch and chain as a reward of merit for his good work in school. Apparently it's useless to endeavor to persuade you to see the wrong you have inflicted on me already without going further & humiliating me all you can in various ways. Surely nothing new has happened in the past 7 years to cause you to use me so. No man alive could do better nor live more correctly than I have in that period.[412]

Okay, well, sure, pal . . . Nine days later, she had evidently responded, and he replied:

> Dear Nettie — Yours came last night. I will drop you a few lines today. I will be checked out from here about August 2 or 3. I think they will give me more work. I am extra agent. Indeed I may get steady work I don't know though.

---

410 Letter, D.W. Bethel to Joannetta Fisher #10, January 7, 1896, from Fisher family papers.
411 Letter, John Edwin Seib to Joannetta Fisher, March 21, 1897, from Fisher family papers.
412 Letter, D.W. Bethel to Joannetta Fisher #22, July 22, 1897, from Fisher family papers.

I'm surprised that Durward should of his own mind conclude not to want a wheel. That is unusual for a boy of his age.

I think you better think that matter over and change your mind about letting him go with me. Remember I will bring him back to you safely. Because I want to be fair with you I have asked you in advance. You can surely allow him alone with me a little bit. I certainly think my request very modest indeed and I think when you think it over? . . .

. . . Write me about him going with me. I've no passes further than Buffalo yet though. Why do you fear to meet me I'll do you no bodily harm I'm sure. I'm not a cannibal. Expect to see you in less than a month.[413]

He was telling folks in Fosston the same story. On July 30, the paper published the following:

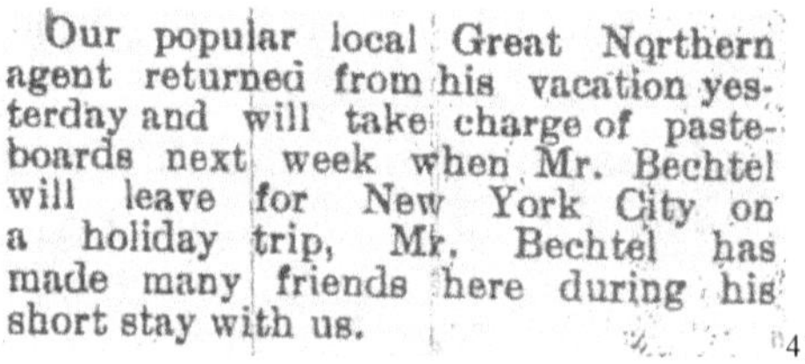
Our popular local Great Northern agent returned from his vacation yesterday and will take charge of pasteboards next week when Mr. Bechtel will leave for New York City on a holiday trip, Mr. Bechtel has made many friends here during his short stay with us.

[414]

Transcription: Our popular local Great Northern agent returned from his vacation yesterday and will take charge of pasteboards next week when Mr. Bechtel will leave for New York City on a holiday trip. Mr. Bechtel has made many friends here during his short stay with us.

Two weeks later, on August 13, the paper mentioned that Willis had traveled to the nearby town of McIntosh and spent the day with a local doctor by the name of McKinnon. He may have been working the doctor/colleague angle, but it went nowhere. This brief mention is the last one we have of Dillon Bechtel in the Fosston paper.

He still wrote to his New York family, but increasingly to Durward, not to Nettie. The last few letters are much shorter, and it's clear that he was losing enthusiasm. On August 16, "Mama wrote papa a very tort letter. I don't know why." He ended it with,

I will try to put you through College. I want you to graduate from Berkely State University in California when you are graduated finally — Be truthful and honest in your studies — Truthful & honest in all things — Don't even tell a small story under any circumstances and you will finally learn and know that

413 Letter, D.W. Bethel to Joannetta Fisher #23, July 31, 1897, from Fisher family papers.
414 The Thirteen Towns, Fosston, Minnesota, July 30, 1897, microfilm from the Minnesota Historical Society, St. Paul.

you are better off for your integrity. When can you go to California to see your little 40 acre ranch?[415]

Honest and truthful, just like dad. Maybe he wanted Durward to attend Berkeley so he could study under his old friend, Dr. Frank Carpenter. Willis wrote two more letters in August, on the 18th and the 23rd, but he wasn't really trying. His August 23rd letter to Nettie read, in part,

> I won't get to Buffalo this month now I'm sure. When does Durward's school begin I would like to know. Have you told him he would see me this fall? I wonder if he will know me? I think I would know him if I should see him. Do you think I would? Did he get his watch set yet? How does his cotton get along? I suppose you will have frost there before long. It's very cool here. I shall arrange for the Pacific Coast before long. I'm not satisfied away from there. Indeed I'm sorry I ever left there. There is the only place in the world to live in my opinion at least.[416]

On September 22, he wrote from Ulen, a small stop in the middle of the western Minnesota plains about 60 miles away. The unfocused letter, which may have been written while he was drunk, was his last to Nettie, and it is transcribed below in its entirety.

> Mrs. Nettie Fisher
> Clarence, NY
>
> Dear Nettie — Seems strange you don't write & answer my letter. I wrote you before I left Fosston & asked you to tell me some matters about Durward. So far not a word from you. If you don't want to write might let him write at least. If you don't care to write me now he surely can?
>
> I asked you to write me at Stephen Minn. as I was to go there from Fosston but not a word.
>
> I suppose Durward is in school again? How is he getting along? After vacation.
>
> I wrote you some time ago & asked for Frank Carpenter's address. I hope you will do me the favor to send it to me.
>
> Did Kate secure an appointment in the Buffalo schools? How does she look since she has grown up? I suppose Bert is quite a good looking girl. She was a

---
415 Letter, D.W. Bethel to Joannetta Fisher #24, August 16, 1897, from Fisher family papers.
416 Letter, D.W. Bethel to Joannetta Fisher #26, August 23, 1897, from Fisher family papers.

prepossessing looking little girl.

I don't know a thing to write you now. Had hoped to have seen you before this but such a torn down letter as you wrote me makes me feel very differently hence I don't think I shall see you. I think you will regret writing me such a letter at some time. No sense in writing any such a letter. I never gave you any occasion to write one like that — and more you will know I never was ill & cross to you as you accuse me. Has Thompson gone home? Love to Durward

Sincerely yours,
D.W. Bethel [417]

The "Sincerely yours," along with the signature, 'D.W. Bethel,' were his way of breaking off communication, although it appears that Nettie had already done that. Only two of the other 26 letters were so signed. Both were from the California period, one when he was basking in the glow of success at Perris, the other when he was begging her to help with his bonding issues. Sometimes he signed "D. Willis Bethel," but usually he went with "Your Own Willis," or simply, "Willis." But he went formal in his exit, a model of offended dignity, martyr for unrequited love that he was.

For years, this was when the stage suddenly went dark, as if the tragicomedy that was the life of Willis Bethel didn't pay its electric bill. After a lot of unsuccessful digging, it became clear to me that he had abandoned not only his birth name but also the alias Dillon Bechtel by September 22, 1897. Without any letters to indicate where he was, it was impossible to know what rock to look under, and in 2016 I thought the rest of his story was gone for good, and I began to write this book. But just as the increasing connective power of the internet had given us the first part of his story, another technology emerged to provide its continuation.

---

[417] Letter, D.W. Bethel to Joannetta Fisher #27, September 22, 1897, from Fisher family papers. This letter is reproduced in its entirety in Appendix IV.

10.

Joseph Patterson Steele

■ **IN 2019, I MADE CONTACT WITH RENEE.** We were DNA matches on Ancestry.com, and our shared matches indicated that we were related through the Bethel branch of my tree. When I had first submitted my DNA to Ancestry for analysis in 2013, my matches were generally unrevealing about my ancestry, but since 2017, with the rise in popularity of these tests, they had become an unmatched source of information. Unsurprisingly, my Bethel line contains the most matches, in part because of the events described in this book.

Reaching out to Renee, I told her a little of the story of D.W. Bethel and asked that if she had any information to please send it along. She replied, "Hi Charles, I'm trying to figure out my family tree. I was adopted so I'm trying to figure out the tree for my biological family as well as ideally find out who my biological father was. So far I know that I'm the daughter of Marie McDermond and granddaughter of William McDermond and Beatrice Steele. I'm sorry I couldn't be of more assistance."[418] If only all of my DNA matches were of that much assistance.

I told myself that our Bethel connection most likely came from her unknown biological father's side of the tree — that would make sense, right? Still, the name Beatrice Steele intrigued me. I knew from the Perris newspapers that Willis's protégé in Perris was named Joe Steele, and I wondered if there was any connection. It was a total longshot, but I was short on research options at that point, so I decided to check it out.

After some poking around, I found that Beatrice's father was named Herbert Benjamin Steele, born near Asheboro, North Carolina on October 25, 1899. Hmm, North Carolina? Didn't sound promising. He was raised, however, in Minnesota, then North Dakota, by his step-grandfather and grandmother, John and Mathilda Tyberg. More research, along with another visit to the Minnesota Historical Society library in St. Paul, allowed me to assemble the next episode of the story.

The Minnesota period was Willis's longest since his early days with Jennie, lasting almost four years in all. It included some of his most outlandish deceptions, and they would be hard to believe if they weren't supported by records and news accounts. This was where his experimentation with aliases would turn identity theft into a way of life for at least the next fourteen years, and likely for the remainder of his days.

Previously, I hadn't paid much attention to the fact that his last letter to Nettie was on

---
418 Message, Renee Johnson to Charles Caldemeyer on Ancestry.com, June 19, 2019.

letterhead of the Northern Pacific Railway, while ones from earlier that summer were on that of the Great Northern. I had just assumed that there was some crossover of temporary employees between the two giant companies. For years as competitors, they dominated rail traffic in their home state of Minnesota, with both outfits providing service to the west coast through North Dakota, Montana, Idaho, and Washington. But in 1893, the Northern Pacific went into receivership, and the business buzzards began to circle. Chief among them was the Great Northern, which incrementally moved to control the assets of its rival through the late 1890's, a goal it finally achieved in 1900.[419]

By September 1897 it must have been clear to Willis that Dillon Bechtel was a flawed alias who was not going to be hired on long term by the Great Northern or any other line. What he needed was a legitimate work history and some institutional bona fides, mainly with a bonding agency. So, what to do? In his most brazen move yet, he applied to the Northern Pacific on September 10, 1897, under the name of his protégé and friend, Joseph Patterson Steele. He likely chose the alias because of Mr. Steele's spotless employment record and bonding history, and because he (Willis) could use a copy of a recommendation letter that he had written for Steele the previous year. He probably chose the railroad because it was a nearby behemoth in financial difficulty, which promised flaws in oversight and opportunities to skim, similar to his plan (although not his outcome) with the Kentucky Union.

The timing of the application, along with other factors, makes it seem likely that Willis and Steele were in communication with each other, although the extent of Steele's knowledge of what his former mentor was up to is unclear. They had been close friends since meeting in Perris in 1895. Willis taught Steele the ropes of the business and was instrumental in getting him his first station, at Hemet, in late 1895/early 1896. Willis lost his position at Rincon in September 1896 and Steele, after being transferred to Riverside, was also dropped by the A.T.S.F. later that fall in a reduction of force. Both men then went to Mexico. We know that Steele began working for the Mexican Central Railway in January 1897, and Willis probably also worked for the company in an effort to make an end run around his bonding problems. A later reference he made to a Minnesota editor about an incident involving a conductor on the Mexican Central may have been the reason he left Mexico, although we don't know the real story.[420]

His correspondence with Nettie and his visit to Ed Seib reveal that he came back to the U.S. in March 1897 to try to clear things up with the National Surety Company. Steele remained in Mexico for a time, but he, too, returned to the States in July. He got a job with the Oregon Short Line Railroad in Wyoming, but he only worked there for two months. On September 13, he left the O. S. L., and he remained out of railroading for the next fifteen

---

419 Hidy, Hidy, Scott, and Hofsommer, *The Great Northern Railway: A History,* pp. 88-96.
420 The Red Lake Falls Courier, as reprinted in the Norman County Index, March 14, 1901, p. 1, microfilm from the Minnesota Historical Society, St. Paul. The information that Joe Steele worked for the Mexican Central in 1897 comes from his application to the N.P. in 1899. Willis's stories usually came from the relatively recent past, and they had a grain of truth at their core, although they tended to be highly exaggerated.

months.[421] Coincidentally (or not), Willis filled out his Northern Pacific application on September 10.[422] Maybe he had gotten word about Steele's plans to go into another business and when that enterprise would begin, and he then felt free to help himself to his former colleague's name and work history. It's also possible that the two men were collaborating.[423]

The job application, clearly in Willis's handwriting, set the tone for the next four years, when he practically dared the world to discover his fraudulence. In the work history section, he couldn't resist listing "D.W. Bethel agt." as Joe Steele's first employer. The real Joe Steele had been married the previous April in El Paso, a wedding Willis may well have attended. But he listed himself as single, although as later events will show, it's possible that he was also a newlywed.

On September 12, 1897, he found himself sporting his brand-new used name at Ulen for the modest salary of $40 per month.[424] It may have made him uncomfortable (or excited?) to be so close to Fosston, which was only about 60 miles away by rail. Because they were serviced by different railroads, the two towns were not in as intimate contact with one another as those on the same lines. Still, there was plenty of local commerce in the area, most of it conducted by rail, and one would think that someone might have noticed that Joseph P. Steele, the genial station agent for the Northern Pacific at Ulen, sure looked a lot like Dillon Bechtel, the genial station agent who had filled in for the Great Northern at Fosston just a few weeks earlier. But if there were whispers in the crowd, no documentation of them survives.

He stayed at the small village for only a couple of months, and we have no news about him while he was there, although later articles indicate that he was, as usual, a popular figure. On November 26, 1897, the Norman County Index, in its section devoted to the small town of Gary, tersely announced that J.P. Steele had been reassigned there.[425] Gary was three stops north of Ulen, about 21 miles up the N.P. line, and even closer to Fosston.

Obviously feeling bulletproof, he made no discernible attempts to avoid publicity. Gary didn't have a newspaper until 1900 but reports of the town's doings from nearby papers indicate that it didn't take long for the old Willis to emerge, and as time rolled on, accounts of his exploits began to appear more frequently. On December 17, the Index reported that our hero had bravely foiled an attempt to burglarize the depot, although since he was the only witness,

---

421 Employment records of Joseph Patterson Steele with the Northern Pacific Railroad, May 25, 1899. Ancestry.com, *U.S., Northern Pacific Railway Company Personnel Files, 1890-1963* [database on-line], and from the Minnesota Historical Society, St. Paul.
422 His application didn't mention Steele's job with the Oregon Short Line or the Mexican Central, instead steering he N.P.'s Superintendent of Telegraphy, Oscar Greene, to verify Steele's credentials with the A.T.S.F., if any checking was to be done.
423 We know that the Steele family remained in Diamondville, Wyoming, for at least the first six months of his time away from railroad work, since his first child, Mary, was born there in February 1898. The only mention we find of his name in the sparse news accounts of the region during that time is a news account from the Anaconda Standard on April 25, 1898, which mentions a Joe Steele working the Whippoorwill mine in the Little Belt Mountains, about 480 miles from Diamondville, in partnership with two other men. If this was, in fact, Joseph Patterson Steele, he probably left his family in the relative safety of a town he knew, near people he trusted, while he pursued riches in the silver fields.
424 A telegram from O. C. Greene to E. H. Williams in the employee folder mentioned his starting salary.
425 The Norman County Index, November 26, 1897, microfilm from the Minnesota Historical Society, St. Paul.

it's easy to believe that he made the story up.[426] In early 1898, residents read that he had spent the previous Christmas in Northwood, North Dakota, probably visiting friends.[427] We don't know who they were, but the inclusion of the item makes it clear that his local celebrity campaign was gaining steam.

An intriguing article from the Twin Valley Times in mid-April, with the Spanish-American War looming, stated that Willis was about to leave "for his old home in Kentucky," and that he would be back "after the war is over."[428] Was he planning to sign up with a Kentucky regiment? That's hard to envision, but it's also hard to know what else it might mean. We know that he wasn't in fighting trim — about a month earlier, the Times had called him "a heavyweight" when reporting on his surprisingly good bicycle-riding skills.[429] No other reference to this trip or its reasons were ever made, and he clearly didn't follow through with an enlistment, or if he did, he was rejected. This was the fake J.P. Steele's earliest claim of Kentucky as his home state — he had correctly listed Missouri, the real Steele's birth state, on his N.P. application. But going forward, he routinely assigned his origins to the Bluegrass State, at least until 1911. And from this and other reports, it appears that for some reason he genuinely had a fascination with the Spanish-American War.

The following article appeared in the Index on May 6:

> A subscription committee has been around gathering money for a new flag and to get a mast put up. The people are enthusiastic over the war and wanted to raise a flag to the honor of the boys, that are fighting for their country. Agent Steele is the one that is the most interested in the war and copies every message that goes over the wire and keeps the people posted on the situations. He will, after this, use three flags; a red one will indicate victory for U. S. and a black one will indicate our defeat, and when neither red or black flags are up, no news is on hand. [430]

Transcription: A subscription committee has been around gathering money for a new flag and to get a mast put up. The people are enthusiastic over the war and wanted to raise a flag to the honor of the boys, that are fighting for their country. Agent Steele is the one that is the most interested in the war and copies every message that goes over the wire and keeps the people posted on the situations. He will, after this, use three flags; a red one will indicate victory for U.S. and a black one will indicate our defeat, and when neither red or black flags are up, no news is on hand.

---

426 The Norman County Index, December 17, 1897, microfilm from MNHS.
427 The Twin Valley Times, January 5, 1898, p. 1, microfilm from MNHS.
428 The Twin Valley Times, April 13, 1898, p. 1, microfilm from MNHS.
429 The Twin Valley Times, March 9, 1898, p. 1, microfilm from MNHS.
430 *Gary News,* The Norman County Index, May 6, 1898, microfilm from MNHS.

Willis's application to the Northern Pacific Railroad as J.P. Steele, September 10, 1897. Note the inclusion of his real name in the employer section at lower left.

---

431 Northern Pacific Railroad employment application of David Wilson Bethel as Joseph Patterson Steele, September 10, 1897, folder #51387. Original records housed at the Minnesota Historical Society, St. Paul. Also accessible online at Ancestry.com. This image is also reproduced full page in Appendix IV.

Of course, it's difficult to view this action other than cynically, as a ploy to win the affection of the locals. If so, it was effective. Over time, he achieved nearly the celebrity at Gary that he had enjoyed at Owingsville and Perris.

Our next reports of him don't come until five months later, in October 1898, when he was mentioned for his role in expanding the Northern Pacific station at Gary. A new floor was added and plans for enlarging the depot were also mentioned. Gary was a growing town, and the paper took this opportunity to advocate for more investment in the place, calling the town "a good business point," that also needed "a bank, a butcher shop, a barber shop."[432] Willis had certainly assumed the role of advocate for the town, just as he had in Perris, although it seems unlikely that he had much influence on the railroad's decision-making.

We get another glimpse of his community status, as well as the beginning of his next seduction, three weeks later. Again, the Norman County Index, which was published at Ada, the county seat 17 miles away, is our source:

> Agent Steele made a flying trip to Ulen last week to attend a social party, at Landlord Stebbins. He returned on the morning train very much pleased with the trip. Mr. Steele seems to take great pleasure in visiting Ulen and he did not go alone this time either.
>
> Agent Steele gave a banquet at the hotel Saturday evening. The table was spread for about 40 and the occasion proved one of the most enjoyable events of the year. Whist was indulged in and when the party broke up all voted Mr. Steele the prince of hosts.

[433]

Transcription: Agent Steele made a flying trip to Ulen last week to attend a social party at Landlord Stebbins. He returned on the morning train very much pleased with the trip. Mr. Steele seems to take great pleasure in visiting Ulen and he did not go alone this time either.

Agent Steele gave a banquet at the hotel Saturday evening. The table was spread for about 40 and the occasion proved one of the most enjoyable events of the year. Whist was indulged in and when the party broke up all voted Mr. Steele the prince of hosts.

George Stebbins ran the brand-new hotel in Ulen where Willis had probably resided during his two-plus months in the town, and the 'social party' was for the birthday of George's daughter.[434] The fact that Willis hosted a banquet for 40 people is interesting. Banquets are expensive,

---

432 *Gary News*, The Norman County Index, October 28, 1898, microfilm from MNHS.
433 *Gary News*, The Norman County Index, November 18, 1898, microfilm from MNHS.
434 The Twin Valley Times, November 23, 1898, p. 4, microfilm from MNHS.

especially on a salary of $40 a month, and how he got the funds to pay for the event are an interesting question that will recur. But for us, the most important item here is the reference about him not going alone. This is probably our first glimpse of Chrestine Hendricks.[435]

She was born in December 1881, most likely in Grant County, Minnesota, to Norwegian immigrants Charles and Mathilda Hendricks.[436] We know nothing more about Charles Hendricks, except that he must have died in the mid-to-late 1880's, because by 1889 Mathilda was in her second marriage, to John Petter Tyberg, a Swedish immigrant twelve years her senior. Like many Minnesota residents at the time, they were part of the Scandinavian influx that turned the prairies of the upper Midwest into prosperous farming communities in the years following the Civil War. The Tybergs had moved the hundred-or-so miles north to Norman County by the mid 1890s. Mathilda was the mother of nine children in all, although only four of them survived until 1910.[437] In addition to Chrestine, Godtfred Hendricks was born around 1885, and John Albert Tyberg and Henry Tyberg were born in 1891 and 1892, respectively.

The Tybergs weren't landowners in the late 1890s. John Petter probably worked as either a hired hand or a sharecropper, moving his family accordingly.[438] Although they generated little news, the accounts that exist tell us that they were favorably regarded in the community for their character, although probably not for the abundance of their resources. Judging from her actions, the headstrong and fun-loving Chrestine was the wild one in a family of honest hard workers. She appears to have been desperately looking for security, both familial and financial, in a world that had taken her father from her when she was young and now offered few exciting, and no lucrative, prospects. Like Annie Reed before her, she was a ready target for the designs of Willis Bethel.

Two months after the banquet, on January 8, 1899, J.P. Steele and Chrestine Hendricks were married by Rev. W. A. Whitcomb in Ada, with only the reverend's wife and her sister as witnesses.[439] The Index implied that the ceremony was driven by certain urgencies. The couple "went right to house keeping at the section house, where they have rented rooms," although the fact that the license was applied for the previous day shows at least some semblance of planning.[440] Chrestine had turned 17 the previous month; Willis was almost 39.

---

435 Her name anglicizes to 'Christine,' of course. But she usually spelled it in the Scandinavian fashion, and we will use that spelling, too.
436 1900 U.S. census, Duluth, St. Louis County, Minnesota, household of Ignatz Freimuth; Marriage Return, James S. Cavanagh and Christina F. H. Mitchell, Seattle, Washington, May 21, 1907, both Ancestry.com. Although this marriage record (her third) lists Gary as her birthplace, both her older and younger brothers were born in the Elbow Lake area, in Grant County. The document was clearly filled out by a clerk, and Chrestine may have been inebriated or past the point of caring about the details of her origins when her marriage to Cavanagh was solemnized.
437 1910 U.S. census, J.P. Tyberg family, Township 159, Range 99, Williams County, North Dakota, Ancestry.com.
438 At the time, the eastern part of Norman County was what is today Mahnomen County, which was part of the White Earth Indian Reservation. The Tybergs missed the 1900 census, but we know they lived "in the eastern part of the county" in 1901 (*Tough on Joseph*, The Gary Graphic, March 9, 1901, p. 4, MNHS), "about five miles south" of Gary in 1903 (The Gary Graphic, October 16, 1903, p. 5, MNHS), and back on the reservation, in Pembina Township in 1905 (1905 Minnesota census, Norman County, Township 144, Range 42, p. 437, Ancestry.com).
439 Marriage license, J.P. Steele and Christine J. Hendricks, Norman County, Minnesota, January 8, 1899, Ancestry.com and records request from the Minnesota Official Marriage System (moms.mn.gov).
440 *Gary Items*, The Norman County Index, January 20, 1899, p. 1, microfilm from MNHS.

The Northern Pacific Section House at Gary, where Willis and Chrestine lived after their wedding.

The marriage proposal must have included the promise of a deferred honeymoon in the spring — actually, it probably included a lot of promises. Chrestine later deposed that Willis "said he had lands in California and Kentucky," that "he was wealthy," and of course, the main promise, that he was an unmarried man.[442]

Main Street, Gary, Minnesota, 1899.

---

441 *Images of Gary, Minnesota*, http://lakesnwoods.com/GaryGallery.htm. The section house was built by the railroad near each station, for employees and guests. This photo was taken around 1886, some 13 years prior to Willis's and Chrestine's marriage.
442 State of Minnesota, County of Norman, District Court case #2698-4-201. Chrestine Hendricks, Plaintiff vs. Joe Steele, Defendant, 1901. Deposition, p. 3.
443 *Images of Gary, Minnesota*, http://lakesnwoods.com/GaryGallery.htm. The pictured gentleman is unidentified. It is probably not Willis, although he and Chrestine lived in the town when this photo was taken.

In March 1899, the gregarious station agent announced his plans to take his latest wife on a trip to see the sunny south. The Index reported that the couple "will visit many of the large cities and may take a trip over to Cuba. They expect to be gone about a month."[444] The desire to visit Cuba, the scene of the brief war won so decisively the previous year, certainly came from Willis. If the army wouldn't take him over there, he could at least be part of the tourist invasion that followed.

Although the trip ended up lasting less than a month, their departure turned out to be a community event. We know that they left sometime after April 21 and that they returned before May 3.[445] On that day, the Twin Valley Times offered the following summary:

> Transcription: J.P. Steele and wife are home from their trip to the south. They went via Chicago down to Tennessee, visited with friends at Memphis, went to Cuba via New Orleans, spent a couple days there, returned the same way and went to Ashville [sic], N.C., where they spent a few days. They returned this week, very much pleased with the trip. The Gary band gave them a warm send-off when they left, which is very much appreciated by them both. Mr. Steele will be glad to tell their friends of what they saw on their trip, especially on the bloody shores of Cuba. They have a host of friends here who are glad to see them home.[446]

It was not much time to visit friends in Memphis, then New Orleans and "the bloody shores of Cuba," and finally to spend a few days in North Carolina. They must have been motivated travelers, or maybe the itinerary was exaggerated to the editor. There was no subsequent mention of who they visited in Tennessee, but it was probably someone he knew from 1893-1894. And the paper confused the better-known Asheville with the Steeles' real

---
444 *Gary Items,* The Norman County Index, March 24, 1899, p. 1, microfilm from MNHS.
445 *Gary Items,* The Norman County Index, April 21, 1899, p. 1, microfilm from MNHS. This issue of the Index included a report that the planned trip was about to begin.
446 The Twin Valley Times, May 3, 1899, p. 4, microfilm from MNHS. The Spanish American War had ended the previous August, making Cuba something of a tourist destination.

destination in North Carolina, Asheboro, a small town near the middle of the state. But there was no confusion about his popularity. With the Gary band turning out to give them a fanfare (probably at Willis's instigation) the admiration of his usual 'host of friends' accompanied him, at least for the time being. Chrestine, an insignificant player in her community prior to the marriage, must have felt like she had been admitted to small-town royalty.

Part of the few days in Asheboro was spent buying a 170-acre farm. Briefly described by Chrestine in her divorce deposition in 1901, it had "one medium size dwelling house in good condition, one medium sized barn and one other building 14x14."[447] Willis seems to have been considering buying land in that area for some time. His long letter, written to Milton V. Richards, Land and Industrial Agent for the Southern Railway, was originally published in the Southern Field, the railroad's companion magazine dedicated to encouraging commercial development in the regions the road served. It was reprinted in a Raleigh newspaper on June 25, and it comes to us via that route. Entitled, *A Fine Country,* and subtitled "Minnesota Man Gives His Reasons for Buying a Farm Near Asheboro, Randolph County, N. C.," Mr. Steele began,

> Some time ago I wrote you telling you about what I wanted in the way of a farm. A very prompt reply from you gave me information about points on your road. After correspondence with parties in the south I determined to visit Asheboro, N. C. I went there and was never more surprised in my life than to find such a delightful country with land at such low prices. I looked over the whole country around there, hence I am not speaking of one or two farms, but of Randolph county, and when I tell you that I have seldom seen nicer land I am not rating it too high.

His farming acumen was so good, after all. He went on to praise the quality of the soil, the diversity of crops, the climate, land prices, educational facilities, and low taxes. He called Randolph County "a favorable place for honest, industrious people to locate."[448] OK, well, he may have been referring to his in-laws.

The paper was glad to use the letter as an advertisement for the region, and they concluded that "this Minnesotan is evidently a man of intelligence." Willis bought his farm for $900, with two different contracts. In the first, under only his name, he paid $300 cash, although how he had that much money on hand when only making $40 a month is, again, a mystery. In the second, Chrestine and he signed a note financing the remaining $600 with a two-year

---

447 State of Minnesota, County of Norman, District Court case #2698-4-201. Chrestine Hendricks, Plaintiff vs. Joe Steele, Defendant, 1901. Deposition, p. 4.
448 *A Fine Country,* The Raleigh Morning Post, June 25, 1899, p. 4, Newspapers.com. We don't know why he wrote this letter. Richards, credited with helping bring industrial development to the South, was a former N.P. employee, although he had moved on by the time Willis arrived on the line. Willis may have been working an angle that didn't materialize, although this would not be his last land acquisition on the eastern seaboard. We know that he was a letter-writing machine, and he probably had multiple deals cooking at any given time.

mortgage from the seller.[449] This must have been purposeful, giving him the option of recovering his cash without her signature, but including her on the instrument that involved debt. Chrestine, a gullible teenager with no clue about finances, probably just signed her name as requested. Less than five months into their marriage, Willis already had the abandonment of his Minnesota wife included in his intentions.

---

[449] Randolph County North Carolina Real Estate Records, Register of Deeds, Book 95, pp. 158-161, and Book 96, pp. 30-31, database online at randrod.com.

11.

"A Smooth One"

▄ ABOUT THREE WEEKS AFTER THEIR HOST OF FRIENDS WELCOMED THE COUPLE HOME, on May 20, 1899, the Northern Pacific transferred Willis to Red Lake Falls, about 40 miles north of Gary. At this point, two strange coincidences intrude upon the story, making it even more complex. On May 25, the real Joseph Patterson Steele applied to the Northern Pacific for a job. After passing the N.P.'s operator tests, he was hired and stationed in the Montana Division, at the small stop of Wilsey. Evidently, the railroad saw no contradiction in the simultaneous employment of two operators with identical first, middle, and last names and similar bonding sureties, work histories, birthplaces, and parentage.

Confusingly, both Willis's and Steele's applications are now found in the same folder, under the same employee number. This must have happened in 1909, when the N.P. overhauled its employee record-keeping, assigned new employee numbers to old records, and began keeping better track of their workers.[450] Someone doing that consolidation, long after both Willis and Joseph had left the company, probably noticed the similarities in the applications and decided that these two Joseph Patterson Steeles must have been the same person.

While the applications have obvious similarities that would explain that decision, there are also some striking differences. The physical description on Willis's 1897 application listed his age as 30 (he was 37), his height as 5'-10", his weight as 180 pounds, and his form as "stout." Less than two years later, he was 27, he had lost two inches of height and 45 pounds and was "slim." Their personal and work history information were similar, except that Willis had mixed up the names of the county and the town in Missouri where Joseph was raised, and Joseph listed his employers since the A.T.S.F. Unlike the first J.P. Steele, the second one was married, and to only one woman, too.[451] The folder contains only three other items: two telegrams of introduction from Oscar C. Greene, the Superintendent of Telegraph for the N.P., to the heads of telegraph in the Manitoba and Montana Divisions, respectively, in which he described Willis's operator skills as "good" and Joseph's as "very good," and the

---

450 Northern Pacific Railway Company employee records, folder #54271. Letter from Alfred N. Page to F. H. Bailey, December 9, 1939, Minnesota Historical Society and Ancestry.com. This letter tells of the reorganization of files that occurred in 1909.
451 As documented in Chapter 9, Steele married Ida Stack in El Paso in April 1897 (El Paso Herald, April 5, 1897).

dismissal notice of the real J.P. Steele from 1902.[452]

Joseph Patterson Steele's application to the Northern Pacific Railroad, May 25, 1899.

---

452 Employment records of the Northern Pacific Railroad for David Wilson Bethel as Joseph Patterson Steele and the real Joseph Patterson Steele, September 10, 1897 and May 25, 1899, folder #51387. Original records housed at the Gale Family Library in the Minnesota Historical Society, St. Paul. Also accessible online at Ancestry.com. It should be noted that a different employee numbering system, now lost, was in use at the time. The real J.P. Steele's employee number while he worked for the N.P. was 7424. Willis's original number is unknown. The number 51387 dates from 1909.

453 Northern Pacific Railroad employment application of Joseph Patterson Steele, May 25, 1899, folder #51387. Original records housed at the Minnesota Historical Society, St. Paul. Also accessible online at Ancestry.com.

For about a year beginning in May 1899, the Northern Pacific had two Joseph Patterson Steeles on its payroll as operators and station agents. I've found no documentation in company records that they ever had a clue about the truth. It's possible that they investigated it at some point, and that the records of that process were kept in a different folder, now lost, but one would think that some notation of it would have found its way into each man's personnel file.

The disorganization of the offices and employee recordkeeping of the struggling N.P., the fact that there was minimal communication between divisions, which operated as semi-autonomous railroads, and the very brazenness of the fraud probably all contributed to its success. Willis had chosen the right railroad to dupe, and the fact that they had also hired the real J.P. Steele was proof.[454]

Both Greene and his immediate subordinate at the time, E.E. Dildine, appear to have been competent in the performance of their duties, judging from their other letters and telegrams. They probably just chalked the name similarity up to coincidence and didn't look deeper, if they even noticed it at all. Maybe the office was especially busy that day.

Oscar C. Greene, St. Paul, Supt. Telegraph N. P. Ry.

Steele had gotten back into the railroad business in December 1898, going to Alabama for a stint with the Kansas City, Missouri & Birmingham. He was there until he applied to the N.P., in May 1899, coincidentally (or not) right after Willis and Chrestine returned from

---

454 The divisions of the Northern Pacific were notoriously insular. Ulen, Gary, and Red Lake Falls were in the Manitoba Division, which ran from its headquarters in Winnipeg to the main line just east of Fargo. The Montana Division, where the real J.P. Steele was employed, was largely on the N.P.'s main east-west line, about 800 miles away. Many divisions, or parts of divisions, began as regional railroads and were acquired by the N.P. over time as the big railroad grew into a giant. Although hires by divisions were allowed, they had to be cleared with St. Paul, and the practice was discouraged. But much of the day-to-day decision-making was left to the divisions. Northern Pacific policies, such as the rule that employees could not ask to transfer between divisions — they had to resign and then reapply in the new division, losing seniority in the process — contributed to the parochialism. The company, however, often reassigned workers as needed. Although Willis's gamble was risky, these factors gave it a greater chance of success.

their southern trip. The timing suggests a connection, but whether there really was one, and what its nature was, is unknown.

It begs all sorts of questions, and unfortunately, few of them have answers. Did Steele know that Willis was working for the N.P. under his name and apply to the company anyway? Did Willis invite him to apply, even though he knew Steele was ignorant of the scam, just to cause havoc? Were they in cahoots? No way to know. Steele's application could have been just one of those innocent coincidences that sometimes find their way into the historical record.[455] The truth surrounding these events involves some of the most interesting of the many unanswered questions in the story of David Wilson Bethel.

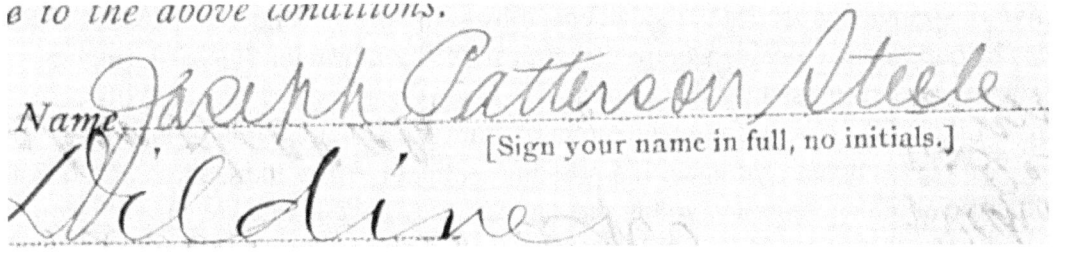

Above: The signature of D.W. Bethel as Joseph Patterson Steele on his employment application from 1897. Willis seems to have altered his handwriting to include an elaborate bottom loop on the 'J' to imitate somewhat the writing of his friend. Below: The signature of the real J.P. Steele on his application. The two signatures are similar in the formation of some letters, although Willis's handwriting is certainly more chaotic.

[456]

---

[455] Steele was employed by the N.P. in Montana for about three and a half years. In late 1900, he was the subject of a character-assassination attempt by another agent, Thomas Cary, that included charges of fraud and drunkenness. The investigation the N.P. launched cleared Steele of wrongdoing and resulted in Cary being fired, and the letter exchanges in Cary's personnel file (#51291) give us a rare look at how the company viewed both employees. Steele was "a good agent both for the public and for the company," who "performed some very good service for us," (letter, H. J. Horn, Jr. to O. C. Greene, 18 Feb 1901). He was praised for resisting an opportunity to enrich himself at company expense, and generally for his honesty and his integrity, although he was "a little hot headed at times," (letter, H. J. Horn, Jr. to O. C. Greene, 14 Jan 1901). Steele remained with the Northern Pacific for almost two years after Willis fled Minnesota. He was fired for "violation of Rule 8," the company's prohibitions the consumption of alcoholic beverages and the frequenting of saloons, in December 1902. He ended up back in his native state of Missouri, working for the Terminal Railroad Association in St. Louis, where he died of heart disease in 1910, at the age of 45.

[456] Signatures are cropped from the Northern Pacific Railroad employment folder #51387. Original records housed at the Minnesota Historical Society, St. Paul. Also accessible online at Ancestry.com.

Some circumstances hint at communication between the two, and possibly point to collusion. First, there was the timing of Willis's application to the N.P. on September 10, 1897, at almost the same time that Steele exited railroading. Then there was the coincidence of Steele applying to the company right after Willis returned from a trip that took him close to Steele's home at Carbon Hill, Alabama.[457] An indication that Steele may have known about Willis's secret is his listing on his application of the exact date of his departure from the Oregon Short Line — September 13, 1897 — possibly a hint that it could not have been he who had applied to the N.P. on September 10. I mean, who does that on a job application, in only one place, two years later? All the other job changes in his work history were specific only to the month. He also listed the American Surety Company, along with the National Surety Company, as his bonding agencies. These weak gestures may indicate that the real Steele was trying to differentiate himself from the one who already worked for the N.P., or to get them to check with a different agency, and so was in on the scam.

On the other hand, Steele had a young family to support in 1899, and one would think that would have kept him from playing pointless games with his employment. He was also generally known to be an honest employee. For Willis's part, if he really put this deception together, it would show more planning of his escapades than he had demonstrated previously, at Owingsville and Lexington. Willis's motto, as we know, was "the only way to keep a secret is never to let any one suspect that you have one," and if he didn't orchestrate Steele's application, he would have been laughing up his sleeve to discover that his old friend had also joined the N.P., but that his secret was still safe. He thrived on chaotic, complex confusions, especially those of his own making.

Despite his motto, keeping his identity a secret does not seem to have been his main objective in spring/summer 1899, as evidenced by some of his conduct at Red Lake Falls, and also by our second coincidence. In July, almost two months after Steele's hiring, the N.P. hired another Bethel as a station agent/operator. Rossco Conkling Bethel was Willis's second cousin.[458] Like Willis, he was born in southern Harrison County, Ohio, although in 1878, making him eighteen years younger. It's possible that both Willis and George Smith Bethel were long-time influences on the young man, and he may have learned telegraphy from one or both of them. He began his agent/operator career at age 19, working for the Cleveland, Lorain & Wheeling Railroad, the same line (having been renamed in the interim) where Willis started. But he soon went to the booming northern Midwest, serving at various stops in Illinois, Wisconsin, and Minnesota. In early summer 1899, he was in St. Paul, working for

---

457 Carbon Hill, Alabama, where Steele worked, was easily reachable from any of the three southern cities (Memphis, New Orleans, and Asheboro) mentioned as part of Willis's and Chrestine's itinerary. The first coincidence might be explained by Willis and Steele still being in letter communication, but the fact that Steele applied to the N.P. when he did makes the timing suspicious.

458 Rossco Conkling Bethel was the son of David Ridgely Bethel, who was the son of Braudus Bethel, Willis's grandfather Norris Bethel's older brother. Willis's and Ross's common ancestor was their great-grandfather, the family patriarch, Henry Bethel.

the Great Northern, and on July 10 he applied to the Northern Pacific.[459]

While it's unknown if Willis invited the real J.P. Steele to join him on the N.P., it is almost certain that R.C. Bethel came to the company with his encouragement. Greene had him take the operator's test (he was rated "about average"), and then stationed him at a temporary post at Grand Forks, North Dakota, about 40 miles from Red Lake Falls, also in the Manitoba Division.[460] The appointment came to an end three weeks later, and Ross (as he was known) requested to be allowed to go to Red Lake Falls and stay with Willis until something else opened up for him. A telegram from O.C. Greene to F.E. Potter, the Division Operator at Winnipeg, makes it clear that their relationship was no secret.

[461]

Transcription: Aug 4 – 99. To: F. E. Potter, Wpg (Winnipeg), Bethel goes to Red Lake Falls tonight to wait until you can use him. Agt. Steele is a cousin. O.C. Greene

To welcome his cousin to town, Willis made sure to have a conversation about him with the editor of the Red Lake Falls Gazette.

---

459 Northern Pacific Railroad employment records of Rossco Conkling Bethel, folder #62205, July 10, 1899, Original records housed at the Minnesota Historical Society, St. Paul. Also accessible online at Ancestry.com; 1880 U.S. census, David R. Bethel family, Freeport, Harrison County, Ohio, Ancestry.com.

460 Northern Pacific Railroad employment records for Rossco Conkling Bethel, July 10, 1899, folder #62205, p. 46. Original records housed at the Minnesota Historical Society, St. Paul. Also accessible online at Ancestry.com.

461 Ibid., p. 34.

> R. C. Bethelweet, a cousin of J. P. Steel, our N. P. station agent, arrived in the city yesterday on a brief visit.[462]

Transcription: R.C. Bethelweet, a cousin of J.P. Steel [sic], our N.P. station agent, arrived in the city yesterday on a brief visit.

Either the adulteration of their common surname was an inside joke with Ross, or Willis was playing games with the editor.[463] This was neither the first nor last time he told the Gazette's Phil Kaufer that a visitor's name was something other than what it was. Two weeks earlier, on July 20, he had told Kaufer that his visiting father-in-law's name was "Jacob Therebuy," instead of John Tyberg.[464] He was handing out aliases to everyone.

J.P. Tyberg's trip to see his son-in-law and stepdaughter in Red Lake Falls must have coincided with Chrestine's departure to the farm in North Carolina. We know that the Tybergs worked the acreage in 1899, and that Chrestine gave birth to Herbert Benjamin there in October.[465] Since she was six months pregnant in late July, it's almost certain that at least one member of her family escorted her. Willis's renaming antics with editor Kaufer began with the July 20 issue, right after "Jacob Therebuy" and Chrestine headed south. He must have felt free to be his old mischievous self again as soon as his wife and father-in-law left town.

Somewhat strangely, given those circumstances, he was the subject of only a couple of minor items in Kaufer's paper in fall 1899. Maybe he was chatting more with John King, the editor of the Red Lake Falls Courier, whose newspapers are now lost. But Kaufer's paper did cover J.P. Steele's big news of the year, in its November 2 issue:

> On Thursday, the 26th ult., our popular N.P. station agent, J.P. Steele, received a telegraphic message from Ashboro, [sic] N. C., to the effect that J.P. Steele

---

462 The Red Lake Falls Gazette, August 3, 1899, p. 4, microfilm from MNHS.
463 Rossco Conkling Bethel crossed paths with his cousin several more times before Willis finally left Minnesota, and his presence created some interesting situations. In late August, Potter again called on him, and stationed him in North Dakota. He was back in Red Lake Falls in January 1900 to relieve Willis while the latter took a trip to North Carolina. Over the next few months, the N.P. moved him to various points in North Dakota and Minnesota, and in September he was assigned to temporarily replace the agent at Gary who had replaced Willis. He received the permanent position at Gary in November 1900. With Chrestine still coming and going from the area by train when she visited her family, there may have been some awkward moments. Ross remained at Gary through 1903, and like his cousin he made the local news often. At 6'-1 1/2" and left-handed, he was an imposing pitcher on the Gary baseball team, and from all accounts he was well-liked in the town. He captained several stations in the area, including the nearby towns of Fertile, Mahnomen, and Bemidji, during his long career with the Northern Pacific, which included re-employment after participation in the operator's strike in 1905. In 1912, his wife Anna died after giving birth to their third child. Ross seems to have taken a break from railroad work around that time, and for a number of years he tried his hand as a merchant in Morrison County, but he returned to station work in his 40's. His older sister Maude, who remained single throughout her life, lived with him, and helped him raise his children. He died in Bemidji in 1942 at the age of 63.
464 The Red Lake Falls Gazette, July 20, 1899, p. 2, microfilm from MNHS.
465 The Gary Graphic, March 31, 1900, p. 5; The Red Lake Falls Gazette, February 5, 1900, p. 3, both from microfilm from the Minnesota Historical Society, St. Paul; All official records of Herbert Benjamin Steele's life list his birthplace as Asheboro, North Carolina.

Jr. had that day made his bow to the world. Mr. Steele feels a little proud of the fact but still in his good natured way continues to speak to people less fortunate.[466]

The Gazette referred to Joe and Chrestine's child three times over the next six months, calling him J.P. Steele, Jr., Little Joe, and Joe Steele, Jr.[467] Herbert must have originally been named Joseph after his father (or, more precisely, after his father's old friend), and Chrestine probably changed the name after Willis was no longer in the picture.[468] North Carolina did not require birth registrations prior to 1913, and there are no contemporary newspapers available from the area, so there is no way to know for sure.[469]

Despite the relative dearth of coverage, Willis must have realized that he had a valuable, gullible mark on his side in Kaufer, and he worked a few angles to ingratiate himself. On November 30, the following item appeared:

> J. P. Steele, the genial Northern Pacific station agent, is a philanthropist as well as a first class railroad man—as evidenced by the fine dressed gobbler he presented the editor for the Thanksgiving dinner. May his kind increase, for a soft berth is reserved for such as he in the editor's heart.[470]

Transcription: J.P. Steele, the genial Northern Pacific station agent, is a philanthropist as well as a first class railroad man — as evidenced by the fine dressed gobbler he presented the editor for the Thanksgiving dinner. May his kind increase, for a soft berth is reserved for such as he in the editor's heart.

It paid off. Later stories in the Gazette demonstrated the editor's ongoing lack of critical thinking skills and his willingness to believe whatever information Willis fed him. Unlike at Owingsville, where things got out of control, he was now a master at manipulating the press and controlling his image.

The December 14 issue of the Gazette reported that he would make a trip to North Carolina to see his latest child "in the course of a month."[471] But before he went, in the December 28 issue, he gave the editor one last alias to publish, and this one was the finest of them all:

---

466 The Red Lake Falls Gazette, November 2, 1899, p. 3, microfilm from MNHS.
467 Ibid.; also, December 14, 1899, p. 5; May 10, 1900.
468 Chrestine's divorce deposition, made in March 1901, when her son was sixteen months old, lists his name as Herbert Benjamin Steele.
469 Information about North Carolina birth records comes from North Carolina, U.S. Birth Indexes, 1800-2000, Ancestry.com.
470 The Red Lake Falls Gazette, November 30, 1899, p. 3, microfilm from MNHS.
471 Ibid., p. 5.

> D. W. Bethel and G. B. Ogsburg, traveling auditors of the N.P., were here making one of their periodical checks of the station and express accounts Wednesday and Thursday[472]

Transcription: D.W. Bethel and G.B. Ogsburg [sic], traveling auditors of the N.P., were here making one of their periodical checks of the station and express accounts Wednesday and Thursday.

Well, we know that he had always wanted to be an auditor. The traveling auditors often worked in teams of two on the N.P., and Gurdon B. Ogsbury, a station agent who also served in the company's accounting wing, was well known in the region. We don't know the real name of the accountant Willis bestowed the honor of wearing his own given moniker (maybe it was the real J.P. Steele? Not possible, just kidding), but he was clearly giving the man a tremendous compliment.

On January 4, the Gazette reported that Ross was in town to fill in for Willis at the depot, and he left, ostensibly for Asheboro, to see Chrestine and "Little Joe."[473] We know that he was back in Red Lake Falls before January 15.[474]

It should come as no surprise to anyone that, in addition to being a wannabe auditor, Willis also harbored theatrical pretensions, and he must have come back to a busy schedule. He was cast in a local musical production, *Esther, the Beautiful Queen*. The cantata's two-day run in Red Lake Falls, "produced entirely by local talent" under a traveling director from Chicago, opened on January 26, 1900. The Gazette only mentioned the production once, on January 25, with the ringing endorsement, "Through the cooperation of Red Lake Falls' musical people a cast of characters of fair ability is presented."[475] There is no record of which character in the biblical drama Willis played, and, probably mercifully, no review or further mention of the musical was published in the Gazette. Other than getting to laugh at their neighbors' lack of singing ability, I'm betting it was a terrible experience for most of the townsfolk who paid the 35-cent admission.

Beginning in early January, hints had appeared in the Gazette that Willis was trying to get farmers in the area to buy land in Randolph County, North Carolina. Several men went south to check the place out, and at least two Red Lake Falls area residents, Fred Gooding and N.P. Nelson, bought property near Willis's farm.[476] Nelson moved his family to the area and remained there for the rest of his life. He reported that his yields were excellent.

---

472 The Red Lake Falls Gazette, December 28, 1899, p. 4, microfilm from MNHS.
473 The Red Lake Falls Gazette, January 4, 1900, p. 3, microfilm from MNHS.
474 The Red Lake Falls Gazette, January 18, 1900, p. 3, microfilm from MNHS. This issue of the paper, which was published on Thursdays, reported that Ross Bethel had gone home to Ohio for a visit the previous Monday.
475 The Red Lake Falls Gazette, January 25, 1900, p. 3, microfilm from MNHS.
476 The Red Lake Falls Gazette, January 4, 1900, p. 3; February 22, 1900, p. 5; The Red Lake Falls Gazette, May 31, 1900, p. 3, microfilm from MNHS. Kaufer reported that Nelson bought about 130 acres near Asheboro. Nelson and his family lived in the area for the rest of his life, buying and selling many other properties in the Asheboro area before his death in 1911.

But the Tybergs did not share that view, calling the land "so poor they couldn't see their way clear to making a living" upon their return in March 1900.[477] Maybe their assessment of the land was actually a reflection of their opinion of the landowner. Their reasons would have dated from the previous month, when Chrestine had come back north, nursing both her four-month-old baby and a serious case of wifely anger.

In her divorce deposition the following year, she claimed that she first discovered Willis's bigamy "in February 1900," when she found some letters from "his first wife" . . . "in defendant's possession." It's possible that Willis left some items, including the letters, at the farm in early January. Or, Chrestine may have discovered them in his things after her return to Red Lake Falls. The truth of their discovery is unknown, and it's possible that Willis planted them for her to find. The deposition also reveals that the 'first' wife had come to Gary looking for Willis in February 1900. A little surprisingly, we have not met her yet. According to Chrestine, her name was Gertrude. Gertrude Bethel.[478]

Just to recap, the first names of Willis's other wives to this point (that we know of) were Jennie, Nettie, Matilda, Minnie, and Annie. There is no record of any marriage to Gertrude in the online archives that have been published, at least as of 2021.

Chrestine arrived in Red Lake Falls on February 13, and Gary's new newspaper, the Graphic, reported her passage through town.[479] I'm sure that Willis tried to calm her down and regain control of the situation, but she wasn't having any of it, and by the 21st she had returned to Gary, staying with Gust and Mathilda Saker.[480] The Sakers were Swedish immigrants, newlyweds in their early thirties, who like Chrestine had just welcomed their first child. Like Willis, Gust worked for the Northern Pacific as the section foreman at Gary, but that's where the similarities ended.[481] Similar to the Fishers some ten years earlier, his working-class background and hardscrabble immigrant experiences must have made him distrustful of fast-talking smoothies like J.P. Steele. It's possible, even likely, that Gust, working as he did out of the Gary station, was the source of the information that Gertrude Bethel had been nosing around looking for Willis. Chrestine and her son probably remained with the Sakers through the month of March, when, as mentioned earlier, the Tybergs returned to the north country.

Kaufer's paper had characterized the reason for Chrestine's abrupt departure in February, so soon after her arrival, as visiting "with old time acquaintances."[482] The editor, like others before him (W. A. Hunt, W. S. Wise) was the station agent's willing dupe by this time, and he

---

477 The Gary Graphic, March 31, 1900, p. 5, microfilm from MNHS.
478 State of Minnesota, County of Norman, District Court case #2698-4-201. Chrestine Hendricks, Plaintiff vs. Joe Steele, also known as Dave Bethel, Defendant, 1901. Deposition, pp. 2-5. The only evidence we have of Gertrude's identity comes from this deposition. Chrestine, in her Nordic way, referred to the woman as "Gertrid." I have anglicized the name in this book, since that is how it appeared in later references in the court documents.
479 The Gary Graphic, February 17, 1900, p. 5; The Red Lake Falls Gazette, February 15, p. 3, both from microfilm from MNHS.
480 The Twin Valley Times, Gary news, February 21, 1900, p. 4, microfilm from MNHS.
481 Northern Pacific Railroad employment records for Gust Saker, folder #15728. Original records housed at the Minnesota Historical Society, St. Paul. Also accessible online at Ancestry.com. Section foremen oversaw local construction projects and headed the crew that maintained the track between stations.
482 The Red Lake Falls Gazette, March 1, 1900, p.5, microfilm from MNHS.

reported it with a straight face, even though the couple had been living apart for about half of their first year of wedded bliss. Attentive readers might have wondered at the quality of a marriage that thrived on separation.

Willis, meanwhile, seemingly unconcerned, was living life as normal in Red Lake Falls. The only report of his doings came on March 15, when the Gazette related that he had made a Saturday trip to Grand Forks, evidently another stop on the traveling director's circuit, to see the cantata in which he had acted two months earlier. He told Kaufer that "he could not see much of the grandeur of the play when it was shown here, he being one of the characters."[483]

That was how things stood in 1900 as the Minnesota winter gradually gave way to spring — Chrestine in Gary, wondering how to proceed with her fractured life, while Willis went on as usual 40 miles up the track in Red Lake Falls. She had the evidence and the motivation to sue him for divorce and damages, and to have him arrested for bigamy, but she demurred. And in a strange lull in the action, he made no immediate move. He continued to leave himself exposed, daring someone to catch him.

That attitude lasted until May 9. The following redundant piece appeared in the Gazette the next day:

> J. P. Steele, the popular N. P. station agent, started yesterday on his trip to Asheboro, N. C., which he has had in contemplation for some time. He will be gone until about the first of June, during which time he expects to get acquainted with Joe Steele Jr., whom he has not yet had the pleasure of meeting. Mr Steele will be joined in St. Paul by N. P. Nelson and Joe Dwyer, who are looking up locations as neighbors to Steele's plantation in North Carolina.[484]

Transcription: J.P. Steele, the popular N.P. station agent, started yesterday on his trip to Asheboro, N.C., which he has had in contemplation for some time. He will be gone until about the first of June, during which time he expects to get acquainted with Joe Steele Jr., who he has not yet had the pleasure of meeting. Mr. Steele will be joined in St. Paul by N.P. Nelson and Joe Dwyer, who are looking up locations as neighbors to Steele's plantation in North Carolina.

I wonder if Kaufer had an eerie sense of déjà vu when he published this garbage. Willis had already gone to North Carolina to see his son the previous winter, after all, or at least, he said he did. Three months earlier, the Gazette had published the news of Chrestine's return to Minnesota, and the Tybergs had returned in March. Nobody was at the farm in May 1900. Willis, Dwyer, and Nelson likely stayed there while the latter two looked for land, and the Gazette reported that Nelson purchased his farm in late May.[485]

---

483 The Red Lake Falls Gazette, March 15, 1900, p. 3, microfilm from MNHS.
484 The Red Lake Falls Gazette, May 10, 1900, p. 3, microfilm from MNHS.
485 The Red Lake Falls Gazette, May 31, 1900, p. 3, microfilm from MNHS.

Despite the paper's stated expectation that Willis would be back by June 1, it turned out that he was done with Red Lake Falls, and with the Northern Pacific. On May 24, Kaufer announced that J.P. Steele had officially resigned his post. His whereabouts for the next six months remain unknown. Maybe he went somewhere to try to patch things up with Gertrude.

Somewhat strangely, given her situation, Chrestine was also on the move. Later that spring, on June 6, she was living in Duluth, unencumbered by her child, where she worked as a domestic, a "second girl," in the home of Ignatz Freimuth, a successful department store owner with a large family. Freimuth was an important figure in the burgeoning city at the time, and it's unknown how she secured the appointment. Young Herbert, only six months old, must have remained in the Gary area with the Tybergs.[486] Chrestine probably wanted a fresh start, and her baby may have been a painful reminder of her association with Willis, but this is our first glimpse of the me-first behavior that would increasingly characterize her life going forward. She was probably coming under the spell of the demons — substance abuse supported by revelry — that would later consume her, and it appears that she largely abandoned her son's care to her mother and stepfather. Over the next few years there were several references to her residence in the Duluth area, doing domestic work, and occasionally visiting her son and birth family in Norman County. There were also periods when she lived "with her parents in the eastern part of the county."[487] Willis's departure seemingly meant that any opportunity to make him pay for his deceit had eluded her. But that was about to change.

On November 15, the Bemidji Pioneer reported that Willis, still going by the name Joseph Patterson Steele, was back with his first Minnesota employer, the Great Northern, and in charge of the Bemidji station.[488] The G.N. management evidently saw no resemblance between J.P. Steele and Dillon Bechtel, the man who had worked for them at Fosston, about 45 miles down the line, three years earlier. He was probably one of the few people ever hired twice by the same company under two different aliases. On hearing the news Chrestine, no doubt spurred on by her parents and friends, retained the law firm of Moen and Matson, out of Ada, and filed suit. Peter Matson, a newly minted attorney and the firm's junior partner, personally served Willis with a summons on January 28, 1901.[489] It gave him twenty days to respond.[490]

When news of the case hit the press in late February/early March, it was a regional sensation, published in papers from Huron, South Dakota to Minneapolis. Most of the stories were

---

486 U.S. census, 1900, Duluth, St. Louis County, Minnesota, Ignatz Freimuth family, Ancestry.com. The page of the census is dated June 6, 1900. There is no record in it of Herbert living with Chrestine in Duluth, and her employers would not have wanted their servant to have a baby in the house, anyway. Herbert is not recorded as living with the Sakers, although it is possible that he was just missed by the census taker. The Tybergs dodged the 1900 census, and it seems likely that they were caring for their grandson, even at his young age, as best they could.
487 The Gary Graphic, September 29, 1900, p. 5; The Gary Graphic, February 27, 1903, p. 5; The Gary Graphic, August 14, 1903, p. 5; The Gary Graphic, October 16, 1903, p. 5, all microfilm from MNHS.
488 The Bemidji Pioneer, November 15, 1900, Newspapers.com; The Red Lake Falls Gazette, November 22, 1900, p. 5, microfilm from MNHS.
489 State of Minnesota, County of Norman, District Court case #2698-4-201. Chrestine Hendricks, Plaintiff vs. Joe Steele, also known as Dave Bethel, Defendant, 1901. Summons and Complaint, p. 1
490 Ibid., p. 2

identical, boiler plate write-ups that circulated over the wires. Kaufer went with this option in his paper's account on March 7, rather than personalizing the story about his friend.

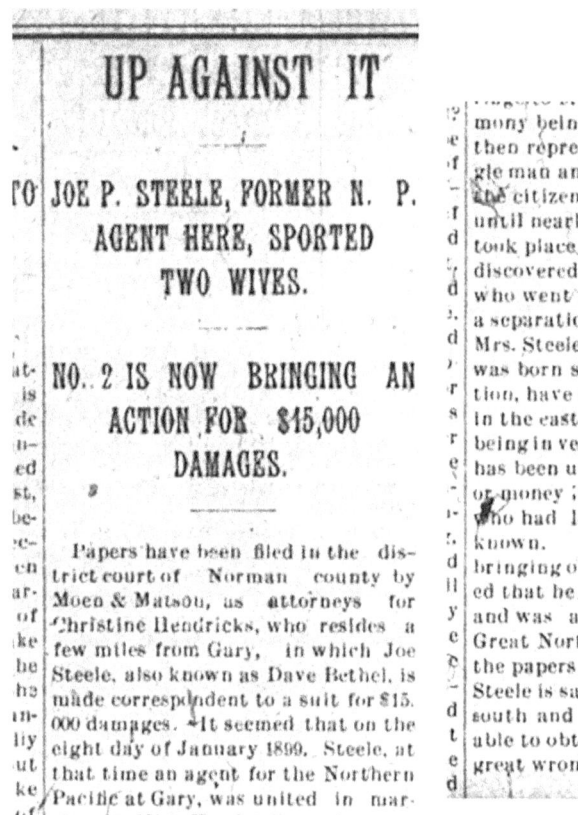

Transcription: Papers have been filed in the district court of Norman County by Moen & Matson, as attorneys for Christine Hendricks, who resides a few miles from Gary, in which Joe Steele, also known as Dave Bethel, is made correspondent to a suit for $15,000 damages. It seemed that on the eight [sic] day of January 1899, Steele, at that time an agent for the Northern Pacific at Gary, was united in marriage to Miss Hendricks, the ceremony being performed at Ada. He then represented himself to be a single man and passed as such among the citizens of Gary, and it was not until nearly a year after the marriage took place that the then Mrs. Steele discovered that he had another wife who went by the name of Bethel, and a separation followed. Since then Mrs. Steele, along with her son, which was born shortly before the separation, have resided with her parents in the eastern part of the county and being in very moderate circumstances has been unable to spend either time or money in an effort to locate Steele who had left Gary for parts unknown. A few days prior to the bringing of this action, it was learned that he had returned to the state and was acting as agent for the Great Northern at Bemidji, where the papers were served on him. Steele is said to have property in the south and Miss Hendricks may be able to obtain some redress for the great wrong done her.

---

491 The Red Lake Falls Gazette, March 7, 1901, p. 1, microfilm from MNHS.

Kaufer's competition at the Red Lake Falls Courier, however, had some juicier details that are worth sharing. Unfortunately, copies of the Courier from 1900-1901 are unavailable today, but luckily for us, the Norman County Index eschewed the story from the wires and reprinted the Courier's account, along with an addendum from the Crookston Times, on March 14:

A SMOOTH ONE.

J. P. Steele, Formerly of Gary, Turns Out to be One of The Best in the Business.

Just at present J. P. Steele, formerly of this city, is greatly in demand, even more so than when he was N. P. station agent here. His wife (for one of them) who resides at Gary, Minn., has sued him for $15,000 damages, alleging that he is a gay deceiver. She also alleges that he has been married before under the name of Dave Bethel; that his former wife was living and not divorced at the time he wedded the young lady from Gary. It has developed that Steele is a man with a history. His experiences have been many and varied. He has traveled in nearly every walk in life. He has a physician's diploma under the name of Dr. Tucker. At one time he studied for the ministry and is by education better qualified to hold forth than many who now occupy pulpits. But evidently a long spell of goodness conflicted with his morals, or lack of them. At another time he rose high in the councils of the Mexican Central R. R. Co. becoming Assistant Superintendent. Trouble with a conductor resulting in a shooting caused him to seek a cooler climate in the north. East, west, south and north have been alike, a field for his endeavor and a friendly public have always been ready to welcome him—for a time. It is said that wherever he has gone the ladies have been especially eager to lend a willing ear to his beguiling tongue—and have rued it later. While at Red Lake Falls his smooth, ingratiating ways made him many friends and he moved in good society. Recently he has been station agent at Bemidji but his present whereabouts are unknown.—Red Lake Falls Courier.

The people on the east say that while J. P. Steele, the man who is wanted for marrying a Norman county girl, when he already had a wife, was station agent at Bemidji, he did not conduct himself in a manner to land him in the office of deacon in any of the churches, his last official act being to appropriate for expense money, $40 deposited with him for a ticket to Spokane.—Crookston Times. [492]

Transcription: Just at present J.P. Steele, formerly of this city, is greatly in demand, even more so than when he was N.P. station agent here. His wife (for one of them) who resides at Gary, Minn., has sued him for $15,000 damages, alleging that he is a gay deceiver. She also alleges that he has been married before under the name of Dave Bethel; that his former wife was living and not divorced at the time he wedded the young lady from Gary. It has developed that Steele is a man with a history. His experiences have been many and varied. He has traveled in nearly every walk in life. He has a physician's diploma under the name of Dr. Tucker.

At one time he studied for the ministry and is by education better qualified to hold forth than many who now occupy pulpits. But evidently a long spell of goodness conflicted with his morals, or lack of them. At

---

[492] The Norman County Index, March 14, 1901, p. 1, microfilm from MNHS.

another time he rose high in the councils of the Mexican Central R.R. Co. becoming Assistant Superintendent. Trouble with a conductor resulting in a shooting caused him to seek a cooler climate in the north. East, west, south and north have been alike, a field for his endeavor and a friendly public have always been ready to welcome him — for a time. It is said that wherever he has gone the ladies have been especially eager to lend a willing ear to his beguiling tongue — and have rued it later. While at Red Lake Falls his smooth, ingratiating ways made him many friends and he moved in good society. Recently he has been station agent at Bemidji but his present whereabouts are unknown. — Red Lake Falls Courier

The people on the east say that while J.P. Steele, the man who is wanted for marrying a Norman county girl, when he already had a wife, was station agent at Bemidji, he did not conduct himself in a manner to land him in the office of deacon in any of the churches, his last official act being to appropriate for expense money, $40 deposited with him for a ticket to Spokane. — Crookston Times.

The tone of this account, calling him "a smooth one," "one of the best in the business," and "a gay deceiver," is almost admiring. Willis must have had much more interesting conversations with John E. King, the Courier's editor, who may have harbored a secret desire to live as free of responsibility as did Willis, than he did with the straitlaced and gullible Kaufer. It is from this source that we get our information that he had been with the Mexican Central in early 1897. It's doubtful that he was Assistant Superintendent of the road, though. And there is no verification of his story about "trouble with a conductor resulting in a shooting" that chased him from Mexico, although that didn't stop me from adapting those particulars into the fictional piece that precedes Chapter 9.

Clearly, Willis had a plan of action if Chrestine filed suit. In fact, he may have returned to Minnesota using the Steele alias just to bring about this result, in an ultimate display of bravado. On February 7, ten days after Matson delivered the summons with its twenty-day deadline, and about a month before the case was publicized, the Bemidji Pioneer ran the following item:

> Station Agent J. P. Steele severs his connections with the Great Northern this week and goes to his old home in North Carolina. Mr. Douglas, of Butte, Mont., has been assigned to this station. [493]

Transcription: Station Agent J.P. Steele severs his connections with the Great Northern this week and goes to his old home in North Carolina. Mr. Douglas, of Butte, Mont., has been assigned to this station.

For once, he told the editor the truth, and he headed straight for Asheboro, but only to get what he could for the acreage there. On February 11, only four days after the Pioneer's announcement, he sold his interest to Ida C. Nelson, N.P.'s daughter, and got his $300 back.[494] He may have had an arrangement with her already in the works. As for the mortgage Willis

---

493 The Bemidji Pioneer, February 7, 1901, p. 9, Newspapers.com.
494 Randolph County North Carolina Register of Deeds, Book 99, pp. 440-441.

and Chrestine had signed financing two-thirds of the price of the property, it was foreclosed upon later that year, in July, with the missing of the final payment.

Joe Steele/Dave Bethel was somebody else by the time Chrestine gave her deposition on March 5. Like Annie's lawsuit the following year, her testimony reveals a naïve young woman who had been welcomed to the adult world in an exceptionally rude manner. A special term of the district court, convened at Crookston, decided the case in Chrestine's favor on March 8 and awarded her custody of Herbert Benjamin and $7,500 plus costs.[495] In theory. In actuality, all she got out of it was her maiden name.[496]

Willis's Minnesota excursion was his first experiment with living an absolute lie, and it raises a number of questions.[497] First, since his real identity was no secret to some people, like his cousin Ross, how many others were in on it, and how much did they know? We know that William and Mary Bethel maintained enough contact with their son to know that he was still alive, and they were probably aware of his whereabouts and more. Did others of his extended family and his many friends across the country know what he was doing? If I were to guess, I would say the number was higher than we would think, and that a code of silence, and possibly secret admiration, kept anyone from saying anything. It's worth remembering that this era in American history was characterized by an upswell of antiauthoritarianism, and a healthy distrust of the robber baron class (which the railroads epitomized in the eyes of many) may have contributed to his ability to keep his identity a secret for so long.

And who was Gertrude? We know that he married her under his given name, so it's likely that she entered the picture before he became Dillon Bechtel at Fosston in June 1897. She may have been the 'Mrs. David Bethel' from Canada, but we also know that Willis spent time in Mexico in early 1897, and we have no information about his time in Rincon, New Mexico from July through September 1896. It makes sense that the marriage took place at one of those times and places. Gertrude is a Germanic name, and there was a growing German community in Mexico, and in the southwestern U.S., at the time. It will be interesting to see if any records ever emerge to clarify things. So many wives, so few answers.[498]

---

495 State of Minnesota, County of Norman, District Court case #2698-4-201. Chrestine Hendricks, Plaintiff vs. Joe Steele, also known as Dave Bethel, Defendant, 1901. Judgment book, p. 557. This document is the first mention we have of Herbert Benjamin Steele's name.

496 State of Minnesota, County of Norman, District Court case #2699-4-202. Chrestine Hendricks, Plaintiff vs. Joe Steele, also known as Dave Bethel, Defendant, 1901, Findings and Decree.

497 It was also the one stop in his career where he exercised complete control of the situation.

498 No record of the Canadian marriage is available, and the only information we have about the Mrs. David Bethel in Innisfil comes from the census conducted on April 11, 1901. At that time, she was 40 years old, about the same age as Willis. Even though she was the only person living in the dwelling, the information may have come from another (a neighbor, for example), because the date and year of her birth are listed as "Don't Know," odd considering that her age was designated. The census related that she was a Methodist. Innisfil was a railroad town on the western shore of Lake Simcoe. Lumber (year-round) and ice (in the winter) were harvested and moved to various points, mainly south to Toronto and west to Michigan and beyond (Andrew Frederick Hunter, *A History of Simcoe County*, pp. 317-318). It's possible that Willis picked up some temporary work across the border in 1896 or 1897 and married her in one of his typical whirlwind romances. Given his continuous presence in Minnesota from 1897 through early 1901, and his documented presence in Perris until May 1896, there was really no other opportunity for this union, unless it came from years earlier (1892-1893, for example), which seems unlikely. He was obviously long gone by the time of the census of 1901, and not expected to return, since "Mrs. David Bethel" was listed as the head, and only member, of her household. The woman had disappeared by the 1911 census and is not found in any other existing records.

A question I continually asked while researching these chapters was how he got away with his deceptions. They were so many and so blatant, and he dropped enough clues that his identity was false, it seems that someone along the way should have noticed. He changed aliases and remained in the same general area, freely interacting with people in his charming way, yet nobody ever knew, even though these were small, rural towns with plenty of commerce between them. Abrupt name changes tend to be difficult to explain, but as far as we know, he never had to try. He mentioned his own real name at least twice — once on his N.P. application in 1897 and again in Kaufer's Gazette in late 1899, yet nobody knew it until Chrestine's divorce suit in 1901. He went out of his way to add complications to the situation, inviting Ross Bethel's application to the N.P. and possibly orchestrating the real Steele's, yet neither event resulted in his apprehension. Chrestine's discovery of letters from Gertrude should have sent him running, yet he remained in Red Lake Falls for three months, daring her to report him to the law. And he returned to Bemidji six months later, after he had already escaped, again going through a hiring process with the Great Northern that could have revealed his identity, or at least his first alias. Even after he was served with notice of Chrestine's divorce filing, and threatened with the inevitable revelations it would bring, he remained in Bemidji for ten days.

It all points to a man who was taunting his marks, purposely baiting any and all authorities to discover his frauds. But he also wanted to get away, laughing all the way out of town. It seems likely that he had his new identity, like a getaway car, all ready and waiting, and he simply hopped into it in February 1901 and disappeared. The fact that he moved on from Minnesota unscathed after almost four years of play-acting probably confirmed in his mind that he was the smartest guy out there. He must have felt vindicated after all the terrible injustices, from his point of view, that D.W. Bethel had suffered at the hands of trotting registries, railroad and bonding companies, and by extension, his many wives.

Five years earlier, at Owingsville, his last big con, he had played things more spontaneously, and his schemes failed because he didn't take into account the ripple effects of his actions and couldn't maintain a poker face. He had not attempted a big scam since (that we know of), but the decisions by the National Surety Company and the A.T.S.F. must have motivated him to get back into the conning game and to do it right this time. Unlike his time in Kentucky, when things quickly got out of hand, Willis exercised control over the Minnesota situation throughout his time there. Better planning certainly played into his success, and it also appears that he just got lucky at times. A laughing countenance and a devil-may-care attitude insulate many sociopaths from the consequences of their actions.

Finally, maybe most importantly, where did he get his money? In his letters to Nettie in early 1897, he claimed that he was almost broke because of his bonding issues, and the only work he could get was low-paying, as a temporary operator.[499] Adopting the alias of J.P. Steele allowed him to get full time employment, but because pay on the N.P. was notoriously low, and station agents could only skim so much before the auditors got wise, it probably didn't help him much. Adjusted for inflation, his salary was the equivalent of between $15,000 and

---

499 Letters, D.W. Bethel to Joannetta Fisher #14, May 2, 1897, and #16, May 16, 1897, from Fisher family papers.

$20,000 per year in today's money, hardly cash you could flash, even allowing for a little extra income from a skim or two.[500] We know that he spent lavishly when he wanted to — the banquet at Ulen must have cost some money, he paid $300 in cash in 1899 to purchase the farm in North Carolina, and he must have made another $300 payment on the mortgage for the place in 1900. He represented himself as a wealthy man to Chrestine, and probably to everybody else, and that would have required a show of resources from time to time. He may have lived on credit, although there is no record of creditors pursuing him. It's worth noting that Minnesota at the time was not far removed from the Old West, and there were many reports in the papers of unsolved thefts, robberies, and murders for the purpose of robbery in nearby areas during all of Willis's Minnesota stops. Was he responsible for any of those? It's an interesting question that would take our view of him to a different level if it could be ascertained. To be clear, I have no evidence that he committed any crimes more violent than those we are exploring in this book. But he had to get his money somehow.

---

500 Inflation calculator, westegg.com/inflation/.

12.

Dr. George Wilson McGuire

■ THE DNA MATCH THAT FIRST REVEALED WILLIS'S PRESENCE AFTER SEPTEMBER 1897 had come along in spring 2018, when Caitlin showed up on my list of cousins. As we corresponded, it became clear that her great-grandfather, George Wilson McGuire, was the same man as my great-grandfather, David Wilson Bethel. Her grandfather, Marcus Wilson McGuire, was born in the Oklahoma Indian Territories in 1903.

Like Joseph Patterson Steele, George W. McGuire was a stolen, not an invented, alias, but Willis added his own personal touch to this one. He had known George *Walker* McGuire at least since the early 1880s, and possibly before, and both worked as a telegraphers in the same office at some point.[501] Born in 1857, George's early life was spent on a farm in Guernsey County, right across the Belmont County line from Flushing.[502] He was orphaned around age ten, and Joseph Bailey, a Quaker farmer who lived near Flushing, assumed guardianship duties for him.[503] George considered Flushing his hometown and he felt an attachment to the strong community of Friends there, of which David Deselms, Willis's step-grandfather, had been a member. An industrious student, he graduated from Miami Valley College, a Quaker school near Dayton, in 1877. He then matriculated to Case Western Reserve Medical School.[504] His official graduation date was in 1881, but we find him already listed as a physician in Flushing in the 1880 census.[505] Fifteen pages away is 20-year-old David Wilson Bethel, a garrulous local schoolteacher.[506] In the 1880s, George moved right on top of Willis's roots, to the village of Rock Hill, where he became a prominent local figure, active in Republican politics. He even ran for Belmont County coroner in 1887.[507]

---

501 The Shawnee News, October 25, 1907, Newspapers.com. This information comes from a later letter, relayed in Oklahoma newspapers in 1907. We don't know if they worked together in the early 1880s, when Willis and George were young men not yet established in career paths, or in the early 1890s, when George was leaving medicine and Willis was in transition after losing his position in Lexington with the Kentucky Union.

502 1860 U.S. census, John McGuire family, Londonderry Township, Guernsey County, Ohio, Ancestry.com. This census is the only record we have of George's childhood, when he was three years old. The other three members of the household were John (age 64), Anna (44), and Rachel (19). George could have been John and Anna's son, but it seems more likely that he was Rachel's illegitimate offspring. No other records provide any clarity about his birth situation.

503 *Probate Court,* The Belmont Chronicle, February 25, 1875, Newspapers.com. Willis's step-grandfather, David Deselms, was active in the Quaker community in Flushing, and Bailey and he may have met early in life.

504 The information about George's education comes from an email from Julia Teran, Archivist, Case Western Reserve University Archives, to Charles Caldemeyer, November 6, 2019.

505 24JI 4, George Walker McGuire, MED1881, documents, Case Western Reserve University Archives.

506 U.S. census, 1880, George W. McGuire, Flushing village, Belmont County, Ohio, p. 30/35; 1880 U.S. census, William S. Bethel family, Flushing Township, Belmont County, Ohio, p. 15/35, Ancestry.com.

507 The Belmont Chronicle, September 1, 1887, Newspapers.com.

But medicine, which by the 1880s was getting increasingly hard to practice without frequently updating one's knowledge, likely left him behind. By 1889, like another George, Willis's Uncle Doc, he had abandoned his practice and was working for the Cleveland, Lorain & Wheeling Railroad as agent at Bridgeport, Ohio, in eastern Belmont County just across the Ohio River from Wheeling.[508] By 1900, he was station agent/operator for the Baltimore & Ohio Railroad at McMechen, West Virginia, on the river's east bank, where he remained until his death in 1914.[509] He never went back to medicine.

Of course, Willis was aware of these particulars. He may have visited his old colleague after leaving Minnesota, possibly even stealing some of his medical testimonials in the process. His plan, similar to his Kentucky days, must have been to move to a place where doctors were so unregulated by the authorities that minimal evidence of competence was necessary. Sometime after February 1901, once he had completed his business in North Carolina and made certain that Chrestine could get nothing from their marriage, he showed up in Wister, in the Choctaw Republic, as Dr. George Wilson McGuire. The tiny town was a new railroad stop in what was then known as the Indian Territories, in the far eastern part of present-day Oklahoma.[510]

It probably seemed to him like the perfect alias. George's middle initial even allowed him to use his own middle name. The only potential drawback would be that, as a physician, he might be expected to actually heal people's ailments. In the nine years since his last attempt at medicine, in Owingsville, even the public in the rural West had become more demanding of proficiency from their doctors.

Soon after Dr. McGuire's arrival in Wister, he went into partnership with Dr. Andrew Jackson Snelson. Snelson was born in Arkansas in 1862 and like Willis, he had begun his professional life as a teacher.[511] But he had always had an interest in the healing arts, and after years in the schoolhouse, he shifted gears and studied at the University of Arkansas, receiving his medical degree in 1898. He then moved his wife and six sons to the new town of Wister and hung out his shingle.[512] Willis probably cultivated Snelson for a partnership in order to cement his own credentials and, more importantly, to have a real doctor nearby in case some expertise, or anything besides charm and rudimentary first aid skills, were needed.[513]

Sometime between late October and mid-December 1901, he relocated to Checotah,

---

508 24JI 4, George Walker McGuire, MED1881, documents, CWRU Archives; The Wheeling Register, February 6, 1890, p. 4, GenealogyBank.com.
509 U.S. census, 1900, George W. McGuire, McMechen, Marshall County, West Virginia; 1910 U.S. census, George W. McGuire, McMechen, Marshall County, West Virginia, both Ancestry.com.
510 Wister, like most small communities, had no newspaper in 1901. We know that Willis began his Oklahoma period there because of later references in the Checotah Enquirer (February 14, 1902) and the Checotah Times (February 4, 1910), Newspapers.com.
511 Biography, Andrew J. Snelson, M. D., included in *Muskogee and Northeastern Oklahoma*, by John Downing Benedict.
512 Obituary, Andrew Jackson Snelson, Eufaula Indian Journal, May 8, 1952, Newspapers.com.
513 The Checotah Times, on February 4, 1910, Newspapers.com. An account of their partnership was published as part of a section entitled, "Eight Years Ago," a popular feature of newspapers of the day, allowing readers, especially in rapidly growing places, to reminisce about the good old days. The brief account relates that McGuire and Snelson were partners in Wister for "a term of years," which is clearly impossible, since Willis left Minnesota in February 1901 and left Wister by December, at the very latest. As usual, misinformation concerning D.W. Bethel that made its way into the papers likely came from D.W. Bethel — it was to his advantage to represent his experience as a doctor as more extensive than it was. The selection quoted was taken from the March 20, 1902 edition. Unfortunately, no copies of the original Times from 1901-1902 remain.

in McIntosh County in the Creek Nation.[514] The move was probably Snelson's idea, and McGuire, unencumbered by family, just ran ahead in an effort to keep his new best friend and associate from escaping him. Early reports were that Snelson would, indeed, join him in Checotah, and the advertisement of their partnership ran in the paper from December 1901 through early April 1902. But the editor got all of his information from McGuire, and Snelson seems to have been less enthusiastic about the arrangement. He visited Checotah a couple of times over the winter, and on April 1 he moved his family there, but not for long.[515] Around the middle of the month the partnership was dissolved, and by April 25 each advertised separately, although they maintained rooms in the same office, and they shared an office phone. To make things clear to all, Snelson's ad made sure to direct his patients to the first door on the right.[516] In less than two months, Snelson had built a house and moved to nearby Oktaha, and by mid-summer he had his practice there up and running.[517] Although he visited from time to time, he did not return to Checotah to live until 1908, the year following Willis's departure. It's unknown if there is any causality between these events, but the timing is suspicious. Snelson was an upright citizen who harbored political aspirations. If he had worked closely with McGuire, he certainly would have come to suspect that the latter was a fraud, and so would have wanted nothing to do with him.[518]

Dr. Andrew Jackson Snelson, circa 1900.

---

514 There are no remaining issues of any Checotah paper between October 18 and December 13, 1901. The December 13 issue of the Checotah Enquirer has an advertisement for "McGuire & Snelson, Physicians and Surgeons," which is not present in the October 18, or any previous issue. This leads us to the conclusion that Willis arrived in Checotah between those dates.
515 The Checotah Enquirer, February 14, 1902, p. 4; March 14, 1902, p. 8; April 4, 1902, p. 8, Newspapers.com.
516 The Checotah Enquirer, April 25, 1902, p. 6, Newspapers.com.
517 The Checotah Enquirer, August 15, 1902, p. 3, Newspapers.com.
518 A. J. Snelson went on to become an important figure in the region's society, politics, and medicine, and he remained in the area for the rest of his life. He was elected the first mayor of Oktaha, and he served in the state legislature, and also on medical boards, throughout his career. He died in Eufaula, the McIntosh County seat, in 1952 at the age of 90. (Biography, Andrew J. Snelson, M. D., included in *Muskogee and Northeastern Oklahoma*, by John Downing Benedict).
519 From Snelson Family Tree, public tree on Ancestry.com, managed by william_rogers_3. First published on July 14, 2016.

Dr. McGuire seems to have been sensitive about the possibility that people, especially those in the medical community, would be skeptical about his skills and qualifications. This was his most ambitious con yet, and some problems can't be just talked away. If he was labeled as a phony from the outset, he knew he would never live it down. That might explain the following unusual item in the Checotah Enquirer on January 3, 1902:

> Dr. G. W. McGuire is very much pleased this week over a letter he received from his friend, Dr. N. H. Walthem, dean of the Kentucky School of Medicine, congratulating him on having secured so good a location. [520]

Transcription: Dr. G.W. McGuire is very much pleased this week over a letter he received from his friend, Dr. W.H. Walthem [sic], dean of the Kentucky School of Medicine, congratulating him on having secured so good a location.

It stinks of a Willis public relations gambit, implying his own unquestionable credentials while at the same time complimenting the town, something the editor and his readers would have enjoyed. William H. Wathen was, in fact, dean of the Kentucky School of Medicine in Louisville. He was an accomplished physician, professor of Obstetrics, Abdominal Surgery, and Gynecology at the school and a pioneer in gynecological surgery.[521] Willis had probably met him, and he certainly envied him, but I doubt they were friends in the usual sense.[522] But as we will see, Willis had somehow formed a connection with Wathen's school. He encouraged at least one young man to attend the place, and Wathen, whose position also required recruitment, no doubt appreciated the business his Oklahoma correspondent supplied. Willis may have sent the dean a letter crafted to elicit a congratulatory reaction like the one above, in an effort to reassure the townspeople how connected, and by extension, how competent, he was. Critical thinkers in the area, however, might have wondered why a middle-aged doctor, who supposedly graduated over twenty years previously, would be "very much pleased" by such a letter.

While Snelson's rejection, and possibly public suspicion, probably inconvenienced his plans, nothing was as much of a threat as the following item, published in the papers on multiple dates in late 1901:

---

520 The Checotah Enquirer, January 3, 1902, Newspapers.com.
521 Howard A. Kelly and Walter L. Burrage, *Dictionary of American Medical Biography*, pp. 1270-1271. Bio by Wathen's son, Dr. John R. Wathen.
522 Willis probably called everyone he met his friend.

> **Notice to Physicians.**
>
> Notice is hereby given, that all physicians practicing in the Creek Nation, without license, must secure same on or before Janurary 7, 1902, or suffer the penalty as provided by law. Graduates of reputable schools may obtain license by registering their Diplomas with any member of the board, but non-graduates must appear before the board, at Dr Callahan's office in Muskogee, Indian Territory for examination, on Tuesday, January 7th.
>
> Fees for Registering Diploma $5.00
> Fees for Examination $25.00
> J. O. Callahan, Pres., Muskogee, I. T.
> G. R. Rucker, Sec'y., Checotah, I. T.
> J. C. W. Bland, Treas., Red Fork, I. T.
> Creek Medical Examining Board.[523]

Transcription: Notice is hereby given, that all physicians practicing in the Creek Nation, without license, must secure same on or before January 7, 1902, or suffer the penalty as provided by law. Graduates of reputable schools may obtain license by registering their Diplomas with any member of the board, but non-graduates must appear before the board, at Dr. Callahan's office in Muskogee, Indian Territory for examination, on Tuesday, January 7th.

Fees for Registering Diploma $5.00

Fees for Examination $25.00

J. O. Callahan, Pres., Muskogee, I. T.

G. R. Rucker, Sec'y., Checotah, I. T.

J. C. W. Bland, Treas., Red Fork, I. T.

Creek Medical Examining Board.

Up popped the devil![524] As more and more 'respectable' folk, instead of the kind Oklahoma was famous for, moved into the Territories, regulations naturally increased. A statehood application was on the horizon, and one problem authorities were grappling with was medical quackery.[525] Willis didn't show up at Dr. Callahan's office to be examined on January 7, but he made some effort to respond to the requirements in his own way. On January 18, 1902, he sent a notarized affidavit to Case Western Reserve Medical College, swearing under oath that his diploma had been destroyed by a fire, and could they please send him another. The college reviewed their records, and assuming he was the real George W. McGuire, sent him a certificate of graduation, their sensible policy being to not issue more than one diploma per graduate. The certificate was enough to procure a license, but it's clear that doubts remained about Dr. McGuire's qualifications among the territory's medical professionals.[526]

---

523 The Checotah Enquirer, December 13, 20, and 27, 1901, Newspapers.com.
524 My father used to say this to me when my plans, especially while playing card or board games, became unexpectedly complicated, usually because of a move he had just made.
525 *Medical Education*, The Encyclopedia of Oklahoma History and Culture, Oklahoma Historical Society.
526 24JI 4, George Walker McGuire, MED 1881, documents, CWRU Archives, letters 1, 2.

January 1902 was a busy month. The week after he sent off his affidavit, on the 23rd, he married local widow Sophia Price Johnson. Sophia, who went by 'Chippie' to family and friends, was born in 1876 in Texas but had moved with her birth family to the Creek Indian Territory by 1892.[527] Her first husband, Wellington Lott Johnson, died suddenly in 1898, leaving her to care for their two sons, Clay (b. 1895) and Todd (1896).[528] The Johnsons had a farm just west of Checotah, and Wellington must have also left her some assets. For almost four years she remained unattached, a long time for a young woman with children to be widowed in that era. Sophia was one-sixteenth Creek Indian, and she also owned an allotment of land in the territory, courtesy of the U.S. government.[529]

The distinguished, charming, and voluble Dr. McGuire evidently checked off enough boxes on her 'perfect man' list to make her rethink unmarried life. For his part, marriage to such an upright and respected citizen helped to cement his status in Checotah society. Their courtship must have been of the whirlwind variety, given how recently he had arrived in town. The wedding ceremony took place on his 42nd birthday. Sophia was about 24.[530]

Married Last Night.

A very beautiful wedding ceremony was performed last night by Rev. J B. McDonald at the home of the bride, the contracting parties being Dr. G. W. McGuire and Mrs. Sophia Johnson. Mrs. Johnson has resided in Checotah for several years, and is highly esteemed and beloved by everybody who knows her. She is a lady of many noble traits of character, and a most lovable disposition.

The groom, Dr. G. W. McGuire, is one of the leading physicians of Checotah, and has made a large number of friends since he has been here. He is a native of Kentucky, having been born and raised at Walnut Cove, in that state. He is an A. M., M. D., being a graduate of Cornell University Scientific Department, He is also a graduate of the Ohio Medical College, Western Reserve University, Medical Department, of Cleveland, Ohio. Dr. McGuire is a pleasant, agreeable gentleman, and from the testimonials he brought with him to Checotah is well worthy the love of this amiable woman who has placed her future in his keeping.

[531]

Transcription: A very beautiful wedding ceremony was performed last night by Rev. J.B. McDonald at the home of the bride, the contracting parties being Dr. G.W. McGuire and Mrs. Sophia Johnson. Mrs.

---

527 This information comes from her application for allotment to the Commission of the Five Civilized Tribes in 1900, in which Sophia said that she had lived in the Creek Nation for eight years.
528 The Muskogee Daily Phoenix, March 17, 1898, Newspapers.com.
529 "Allotment, the federal policy of dividing communally held Indian tribal lands into individually owned private property, was the culmination of American attempts to destroy tribes and their governments and to open Indian lands to settlement by non-Indians and to development by railroads. It was a necessary prelude to statehood for Oklahoma and Indian territories." From the Oklahoma Historical Society website.
530 Marriage license, George W. McGuire and Sophia P. Johnson, Indian Territory, Northern District, January 23, 1902, Ancestry.com. Sophia's birthday was listed on her Death Certificate as October 22, 1877, which, if correct, would have made her 24 years old. Other documents in her life, however, list her birth year variously.
531 The Checotah Enquirer, January 24, 1902, p. 4, Newspapers.com.

> Johnson has resided in Checotah for several years, and is highly esteemed and beloved by everybody who knows her. She is a lady of many noble traits of character, and a most lovable disposition.
>
> The groom, Dr. G.W. McGuire, is one of the leading physicians of Checotah, and has made a large number of friends since he has been here. He is a native of Kentucky, having been born and raised at Walnut Cove, in that state. He is an A.M., M.D., being a graduate of Cornell University Scientific Department. He is also a graduate of the Ohio Medical College, Western Reserve University, Medical Department, of Cleveland, Ohio. Dr. McGuire is a pleasant, agreeable gentleman, and from the testimonials he brought with him to Checotah is well worthy the love of this amiable woman who has placed her future in his keeping.

That he was referred to as "one of the leading physicians of Checotah" probably says more about the close relationship he had already formed with K.W. Whitmore, the Checotah Enquirer's editor, than it does about the quality of the doctors in town, although if I were one of the other six I might have taken offense.[532] The real George McGuire had been born in Ohio, but Willis didn't see any reason not to be creative with his new moniker, and Kentucky was a special place for him.[533] He had claimed the state as his birthplace on his licenses to marry Nettie and Matilda, and he also told Chrestine he was born there, and that he owned land there.[534] He now claimed it as George's birthplace. On later documents, he said that George Wilson McGuire was born in Mount Sterling, about 14 miles from his old haunts at Owingsville, where his first ambitious con, the Dictawood horse breeding scheme, had blown up in his face so spectacularly ten years earlier. Maybe this was an acknowledgment of his true birthplace — where the completely dishonest, devious person he had become was hatched. Interestingly, he kept his true birthday of January 23, 1860, throughout his time as George W. McGuire, to his detriment, as we will see.[535] As far as the degree from Cornell was concerned, well, hey, why not slap a little lipstick on the real Dr. McGuire's pig of a resume? And wouldn't it be interesting to know what testimonials he brought with him to Checotah, and how he got them?

After the ceremony, Willis moved into Sophia's house with her and her two sons — there are no reports of him building or buying a place, and we know that they lived on a farm outside of town, just as she did prior to their marriage. The papers, in the typical paternalistic fashion of the era, simply began referring to the place as "the Dr. McGuire farm west of

---

532 The January 24 issue of the Checotah Enquirer lists seven physicians' advertisements, including both McGuire's and Snelson's. Also practicing in the town at the time was Dr. George R. Rucker, secretary of the Creek Medical Board. Source: Newspapers.com.
533 No community named Walnut Cove exists in Kentucky today, but it is possible that there was a place by that name near Bowling Green, a birthplace he had claimed on his license to marry Matilda. There is a Walnut Cove in North Carolina, about thirty miles from Asheboro. It's possible that Willis just said the first community that came to his mind when he was asked where he was born. Source: Robert M. Rennick, *Kentucky Place Names*.
534 In all the documents that Herbert Benjamin Steele filled out that required his father's birthplace, including his employment application to the War Department and to the Civilian Conservation Corps, it was listed as Kentucky. It was also so listed on his death certificate. The Minnesota papers had also made passing reference to Kentucky as J.P. Steele's home state.
535 Application to Muskogee County Medical Society, Case Western Reserve University Archives; Registrations of an American Citizen in Mexico, George W. McGuire, Tampico, August 11, 1908; San Luis Potosi, August 28, 1909; Chihuahua, March 24, 1911, Ancestry.com. The real George W. McGuire was born in May.

Checotah," or something similar.[536] In the same spirit, he probably also assumed control of Sophia's funds.

As he had at many of his previous stops, he made sure to acquire an apprentice early, although passing along the necessities of medicine must have been far less natural to him than communicating the requirements of a being a railroad station agent/operator.[537] He probably had a hidden agenda this time. The young man's name was Harry Bertram Kniseley, and he was the younger brother of Herman Kniseley, who ran a drug store in Checotah. Willis's office was above the store.

Harry was an accomplished musician, popular with the younger crowd, and his name appeared in the papers often. He had served in the army during the Spanish-American War, and after he came back he worked in town as a jeweler. In February 1902, just a few months after Willis arrived in town, Kniseley began attending Wathen's Louisville school, and it seems likely that Willis helped him make the decision to go there. That summer, while on break from his studies, he began tagging along on Dr. McGuire's calls.[538] Two not-quite-doctors are better than one any day, after all. Willis's intention was likely to get the flow of information going both ways, and he must have pumped the young student for all the up-to-date knowledge about medical practice he could glean.

In early July, the two men "removed an immense bug from the ear of Mrs. W.T. Green." Whitmore wrote that "the bug had to be taken out in pieces," and continued, "While the bug was in Mrs. Green's ear she suffered indescribable agony, but its removal afforded immediate relief, and at last report she was getting along nicely."[539] Ah, life in rural America in the early twentieth century! I mean, how many times have you gotten a giant bug stuck in your ear? Two days later on the fourth, both men, along with McGuire's family, attended a picnic of over 40 people hosted by one of Mrs. Green's neighbors, and they reported that "they never spent a more pleasant day," although George also said that the chiggers had made him "a special victim."[540] Maybe the bugs were getting their revenge. In case you're wondering what happened to the bug that started it all, Whitmore informed his readers that McGuire and Kniseley, as proud of themselves as big game hunters, kept it as a trophy, preserved it in alcohol, and put it on public display in the older Kniseley's drug store.[541]

Not all the news that month was happy. One week later, on July 11, the paper reported that Mrs. C.C. Phillips, who was "living on the Dr. McGuire farm west of Checotah," had

---

536 The Checotah Enquirer, July 11, 1902, Newspapers.com.
537 At Owingsville, he had taken Leslie Wilson under his wing, and at Perris, of course, Joe Steele. We have not mentioned Frank Boudreault, but he had learned the station agent's job from Willis at Red Lake Falls, although he was not as close to Willis as the other two.
538 The Checotah Enquirer, February 7, 1902; February 14, 1902; July 4, 1902, Newspapers.com.
539 Ibid., July 4, 1902
540 Ibid., July 11, 1902
541 Kniseley did not complete his education at the Kentucky School of Medicine, rather, he graduated from Washington University Medical School in St. Louis in 1906. His time of tagging along on Dr. McGuire's calls evidently did not last past the summer of 1902, and he may have distanced himself, just as Snelson had. Kniseley went on to practice in Tishomingo, Oklahoma, about 120 miles from Checotah, for 21 years before moving to Norman, where he practiced until a year prior to his death in 1942. His obituary listed him as a "pioneer state physician." (*Dr. H. B. Kniseley Dies at Norman,* The Daily Oklahoman, March 2, 1942, Newspapers.com)

died suddenly of "a congestive chill."[542] The papers did not elaborate on the cause of her illness, why she was living on the farm in the first place, or what her relationship was to the McGuires. Even though people routinely died of such causes during this period, this event could not have been positive for Dr. McGuire's reputation. It must have caused some of the serious doctors in the area to exchange some knowing glances.

The following month, George's brother-in-law, Chaney Minton, needed an operation of some kind. Luckily for Mr. Minton, Dr. McGuire did not attempt to perform it himself. He did, however, accompany Minton to Dallas for the surgery, and he dutifully reported to the local papers that all went well.[543] McGuire was also present to record the delivery of the Mintons' child the following year, although it's likely that a midwife, as usual, did most of the work.

Speaking of progeny, Willis and Sophia were also busy on that front. On August 9, 1903, Marcus Wilson McGuire became the fifth inhabitant of the farmhouse. Willis served as the doctor present, and the paperwork was in his handwriting.[544] The event must have been noticed by the local papers, but none from 1903 survive to give us a report. Interestingly, Marcus would go by his middle name of Wilson, just as his father had, as a child and young adult.[545]

Like his mother and half-brothers, the boy was entitled to an allotment of land in the Creek Nation because of Sophia's ancestry. The law allowed families to select their parcel within four years, and it fell to Marcus's father to do the choosing.[546] In 1905, he was awarded 161.2 acres in Section 1, Township 18, Range 11, in Creek County "between Tulsa and Sapulpa." The government estimated the land was worth $646.61.[547] Willis probably chose the site because the St. Louis & San Francisco Railway ran across the land. That was a smart move, but most of its later value came from what lay beneath it. Oil was discovered soon after the tract was allotted, and those leases, and the subsequent investments they enabled, eventually made Marcus Wilson McGuire a millionaire before his maturity, and raised the standard of living of the entire household.

Between 1902 and 1907, we find frequent references to the McGuires in the spotty newspaper coverage of the day. They enjoyed the bucolic lifestyle as prominent community members in what was to become eastern Oklahoma, and articles reporting deliveries of babies and basic medical procedures, as well as visits to nearby towns and minor health issues, often mentioned the doctor. As at his previous stops, he was a respected local professional, with many friends.

In 1904, Willis was appointed to the three-member Board of Examiners for the local

---

542 The Checotah Enquirer, July 11, 1902, Newspapers.com.
543 Ibid., August 1, 1902. Chaney Minton had married Sophia's sister, Ida Price, in 1890 (Luther B. Hill, *History of the State of Oklahoma*, p. 139).
544 Birth affidavit, Marcus Wilson McGuire, Department of the Interior, Commission to the Five Civilized Tribes, Creek Nation, August 9, 1903, courtesy Caitlin McGuire Reid.
545 U.S. census, 1920, Muskogee Ward 4, Oklahoma; U.S. Passport application, April 15, 1925, both Ancestry.com.
546 D. S Otis, *The Dawes Act and the Allotment of Indian Lands*, pp. 5-6
547 Department of the Interior, *In the Matter of the Allotment of the Lands of the Creeks,* Roll No. 40, August 11, 1905, Ancestry.com; *Was Born in Checotah,* The McIntosh County Democrat, July 29, 1915, Newspapers.com.

schools, the body charged with examining teachers for competence and, of course, good moral character. Feel free to insert your own ironic line in this spot. He served until 1906.[548] Equally grotesque was his selection as treasurer (really?) of a new telephone company formed in Checotah in December 1906.[549] There is no mention in the records as to whether or not it stayed in business.

Willis also maintained, and expanded upon, his medical connections, at least those in western Kentucky. It's hard to know how, or when, he had established his attachment to the Kentucky School of Medicine. Co-founded by Wathen after his own graduation from the University of Louisville medical school in 1870, the dean had built the school into a respectable institution that attracted prospective doctors from across the south. Wathen ran the place for over three decades before it was absorbed by his alma mater around 1908.[550] Willis may have met Wathen during his brief partnership with J.T. Catlett in Owingsville in 1892. But since Dr. Wathen likely knew him as George Wilson McGuire, as Harry Kniseley certainly did, it seems more likely that his relationship with the Louisville college was a post-J.P. Steele event. He may have spent some time in Louisville building his connections with the medical community before he went to Oklahoma in 1901. It would have been a smart move to help establish some credibility and forestall the questions he no doubt knew would surface.

In addition to sending Kniseley their way and corresponding with Wathen, a number of other references were made to the school in the Checotah papers of the day, and all of them connect back to Willis in some way. Dr. Robert Crawford Farris, another K.S.M. grad, moved to the Creek Nation in late 1906, probably at Willis's urging. Born on a farm near Salem, Kentucky in 1873, a stone's throw from Fredonia and Baker station, it seems likely that Farris knew the Baker family and Willis during his time in the area in the early 1890s. In the 1900 census, Farris was living with his birth family and teaching school. Soon thereafter, he must have enrolled in Wathen's medical college. He practiced in Fredonia for a couple of years after he graduated in 1903. Then he went west, staying at the McGuire farmhouse while he made arrangements to live and practice in nearby Porum. Since Farris probably knew him as David Wilson Bethel, it's interesting to imagine the conversation they would have had about the importance of keeping things like aliases secret. It's possible that Farris was a source of information about Dr. McGuire to the Oklahoma medical authorities, although there is no way to know for sure. Willis, Farris, and another Kentucky transplant, an educator named John A. Jackson, whom he probably met through his association with the Checotah schools, went hunting and camping a couple of times in 1907. They even took four-year-old Wilson camping with them on one occasion.[551]

---

548 The Checotah Times, June 9, 1904; August 4, 1904; August 25, 1905, August 3, 1906, Newspapers.com.
549 The Checotah Enquirer, December 7, 1906, Newspapers.com.
550 Howard A. Kelly and Walter L. Burrage, *Dictionary of American Medical Biography,* pp. 1270-1271. Biography of William Wathen by his son, Dr. John R. Wathen.
551 The Checotah Times, October 5, 1906; May 17, 1907; June 7, 1907; June 14, 1907, Newspapers.com.

Left to right: William H. Wathen, Harry B. Kniseley, Robert C. Farris. Wathen's photo dates from 1906 and Farris's from 1903. Kniseley's photo is undated, but probably was taken around the time he knew Willis in Checotah.

In all, Willis was able to pilot his new scam, apparently unmolested, for six years. But doctors in the area, possibly tipped off by Farris or Snelson, local medical board member George Rucker, or even members of the community, couldn't get the smell of a rat out of their noses. The territorial medical board repeatedly asked him to stand for examination, not believing that he was the George McGuire who had graduated from Case Western, and he kept delaying them. They began investigating his background. Those materials would be interesting reading, but the only item remaining is the letter on the following page, sent in fall 1906, from the Muskogee County Medical Society to Case Western Reserve.

As with the Dictawood horse scandal, these wounds were self-inflicted, a product of hubris. He didn't need to apply for membership in the Muskogee County Medical Society — Checotah was in McIntosh County. He must have just been trying to increase his regional celebrity. He even used his real birthdate, January 23, 1860, on the application (the real George W. McGuire was born in May 1857), which tipped off the already suspicious doctors that something was wrong — they knew this guy was no child medical prodigy, after all. Willis built George Wilson McGuire's coffin all by himself, almost begging someone to bury his borrowed alias in it, and the serious doctors in the territory were only too happy to oblige.

---

552 The photographs of Wathen and Farris are from the Kentucky School of Medicine graduation photos, published online by the University of Louisville Libraries, Kornhauser Health Sciences Library, digital.library.louisville.edu. The picture of Kniseley is from the Griffin Family Tree on Ancestry.com, originally shared by Ken Griffin on October 31, 2015.

Muskogee, I.T. Nov. 13, 1906.

Dr. B. L. Millikin,
    Dean of Western Reserve University Medical College,
        Cleveland, Ohio.

Dear Doctor:

    We have an application for membership to our County Medical Society from Dr. Geo. W. McGuire of Checotah, Indian Territory in this he states he graduated from your College on the 9th of March 1881, and gives his date of birth as the 23rd day of January, 1860.
    It has been reported that the applicant is not Geo. W. McGuire, but that his real name is Blair. I understand that he has no diploma from your School but has a certificate of graduation, claiming that his diploma has been destroyed by fire.
    It would oblige us greatly if you can give us any information regarding the age and present location of Geo. W. McGuire who graduated from your College in 1881. In the application he made to the Western District Medical Society one year ago, he gave his age as 44 years; this would have made him only 20 years old in March 1881, the date on which he claims to have graduated.
    I am,

                Fraternally yours,

                      Secretary.
              Muskogee County Medical Society.

Transcription: Muskogee, I. T. Nov. 13, 1906

Dr. B. L. Millikin, Dean of Western Reserve University Medical College, Cleveland, Ohio.

Dear Doctor:

We have an application for membership to our County Medical Society from Dr. Geo. W. McGuire of Checotah, Indian Territory in this he states he graduated from your College on the 9th of March 1881, and gives his date of birth as the 23rd day of January, 1860.

It has been reported that the applicant is not Geo. W. McGuire, but that his real name is Blair. I understand that he has no diploma from your School but has a certificate of graduation, claiming that his diploma has been destroyed by fire.

It would oblige us greatly if you can give us any information regarding the age and present location of Geo.

---

553   24JI 4, George Walker McGuire, MED 1881, documents, CWRU Archives, letter 2.

W. McGuire who graduated from your College in 1881. In the application he made to the Western District Medical Society one year ago, he gave his age as 44 years; this would have made him only 20 years old in March 1881, the date on which he claims to have graduated.

I am, Fraternally yours,

P.P. Nesbitt, M.D.

Secretary, Muskogee County Medical Society

The letter also gives us a peek at another one of his aliases, ". . . it has been reported . . . that his real name is Blair." It was likely a reference to James Martin Blair, whom we heard about in Chapter 7. You may remember that he was going to join our boy in Perris, but it didn't work out. Willis may have used Blair's name as a temporary alias, possibly before deciding that George W. McGuire was a better bet because their ages were closer. Or maybe he just changed names like most of us change clothes. We know from later events that Willis was still in touch with Blair during his time in Oklahoma and his friend must have known that he was going by the name of George W. McGuire. Blair was an active and outspoken member of Eugene Debs' Socialist Party, which was growing in popularity in 1906, and he may have privately delighted that Willis was sticking it to the system, although he probably would have been less enthusiastic over the theft of his name.[554]

After receiving the above letter, Case Western Reserve may have found and contacted the real George W. McGuire, still running the B.&O. station at McMechen, West Virginia, and told him (no doubt to his surprise) that he was practicing medicine in Oklahoma. At some point in 1907, the real McGuire wrote the letter to the territorial board of health that is mentioned in the second article below. After gathering this documentation and other evidence from the appropriate sources, the board completed its investigation. The press got wind of it, and on October 24, 1907, the following unusual item appeared in the Muskogee Times-Democrat:

---

[554] Debs ran for President in 1904, 1908, 1912, and 1920, the last time while he was in prison for sedition after urging young men to resist the draft for World War I. In the 1908 election, he won 2.83% of the vote nationwide and in 1912, six percent. Blair ran for Richland County (Ohio) marshal, judge, and prosecuting attorney on the Socialist ticket in 1903, 1905, and 1908, respectively.

Dr. McGuire's Identity The Question

Is Dr. G. W. McGuire of Checotah a physician, is he really Dr. McGuire or another man? These are some questions which will be settled in the next few days.

The territorial board of health believes that Dr. McGuire succeeded in getting hold of a diploma belonging to a man of that name and that his real name is Bethel. He came to Checotah several weeks ago and hung up his diploma. The state board of medicine requested him to pass an examination, but he kept asking for more time. Finally it became evident to the board that he did not intend to take any examination. The board then made some inquiries which resulted in the gravest suspicions being thrown upon Dr. McGuire's identity.[555]

Transcription: Is Dr. G.W. McGuire of Checotah a physician, is he really Dr. McGuire or another man? These are some questions which will be settled in the next few days. The territorial board of health believes that Dr. McGuire succeeded in getting hold of a diploma belonging to a man of that name and that his real name is Bethel. He came to Checotah several weeks [sic] ago and hung up his diploma. The state board of medicine requested him to pass an examination, but he kept asking for more time. Finally it became evident to the board that he did not intend to take any examination. The board then made some inquiries which resulted in the gravest suspicions being thrown upon Dr. McGuire's identity.

The answers to these questions began hitting the papers the very next day. Except in Checotah, where the editors must have been trying to save Sophia and the boys some embarrassment, the following article appeared throughout the territory:

---

[555] The Muskogee Times-Democrat, October 24, 1907, Newspapers.com. The article is mistaken only in that Willis had been in Checotah for years, not weeks, and we know he had a certificate of graduation instead of a diploma.

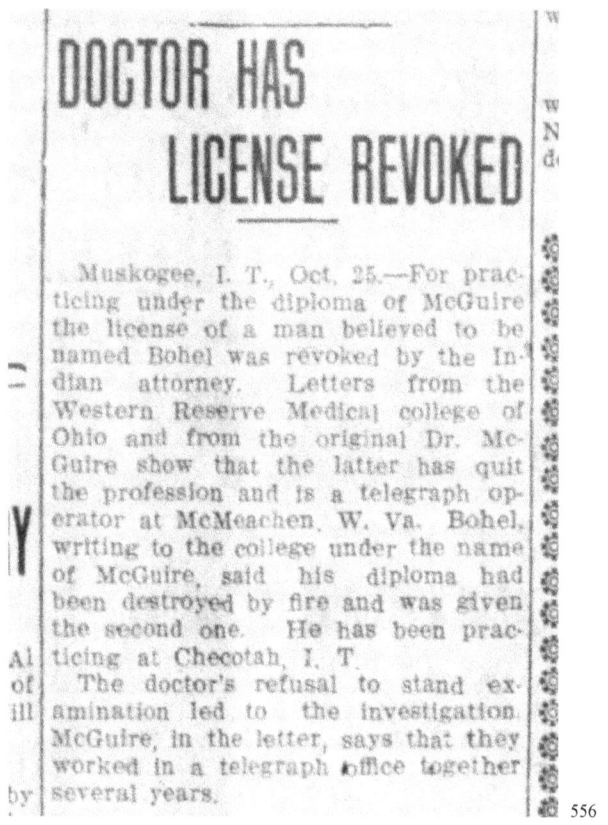

Transcription: Muskogee, I. T., Oct. 25 — For practicing under the diploma of McGuire the license of a man believed to be named Bohel [sic] was revoked by the Indian attorney. Letters from the Western Reserve Medical college of Ohio and from the original Dr. McGuire show that the latter has quit the profession and is a telegraph operator at McMeachen, W. Va. Bohel, writing to the college under the name of McGuire, said his diploma had been destroyed by fire and was given the second one. He has been practicing at Checotah, I.T.

The doctor's refusal to stand examination led to the investigation. McGuire, in the letter, says that they worked in a telegraph office together several years.

Willis left Oklahoma that week.

---

556 The Shawnee News, October 25, 1907, Newspapers.com. All of the boiler-plate news reports incorrectly listed his real name as "Bohel" instead of Bethel. This was likely a typo from the newswires. The previous story in the Muskogee Times-Democrat did get his real surname right. We don't know when George and Willis worked together. It could have been in the early 1880s, when both were young men not yet established in career paths, or in the early 1890s, when George was leaving medicine and Willis was in transition after losing his position in Lexington with the Kentucky Union.

13.

The Death of Dr. George W. McGuire

■ **IN HER DIVORCE PETITION THREE YEARS LATER,** Sophia charged only that her husband "willfully abandoned the plaintiff without any cause whatever" on November 1, 1907.[557] It seems to me that running away from a sure-fire fraud conviction is a pretty good cause, but the suit didn't mention it. There was also no mention that her and her son's last name should have been Bethel, not McGuire. Neither was that information included in any of the thousands of pages of guardianship documents generated by the courts concerning Marcus Wilson's estate. It's impossible to believe that Sophia was ignorant about what was written about Willis in the papers and the reasons he had left the area. Most likely, the decision to keep the fraud scandal out of the divorce case came from her lawyers, who determined that dredging up the fact that McGuire was an alias was an unnecessary complication to the open-and-shut abandonment case. Sophia was not seeking any damages — she must have known they would be uncollectable, anyway. By late 1910, she just wanted out.

As for the omission of the name Bethel, or any mention of the identity fraud, from the guardianship papers, it remains a mystery — the documents referred to Willis as "Dr. McGuire" whenever he was mentioned. Sophia may have asked her attorneys and the court to maintain this designation to protect her son. Marcus was four years old when Willis left, an event that was traumatic enough for the boy, and she would have been anxious to avoid disrupting his life further. Like Herbert Benjamin Steele, he kept his fallacious surname throughout his life, and there is no evidence that he ever discovered the truth about his father. It all must have taken a toll on Sophia, who also maintained the last name of McGuire until she remarried in 1913. Subsequent events make it clear that she was at least somewhat conflicted, and that she retained feelings for Willis and a desire to believe his stories, along with the healthy skepticism they deserved. She corresponded with him and delayed divorce proceedings until late 1910. But then she moved on.

Since he was already unmasked, it also seems mysterious that Willis did not ditch his

---

557 In the District Court of McIntosh County, Oklahoma, Sophia McGuire, Plaintiff, vs. George W. McGuire, Defendant, case #495, Petition for Divorce, p. 1. Records requested from the McIntosh County District Court. Marcus Wilson McGuire was four at the time, and Clay and Todd Johnson were 12 and 11, respectively.

alias on November 1, 1907. Instead, he put the George McGuire face back on and said to the world, essentially, "Pay no attention to the man behind the curtain!"[558] He stayed in contact with Sophia via one of his habitual letter-writing campaigns for more than three years, and if his fraud was ever referred to in the findings of the territorial board, those passages were not transcribed into the guardianship records.[559] Maybe, because the play in the Creek Nation hadn't ended to his liking, he wanted to take it on the road and act the part of George McGuire for a few years longer. Or, as we will see, he may have had a darker motive. In the process, some familiar players and plot lines showed up on stage for encores, along with a few new twists.

D.W. Bethel's story gets increasingly hazy at this point due to lack of records, crazy events, language and cultural barriers, and an absence of DNA matches. We can track his shadow and guess about everything from his actions to his motives, but then we lose him completely in a cloud of disinformation and foreign revolution. If, when, and where he emerged from that cloud, and what he was calling himself when he did, is anybody's guess as of this writing.

He must have begun his exile from Oklahoma with a trip to Virginia, after which he left for Tampico, a coastal city on the Gulf of Mexico in the Mexican state of Tamaulipas, arriving on January 28, 1908, for the purpose of "practicing medicine."[560] Tampico was beginning an oil boom, and many American and British interests were pouring into the area. We don't know what company he worked for, but it seems certain that he was employed by some American industrial interest. The folks doing the hiring probably hadn't read the Oklahoma newspapers lately.

Mexico was a sensible place to run off to. Oversight of Americans was left largely to the companies they worked for, and they had little time to run down a man's past, especially if he did his job passably. Willis had a history with the country dating all the way back to the early 1890's, if not before, and he undoubtedly had connections in the large American expatriate community, and possibly among some of the locals. He may have spoken Spanish. Living was cheap, Americans were well paid, and there were other business opportunities for those who wanted them. The Checotah papers of this period trumpeted the stories of at least three local doctors who divided their time between Oklahoma and Mexico and were making their fortunes there. Willis certainly would have read about the successes of Robert L. Stewart, Charles H. Davis, and George R. Rucker. Stewart had gone into practice in Chihuahua in 1899 and had "extensive coal interests down in that country."[561] Davis and Rucker reported similar opportunities, developed while they worked as doctors and surgeons for Willis's old employer, the Mexican Central Railroad.[562] Both the Checotah Enquirer and the Times published these doctors' letters as well as their glowing reports when they came back to town for

---

558 I feel foolish putting in a footnote here because it's common knowledge to most Americans of my generation, but for those who may not know, this is a reference to *The Wizard of Oz*.
559 We do not have the actual letters, but selected quotations from them appear in the reports from Sophia's lawyers that are included in the guardianship papers of Marcus Wilson McGuire.
560 Certificate of Registration of American Citizen, Tampico, Tamaulipas, Mexico, August 11, 1908, Ancestry.com.
561 *Back from Mexico,* The Checotah Enquirer, February 14, 1902, Newspapers.com.
562 *Off for Mexico,* Ibid., December 14, 1906.

visits. They related how much they liked the work, the people, and the climate.

As members of the small medical community in Checotah, Willis would have known all three men personally. In March 1902, the Enquirer noted that Dr. Davis was exhibiting the "curios and souvenirs" he had acquired "during his year's residence at Cardenas" in the window of a Checotah drug store.[563] Given his history, these items must have attracted Willis's interest, and it would have been out of character for him not to strike up at least a few conversations about the country with his fellow physician, relating his own stories (true or not) in the process.

Rucker, for his part, was even more closely tied to Dr. McGuire, and it seems certain that they were well acquainted, although there was probably not a lot of regard in either direction. Rucker was secretary of the Creek Medical Examining Board in 1902 and was probably one of the real doctors who busied himself looking into, and questioning, Willis's qualifications.[564] He was a physician for the Missouri, Kansas & Texas Railroad while in Oklahoma, but he moved to Mexico for his health.[565] In early 1907, nine months before Willis's departure, the Times published a long letter from Dr. Rucker about his experiences, written from Jimenez, Chihuahua, on the Mexican Central line just north of Joe Steele's (and probably Willis's) old haunts at Yermo. "I treat nearly every disease you can think of and a great number of unmentionable ones," he wrote. Well, Willis had likely had some experience with those. "Able American doctors," Rucker went on, "are thought much of here but they must be capable men."[566] It's easy to believe that he was directing this comment toward Willis, whom he knew would read the article, and who had probably expressed an interest in following in his footsteps. It seems likely that Mexico was already in his plans as a getaway destination.

Three days after he registered with the consulate at Tampico, and three months after leaving Oklahoma, he wrote his first (that we know of) letter to Sophia. In it, he said "that he had purchased a farm in Virginia, Three Hundred and two (302) Acres, ten room house, as a home."[567] The place was located near the thriving community of Keysville, and it had a purchase price of $7,000, equal to over $200,000 in today's money.

Over the next three years, he sent along detailed descriptions and photographs of the place. "This is one of the nicest farms I ever saw,"[568] he bragged in 1909, and he went on at length about the quality and value of its yields and how much rent he was collecting from his tenants, making comparisons to the relatively paltry returns of Sophia's place near Checotah. He was trying to get her to move to Keysville. "I thought you were in earnest when you wrote me that you wanted to get away from Checotah, that it was hateful to you. I being in dead

---

563 Ibid., March 28, 1902. This Checotah drug store was not Herman Kniseley's, but Ira Marsh's.
564 Ibid., December 13, 1901.
565 Herman Kniseley, Harry's brother and owner of the drug store over which Willis kept his office, was one of the pallbearers at Rucker's funeral in 1908. Rucker was a respected man in town, and Willis and he would have crossed paths often (*Death of Dr. Rucker,* Ibid., February 21, 1908).
566 *From Old Mexico,* The Checotah Times, February 1, 1907, Newspapers.com.
567 Oklahoma Wills and Probate Records, in the County Court in and of the County of Muskogee, Guardianship Records of Marcus Wilson McGuire, case #1644, Ancestry.com. Report of W. C. Jackson, attorney at law, to the court, summarizing the contents of McGuire's effects and letters, April 1913, p. 2.
568 Ibid. Report of W. C. Jackson, attorney at law, to the court, summarizing the contents of McGuire's effects and letters, April 1913, p. 3, quoting letter from George W. McGuire to Sophia McGuire, October 3, 1909.

earnest went ahead and bought a piece of land, 8 room house, good house cellar, good fruit and good land, and I had the deed made in your name," he wrote on September 25, 1909. He continued, ". . . in as much as you don't care to join me suppose I will have to stay here another year — if I can save as much in a year as I have heretofore I can pay it out in one year. Then I can work one more year and I have enough to stock it good."[569]

On October 3, he kept things rolling:

> There is on the farm an eight room house, pantry and closets. Two tenant houses, each much better than the house on your farm. Three barnes, hog house, ice house, two chicken houses, two tobacco barnes, 7 or 8 springs of very fine water. Several branches. We can have our own fish, for I'm going to put in a pond as soon as I get there. I enclose you a portion of letter I got from Miller telling about the town and people. On this farm there is 50 acres of fine bottom land. 70 acres upland cleared also, both in high state of cultivation. There are 86 acres of fine timber, oak, hickory, beech, chestnut, etc.[570]

Sounds like paradise, but Willis, clearly angling to become a Virginia land baron, wasn't finished. On January 30, 1909, he bought 300 acres in Nottoway County near the town of Blackstone, about 35 miles east of Keysville.[571] The following year he ranged wider, buying almost 100 acres in Bedford County, near Lynchburg, from John A. Thaxton, who (surprise!) was attending the Kentucky School of Medicine at the time.[572] Willis described the Blackstone farm in much the same way as the one near Keysville, as having a "large house, orchards, and well stocked." And the Bedford County place had "good improvements."[573]

As with so many things involving Willis Bethel, the reality turned out to be just a little different than the stories. In April 1913, after finally receiving his effects, which included some deeds and other papers, from the American consulate at Chihuahua, Sophia was intrigued to find out more about the Virginia land her husband had raved about in his letters. She petitioned the Muskogee County court to allow her attorney, W. C. Jackson, to travel there and investigate. She believed "that Dr. Geo. W. McGuire had a valuable estate in three counties in the State of Virginia, and the interest of her ward needs protection, and an investigation

---

569 Ibid., p. 4, quoting letter from George W. McGuire to Sophia McGuire, September 25, 1909.
570 Ibid., p. 3, quoting letter from George W. McGuire to Sophia McGuire, October 3, 1909.
571 Nottoway County Virginia Land Records, W. I. Jones & others to G.W. McGuire, Deed Book 25, Page 481, Nottoway County Clerk of Circuit Court.
572 Bedford County Land Records, John F. Thaxton and Lelia J. Thaxton to George W. McGuire, Page 466, court.state.va.us. Willis's ongoing connection to the Kentucky School of Medicine stands out in the bare-bones records of this period, and it is a little puzzling. He may have made Thaxton's acquaintance there, but since Thaxton did not matriculate until 1909, it seems more likely that he just encouraged the younger man (Thaxton was born in 1885) to attend the place while he was looking over the Bedford County land, and that Thaxton took the advice. He may also have met Thaxton through some mutual acquaintance who had ties to the Louisville school. One would think that Willis would have stayed away from the medical college during his stateside visits, not knowing if news of his Oklahoma embarrassment had reached their ears.
573 Oklahoma Wills and Probate Records, in the County Court in and of the County of Muskogee, Guardianship Records of Marcus Wilson McGuire, case #1644, Ancestry.com. Letter from Sophia McGuire to Judge Thomas Leahy petitioning for allowance of $200 for her attorney to investigate McGuire's Virginia land holdings, April 12, 1913.

should be made at once."[574] The court agreed, and Jackson drove off to Virginia. His descriptions varied slightly from Willis's.

> In the town of Blackstone, Nottoway County, I received the following information in regard to the Three Hundred acres purchased by George W. McGuire, and also examined his bank account at that place, and found no balance in his favor. And went from there to Nottoway Court-house, County seat of Nottoway County, and carefully examined the records and found them as follows: That on March 15, 1909, George W. McGuire conveyed to Thomas G. Philbert one undivided one-half interest in this Three Hundred acre tract. That McGuire and Philbert executed a Deed of Trust on the land to T. F. Epps, Trustee, who sold the land at Trustee sale, and the same was bought by Ross Philbert on default payment of Fifteen Hundred and Twenty-five Dollars ($1525.00) and interest.[575]

Hmm. Okay, so he had defaulted on one of the properties, but there were two others, right? What about the first one, the nicest farm he'd ever seen, his home place near Keysville? Jackson's report continued:

> From Nottoway Court-house I went to Keysville in Charlotte County, Virginia, where he wrote to both his wife and child a number of letters, stating that he had a very valuable farm for which he paid the sum of Seven Thousand ($7000.00) Dollars. Upon investigation I found no one connected with the Bank, real-estate people, Sheriff or any county official that knew anything in regard to said farm of George W. McGuire.
>
> I then drove to Charlotte Court-house, the County seat, a distance of ten miles in the country and made a thorough examination of the County Records, and found no conveyance to George W. McGuire, Sophia McGuire, or Marcus Wilson McGuire.
>
> I got in telephone communication with Sameul [sic] T. Miller of Washington, D.C., he formerly lived at Keysville, and whom Dr. McGuire stated in his letter was collecting the rent for him. He replied that he had a number of letters of inquiry in regard to the property from Dr. McGuire, but that he never came there and never purchased any property to his knowledge in that part of the State.[576]

---

574 Ibid.
575 Ibid. Report of W. C. Jackson, attorney at law, to the court, summarizing the findings of his trip to Virginia, April 1913, p. 1.
576 Ibid., p. 2

Willis had used the photos and letters Miller had sent in reply to his inquiries to dupe Sophia into thinking the place was really his. If she had taken the bait and moved her family to Virginia, she would have found strangers living in her beautiful new home, wondering who these folks from Oklahoma might be.

Jackson had only slightly better luck with the third farm, in the mountains of Bedford County west of Lynchburg. He visited the property, "and found none of it under fence. Had been abandoned for about three years, and a very small part of it had ever been in cultivation or susceptible of cultivation . . . Had two small delapidated [sic] log houses on the place, and a few old apple trees."[577] Dr. Thaxton had sued McGuire for chancery in 1912 with the passing of a payment deadline, and since McGuire had died, the suit was now directed toward "his unknown heirs."[578] So much for "Wilson's new farm."[579]

Jackson guessed that, "after paying all court expenses, attorney fees, etc., it will net the minor about Three Hundred and Fifty ($350.00) Dollars."[580] It turned out that he was an optimist. The suit was not resolved until 1918, five years after Jackson's report and eight years after Willis purchased the property, with Marcus Wilson's estate finally collecting $224.54. That, plus the $8.82 in an account at the People's National Bank in Lynchburg, was the extent of his Virginia inheritance.[581] How much of that sum he had to pay to his attorneys is unknown.[582]

In all, Jackson estimated that Willis was out about $2,259.23 in cash payments for his failed Virginia land deals, or about $60,000 in today's money.[583] If you're wondering where he got it, well, so did I at first. Although it's never stated in any of the records, it seems likely that he left Oklahoma with a stash of funds from Wilson's oil leases, which had begun to pay well by late 1907. As father and guardian, of course, Willis had authority over their disposition, and he may have retained some of that control even after Sophia had him removed from those duties. In most of his letters, he referred to the Virginia farms as belonging to Wilson. He must have helped himself to a lot more than $2259, and all the so-called land investments, especially the fictitious Keysville place, were just a cover for outright theft, devised to make the claim to Sophia that he was still acting in his family's best interest.

We know that Sophia asked the Oklahoma courts to appoint Marcus's estate a new guardian in April 1908, some six months after Willis left town, a request the court accepted. In that

---

577 Ibid., pp. 2-3
578 Circuit Court of Bedford County, Virginia, John F. Thaxton vs George W. McGuire, &c., case #4889, filed June 17, 1912, records request from Bedford County Circuit Court.
579 Oklahoma Wills and Probate Records, in the County Court in and of the County of Muskogee, Guardianship Records of Marcus Wilson McGuire, case #1644, Ancestry.com.. Report of W. C. Jackson, attorney at law, to the court, summarizing the contents of McGuire's effects and letters, April 1913, p. 6, quoting letter from George W. McGuire to Sophia McGuire, June 25, 1910
580 Ibid., p. 3
581 Ibid., p. 1
582 In the Circuit Court of Bedford County, Virginia, John F. Thaxton vs George W. McGuire, &c., case #4889, filed June 17, 1912, records request from Bedford County Circuit Court.
583 Oklahoma Wills and Probate Records, in the County Court in and of the County of Muskogee, Guardianship Records of Marcus Wilson McGuire, case #1644, Ancestry.com.. Report of W. C. Jackson, attorney at law, to the court, summarizing the contents of McGuire's effects and letters, April 1913, pp. 1-2. Jackson totaled the payments from the deeds to arrive at this sum. Inflation figures obtained from the U.S. Inflation Calculator, westegg.com/inflation/

petition, she said nothing about her husband's fiduciary actions except that he did "not reside in the state of Oklahoma."[584] It's possible that while she wanted to free her son's estate from Willis's control, she didn't want to cut all ties to him, either, in case he truly was investing the missing money. Sophia was no dummy.

Willis's basic strategy was similar to his letters trying to lure Nettie to his fictitious California property over ten years earlier, but that episode was more on the order of a prank by comparison — it cost him nothing to brag about land that didn't exist. Maybe it was just a warm-up for this more convoluted con. But if his aim was just to steal his son's oil money, why not just grab what he could and start going by the name of some other old acquaintance? The only answer I can devise is that some of those investments must have been yielding ongoing proceeds to him, and so it was to his advantage to maintain them. His darker purpose likely involved the manipulation of Sophia, sending up smokescreens and creating expectations for payoffs that would never happen. If he could entice her to move to Virginia, it might have set up a situation where he could steal Marcus Wilson away, or do her some other injury, or simply laugh at her from afar.

I think that he wanted to 'win' the con in his mind. The Oklahoma Board of Health had outed him, and there's no doubt that he wanted revenge. And as we know, whenever some authority defeated Willis's plans, his wife of the moment had to pay.

After spending eight months in Tampico, he moved to the mining town of Charcas, in the mountains of the state of San Luis Potosi about 300 miles away, in late September 1908.[585] He worked as a doctor at the mines, probably for the American Smelting and Refining Corporation. From the available information, which is sparse, it appears that he remained in Mexico until 1911, except for a couple of months in 1909 to acquire the worthless deed to the ill-fated farm at Blackstone and again in 1910 to sign the deed in Lynchburg with Thaxton.

These were the last years of the rule of Porfirio Diaz, the strong-armed general-turned-politician who, by 1910, had been in power for about 30 years, an era commonly referred to in Mexico as the Porfiriato. Diaz was friendly to foreign investment and the large landowning interests in his country. During the final stages of his rule, especially, Mexico was a country of a few very wealthy haves and a multitude of have-nots. The land holdings of the Terrazas family, for example, have been estimated at between 4.8 and 6.6 million acres, while the only dirt most peons owned was what was on their hands and clothes.[586] Local institutions were corrupt, and officials were easily bribed. While foreigners brought needed capital into the country and developed the infrastructure to tap into its abundant natural resources, they also brought ethnocentrism and double standards, and their presence created resentment among

---

584 Oklahoma Wills and Probate Records, in the County Court in and of the County of McIntosh, Guardianship Records of Marcus Wilson McGuire, case #1644, Ancestry.com. Petition to appoint guardian, April 16, 1908.
585 Certificate of Registration of American Citizen, San Luis Potosi, Mexico, August 28, 1909, Ancestry.com.
586 Michael C. Meyer, *Mexican Rebel: Pascual Orozco and the Mexican Revolution, 1910-1915*, p. 11. These numbers approximately equal the total land area of Maryland, Rhode Island, Connecticut, and Delaware combined.

the populace, most of whom saw no path to prosperity.[587]

In June 1910, Diaz was again elected in a landslide. The following article summarizes the situation in the small village of Miñaca, in Chihuahua, the Mexican state directly south of New Mexico and western Texas.

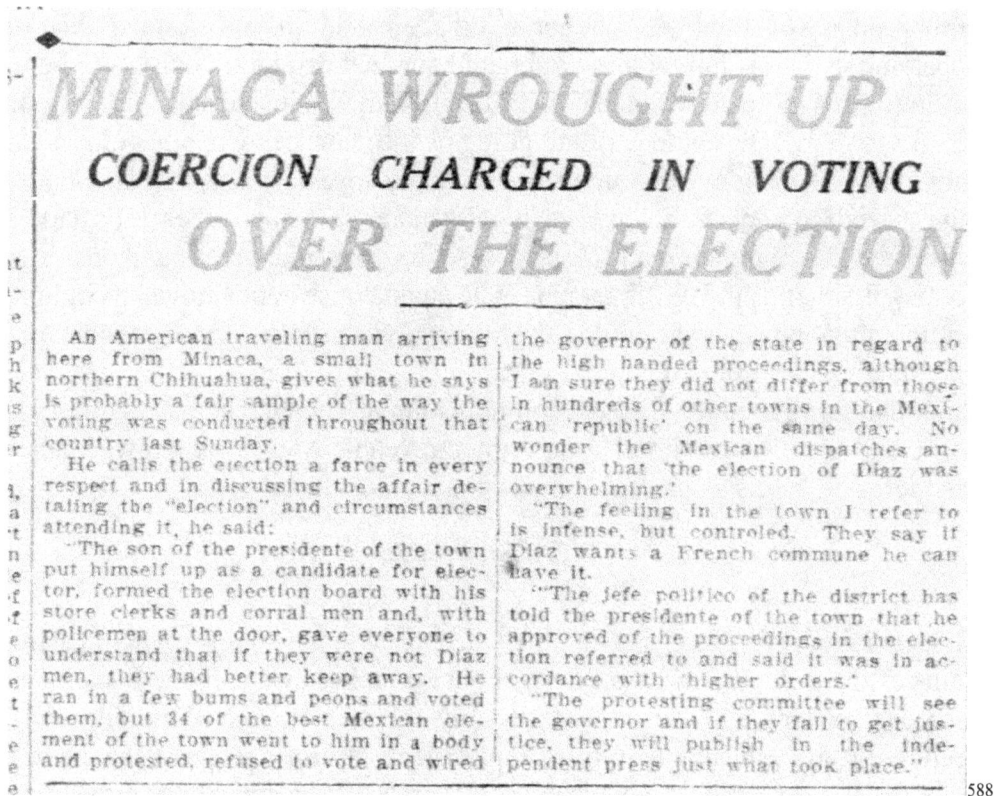

Transcription: An American traveling man arriving here from Minaca, a small town in northern Chihuahua, gives what he says is probably a fair sample of the way the voting was conducted throughout that country last Sunday.

He calls the election a farce in every respect and in discussing the affair detailing the "election" and circumstances attending it, he said:

"The son of the president of the town put himself up as a candidate for elector, formed the election board with his store clerks and corral men and, with policemen at the door, gave everyone to understand that if they were not Diaz men, they had better keep away. He ran in a few bums and peons and voted them, but 34 of the best Mexican element of the town went to him in a body and protested, refused to vote and wired the governor of the state in regard to the high handed proceedings, although I am sure they did not differ from those in hundreds of other towns in the Mexican 'republic' on the same day. No wonder the Mexican dispatches announce that 'the election of Diaz was overwhelming.'"

"The feeling in the town I refer to is intense, but controled [sic]. They say if Diaz wants a French commune

---

587 Alan Knight, *The Mexican Revolution, Volume I*, pp. 15-36.
588 The El Paso Herald, June 29, 1910, Ancestry.com.

he can have it.

"The jefe politico of the district has told the president of the town that he approved of the proceeding in the election referred to and said it was in accordance with 'higher orders.'

"The protesting committee will see the governor and if they fail to get justice, they will publish in the independent press just what took place."

It turned out that Miñaca, in Chihuahua's Guerrero Municipality, was at the center of an unfolding crisis in Mexico. About 300 miles south of El Paso and 100 miles west of the state capital of Chihuahua city, the tiny hamlet had become a railroad center since the Mexico Northwestern Railway and the Kansas City, Mexico & Orient had built lines through the place in the early 1900s. The Mexico Northwestern was an especially important player in the area, built and run by foreigners to serve the lucrative mining and lumber interests of the companies founded and run by F. S. Pearson. The railroad referred to Miñaca as "an important outfitting, forwarding and receiving point for a rich mining district."[589]

The general inequities in the country's social fabric and the tensions over land ownership boiled over about five months after the bogus election, in the series of conflicts that came to be known as the Mexican Revolution. For the next ten years, the country descended into intermittent, then almost constant chaos, and murder and robbery became commonplace. Francisco I. Madero, the leader of the Anti-reelection Party and 'loser' of the election, was arrested for "insulting the President and fomenting rebellion" soon after the rigged results were announced.[590] He escaped and went into exile in the U.S. in October 1910. Madero called for an armed uprising against Diaz to begin on November 20. On that day, most of Mexico remained quiet, though seething, but it was a different story in the Guerrero Municipality. Pascual Orozco, a muleteer from nearby Guerrero City and Madero's most effective general in the early stages of the rebellion, led his band of angry peons against the Federal garrisons in the area and swept them away one by one. The first town to fall, early on the morning of the 20th, was Miñaca.[591]

The entire Guerrero Municipality was firmly under the control of Madero's revolutionaries by spring 1911. Thanks to the military prowess of Orozco and Pancho Villa, most of the rural areas in western Chihuahua had been subdued, and the Federal presence was mostly limited to the large population centers, specifically Chihuahua city and Juarez, in the eastern and northern parts of the state. But while the rebels controlled travel on the railroads, and the foreigners operating them were required to work under their direction, Madero was explicit that his fight was with Diaz and his supporters, not foreign business interests. As soon as Orozco and Villa had made it clear who was in charge by tearing up some track and burning some bridges, the mines, sawmills, and railroads were all allowed to return to a semblance of normalcy. Except for relieving them of their weapons in the name of the cause and requiring

---

589 "The Road to Wealth," a promotional brochure published by the Mexico Northwestern Railway Company, November 14, 1909, p. 3.
590 Alan Knight, *The Mexican Revolution, Volume I*, p. 75.
591 Michael C. Meyer, *Mexican Rebel: Pascual Orozco and Mexican Revolution, 1910-1915*, p. 19.

that their trains not carry Federal soldiers, foreigners were treated politely and largely left alone. Madero gave strict instructions to his commanders to that effect. The murder and looting that characterized later stages of the conflict were not much of a problem in 1911, thanks to Madero's orders and the ruthless control Orozco, Villa, and other field commanders exercised over their forces.[592]

Why, you might be asking, has this book suddenly gone from discussing the sociopathic behavior of a bigamist telegrapher-turned-poser-doctor to examining the role of a village in western Chihuahua in the early stages of the Mexican Revolution? Well, because Dr. George Wilson McGuire died in Miñaca on April 5, 1911.

Before you cry too much, I should tell you that I believe his death was faked. More specifically, I think that the alias George Wilson McGuire died, but that the man who was wearing that alias, David Wilson Bethel, did not. I also think there is an outside chance that someone else, an unknown but real human being, died, too.

Willis had registered at the American consulate in Chihuahua city on March 24. His new job was with the Sierra Consolidated Mining Corporation in the Ocampo Municipality, about 190 miles west. According to the consular report of his death, "Deceased was enroute to Ocampo, Chihuahua, to take position as mining physician and died suddenly from heart failure, probably hastened by excessive altitude." The death occurred at a hotel operated by Clemens Jungk, a German American expatriate with longtime business interests in the area.[593] Jungk arranged for McGuire's burial in Miñaca and retained his trunk and its contents in good order. He even paid money out of his own pocket to help finance the funeral, since the amount McGuire had on his person was not enough. The consulate asked Mr. Jungk to forward Dr. McGuire's effects to them, and he complied.

All of this is perfectly plausible. Miñaca was on the railroad route from Chihuahua city to the mines, and it was logical for the doctor to be staying there in early April, especially with the intermittent train service resulting from the social unrest. Jungk was known to be a stand-up member of the expatriate community, and he would have unquestioningly arranged for the services needed, and paid what was required, to have his poor, deceased fellow American properly buried. Why then, Mr. Caldemeyer, do you think this death was a put-up job?

---

592 Alan Knight, *The Mexican Revolution, Volume I*, pp. 171-242
593 Report of the Death of an American Citizen, American Consular Service, Chihuahua, Mexico, April 29, 1911, Ancestry.com.

14.

"March 28, 1920"

■ THE FACE STARED OUT OF THE PICTURE AT ME, almost begging for recognition. It was the summer of 2010, and I was going through some old photographs, rediscovered by Jim and Kari in Aunt Marilyn's basement, with my mother, who was 93 at the time. We had come across a group of three pictures taken in the back yard of Durward and Alida Fisher's house in Wenatchee, Washington. In one, Alida stands with her only two children at the time, Durward Frederick, Jr. (whom the family called Fred) and Ida. They are bundled in coats, and my mother holds an enigmatic sheet of paper in her right hand, while her left clutches her mother's. Fred is on Alida's other side. The young family smiles shyly for the camera. The back of one of the copies is labeled, in Alida's handwriting, "Just home from Sunday School," the date, and "Get the grins."

The other two pictures are labeled only with the date, March 28, 1920, also in Alida's wispy hand. In one, the same three figures stand with an unidentified man, who is holding Fred's hand. Alida, still holding Ida's, stands to the right with a forced smile. The man is elderly, dressed in good clothes and an overcoat, with the dusty shoes of a traveler. He wears a nice pin of some sort in his tie and has a pinky ring on his left hand, the same hand to which Fred clings, his smiling expression now replaced by sullenness. The third photo has the same composition, but Durward has replaced Alida, as they had evidently switched cameramen. I asked my mother who the gentleman was, and she said, "I think that is Professor Eustace, my dad's mentor from Michigan State."

We continued through the stack until we came to another shot of Durward and Alida with four men, standing before a hedge with the same two children in front. In addition to the date (June 12, 1921), Alida had listed the names on the back of this one, as was customary for her, and in the middle was Professor Eustace. But it wasn't the same guy as in the previous set of three. I called my mother's attention to this, and we went back to the three pictures.

"Could that be him?" I asked. She didn't have to ask me who I meant by 'him,' since I'd been looking for information about her recreant grandfather, David Wilson Bethel, for over a decade by this time. All those years she had said she didn't know a thing about him.

"Nah . . .!" she said, with more vehemence than was usual for her soft-spoken demeanor, and certainly more than was called for. "I thought it was Professor Eustace, but if it's not him, then I don't know who it is." She waved her hand dismissively, and it was pretty clear she wasn't going to talk about it anymore. She was disgusted with me for ruining a sweet family history moment by bringing the subject up.

I took the photos back to Ohio with me. I scanned them and isolated the face of the man and put it side by side with the known picture of David Bethel from 1886. They *could* be the same person, separated by over 30 years. I overlaid the two faces in Photoshop. Although they were both about three-quarter views, they stared off center in different directions. But I was lucky, and the angles were about equal except for a difference in the tilt of the head. After flipping one of the images, the features of the frontal face matched exactly — eyes, nose, cheekbones, eyebrows, mouth, chin — all the frontal prominences of the face stayed in the same places as I moved the transparency slider. Finally, after over two decades of searching, first by Harry and then by me, here was evidence of David Wilson Bethel's existence after 1897, after 1911. It had been in our family's possession, buried in a stack of old photos, the whole time.[594]

Written on the back: "Just home from Sunday School
March 28, 1920 — Get the grins."

---

[594] The two photographs have been forensically compared, and while there is insufficient evidence (such as profile views) to definitively conclude they are the same person, "Observations support that to some extent the evidence image and the unknown person within the reference photo are consistent with being the same individual. A fair amount of agreement was observed in limited class features.
This conclusion is based on the following premises:
• There are multiple local class features in agreement between David Wilson Bethel and the unknown person within the evidence image. The strongest of these are the similarities drawn between the distinctive details of: - General curvature of face - Relative size of mouth - Relative size of nose - Jaw line - Eye distance - Neck shape
Thus: • Both individuals have some agreements in many local and global class features." (Focal Forensics Report Reference FMAP_20180716_ZG, *Facial Comparison*, July 17, 2018)

"March 28, 1920"

"March 28, 1920"

The photographs must have been taken to commemorate a visit by an insistent grandfather to a reluctant son and daughter-in-law and their young family. My grandmother Alida, clever and understated as always, marked the occasion with only a date — no name or other declaration of context, contrary to her usual practice — daring future generations to figure it out. If she were here, she might just smile and shrug, and quietly remark that she just didn't know which name she should have written down.

---

595 Photographs from Fisher family papers.

This composite progression was developed by overlaying the flipped image from 1886 onto the one from 1920 and adjusting the transparency setting.

This composite image is taken from the overlays above. It approximates what D.W. Bethel may have looked like around 1911. If it resembles an old photo of one of your ancestors, please contact the author.

Some aspects of the story of McGuire's death are fishy, making it believable that it was staged. To start with, if someone wanted to fake his death, Miñaca was one of the best places in the world to do it at the time. Whatever lax federal authority there was that normally oversaw the expat community had been chased away by Orozco, and the rebels didn't care to record such things as the deaths of foreigners, especially since they were responsible for some of them. The report from the consulate said that McGuire had "died suddenly from heart failure, probably hastened by excessive altitude." Miñaca's altitude is 6918 feet above sea level. High up in the mountains, for sure, but he had spent the previous two-and-a-half years at Charcas, with its 6627-foot altitude. Of course, he still could have had a heart attack, but he was certainly acclimated to the conditions. There were American doctors in the area at the time, but McGuire's death was not certified by one, in fact, the only known witness was Jungk. The death was not reported to the American consulate until April 29, over three weeks after the burial.[596] Local laws prohibited any exhumation of the body for at least five years.[597]

The timing, conveniently occurring right before the Oklahoma divorce decree became final on April 26, seems to be saying, "You can't divorce me — I'll die instead!" Willis may have waited to 'die' until he was sure that Sophia was not going to drop the suit. We know that he hated to be divorced by any of his wives, and he probably strung her along for as long as he could. Twice in December 1909, as he had previously with Nettie and Durward, he had given instructions for the disposition of his properties after his death. In his letter of December 6 he wrote, "the deed to farm, insurance papers, title guarantee, and said notes are all in one big envelope in my trunk, should I not live they will be sent to you together with what I have here." On the 28th he wrote, "I sent you those certificates so that in the event I died no shark could steal them — while they are worth about Sixteen Hundred ($1600.00) Dollars now you could not sell them unless I am dead, and you would then be Administrator, but I guess I won't die this time."[598] It appears likely that George Wilson McGuire's demise was on his list of things to do over a year earlier, just awaiting the right time for its execution.

Also, for what it's worth, April 5 was William and Mary Bethel's wedding anniversary. Willis may have chosen the date to honor his parents, or more likely, to commemorate his own precious conception.

Another piece of evidence, found buried in the documents retained by my family, contributes to the belief that D.W. Bethel may have survived his stolen moniker. In 1915, as Durward and Alida were establishing their professional lives in Wenatchee, Durward visited an old character in this story. Our only information about the event is contained in a letter Nettie wrote to her son and daughter-in-law on June 8.

> By what you say about Dr. Frank Carpenter & other things I judge that university is in Berkely [sic]. I'm glad you enjoyed his visit any way that's most always the case people we most fear are the most pleasant & easy to become acquainted with. I do hope there were no accidents on that picnic trip or any other trip.

---

596 It is entirely possible, given the unrest in the area at the time, that such a delay was justified, but the passage of time would have made it more difficult for anyone from the consulate to ascertain what really happened, if, in fact, they had been suspicious. And with all the upheaval in the country, Willis would have been pretty sure they had their minds on other matters.
597 *Report of the Death of an American Citizen*, The American Consular Service, Chihuahua, Mexico, April 29, 1911.
598 In the County Court, Muskogee County, Oklahoma, in the matter of the Guardianship of Marcus Wilson McGuire, Sophia McGuire, Guardian, case #1644. Report of W. C. Jackson, attorney at law, to the court, summarizing the contents of McGuire's effects and letters, April 1913, p. 2-3, quoting letter from George W. McGuire to Sophia McGuire, December 28, 1909 and letter from George W. McGuire to Sophia McGuire, December 6, 1909, Ancestry.com.

Nettie's letters to her only child during this period in her life are full of run-on sentences, bad spelling and grammar, and scattered thoughts, and they are riddled with cloying insecurities that would only get worse as she aged. We know that Durward was applying for a position at the University of California at Berkeley at the time. Evidently, he visited Dr. Carpenter, who taught at the university and maintained his family and a thriving practice in Berkeley. It appears that the Carpenters took him on a picnic.

Nettie and the rest of the Fisher family were well-disposed toward Dr. Carpenter — they considered him an old friend. Willis was the only person in Durward's life who would have ginned up any "fear" of the doctor in the young man. Durward had evidently told his mother about a minor accident that had occurred previously on the trip. She may have just been playing the part of a hand-wringing distant mother, but her cryptic reference to an accident that didn't occur at the Carpenter picnic may also have been a reference to the threats that D.W. Bethel had made against Carpenter. If so, it would indicate an awareness on her part that he was still alive. Nettie never mentioned Durward's biological father in her letters — she was in full denial by this point in her life. An oblique reference such as this would have been the closest she would have come.

We also have the memories, indistinct though they were, of Durward and Alida's son, my uncle Harry, that his father made periodic visits to see his father, wherever he may have been living, in the 1920s. All of these indications, considered along with the photographs and the events described in the coming pages, point at least to the possibility that Willis's death at Miñaca in 1911 was a fiction.

So, who the heck was Clemens Jungk, and what was his role? We know that he was born in Germany in 1852 and immigrated to the U.S. in 1882. He established a home in New Mexico and became an American citizen in 1887. He had a background in mining operations — when he first arrived in America he worked as a clerk for the Arkansas Valley Smelting Company at Leadville, Colorado. His cousin, Justus Jungk, was treasurer of the company and remained a prominent businessman in Salt Lake City throughout his life. Clemens first went to Mexico in 1897 to work for the Kansas City Smelting and Refining Corporation in Sonora, and later he was at Santa Eulalia, just east of Chihuahua city. But he had been at Miñaca, running his hotel and store, since 1902. It appears that when he was working for the mining companies, he was nothing more than a clerk, despite the lofty positions held by his cousin and some other relatives. He probably enjoyed the autonomy, authority, and income of being a prominent expat businessman in a small but lucrative frontier town like Miñaca. While living in Mexico, Jungk, who was married with two sons, claimed El Paso as his home address, and his family usually stayed there, traveling back and forth between Miñaca and the U.S. With the unrest in the country, they were almost certainly in El Paso in early 1911.

Clemens Jungk's passport photograph from 1920.

Jungk's strong friendships with the expat community in Mexico were illustrated by an event that had occurred just three months before Dr. McGuire died at his hotel. William Burling Tucker, a young mining engineer from California, was accused by "a squad of half-drunken revolutionists" in Miñaca of spying for the Mexican government. The article said that Tucker,

> was saved from being executed only by the devotion of a brave German storekeeper named Junk [sic]. Four times Tucker was stood up to be shot and as many times Junk by the most vehement protestations secured delays and finally saved his friend's life. Junk was asked if he would stake his own life in guaranteeing the neutrality of Tucker. "If we catch him doing anything that looks like assisting the government we will line you up with him and shoot you both. Do you agree?" Junk was asked. "I guarantee him with my life," replied the German and the shooting party was postponed indefinitely.[600]

So, Jungk was both loyal and brave. If he was also unprincipled, it would give him all the necessary attributes to pull off this deception. As an expat American hotel owner in rural Mexico, he may well have known D.W. Bethel, and by his real name, from the latter's previous travels south of the border. If Willis had come to him with a plot to escape his evil wife (as he certainly would have portrayed Sophia) and provide his son with some imaginary insurance money, Jungk probably would have said yes, especially if there was a payout involved.

Jungk reported that he found only $75.50 in Mexican currency on McGuire's person, which he put toward the burial. He submitted a bill to the consulate, which presumably was passed on to Sophia, for $66.30 (again, in Mexican money) for his other out-of-pocket burial expenses. Any receipts that came with the "itemized bill" would have been easy to falsify.

---

599 Passport application, Clemens Jungk, 1920, Ancestry.com.
600 The El Paso Times, January 2, 1911, Newspapers.com.

The cash in McGuire's trunk totaled $1.61 in American and Mexican coins. Just over a year earlier, Willis had written Sophia that he had "about Five Hundred and Fifty ($550.00) Dollars cash here in U.S. money — About One Hundred ($100.00) Dollars Mexican money."[601] He could have been exaggerating, but if this is any indication of the amounts he usually carried, the sum quoted by Jungk seems to be on the low side. Maybe Willis held onto some walking away money, or gave Jungk a payoff.

It's also possible, although I think much less likely, that Jungk was not involved, and that the only person in on the plot was Willis. This scenario would mean that someone unknown to Jungk, likely a traveling companion of Willis's that he had befriended at an earlier stop, died at the hotel in Miñaca, and that Willis switched trunks to make the deception stand. It would require a huge coincidence: the man dying at exactly the right time and place to suit Willis's plans. It's only plausible if we think he was capable of murder, likely by some poison that would mimic a heart attack. I think he probably was.

Willis's last letters as George W. McGuire had been to Wilson early in the year, his final, likely ineffectual, attempts to rattle his Oklahoma wife's cage. As he had in his last communications to his New York family, he focused on his seven-year-old son after negotiations with Sophia had broken down. On January 26, he wrote that his old buddy, attorney James M. Blair, would be visiting Checotah to arrange for a new guardian to assure that Wilson's "interests were safe," a clear shot at Sophia's choice for the job, Adolph O. Johnson. It was Willis's last chance to assert his fatherly authority, and it failed — once again, Blair didn't show up. He may have had enough of D.W. Bethel's games by that point (after all, there were reports that Willis had once used his name as an alias), or maybe he was a person who tended to promise more than he delivered.

On February 27, Willis sent his last letter to his Oklahoma son, "Since I wrote you before I've been well while I have had considerable cold I've been on the go and I'm thankful for that."[602] As usual, he was happiest when he was traveling (and working his loved ones for sympathy about his health). It's unknown where he wrote from, but he landed in Chihuahua city, probably sometime in March. He registered at the American consulate there on March 24 for his job at the mines in the Ocampo district.[603] We don't know how or where he applied

---

601 In the County Court, Muskogee County, Oklahoma, In the matter of the Guardianship of Marcus Wilson McGuire, Sophia McGuire, Guardian, case #1644. Report of W. C. Jackson, attorney at law, to the court, summarizing the contents of George W. McGuire's effects, April 1913, p. 3, quoting letter from McGuire to Sophia McGuire, December 28, 1909, Oklahoma Probate Records, Ancestry.com.

602 In the County Court, Muskogee County, Oklahoma, In the matter of the Guardianship of Marcus Wilson McGuire, Sophia McGuire, Guardian, case #1644. Report of W. C. Jackson, attorney at law, to the court, summarizing the contents of George W. McGuire's effects, April 1913, p. 7, quoting letter from McGuire to Sophia McGuire, December 28, 1909, Oklahoma Probate Records, Ancestry.com.

603 Certificate of Registration of American Citizen, Chihuahua, Mexico, George W. McGuire. March 24, 1911, Ancestry.com.

for the job, but it seems clear that nobody at the mines had met him personally, since the consular death report states that he was "enroute to Ocampo, Chihuahua, to take position as mining physician," and since Robert Linton, the general manager of the place, did not write a letter of condolence to Sophia and Marcus until July 21. Linton probably received notice of the death from the consulate. By far the fastest route from Chihuahua city to the mines was via the Mexico Northwestern Railway, which went the one hundred or so miles to Miñaca, and then the Kansas City, Mexico & Orient, which went the rest of the way.

It just so happens that we have already met the General Manager of the Mexico Northwestern, Henry Carr Ferris. This was the same H. C. Ferris who ran the Toledo & Ohio Central 17 years earlier, in 1894, when Willis had worked for the line in Columbus.[604] As far as we know, Willis exited that employment with a clean record when he went to California in early 1895. Ferris had been hired by the Mexico Northwestern in 1909 to oversee its construction and operations in the state of Chihuahua.[605] His headquarters in Chihuahua city must have been a busy place in early 1911 as the railroad reacted to the destruction wrought by Orozco and his demands that they change their practices to accommodate Madero's revolution. There were a number of communications between the general and the railroad leadership during this period, most of which were designed to prove to Ferris that there was a new sheriff in town, and that if he wanted to keep his line from being completely destroyed, he had better only run the trains where and when he was told and prevent Federal troops from riding them. At the same time, Orozco had a use for the rails for his own army, and Madero did not want to inherit a country without rail infrastructure, so as long as Ferris and his men showed compliance, which they usually did, the rebels turned their attention to their main mission of killing Federals and overthrowing Diaz.[606]

There is no question that the trunk that Jungk shipped to the U.S. consulate in Chihuahua city belonged to Dr. George Wilson McGuire. Aside from the mostly worthless Virginia deeds and some other identifying papers and photos, the inventory produced by the consulate listed a "Physicians and Surgeons outfit consisting of 19 separate pieces," and some other medical paraphernalia. For any deception to work, of course, Sophia had to recognize the trunk and its contents as belonging to her husband.

The total worth of McGuire's possessions was estimated by the consular employees at $160.86 U.S. currency, about $4,100 in today's money. The most valuable items were a Waltham gold watch, the physician's supplies, and three firearms, one of which was a .41 caliber revolver that was claimed by Charles Hawley Hoffman, a mining engineer at Charcas. McGuire must have either borrowed or stolen the gun, and Hoffman must have retrieved it from the consulate when he learned that McGuire had died. One wonders how he knew, but then, the expat community in Mexico was relatively tight, and people heard things. It would

---

604 The El Paso Times, August 31, 1912, Newspapers.com. This article, written on the occasion of Ferris's resignation from the Mexico Northwestern, gives a brief resume.
605 Ibid., August 4, 1909
606 Ferrocarril Noroeste de Mexico records, 1910-1919, archived at the Benson Latin American Manuscripts Collection, University of Texas Libraries, Austin, Texas. Telegrams and letters, mostly between managers, tell of the negotiations with the rebels during the first months of 1911.

be a stretch to conclude that Hoffman was aware of McGuire's plan to die in Miñaca without more information.[607]

The most interesting aspect of the inventory, from our point of view, is the date it was compiled — October 18, 1911, four days after the trunk's delivery to the consulate and over six months after McGuire's death. Jungk himself had been in Chihuahua city the last week of April to renew his own registration with the consulate.[608] It was at this time that he reported the death, but he did not bring McGuire's trunk with him, probably using the ongoing unrest as a reasonable excuse, since there was still fighting going on. But after late May, when Diaz resigned and left Mexico, the trains in Chihuahua again began to run normally on repaired tracks.[609] Although there was the usual occasional brigandage in the rural areas, the state of Chihuahua was largely peaceful, under an interim government, waiting for the free elections that would elect Madero in October.[610] Shipping a trunk the 100-or-so miles from Miñaca to Chihuahua city would have been no problem, but for some reason, Jungk delayed doing it. This timing, as you may have guessed, plays into a suspicious scenario.

On October 9, under the headline "Absconding Minaca Agent Still Among the Missing," the El Paso Times ran the following article:

> Chihuahua, Mex., Oct. 8 — The railroad and express agent at Minaca station, who skipped town about two weeks ago, is still skipping somewhere between that place and South America, according to a dispatch received from that place on Thursday. He was joint agent for the Northwestern, and Kansas City, Mexico & Orient railroads, besides handling the express matter for the Mexican Express company. In all the absconder secured about $2000, most of which belonged to the express company. Detectives are on his trail.[611]

The El Paso Herald published a similar story. Neither paper gave any other details about the agent — his name, even his nationality, remained unmentioned. It's possible that I'm barking up the wrong tree, but what if that agent was Willis? The station agent position at Miñaca had been notoriously hard to staff for the previous year because it was at the epicenter of the conflict. An account from December 1910 told of the agent there abandoning his post and joining the revolution, and the traveling auditor on the Chihuahua division of the

---

607 *Report of the Death of an American Citizen*, The American Consular Service, Chihuahua, Mexico, April 29, 1911. *Inventory of Personal Effects of Dr. George W. McGuire, Decd.*, October 18, 1911, Ancestry.com. Hoffman, like many Americans who worked and lived in Mexico at the time, is a somewhat elusive character, and we don't know much about him. Born in 1865 in California, he had been at Charcas since 1899. He was married to a Mexican woman from Zacatecas, and he died in San Luis Potosi in 1916.
608 Certificate of Registration of American Citizen, Chihuahua, Mexico, Clemens Jungk, April 22, 1911, Ancestry.com.
609 William H. Beezley, *Insurgent Governor: Abraham Gonzalez and the Mexican Revolution in Chihuahua*, p. 67
610 Alan Knight, *The Mexican Revolution, Part I*, p. 257
611 The El Paso Times, October 9, 1911, Newspapers.com

railroad, Frederick J. Clark, had to fill in because there was no one else available.[612]

A plausible (and at the same time, outlandish)[613] scenario might have gone something like this: In March, Willis was in Chihuahua city to register at the consulate for his job with the Sierra Consolidated Mining Company in the Ocampo district. At the same time, he applied to the Mexico Northwestern for the agent position at the Miñaca station, with the intention of exchanging the George McGuire alias for a different one. He might have looked up an underling on Ferris's staff whom he knew from the old days in Columbus and who had accompanied Ferris to Mexico, or he may have contacted Ferris directly. Either way, the railroad, desperate to staff the station, hired him readily. At Miñaca, he conspired with Jungk, whom he probably had known for years, to stage McGuire's death at the hotel. Then he simply walked over to the depot, took control, and began skimming money. The Guerrero mining district produced precious metals in abundance, which were shipped from the station. It also had plenty of mine workers who needed to be paid, so a good bit of cash also flowed through the depot. The theft may have involved many small sums over time or one big withdrawal in late September, or both.[614] During this time, he retained his trunk, and he may have lived at Jungk's hotel. Six months later, after he had accumulated enough to recoup his losses from the Virginia land deals, he pulled the good old Willis disappearing act. He may have gone to South America, as the El Paso Times suggested, or he may have left indications to that effect as a smokescreen and headed back to the States.

---

612 J. F. Hulse, *Railroads and Revolutions: The Story of Roy Hoard,* pp. 33-34. An account from the book illustrates how dangerous and fluid the situation was in the Miñaca area during this time, and the difficulties the railroad had in maintaining station agents there:
>   Clark's experiences with some of the people with whom he had contact were most unsatisfactory. He was accompanied to Miñaca by a Wells-Fargo agent, who soon left after requesting Clark to look after the Wells-Fargo business as well as the railroad business. About the same time the revolutionary paymaster stationed there approached Clark, suggested that they leave Miñaca and go overland to the West Coast on horseback. The paymaster, who was drunk at the time, said he had plenty of funds for the two of them. Clark told him it was out of the question for, other than himself, there was no one to leave in charge of the station. He was also responsible for looking after the Kansas City, Mexico and Orient railroad trains running from Miñaca to Sanchez, and he felt he could not walk away and leave the two railroads without an agent.
>   The next day the paymaster loaded his horse and saddle in an empty stock car ready to leave on the 1:00 P.M. Orient train. He insisted Clark go with him, and Clark, to pacify him, pretended to go. However, just as the train was leaving, two revolutionary officers rode up and ordered the engineer to stop. The officers had orders to bring the paymaster to headquarters, dead or alive, but he refused to go with them. The officers went to their horses to get their rifles, giving the paymaster and Clark the opportunity to jump from the train and hide behind a nearby building.
>   At this moment the paymaster's two brothers rode up with drawn guns, and their intercession permitted the paymaster to jump aboard the train, which then pulled out. The revolutionary officers telegraphed to the first station beyond Miñaca on the Orient railway to have the paymaster arrested and to send him back on the first train. He was sent back to Miñaca, where the revolutionists stretched him across a barrel and beat him with a sword, following which they ordered him placed in the front ranks when they attacked the Federals at Cerro Prieto.

These events took place during the height of the early stages of unrest, in December 1910/January 1911. Unfortunately, the book mentions nothing about the "absconding agent" from Miñaca in the fall of 1911.

613 It is typical of the events in D.W. Bethel's life to be both plausible and outlandish.

614 Since the newspaper specifically mentioned that $2000 was stolen, it seems likely that most of it came from one big theft, although he was probably skimming smaller sums as he went along. It's also possible that the auditors did not determine the total until after his abrupt departure.

Interestingly, on October 11, the San Antonio Express reported the following item:

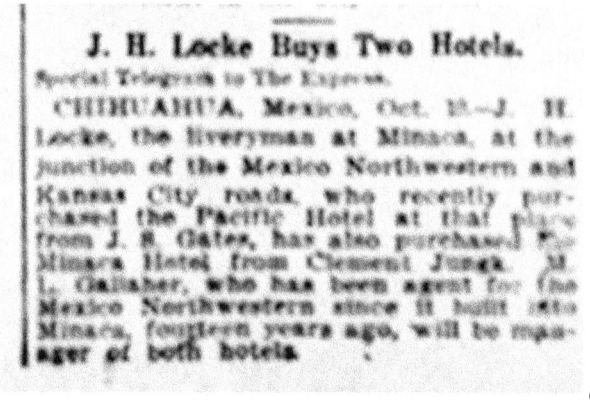

Transcription: Chihuahua, Mexico, Oct. 10 — J.H. Locke, the liveryman at Minaca, at the junction of the Mexico Norwestern [sic] and Kansas City roads, who recently purchased the Pacific Hotel at that place from J.S. Gates, has also purchased the Minaca Hotel from Clement Jungk. M.L. Gallaher, who has been agent for the Mexico Northwestern since it built into Minaca, fourteen years ago, will be manager of both hotels.

So, the agent skipped town in late September, Jungk sold his hotel on October 10, and four days later, on October 14, McGuire's trunk was finally delivered to the consulate at Chihuahua. The unrest in the country gave all parties involved the perfect excuse for the delay, allowing Willis to use his items while he embezzled funds from the railroads, but once he left Miñaca the trunk was sent on its way to fulfill its role in the deception. Because of a renewal of the fighting in 1912, it ended up sitting at the consulate for another year and a half before finally making its way to Oklahoma in April 1913, two years after Dr. McGuire's death.

Given some of the other bizarre stunts that D.W. Bethel pulled off in his life, this scenario is certainly believable. If so, it argues that Jungk was in on the plot all along. He may have sold his hotel to keep the detectives who were sent to investigate the theft from asking too many questions. They would have been looking into the disappearance of either D.W. Bethel or whatever alias he had adopted to get the Mexico Northwestern job, but Jungk may have decided that he needed more distance between himself and Bethel/McGuire, especially if Willis had been staying at his hotel for the previous six months. By the way, the reference to "M.L. Gallaher" in the article above is either a mistake or a red herring. We know that the Miñaca station had not been staffed contsistently for at least the previous eleven months. Maybe this was the alias Willis had used while in Miñaca, and Jungk (or Locke) fed it to the news media for fun. I continue to believe that my great-grandfather maintained a secret cadre of co-conspirators, men who cooperated with his plans just to have a good laugh.

---

615 San Antonio Express. (San Antonio, Tex.), Vol. 46, No. 284, Ed. 1 Wednesday, October 11, 1911, San Antonio, Texas, the University of North Texas Libraries, The Portal to Texas History, crediting Abilene Library Consortium.

I think the 'absconding Miñaca agent' was probably D.W. Bethel, but it's only a supposition — all of these coincidences also could have happened innocently. As far as where he went and what name he was calling himself after 1911, it's impossible to know as of this writing. There are almost 9 years, between April 1911 and March 1920 (Willis's appearance in Wenatchee with Durward's family), when D.W. Bethel's chosen identity and whereabouts are unknown. We also remain ignorant, of course, about how long he lived afterward, and when, where, and how he died.

The Railroad Skunk's trail has gone cold again, as it has so many times over the past twenty-odd years, and only a few avenues of pure conjecture, which we will address in the epilogue, remain. But first, we need to catch up with some of the other people in the story.

―――◇―――

Willis eased out of the back door of the car and softly lowered himself to the gravel, fairly sure that none of the passengers had noticed. He had been obvious about boarding the train, which was bound for Chihuahua city, and he knew that several people at the depot had seen him as planned, but his departure from the car was as stealthy as he could make it. He moved along the siding in the twilight and ducked into the barn where he had hidden the mule. As the sun was going down over the mountains and the train was pulling out east, he surreptitiously coaxed his mount into the hills northwest of Miñaca. He camped that night in a small ravine, with only a few cold tortillas for a dinner.

The next day, he headed north on the back mountain paths. By nightfall, he made it to a small farm just south of Tejolocachi. The farmer was surprised at this gringo's sudden appearance, but Willis's easy-going demeanor and his Spanish were enough to lower the man's defenses, and soon enough he was enjoying a hot meal and laughing with the man's family. Willis told them he was mining engineer who worked for the Pearson companies, and he had gotten turned around in the hills while scouting a site. He was glad to get a good night's sleep. The following day, he paid the man handsomely for his trouble, and by sundown he made it to Temosachic. He spent the next few days laying low at the house of his old friend, Lee Lindley, and his Mexican wife, Maggie. Lindley, who ran a store in town, found a buyer for his mule. On September 29, a week after he had skipped from Miñaca, Willis hopped on a train for Ciudad Juarez, confident that he was not being followed.

He befriended a man named Arnold Shipman, who was the most prosperous-looking American in the passenger car. Shipman was on his way to Nueva Casas Grandes to shore up his company's supply chain from the damage caused by the revolution. As they sat together, drinking whiskey and talking about the lumber business, Willis managed to slip a mickey into his companion's glass. Shipman soon fell into a deep sleep, and Willis rifled his pockets for his identification, and he also found about $150 more cash to add to his collection. He got off at Dedrick, secure in the knowledge that Shipman wouldn't be able to put the rurales on his trail until El Rucio, over 90 miles away, and to cross them up further he took the next train north again. As it passed El Rucio, he saw Shipman sitting on the platform, still looking *dazed. When they pulled into El Paso Willis used the man's papers to get across the border, but then he tossed them, knowing the cops would be looking for him soon enough. He stayed for several nights at the St. Regis Hotel, long enough to see the account of "absconding agent" from Miñaca in the El Paso papers. His plan to make them think that he had gone to South America had evidently worked, and they seemed to have swallowed it whole. He had talked up Colombia as a good destination for several weeks before he had left town, and he had purposely discarded a crumpled schedule of Gulf coast travel connections in the trash under the counter at the depot. "What a jolly time this revolution has been," he thought with satisfaction, but he was glad to leave Mexico before it got too dangerous. The next day, Mr. James Bryant caught a train for Colorado, where he had heard there were openings for good station agents.*[616]

---

616 *Bryant was an old acquaintance from Tennessee, whom Willis knew from his time with the Newport News & Mississippi Valley Railroad in 1893. He had once written young Bryant a reference letter, and he now used a copy of it, which he had assiduously kept, to assume the man's identity.*

15.

The Wives of Willis

■ WHILE WE HAVE ALL SORTS OF EVIDENCE THAT WILLIS BETHEL WAS INDIFFERENT to his procreative responsibilities, the opposite was generally true of the women he abandoned. Willis's first four wives, along with his eighth, Sophia Price, were fiercely protective mothers who were responsive to the needs of the children they ushered into the world. Annie Reed and Chrestine Hendricks, while not strong mothers, can be partially excused because of their youth. We don't know whether Willis had any children by Gertrude (probably his sixth wife), or how she handled the difficult position in which he no doubt left her.

Most of the evidence we have indicates that Willis's wives were naïve and conspiratorially rebellious, in the general tenor of both their young ages and the age in which they lived. Willis let them in on enough of his secrets to make them feel like participants who were bound to help and defend him, and their loyalty allowed him to victimize them. Once they had a young life to protect, however, most of them developed some ferocious mothering skills. This fact leads us to understand him a little better — he usually chose women whose gullibility made them vulnerable, but who also ultimately understood their obligations and were generally responsible people.[617] Despite the trauma and hardship his actions caused, these mothers were resilient, and they were able to guide the young lives he left to their care with determination and support them emotionally, financially, and morally. His children had only one parental role model, and yet most of them became good, and even exemplary, citizens.

We have already covered some aspects of the lives of the wives of Willis, but in this chapter I would like to tell as much of the rest of their narratives as we can ascertain. Much of the information about them is lost, but I have tried to build their stories from the records that are available and, when possible, testimony from relatives. Interestingly, of all his wives, only Sophia had any children with other men. One (Nettie) succeeded in having her marriage to him annulled, although she was emotionally impaired as a result. Two others (Chrestine and Sophia) succeeded in divorcing him, although Chrestine's long slide into substance abuse and debauchery began under his tutelage. Two (Jennie and Annie) tried to divorce him without success. Matilda and Annie both died young, the stress of their failed marriages probably a contributing factor. Both Jennie and Minnie lived out their long lives as D.W. Bethel's

---

[617] The exceptions to this generalization were Annie, who was self-centered, and Chrestine, who appears to have been criminally minded, but both of them abandoned their children to relatives.

widow, and neither (as far as we know) attempted to have him declared dead, despite the years that passed with him absent. It's fair to say that David Wilson Bethel left indelible marks on the lives of all of the women in this chapter.

Eliza Jane (Jennie) Howell (1849–1939)

Jennie and Bessie both remained in Flushing all their lives. They lived together until Jennie's death in 1939 at the age of 90, and Bessie remained in the same house on High Street almost until her own death in 1968.

There is some evidence that Eliza Jane (Jennie) Howell Bethel was estranged from other men in her life besides her husband. We have already glimpsed Willis's negative attitude toward her, and it appears that her own father did not regard her highly, either. Hiram D. Howell had three children by his first wife, Eliza Kirk (Jennie, born in January of 1849, was the third). Their oldest, Joshua, was killed in the Civil War, and their second, John Gilmer Howell, became a prominent doctor in southern Harrison County. Eliza Kirk Howell died in 1850 and Hiram remarried, and he had five additional children with his second wife, Martha. His will, executed after his death in 1894, provided for his estate to go to Martha until her death, after which it was to be divided among his seven remaining children, "That all of my said children above named shall share my said estate, both real and personal, equally, save and except my daughter Eliza Jane Bethel, whom I desire to have only one half (1/2) as much as <u>either</u> of my other children above named and no more."[618] We don't know what Jennie had done to deserve being singled out in such a manner. It's possible that Hiram had helped her financially after Willis left her, and so her inheritance came early in his eyes, but the emphasis seems to reveal that he regarded Jennie as a failure. Maybe he resented that she had not been able to get along with Martha. In the 1860 census Jennie, age eleven, was the only of Hiram's children not living in his home. Instead, we find her with Robert and Hester Kirk, her maternal grandparents.[619] It seems likely that Jennie may have been considered a difficult person, and by the standards of her day a woman who went her own way and voiced her true opinions would have qualified for such a designation. She may not have been submissive enough to suit either Hiram or Willis.

In the 1870 census Jennie, then 21, was back under Hiram's roof, helping Martha keep house, but probably nobody was happy about it. In the next decade, she didn't go on to marry a prosperous man, the fondest home that most nineteenth-century fathers held for their daughters. Instead, she may have reveled in her independence. By 1880, she was a servant in

---

618 Last Will and Testament, Hiram Howell, Flushing Township, Belmont County, Ohio, pp. 2–3, Ancestry.com.
619 U.S. Census, 1860, Flushing Township, Belmont County, Ohio, Hiram Howell family, Robert Kirk family, Ancestry.com.

the house of Simeon Pickering, likely a cousin to some degree of Willis's old friend Dillon Pickering, who lived just one farmhouse away.[620] She may have looked at her marriage to David Wilson Bethel, the devil-may-care young schoolteacher who would soon become a successful railroad office worker on his way up the ladder, as her way out of a servile life. But we know how that turned out.

While her relationships with men may have been rocky, she was, from all indications, a good mother. Jennie may have instructed her young daughter to be mistrustful of men, and she may have been needy, monopolizing Bessie's attentions. In all the census records, even later ones when Bessie was the only income-producing member, Jennie was listed as the head, although this may have simply been a gesture of respect.[621] Their relationship seems to have been a harmonious one, and one gets the feeling that they regarded themselves as a team. After Jennie died, Bessie maintained the same life course as she had before, so it's clear that her mother was not an impediment to some secret yearning. Jennie nurtured her daughter, and modeled a faithful, honest, and ethical approach to life. And as we will see in the next chapter, Bessie turned out great.

[622]

Jennie Howell Bethel sitting in her garden holding a chicken, about 1920.

---

620 U.S. Census, 1870, 1880, Flushing Township, Belmont County, Ohio, Eliza Jane (Jennie) Howell, Ancestry.com.
621 U.S. Census, 1900, 1910, 1920, 1930; Jennie and Bessie Bethel, Ancestry.com.
622 Photo originally shared on Ancestry.com by LynnGoodman2457, December 25, 2012

After Willis left, Jennie went back to cleaning houses for a living. The late 1880s and 1890s must have been especially difficult for her. As we have mentioned, she tried to divorce Willis in 1892–1893, but wound up with no outcome, and had to pay court costs of $2.84.[623] She seems to have found comfort in the Flushing Methodist church, and faith became an important element of her life.

The Flushing United Methodist Church, at 301 E. High Street, in 2002.

---

623 *Bethel vs. Bethel*, Belmont County Circuit Court documents, 1893, photographed at the Belmont County Courthouse, St. Clairsville. The sum would be about $82 in today's money (The Inflation Calculator, westegg.com)
624 Photo by Charles Caldemeyer, 2002

She worked until Bessie was old enough to work, then the two of them must have lived on Bessie's income, plus whatever inheritance Jennie acquired after the death of her stepmother in 1915.[625] The mother and daughter probably lived frugally, but they had some active friendships, and they maintained relationships with a number of relatives, including some members of the Bethel clan. They were well known in Flushing community life, and if more issues of the local newspaper were available we would undoubtedly see more mentions of their activities.[626]

[627]

Jennie Howell Bethel sitting on the front porch of her house on High Street, Flushing, about 1930.

---

625 Death Record, Martha Howell, Ancestry.com and Ohio Department of Health. *Ohio, U.S., Death Records, 1908–1932, 1938–2018* [database online]. Provo, UT, USA: Ancestry.com Operations Inc., October 2, 1915.
626 The only preserved issues of the Flushing News are from 1924–1926, on microfilm at the Ohio Historical Society Library, Columbus. Bessie and Jennie are mentioned twice, once for their attendance at a birthday party for Jennie's cousin, Walton Howell (December 18, 1924), and once when Bessie had an old tree on their property removed (November 13, 1924).
627 Photo originally shared on Ancestry.com by LynnGoodman2457, December 25, 2012

In the 1930 census she was listed as widowed. This was the first time since 1900 she had been so designated, and it's possible that she somehow found out that Willis had passed away during the 1920s. In February 1939, Bessie hosted a ninetieth birthday dinner party for her mother, attended by eight of Jennie's closest friends and relatives.

> **ENTERTAINED FOR MOTHER**
>
> Miss Bessie Bethel was hostess Monday evening at her home on High street to a number of guests honoring the ninetieth birthday anniversary of her mother, Mrs. Jennie Bethel. Following the six o'clock dinner a social evening was enjoyed. Mrs. Bethel, although ninety years of age, still enjoys good health. She does most of her housework and is a faithful member of the Methodist church.
>
> She was the recipient of a number of greeting cards during the day.
>
> Dinner guests were her close friends, Mesdames Ada Birney, W. R. Oglevee, Mary Oglevee, Edward Shallcross, Ward and William Bethel and Misses Alice Oglevee and Helen Shallcross. [628]

Transcription: Miss Bessie Bethel was hostess Monday evening at her home on High street to a number of guests honoring the ninetieth birthday anniversary of her mother, Mrs. Jennie Bethel. Following the six o'clock dinner a social evening was enjoyed. Mrs. Bethel, although ninety years of age, still enjoys good health. She does most of her housework and is a faithful member of the Methodist church.

She was the recipient of a number of greeting cards during the day.

Dinner guests were her close friends, Mesdames Ada Birney, W.R. Oglevee, Mary Oglevee, Edward Shallcross, Ward and William Bethel and Misses Alice Oglevee and Helen Shallcross.

Although she was in good health then, less than two months later, on March 21, 1939, Eliza Jane Howell Bethel died after contracting influenza. She was buried in Flushing Union Cemetery behind her beloved Methodist Church, which had given her so much comfort during her life. A prominent headstone (pictured in the next chapter) marks the spot. There was no mention of David Wilson Bethel in her obituary.

---

628 *Entertained for Mother*, The Belmont Chronicle, February 3, 1939, Newspapers.com.

BETHEL SERICES

Funeral services were held Friday afternoon at two o'clock for Mrs. Eliza Jane Bethel who passed away late Tuesday evenng at her home on High street, following a ten days illness of influenza and pneumonia.

She was born at Flushing, Jan. 24, 1849, the daughter of Hiram and Eliza Kirk Howell and lived her entire life in this community, where she was an active member of the Flushing M. E. church and a faithful worker in the missionary societies and other church activities.

She is survived by one daughter, Miss Bethel, cashier in the Flushing Savings and Loan Company, and one half-sister, Mrs. E. W. Shallcross, also of this place, also a number of nieces and nephews.

The remains were taken to the Romich funeral home and later removed to the family home where services were conducted Friday afternoon by Rev. A. A. Gilmore, pastor of the Flushing M. E. church, and burial was made in Union cemetery, Flushing.

Transcription: Funeral services were held Friday afternoon at two o'clock for Mrs. Eliza Jane Bethel who passed away late Tuesday evening at her home on High street, following a ten days illness of influenza and pneumonia.

She was born at Flushing, Jan. 24, 1849, the daughter of Hiram and Eliza Kirk Howell and lived her entire life in this community, where she was an active member of the Flushing M.E. church and a faithful worker in the missionary societies and other church activities.

She is survived by one daughter, Miss Bethel, cashier in the Flushing Savings and Loan Company, and one half-sister, Mrs. E.W. Shallcross, also of this place, also a number of nieces and nephews.

The remains were taken to the Romich funeral home and later removed to the family home where services were conducted Friday afternoon by Rev. A.A. Gilmore, pastor of the Flushing M.E. church, and burial was made in Union cemetery, Flushing.

---

629 *Bethel Serices* [sic], Eliza Jane Howell Bethel, The Belmont Chronicle, March 29, 1939, Newspapers.com.

Joannetta Henrietta (Nettie) Fisher (1860–1929)

Because she was my direct ancestor, I have more documentation of Nettie's life than some of the other women in this chapter. Most of the information and documents that began this investigation were saved and passed down by Nettie. That she kept any of it at all tells us something about her, and how much she valued her relationship with David Willis Bethel.

Joannetta and Durward Fisher, about 1894.

After her final farewell to the man of her dreams in 1897, money was probably tight, and since she suffered from a fragile temperament anyway, she was probably depressed. She

---

630 Photo from Fisher family papers.

had done housework and cared for Alathera Whipple prior to the latter's death, but we don't know how often she went out to clean other houses in the 1890s, although Willis referred to it in one of his letters.[631] We don't know what happened to the Whipple's house after she inherited it, but she may have sold it to meet expenses. The 1900 census finds her working as a cook and living at the Buffalo Homeopathic Hospital to make ends meet. Eleven-year-old Durward was still in Clarence, living on his Uncle Jake's and Aunt Sarah's farm while he attended school.[632]

Nettie was fortunate to have the safety net provided by the strong family ties that united German immigrant communities of the time. Her mother, brothers, sisters, and cousins were a constant source of support for her. Only excessive selfishness, irresponsibility, or laziness could get a member kicked out of these family units, and while young Joannetta had taken herself to the brink of that result, she had not crossed the threshold. But by 1900 it must have seemed to her that her life decisions had led her down a dark road.

This photo, dating from 1915, shows Eva Catherine Speith Fisher and her children. These individuals and their families provided the support system for Nettie. Front row (L-R): Nettie Fisher Helwig, Eva Catherine Speith Fisher, Katherine Fisher. Back row (L-R): Charles Fisher, Jacob Fisher, Anna Fisher Schurr, Bertha Meyer, George Fisher, Frederick Fisher, Jr.

---

631 Letter, D.W. Bethel to Joannetta Fisher #16, May 16, 1897, from Fisher family papers.
632 U.S. Census, 1900, Joannetta Fisher, Buffalo, Erie County, New York; Durward F. Fisher, Clarence, Erie County, New York, both Ancestry.com.
633 Photo from Fisher family papers.

As her younger sister Anna wrote in 1949, "It was a mess all thru until she met Uncle John."[634] That was John G. Helwig, a farmer and builder some nine years her senior who had been widowed in 1898, and whom Nettie married in 1901 at the age of 41.[635] He was a long-time friend of the Fishers and a member of their extended family by marriage to his first wife, Anna Seib.[636] The marriage allowed Nettie to reunite with her son on a full-time basis, relieving her siblings of the responsibilities of caring for him, and she proceeded to cement herself as a productive member of the Clarence community. Like Jennie, Nettie seems to have found comfort in her faith and the community of the German Reformed church in Clarence, for which she was Sunday School superintendent "for a time," as well as in some social causes. We know from her letters that she was active in both the women's temperance and the women's suffrage movements and was a member of the Ladies of the Maccabees Lodge, the women's auxiliary of Knights of the Maccabees, a group dedicated to lowering insurance costs, and the Rebekah Lodge, the women's arm of the International Order of Oddfellows.[637] The letters also reveal a strong love of gardening and animal husbandry, an affirmation of the farming background she was once so anxious to escape. She was sociable and had many friends — her later letters were filled with news about, seemingly, everyone in Clarence.[638]

The 1905 New York state census finds the Helwigs farming in Clarence, with John's mother and sister joining Nettie and Durward in the home.[639] By 1910, it was just John and Nettie. Durward was also listed as living in the home, although he was attending Michigan State Agricultural College at the time.[640]

---

634 Letter, Anna Fisher Schurr to Eva Katherine Wiley, September 27, 1949, from Fisher family papers.
635 Daniel C. Fisher and Irene A. Fisher, *A History of the Family and Descendants of Frederick and Catherine Speith Fisher (1825–1978)*, p. 13, from Fisher family papers.
636 The Seib extended family, which included Nettie's cousin and Willis's friend, Ed Seib, immigrated en masse from Germany around the same time as the Fishers, prior to the middle of the nineteenth century. Maria Barbara Seib was Nettie's paternal grandmother.
637 Joannetta Henrietta Helwig's letters to Durward and Alida Fisher, 1912–1928; Daniel C. Fisher and Irene A. Fisher, *A History of the Family and Descendants of Frederick and Catherine Speith Fisher*, from Fisher family papers.
638 Joannetta Henrietta Helwig's letters to Durward and Alida Fisher, 1915, from Fisher family papers.
639 New York census, 1905, John G. Helwig family, Clarence, Erie County, Ancestry.com.
640 U.S. Census, 1910, John G. Helwig family, Clarence, Erie County, New York, Ancestry.com.

Joannetta and John Helwig, about 1910.

Nettie probably found the most meaning in her life through the activities and achievements of her only child. Durward went directly into his U.S.D.A. employment after college, and the job moved him all the way across the country, to Washington state. We have many of her letters to Durward and his family. She wrote to them religiously, once every week. They are difficult to read — newsy to a fault, increasingly repetitive, and manipulative, especially as she aged, but they also show a generally positive attitude and document her helpfulness to others and her dedication to family. She and John made several trips to Wenatchee to visit Durward and his family during the time he was stationed there, and we also have photos that document their trips to Clarence.

---

641 Photo from the Fisher family papers.

The Durward Fisher family on a visit to Clarence, New York, about 1929. (L-R): Fred, Harry, Nettie, Durward, Ida, Evan (holding the dog), Alida, John Helwig. Nettie would pass away soon afterward.

By 1920, John had retired, and the couple lived alone, although both remained as active as their health would allow.[643] As she aged, Nettie began a slow descent into maudlin neediness and, eventually, what her nephew, Dr. Daniel Fisher, described as a disorder with "vague, unexplained symptoms" that, "In some respects . . . resembles a melancholia, in some a depressive psychosis, and then again it may be a psychoneurosis or even an early

---

642 Photo from Fisher family papers.
643 U.S. Census, 1920, John G. Helwig family, Clarence, Erie County, New York, Ancestry.com.

senile psychosis."[644] We will discuss this in more detail later, but it's clear that the last years of Joannetta Henrietta Fisher's life were filled with mental anguish, and that she placed some difficult demands on her relatives. Nettie died of a stroke on August 27, 1929, at the age of 69, and she was buried in the Fisher plot in Clarence Fillmore Cemetery. Her obituary spoke warmly of her importance to family and friends, her community involvement, and her marriage to John Helwig. No mention was made of David Willis Bethel.[645] John lived in Clarence until 1946, passing away at the age of 95. He was also buried in Clarence Fillmore Cemetery, although in the Helwig plot next to his first wife, Anna Seib Helwig. It seems likely that, although their marriage was a comfortable one, he was never able to replace Nettie's first husband in her eyes, and that the reverse was true, as well.[646]

OBITUARY

MRS. JOHN G. HELWIG

The end of the earthly existence of Mrs. John G. Helwig came at the family residence at Clarence Tuesday, August 27, 1929, at 3:30 in the afternoon. A long illness preceded the end, and those who were devoted to her saw her slowly slip toward the Better Land in spite of their care.

All her life was spent in this locality. She was born August 11, 1860, in the town of Newstead, the daughter of the late Mr. and Mrs. Frederick Fisher. This community which has known her through the 69 years of life has high praise for the fine traits of character she continually displayed. She was ever cheerful, agreeable and ready to aid in whatever way she was able. Her friends, who are many, feel her loss keenly, and console themselves with the thought that they enjoyed her presence for many years.

Her husband, John G. Helwig, to whom she was united in marriage September 15, 1901, survives to mourn his loss. Also sorrowing for her are one son, Durward Fisher of Wenatchee, state of Washington, who recently gave her great joy by coming for a visit, three brothers and one sister, Frederick, George and Charles Fisher and Mrs. Jacob Schurr of Clarence, and four grandchildren, Frederick, Ida, Harry and Evan Fisher.

Her religious affiliations were with the Reformed church of Clarence, which recently disbanded. Her membership in the W. B. A. and the Rebekah lodge of Clarence was valued by those organizations.

The funeral service will be held Friday afternoon at the family residence in Main street. Rev. Reed of the Methodist Episcopal church and Rev. Riley of the Presbyterian church will officiate. Six nephews will bear her remains to their last resting place in the Fillmore cemetery.

[647]

Transcription: The end of the earthly existence of Mrs. John G. Helwig came at the family residence at Clarence Tuesday, August 27, 1929, at 3:30 in the afternoon. A long illness preceded the end, and those who were devoted to her saw her slowly slip toward the Better Land in spite of their care.

All her life was spent in this locality. She was born August 11, 1860, in the town of Newstead, the daughter of the late Mr. and Mrs. Frederick Fisher. This community which has known her through the 69 years of life has high praise for the fine traits of character she continually displayed. She was ever cheerful, agreeable and ready to aid in whatever way she was able. Her friends, who are many, feel her loss keenly, and console themselves with the thought that they enjoyed her presence for many years.

Her husband, John G. Helwig, to whom she was united in marriage September 15, 1901, survives to mourn

---

644 Letter, Daniel Fisher to Durward Fisher, August 6, 1928, from Fisher family papers.
645 *Obituary, Mrs. John G. Helwig*, probably in The Clarence Bee, August 1929, from Fisher family papers.
646 Memorial #81076630, Helwig plot, Clarence Fillmore Cemetery, Clarence, New York, Findagrave.com; Memorial #29246757, Fisher plot, Clarence Fillmore Cemetery, Clarence, New York, Findagrave.com.
647 *Obituary, Mrs. John G. Helwig*, probably in The Clarence Bee, August 1929, from Fisher family papers.

his loss. Also sorrowing for her are one son, Durward Fisher of Wenatchee, state of Washington, who recently gave her great joy by coming for a visit, three brothers and one sister, Frederick, George and Charles Fisher and Mrs. Jacob Schurr of Clarence, and four grandchildren, Frederick, Ida, Harry and Evan Fisher.

Her religious affiliations were with the Reformed church of Clarence, which recently disbanded. Her membership in the W. B. A. and the Rebekah lodge of Clarence was valued by those organizations.

The funeral service will be held Friday afternoon at the family residence in Main street. Rev. Reed of the Methodist Episcopal church and Rev. Riley of the Presbyterian church will officiate. Six nephews will bear her remains to their last resting place in the Fillmore cemetery.

Joannetta's inscription on the Fisher Monument, Clarence Fillmore Cemetery, Clarence, New York.

---

648 Find a Grave Memorial 29246757, Fisher plot, Clarence Fillmore Cemetery, Clarence, New York, Findagrave.com. Photo credit: Candy.

Matilda Ralston Gilmour (1859?–1893?)

Unfortunately, we don't know much about her, and while we have records of her direct descendants, we have had no contact with them, so few family stories add to this history. It may well be that they would have little to add, anyway. Mary Ralston Bethel was less than two years old when her mother died, so she would have had no memories to share with her own children. We have public records and accounts from other relatives that allow us to track Mary as she made her way through life. But Matilda remains largely enigmatic, due to the poor quality of record keeping in rural Pennsylvania in the late nineteenth century and lack of documentation by her family.

This limitation includes the cause and date of her death, which the reader will remember occurred in August of either 1892 or 1893, with the latter date being more likely. Matilda must have been an emotional wreck when she showed up at her sister's farmhouse in Venango County, Pennsylvania in the summer of 1892 with young Mary in tow. Willis had just left her in Owingsville, without warning or funds, in debt, and with a toddler to care for. Deadly diseases were rampant at the time, but the stress of her ill-fated marriage must have at least contributed to her early demise.

The Ralston siblings had begun to show up in Pennsylvania as early as the 1870's. As with the Fishers in western New York, as soon as one, usually male, family member established himself others followed, and so the family unit was gradually strengthened and enhanced. Unlike the Fishers, who clustered closely together in the Clarence/Clarence Center/Newstead/Amherst area, the Ralstons were a little more adventurous, and spread out wider. While the distances were not great, they were significant given the modes of travel at the time. Throughout the 1880's, Thomas (1848–1902) and Robert (1851–1912) settled in the Brockway area, and William (1853–1911), Joseph (1863–1934), and later, Mary Ann (1846–1915) set up shop in DuBois. But Sarah Jane (1850–1902) and Matilda had arrived earlier, and they pushed farther west, ending up in southern Venango County.[649]

Thompson McGinnes (1835–1899) was a farmer who lived in Scrubgrass Township, near the village of Emlenton. In 1880, he was a widower — his first wife, Sarah Jane Jolley, with whom he had ten children, had passed away the previous year. Thompson, Sarah Jane Ralston, and Matilda Ralston are found on the same page of the 1880 census — the newly widowed Thompson with nine mouths to feed living next door to Sarah Jane Ralston, who like many single female immigrants, did domestic work. Matilda, then about 20, was also working as a domestic in the home of local oil producer James Young.[650]

But that is just what the census taker wrote down, because he needed categories to place

---

[649] U.S. Census, 1910, DuBois, Clearfield County, Pennsylvania, William, Joseph Ralston, Mary Ann Moore; U.S. Census, 1900, Brockway, Jefferson County, Pennsylvania, Thomas Ralston; Death Certificates, DuBois, Clearfield County, Pennsylvania, Mary Anne Ralston Moore (1915), William Ralston (1911), Joseph Ralston (1934); Death Certificate, Brockway, Jefferson County, Pennsylvania, Robert Ralston (1912), all Ancestry.com.

[650] U.S. Census, 1880, Scrubgrass Township, Venango County, Pennsylvania, Thompson McGinnes, Sarah Jane Ralston, James Young, Matilda Ralston, Ancestry.com.

people in, and because America retained some English hierarchical traditions. In actuality, the connections between immigrants, especially Irish immigrants living in the same house, was usually much more egalitarian than the master/servant relationship supposed by English traditions, largely because the members were all relatives. The Ralston girls were cousins to the Youngs, and all had emigrated from the same area of Ireland.[651] Young had come first and had made good both as a farmer and an oil producer, and so he had been able to give his cousins shelter. According to Nell Young Smith, James's daughter, "Sarah MacGinnis and Matilda Bethel lived with my father and mother and was always close friends."[652] It was important that relatives watch out for one another in an environment that could be unforgiving.

After Thompson McGinnes and Sarah Jane Ralston married in the early 1880s they had two children of their own, William Ralston McGinnis (1882–1965) and Jessie V. McGinnis (1883–1955). Matilda was also married around this time, to a man named Gilmour, but the only record we have of it is found on her marriage license to Willis, which gives only her married surname and the information that she was widowed on February 8, 1888.[653] Frustratingly, no other records exist. Jim Sterrett, our source for much of the information about the Ralston family, remembered that his first name was Stephen, but there are several men found in the records with that name (or some variation), and Matilda's first husband could be any, or none, of them.[654]

If, as appears certain from the way he wrote about her, Matilda was the woman in Buffalo whose association with Willis earned him his invitation to leave Clarence, it seems likely that she was already living in the area when she was widowed. If that was the case, then Mr. Gilmour may have been from the Buffalo vicinity, but we don't find any surefire suspects in the records there, either.

The only official records that identify Matilda are the 1880 census and her marriage license to Willis in 1890. Most of the little information we have about her comes from two unreliable sources — Willis, whose agenda in referencing her was to make himself appear blameless, or even a victim, and Ben Perry, whose description of her requires confirmation from another source to be believed. It appears to have been calculated to wring a reaction out of Nettie, possibly for the purposes of town gossip, or to engineer a reunion with Willis. Unfortunately, sources sympathetic to her, such as the letters of Nell Smith and William Ralston McGinnis, don't tell us much about her.

---

651 Conversation with Jim Sterrett, January 6, 2007.
652 Letter, Nell Smith to James Sterrett, April 23, 1965.
653 Marriage license #3, David W. Bethel and Matilda Ralston Gilmour, September 3, 1890, Ancestry.com.
654 Conversation with Jim Sterrett, January 6, 2007.

Minnie Rietman (1869–1965)

Willis's relationship with his Cincinnati family was unusual in that he stayed around for almost four years, long enough to sire two children, twice his usual donation. Part of the reason for this longevity (a relative term when applied to Willis Bethel's love life) was probably that they seem to never have actually lived together. Willis was living in Owingsville with Matilda when Minnie bore Elsie Ruth Bethel on July 30, 1892, which means that he and Minnie were in their relationship around the time Matilda gave birth to Mary on September 30, 1891. He must have continued his trysts with Minnie while he worked at Lexington in the last months of 1892. We don't know exactly where he resided when they were married (Indianapolis, western Kentucky, and western Tennessee are all possibilities) in September 1893. Later, as he worked his way back toward a station agent position, he was based in Chicago, and he was in Columbus for the three or four months prior to going to California. Willis never had to deal with the day-to-day routines of married life with his Cincinnati family. This may have curbed his restlessness for a while, but in the end, of course, he left anyway.

It may also have been that he enjoyed a special bond with Minnie, a fellow telegrapher, and that they had common friends up and down the line. We have already discussed the camaraderie found in the ranks of these workers, "members of a closed, exclusive community."[655] Willis must have felt some of that amity for Minnie, and it's certain that she did for him, as evidenced by the fact that good feelings about him were carried on by their descendants over the years. Minnie was the only one of his wives, not counting the deceased Matilda and the absent Gertrude (about whom nothing is known), who did not try to dissolve her marriage bonds to Willis at some point. Only two of the over 60 records at our disposal, the 1900 census and the notation on her burial record in 1965, list her as divorced.[656] I have been unable to locate any divorce proceedings, and all other records list her as the widow of David Willis Bethel. If Minnie did not think that Willis had died, she at least decided that was the most expedient way to explain his absence. The census taker in 1900 may have just filled in "divorced" when Minnie had no answer as to where her husband was, or she may have been angry that day. The burial record was, of course, also filled out by another. Minnie seems to have been resigned to being Willis's widow, and she was content to simply raise the children he had left her. Her great-grandson notes that she may have harbored some bitterness, and given the way she was used, that would be understandable.

We know that Willis wrote to Nettie, but we don't know if, or for how long, he wrote to Minnie after he abandoned her in 1895. It was safe for him to write to Nettie — he wasn't allowed to be with her, but Minnie was a different story. If he had sent her a letter like the ones he sent to Nettie, with his name printed on the letterhead, or even told her about his

---

655 Tom Standage, *The Victorian Internet*, Kindle edition, Location 1350
656 1900 U.S. census, Minnie Bethel family, Cincinnati, Ohio, Ancestry.com; Interment Record 154093, Minnie Rietman Bethel, Spring Grove Cemetery, Cincinnati, Ohio, April 28, 1965, springgrove.org.

position at Perris, her next question would have been, "So, where are the rail passes for the children and me?" It seems unlikely that he corresponded with her for long, or if he did he must have misrepresented his situation. He may have kept up the illusion that he was coming back, or about to bring his family to him, at least for a while. Maybe he sent some money her way occasionally, as he did with Nettie, but it was likely the same story of promises, excuses, delays, and lack of follow-through. Either she finally concluded that he must be dead, or she heard that news from a friend she trusted. It's even possible that Willis asked one of their friends to get in touch with her and give her the bogus story that he had tragically died.

Minnie was the longest lived of any of Willis's wives in this history, passing away at the age of 95, outliving even their daughter Elsie. Along with first wife Jennie and eighth wife Sophia, Minnie seems to have had a toughness and resourcefulness that some of Willis's other victims lacked. Matilda died within two years of his abandonment, and Nettie and Annie fell apart and were impacted by his "disappearing act" for the rest of their lives. Chrestine descended into a dissolute, and ultimately fatal, lifestyle. But Minnie seems to have gotten up, dusted herself off, and set about the business of raising and supporting her children, alone but for the help of her family.

But her early experiences certainly took a toll on her. Her great-grandson described her as "not a very pleasant person," and followed up with:

> We called her Grandma Bethel most of the time, sometimes Grandma Reitmann. You are right, she was a strong women, never re-married or sought a divorce (I don't think), but she was not warm and fuzzy. My brother said he remembers her as being distant, not mean-spirited, so maybe she just didn't care for me so much. Again, I think you're right, she was probably bitter about how DW deceived her. I wonder how long DW strung her along, thinking she was his one and only. Did he tell her, or just disappear?[657]

She remained in Cincinnati almost her entire life, and we can track her closely with records in censuses, directories, and other sources. Like Nettie and Matilda, she had a strong support system in place in the form of her family and the German American community. People acquired success because everybody chipped in and helped where needed without hesitation. Minnie made an attempt at living on her own, renting a house at 3105 Eastern Avenue beginning in 1899 (the first year she was listed as Willis's widow), and by 1901 her brother George Jr. had joined her and her children. She had a home confectionery business, which she maintained for several years. But George Sr. and Elizabeth were probably never far away, and by 1905 she had moved back with her parents and sister Ella in the family home at 3020 Columbia Avenue. George Rietman, Sr. died in 1907 of lead poisoning, the occupational hazard of house and sign painters of the day. That year, with Elsie and Clarence now 15 and 12, respectively, Minnie went back to her first occupation, telegraphy, at a company

---

657 Emails, Thomas Trapp to Charles Caldemeyer, June 7 and June 8, 2018.

called Postal Telegraph-Cable, where she remained until her retirement. The family continued to live with Elizabeth at the house on Columbia Avenue until 1922, when they moved to a home on Markbreit Avenue.[658]

Our last record of her professional life comes in 1931. She had been promoted to Assistant Traffic Chief at the company, and she still lived at the house on Markbreit with her mother and widowed sister, Ella. Elizabeth died in 1934 and Ella in 1937, but Minnie continued to live at the house through the 1940's, although the 1940 census records her as residing with Elsie and her husband, Herbert Smith, while Clarence and his family occupied the Markbreit Avenue house.[659] It seems likely that "Grandma Bethel" went back and forth between the two families.

By the mid-1950s Minnie, then in her eighties, lived with Elsie and Herbert at 1902 Andina Avenue. But Elsie was widowed in 1958, and both mother and daughter moved to Tampa, Florida. Minnie's sister Cora lived nearby, in Clearwater. Minnie died in her home in Tampa on April 25, 1965, about a month shy of her 96th birthday, and was buried in the Rietman plot at Spring Grove Cemetery in Cincinnati three days later.[660]

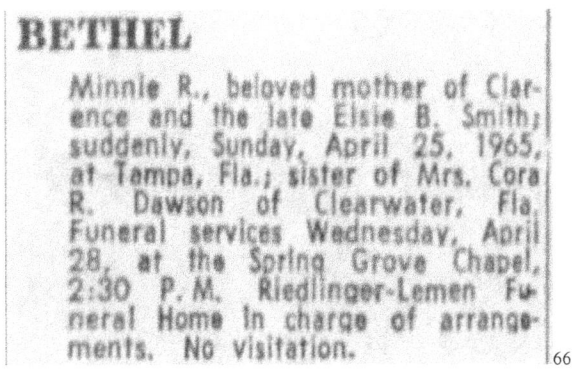

[661]

Transcription: Minnie R., beloved mother of Clarence and the Elsie B. Smith; suddenly, Sunday, April 25, 1965, at Tampa, Fla.; sister of Mrs. Cora R. Dawson of Clearwater, Fla. Funeral services Wednesday, April 28, at the Spring Grove Chapel, 2:30 P.M. Riedlinger-Lemen Funeral home in charge of arrangements. No visitation.

---

[658] U.S. Census, 1900, 1910, 1920, Cincinnati, Hamilton County, Ohio, Minnie Rietman Bethel; Cincinnati, Ohio directories, 1886, 1892, 1895, 1897, 1899, 1901, 1905, 1907, 1909–1910, 1912, 1917, 1921, 1922, Minnie Rietman Bethel, all Ancestry.com.

[659] U.S. Census, 1930, 1940, Minnie Rietman Bethel, Clarence Bethel, Elsie Ruth Bethel Smith; Cincinnati, Ohio, directories, 1923, 1927, 1931, 1936, 1942, 1945, Minnie Bethel, all Ancestry.com.

[660] Interment Record 154093, Minnie Rietman Bethel, Spring Grove Cemetery, Cincinnati, Ohio, April 28, 1965, springgrove.org; Cincinnati, Ohio, directories, 1956, 1958, Ancestry.com.

[661] *Bethel,* Obituary, Minnie Rietman Bethel, The Cincinnati Enquirer, April 27, 1965, Newspapers.com.

Minnie Rietman Bethel holding her great-grandson, early 1950s.

Headstone, Minnie Rietman Bethel, the Rietman plot, Spring Grove Cemetery, Cincinnati, Ohio. Her birth year was inscribed incorrectly – all other records, including her burial record, say she was born in 1869.

---

662 Photo courtesy Thomas Trapp.
663 Photo by Charles Caldemeyer, 2016

Annie M. Reed (1880–19??)

Aside from Matilda, whose association with Willis ended with her death, Annie was among the wives who suffered most from her marriage to the Railroad Skunk. Like Chrestine Hendricks, Miss Uptodate labored under some youthful delusions, and they made her especially vulnerable to his designs. She must have thought she had married the catch of the town, a popular, worldly, confident, and successful man who would provide for her generously and keep her entertained in the process. All of Willis's wives were dreamers to some extent, but Annie's head was in the clouds. The fall back to the hard surface of this planet must have been excruciating for her, and the landing was likely fatal.

We can establish a fairly accurate timeline of Annie's first few years as Mrs. Bethel because of newspaper accounts and directories, but then the view becomes murky, and finally, she disappears altogether. The couple remained in Perris for a few days after their wedding, then they removed to Los Angeles, where the paper said they intended to reside, although Willis's intentions were clearly different from Annie's. In late October, Annie visited friends and relatives in Perris, returning to "her home in Los Angeles" on November 3.[664] But on November 7, 1896, according to later court documents, Willis "left the plaintiff, and has been continuously absent since."[665] He must have said he was going away to look for work, and just kept on going. They had been married for exactly 38 days.

Annie gave birth to Raymond Harry Bethel on July 9, 1897, so she may have been pregnant before the couple even left Perris. It seems likely that she went to Michigan to give birth to her baby. Although no records confirm it, I believe that her mother, Martha Frasier Reed, died in Perris in early 1897 (a descendant of Annie's sister Bessie gave her death year as about 1895, but Mattie Reed is still found in local news accounts in Perris through 1896, although not beyond).[666] Annie's grandmother in Michigan was also dead, but she still had plenty of relatives there, and she probably carried her pregnancy to term in one of their homes. Her uncle Jerome was a prominent farmer in Shiawassee County, just west of Flint, and his wife and two of their daughters were still at home to give Annie some help.[667] Raymond's obituary said that he was born in Detroit, and it is also possible that Martha Frasier Reed had other relatives there who assisted their niece or cousin in her hour of need.[668]

---

664 The Perris New Era, November 5, 1896, microfilm from the California State Library, Sacramento.
665 *Bethel vs. Bethel*, The Superior Court of Los Angeles County, State of California, April 10, 1902, case #38621, p.5, records request from the Superior Court of Los Angeles County.
666 Tidbits about Martha Frazier, courtesy LadyLittle, Seeley Family Tree, Ancestry.com. We know that Martha Frasier Reed did not die prior to 1897 because there are mentions of her in The Perris New Era through 1896. Unfortunately, issues of Perris newspapers after 1896 are missing. She probably died between January and July 1897, with a death date early in the year being most likely.
667 Biography of Jerome Bonaparte Frasier, from *Portrait and Biographical Album of Clinton and Shiawassee Counties, Michigan, 1891*
668 Obituary, Raymond Harry Bethel, Santa Cruz Sentinel, Santa Cruz, California, September 19, 1958, Newspapers.com.

It should be stressed that the Reed family was not one that obsessed about their heritage. The same descendant of Bessie Reed wrote,

> I talked to my great aunts. They remember that Annie was considered to be 'weak'. But didn't know much more than that about her, but then they grew up right down the street from one of their uncles and didn't know they were even related to him till years later.[669]

Whether the description of Annie as 'weak' meant she was prone to illness, friendly with men to a fault, or unable to successfully negotiate the demands of life, is unknown. Probably all three, in varying measures.

All of the Reed children seem to have lived for the moment. They moved every year or so in the late 19th and early 20th centuries, and probably kept few mementoes, letters, or family photos. All family history was passed down by word of mouth, if at all, and if things got a little garbled, well now, close enough. And Raymond spent much of his childhood in orphanages, which could have operated against him knowing or caring about his birth parents, and it appears that he did neither. Under such circumstances, it would not be surprising if Shiawassee County, Michigan became Detroit in family stories over the years. Detroit's in Michigan, too, right?

Soon after Raymond's birth, she took him to California and joined the only family she really knew, her siblings back in Perris. In fall 1897, the five Reed children decided to move to Los Angeles, and there are several accounts of their departure in the Perris section of the Riverside newspapers. If we had the 1897 papers from Perris, no doubt the fanfare would have been greater. The Reed siblings, the salt of the earth, were Perris's kind of people.

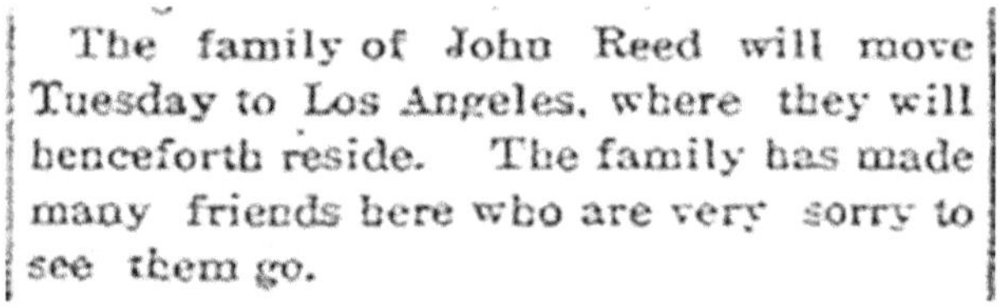
The family of John Reed will move Tuesday to Los Angeles, where they will henceforth reside. The family has made many friends here who are very sorry to see them go.

[670]

Transcription: The family of John Reed will move Tuesday to Los Angeles, where they will henceforth reside. The family has made many friends here who are very sorry to see them go.

669 Note from LadyLittle, administrator of the Seeley Family Tree, Ancestry.com.
670 The Riverside Daily Press, November 23, 1897, GenealogyBank.com.

> Mrs. Bethel, Miss Bessie Reed and John Reed departed for Riverside on Monday. Guy went on wheel at a 2:04 gate on Tuesday evening, and George went on Wednesday morning with a load of goods. They will meet at Riverside and then proceed to their future home in the Angel City.[671]

Transcription: Mrs. Bethel, Miss Bessie Reed and John Reed departed for Riverside on Monday. Guy went on wheel at a 2:04 gate on Tuesday evening, and George went on Wednesday morning with a load of goods. They will meet at Riverside and then proceed to their future home in the Angel City.

> A farewell party was given to Guy Reed and sisters last Monday night at the home of J. W. Porter. A select company enjoyed a merry time until a late hour.[672]

Transcription: A farewell party was given to Guy Reed and sisters last Monday night at the home of J.W. Porter. A select company enjoyed a merry time until a late hour.

The Riverside papers seem to have gotten the timing of the move garbled, but there is no mistaking the respect shown to the Reed family. They were not important people in the usual sense — John and Guy were known to be hard workers, but at menial jobs, Bessie was in school, and Annie and George had accomplished little. It's likely that there was a great deal of feeling for them in Perris since they had recently lost their mother, and for the way Annie had been used by Willis. It must have been obvious to their friends by that point that he was not coming back to her.

According to later court documents, his letters stopped coming soon after the move, on December 7.[673] In 1898 the four oldest Reed children were listed in the Los Angeles directory, living at 1110 E. 8th Street. John worked as a miner and Guy as a clerk at a grocery. Bessie was probably still attending college and working part time. Annie likely remained home with baby Raymond.[674]

---

671 The Riverside Independent Enterprise, November 28, 1897, GenealogyBank.com.
672 The Riverside Daily Press, December 1, 1897, GenealogyBank.com.
673 *Bethel vs. Bethel*, The Superior Court of Los Angeles County, State of California, April 10, 1902, case #38621, p.5, records request from the Superior Court of Los Angeles County. The documents list December 7, 1897 as the date of Willis's abandonment of Annie and Raymond. Since he had been "continuously absent" since November 7, 1896, this must mean that was the date when communication ceased.
674 Los Angeles, California, Directory, 1898, Mrs. Anna M. Bethel (p. 166), Bessie (p. 839), John, Guy Reed (p. 840), Ancestry.com. George seems to have found city life unsuited to his needs, and he returned to Perris, where he remained at least through the 1900 census.

The constant grind of motherhood must have been too much for the eighteen-year-old. Maybe her brothers rebelled at providing for a child they did not create, maybe Annie wilted under the responsibilities, or maybe she just felt robbed of her life as a carefree young woman. Some combination of those factors must have driven her to place Raymond in the Home of the Guardian Angels Orphan Asylum on January 6, 1899, when he was eighteen months old. He was listed in the "half orphan" section of their records.[675] From later events we know that Annie did not really believe that Willis was dead, but she probably had to say he was so the orphanage would accept their son. From her perspective, for all intents and purposes, it was true, too.

Only Bessie is to be found in Los Angeles in the 1899 directory, at a different address.[676] The Reed siblings were each looking to establish themselves in a difficult world, and they had few resources at their disposal. Their lives and their living arrangements were probably fluid, and they may have moved back and forth between Los Angeles, Perris, and other places during this time. Annie may have been living with one of them, but she remained unlisted in the directory for that year. It's also possible that she went somewhere else for a while. But in 1900 she resurfaced in L.A. records. She worked as a waitress, although the census reveals that she was unemployed for half of the preceding year. She resided in a large lodging house at 447 South Broadway with her brother John. They seem to have remained there through 1901.[677]

By 1902, none of the Reed siblings were listed in the Los Angeles directory, but we know that Annie continued to live there, because of a couple of newspaper blurbs that mention her recreations.[678] Bessie, her education completed, had reappeared in the growing nearby town of Long Beach, working as a public stenographer.[679] She recorded for the Long Beach City Council meetings as well as other local legal proceedings, and it was most likely in that capacity that she got to know the Long Beach City Attorney, Alexander C. Lawson.[680]

On April 10, 1902, in the Superior Court of the County of Los Angeles, Annie, represented by Lawson, filed a divorce suit against David Willis Bethel on the grounds of abandonment and desertion. These documents give us the timeline that was discussed above and at the end of Chapter 8. They reveal that "on or about the 7th day of December, 1897," Willis "abandoned the plaintiff with the intention to desert her."[681] They also alleged that, "From

---

675 *Half Orphans and Abandoned Children in the Home of Guardian Angels Orphan Asylum,* Los Angeles, California, compiled by Marilyn Gouailhardou, R.S.M., Regional Community Archivist, Sisters of Mercy/Guardian Angels, July 4, 2009, records request from Guardian Angels.
676 Los Angeles, California, directory, Bessie Reed, 1899, p. 764, Ancestry.com.
677 U.S. Census, 1900, John W. Reed, Annie M. Bethel; Los Angeles, California, directory, 1900–1901, Annie Bethel, p. 145, all Ancestry.com.
678 Los Angeles Herald, September 1, 1901, April 30, 1902. The first entry is undoubtedly Annie — it lists her by her married name as visiting her sister in Long Beach with a friend. The latter entry lists only a "Mrs. Bethel" as assisting at the candy booth at the Masonic Fair. It is likely, but not certain, that this was Annie. Only two men named Bethel are listed in the Los Angeles directory for that year, and both appear to have been single at the time, Newspapers.com/Ancestry.com.
679 Long Beach, California, directory, Bessie Reed, 1902, p. 78, Ancestry.com.
680 The Pacific Weekly Tribune, Long Beach, California, March 21, 1902, August 1, 1902, August 8, 1902, August 15, 1902, microfilm from the California State Library, Sacramento.
681 *Bethel vs. Bethel*, The Superior Court of Los Angeles County, State of California, April 10, 1902, case #38621, page 5, records request from the Superior Court of Los Angeles County.

the said 7th day of November, 1896 to the time of the filing of this complaint, defendant has neglected to supply plaintiff with the common necessaries of life, although he had the ability to do so."[682] In addition,

> There is one child issue of said marriage of plaintiff and defendant, Harry Raymond Bethel, five years of age July 9, 1902, who is now and has continuously been since his birth in the care and custody of the plaintiff, and dependent upon her or her relatives for support.[683]

Well now, Annie, really? At some point, it must have occurred to her that it might be a good idea to have some evidence that the child was really in her care and custody, because some three weeks after the filing, on April 30, she checked Raymond out of the Guardian Angels. It's easy to believe that she only did it for the sake of the lawsuit, but it's also possible that she wanted to take another crack at motherhood. By this time, she was 22, and maybe she felt a greater sense of responsibility. The document went on,

> That the plaintiff was but sixteen years of age at the time of said marriage, and was not robust or strong for her age, and by reason of this fact and the further fact of the birth of said child, its care and custody and the natural trouble and consequent impairment of her mental and physical strength by reason of the said desertion and neglect of her said husband, she has been unable to work or support herself except in very small part since the said November 7, 1896, and has been dependent for her support upon her relatives and friends, wherefore plaintiff prays for a decree of this court dissolving the bonds of matrimony heretofore and now existing between herself and the defendant herein, and decreeing to her the care and custody of the said child, Harry Raymond Bethel and for costs of suit.[684]

Compared to the reactions of some of the other women victimized by Willis Bethel, Annie was making some excuses, and stretching the truth a little. The "care and custody" of her child had not been her problem since January of 1899, after all, and although her abortive marriage may certainly have resulted in the "impairment of her mental and physical strength," with Raymond's care out of her hands nothing really prevented her from getting a job. It seems clear that she was not the industrious go-getter her sister or even her brothers were, and she certainly did not possess the spirit shown by Jennie, Minnie and Sophia. Annie enjoyed dependency and self-pity more than self-sufficiency. Her siblings likely had a running joke about whose turn it was to take care of their "weak" sibling, and John, as the oldest, and Bessie, as her only sister, felt the most responsibility. They all certainly would

---

682 Ibid.
683 Ibid., page 6.
684 Ibid.

have pitied her for the despicable way she had been treated, but they probably also got tired of her neediness.

The divorce documents make it clear that neither Annie nor her family and friends knew that her marriage was bigamous, and so illegal anyway. Had they known, they could have tried to take the course that Nettie did, and seek an annulment, which likely would have required only proof of Willis's and Jennie's (or, for that matter, Minnie's) still-binding Ohio marriage. The documents also listed his name as "David Willis Bethel," demonstrating that Annie, like the three other wives since Jennie, did not even know her husband's real middle name was Wilson. In fact, she probably discovered that she knew very little about him. As Ben Perry had so colorfully put it, ". . . the further along the more of his crookedness come out."

On June 7, 1902, all hope she may have had for a legal solution fell apart when the case was dismissed. No cause was given, but it may have been the same problem that had hampered Jennie's efforts to divorce Willis in Ohio — the officers of the court simply could not find him to serve him with papers. He was three aliases removed from the name D.W. Bethel by that point, living in the Creek Indian Territory with Sophia as Dr. George W. McGuire. Even if the Los Angeles constabulary had contemporary digital tools, he would have been a difficult creep to unearth.

The other possibilities are that Annie either died or disappeared. She is absent from all documents after that date. No entry of her death is to be found in the extremely spotty records of the day and no mention of her is to be found in the newspapers I have been able to review, although contemporary Long Beach papers remain unavailable online. There are several records of 'Mrs. Anna Bethels' and many more of 'Anna Reeds' in California directories and other sources through the first half of the twentieth century, but none look likely. I think it's most likely that she died between 1902 and 1907, since Raymond was admitted to a different orphanage in the latter year. On the orphanage records, his mother's place of death was listed as Long Beach, although the date and circumstances were not recorded. Other information on this document is mistaken (the place of Annie and Willis's marriage, for example, is listed as Chicago), missing, or jumbled, however. The scenario that fits most neatly with the records and the circumstances described by family members is that Annie died in 1902, and the divorce suit was withdrawn at that time.[685] I think it's less likely, although possible, that she just wandered off and abandoned the responsibilities of the life that had so disappointed her. Why not? Willis had.

Raymond's granddaughter, Carole Frances Bethel, wrote that the family story that was passed down was that both of Raymond's parents had died in "a train wreck."[686] Even though it was no doubt invented to simply explain a complex and tragic set of circumstances, it remains a fitting description of Willis and Annie's marriage.

---

685 We have no records or mentions of her in the papers after 1902, and family lore relates that Raymond was raised by "a maiden aunt," i.e., Bessie Reed, who may have put him back in an orphanage in 1907.
686 Letters, Carole Frances Bethel to Charles Caldemeyer, August 5 and September 23, 2009.

Chrestine J. Hendricks (1881–1928)

Chrestine's story is also a tragic one. Like Annie, she married an older man while still in her teens. Both girls were evidently more interested in leisure activities than building a family, and Chrestine (and possibly Annie, too) had difficulty with addictive substances. Both became pregnant within a month of their weddings, and both children were raised by other relatives — Raymond by Annie's sister Bessie and Herbert by John and Mathilda Tyberg.

Unlike Annie, Chrestine did not preoccupy herself with the memory of her first marriage. Five months after the court judgment against Willis, she again pledged lifelong devotion. You have to admire her dedication to the search for true love, but her decision-making abilities didn't improve. Still looking for a fun and easy ride, and possibly a father figure, she turned to another charming con artist over twice her age who turned out to also be a bigamist — Dr. Ferdinand H. Mitchell. Originally from Canada, Mitchell was 46 (she was 19). He was also a tubercular drunk, and although it's never explicitly stated, it's pretty clear that alcohol, and possibly other substances, were a companion in their relationship. Mitchell was not as good at keeping his criminal life a secret as Willis was, but he was the same order of human being. He had at least one conviction for forgery, and he had served a stretch in the Minnesota state prison from 1885–1887.[687] After he got out, his long-suffering wife told the local paper "that she would be pleased to see her recreant husband in his old garb and place at the state prison, his alleged intimacy with a strange woman somewhat increasing Mrs. Mitchell's bitterness." She went on to say, "that he has never purchased her a dress or a pair of shoes and never provided their child with any article of apparel."[688]

Evidently, philandering was one of Mitchell's main hobbies. His attentions to another man's wife had gotten him tarred and feathered by his neighbors in his adopted hometown of St. Paul Park in 1896. In 1897, he married a Wisconsin widow for her money without bothering to get a divorce from his wife first. The following year, when the deception was discovered, he sued his first wife for divorce. At that point, the people of St. Paul Park had had enough of their neighbor and they had him arrested for bigamy.[689] Since the second marriage had already been annulled, the state declined to prosecute, but the people had spoken, and Mitchell made himself scarce. We don't know whether or not his first wife divorced him.

By the early 1900s he was roaming around western Minnesota working a portfolio of con games — from phony land deals to forged mortgages to bogus medical cures — anything to make a dishonest buck. Like Willis, it's questionable if he really had much medical training, but he played the part well enough, hanging out his shingle in Gary in February 1901, right about the time Willis was evacuating Bemidji.[690] The two 'brothers in con' had a lot in common. I've even wondered if they knew each other.

---

687 The St. Paul Daily Globe, May 16, 1885, p. 4, Digital Newspapers, Minnesota Historical Society, St. Paul.
688 The Stillwater Messenger, March 12, 1887, Digital Newspapers, MNHS.
689 *Hot on His Trail*, The Minneapolis Star-Tribune, March 15, 1898, p. 7, Newspapers.com.
690 The Minneapolis Tribune, March 6, 1887, p. 7, Digital Newspapers, MNHS; The Gary Graphic, February 16, 1901, p. 5, microfilm from MNHS.

Chrestine went for it all over again. She married Mitchell on August 15, 1901, but they only lived together for about three months.[691] He abandoned her at their home in Fertile (just up the tracks from Gary) after a local farmer sued him over a swindle.[692] He lived for a time in the tiny village of Faith on the White Earth Reservation, "administering soothing lotion," and other fake cures, to the Ojibwe.[693] From mid-1902 until mid-1903 Mitchell was in the wind, but then he resurfaced at his old home of St. Paul Park.[694] Chrestine, who had moved back to her old haunts in the Duluth area, making occasional visits back to Gary, sued him for divorce, first for "extreme cruelty," which evidently could not be proven and was dismissed, then for abandonment.[695] In addition to leaving her without support, her petition averred that Mitchell had been "in a state of habitual drunkenness" for at least the previous year. The case went to trial in late 1904, and like Willis, Mitchell was a no-show. The court again decided in her favor on January 2, 1905.[696] Again, she got nothing for her trouble. Mitchell was hospitalized the following June and died on September 17.[697] The local paper announced his death tersely, "A man named Mitchell of St. Paul Park died Sunday, of tuberculosis, aged 55 years, at the city hospital. He had no relatives in this part of the country. He was buried in St. Michael's cemetery."[698] My, what a loss for the community.

We don't know where Chrestine lived immediately after the divorce. She certainly preferred the excitement and gaiety of city life, but she may have remained for a while in western Minnesota with the Tybergs and her son. In early 1906, John and Mathilda moved their household to far northwestern North Dakota.[699] John was able to afford a farm, and the family was finally established on their own land. We don't know how much time Chrestine spent there, but it's difficult to imagine her being contented in such remote surroundings. We know that she still maintained some contact with her mother and son, but it's clear that she was firmly in the grips of her demons by this time, and that criminal activity was at least a

---

691 State of Minnesota, County of Polk, District Court case #3219-5-108. Chrestine Mitchell, Plaintiff vs. Ferdinand H. Mitchell, Defendant, 1905, records request from Polk County District Court, Crookston, Minnesota.
692 The Gary Graphic, November 30, 1901, p. 5; The Norman County Herald, December 3, 1901, p. 4, microfilm from MNHS.
693 The Gary Graphic, December 14, 1901, p. 5, microfilm from MNHS.
694 The Gary Graphic, June 5, 1903, p. 8, microfilm from MNHS.
695 The Gary Graphic, March 29, 1902, p. 5; The Gary Graphic, February 27, 1903, p. 5; The Gary Graphic, August 14, 1903, p. 5; The Gary Graphic, October 16, 1903, p. 5, all microfilm from MNHS; The Duluth Evening Herald, May 22, 1903, p. 15, Digital Newspapers, MNHS; The St. Paul Globe, November 26, 1904, p. 2, Newspapers.com.
696 State of Minnesota, County of Polk, District Court case #3219-5-108. Chrestine Mitchell, Plaintiff vs. Ferdinand H. Mitchell, Defendant, 1905, records request from Polk County District Court, Crookston, Minnesota.
697 Death card, F. H. P. Mitchell, Stillwater, Washington Co., Minnesota, September 17, 1905, records request from MNHS.
698 The Stillwater Messenger, September 23, 1905, p. 4, Digital Newspapers, MNHS. The paper lists Mitchell's age as 55, which would put his birth date at about 1850, but most census sources, including the Canadian ones when he was a child, list his birth date as November 1855.
699 We don't know the exact date of their move, but a brief mention in the Twin Valley Times from December 20, 1905 (microfilm from MNHS), makes it clear that the Tybergs were still Minnesota residents at that time. Six months later, on June 19, 1906, John Petter Tyberg made a citizenship application from his new residence in Williams County, North Dakota, records request (records request, Petition for Naturalization, Court of Divide County, North Dakota).

component of her lifestyle.[700]

The next confirmed record we have is her marriage to James S. Cavanagh, in Seattle in May 1907. She listed her residence as Chicago.[701] Chrestine was not above misstating her information on official documents, and no other records confirm that she lived there. Cavanagh also listed the Windy City as his residence, although we know that he had lived in Seattle in 1903.[702] It's possible that both were relatively transient, and they may have moved wherever they could get some easy pickings. On the Marriage Return, Cavanagh's occupation was listed as "bookkeeper," although the kind of books he kept were unstated. Chrestine called herself a "dressmaker."

Cavanagh had once worked for the Northern Pacific Railroad as a laborer. In 1899, he was stationed at Grand Forks, just up the line from Willis's post at Red Lake Falls. He resigned to move to Billings, Montana in late 1899 to work in the same capacity on the Yellowstone Division, and in December he was promoted to car clerk. Two months later, at the age of 32, he achieved his main claim to fame — stealing some paychecks from the depot and forging the agent's signature, for which he was caught, at a local brothel, the same evening.[703] Obviously, a criminal mastermind. The caper netted him fifteen months in the Montana state prison system.[704] Like Willis and Mitchell, he must have been a charming fellow with strong powers of persuasion. Just prior to his release, the Billings sheriff circulated a petition to get his citizenship rights restored. By way of explanation, the local paper related:

> It is understood that Cavanaugh intends to come back to this city and show by his future acts that he means to live a correct life. He had always borne a good reputation in all of the places he is known and it was while drunk and infatuated with a fast woman that he committed the forgery.[705]

Yeah, well, anyway . . . Soon after he got out, the reformed Cavanagh "swindled some outside people out of some money and went west," all but disappearing.[706] There are no confirmed records of him after his marriage to Chrestine, but a man with the same name popped up in various news items across the upper Midwest and West from time to time, mainly for gambling, being drunk in public, and forgery, from 1901 until 1909, when we lose track of him.

---

700 U.S. census, John P. Tyberg family, Williams County, North Dakota, 1910, Ancestry.com. Herbert Benjamin Steele was listed as "Bennie Cavanagh" in this census, indicating that the Tybergs remained cognizant of Chrestine's marital status.
701 Marriage documents, James S. Cavanagh and Christine F. H. Mitchell, Seattle, Washington, May 21, 1907, Ancestry.com.
702 Seattle, Washington directory, 1903, p. 356, Ancestry.com.
703 Northern Pacific Railroad employment records of James S. Cavanagh, October 30, 1899, folder #35986. Original records housed at the Minnesota Historical Society, St. Paul. Also accessible online at Ancestry.com.
704 *Robbery and Forgery,* The Billings Weekly Gazette, February 20, 1900, Newspapers.com.
705 *For Citizenship Papers: Petition in Favor of James S. Cavanaugh, a Forger,* The Billings Gazette, July 5, 1901, Newspapers.com.
706 Northern Pacific Railroad employment records of James S. Cavanagh, folder #35986, letter from H. J. Horn, Jr. to Dan Boyle, July 6, 1907. Original records housed at the Minnesota Historical Society, St. Paul. Also accessible online at Ancestry.com.

His time with Chrestine was likely shorter than Mitchell's. About two months after they exchanged vows, in July 1907, H. J. Horn, Jr., a superintendent for the N.P. in St. Paul, began writing to offices at Billings wondering whatever became of Cavanagh.[707] His reasons for wanting this information, seven years after the man had stolen money from his company and was terminated, were never stated, but letters of this kind usually meant that a tearful wife had showed up at a superintendent's office asking if anyone knew what had become of her adoring husband.

Chrestine ended up in southern Idaho, in the bustling, wide open railroad town of Pocatello. In 1911, she sued the long-gone Cavanagh for divorce, again for abandonment. Three weeks after it was final, remaining completely in character, she married John W. Burns, a boozy plumber and part-time thug.[708] Half Bannock Native American, he split his time between Pocatello and the Fort Hall Reservation, routinely making the newspapers for public drunkenness, assault, and theft, and serving various stretches in the county jail. From 1901–1950, over 45 articles in the Pocatello papers documented his legal problems.[709] Chrestine, 30, was likely prostituting herself to support a substance habit, and Burns may have been acting as her pimp. The wedding was solemnized in Salt Lake City by an elder of the Mormon church.[710]

Several court cases reported in the Pocatello Tribune in 1914 and 1915 may have contained references to Chrestine. In July 1914, Burns savagely beat "a white woman who was associated with him."[711] In fall 1914, a "Mrs. Burns" complained to the courts about a neighbor who was "injuring her character."[712] And in April the following year, Burns was again arrested for beating a woman named Nellie West, which may have been the name Chrestine went by when conducting business.[713] As with many instances of domestic violence, especially in that era, the victims in the assault cases did not show up to testify, so there was no elaboration in the papers.[714] The outcome of the second case was never mentioned, but the paper referred to it dismissively, so it was probably dropped.

Somewhere along the way, she acquired a case of syphilis. It could have come from her profession or, for that matter, from any of her husbands. She was committed to the Southern Idaho Insane Asylum around 1915.[715] The event that triggered the commitment, if there was one, was not mentioned in any of the news coverage that is still available, nor is there any

---

707 Ibid., Letter, D. Boyle to H. J. Horn, Jr., July 20, 1907.
708 Marriage documents, John W. Burns and Chrestine J. Hendricks, Salt Lake City, Utah, November 27, 1911, Ancestry.com.
709 Digital Archives of the Marshall Public Library.
710 Marriage documents, John W. Burns and Chrestine J. Hendricks, Salt Lake City, Utah, November 27, 1911, Ancestry.com.
711 *Police Court,* and *Beat Woman,* The Pocatello Tribune, July 13, 1914, p. 5, Digital Archives of the Marshall Public Library.
712 The Pocatello Tribune, October 5, 1914, p. 5, Digital Archives of the Marshall Public Library.
713 *Woman Was Beaten Up,* The Semi-weekly Pocatello Tribune, April 17, 1915, p. 2, Digital Archives of the Marshall Public Library.
714 The Pocatello Tribune, July 28, 1914, p. 5, Digital Archives of the Marshall Public Library.
715 According to her death certificate, Chrestine was admitted to the asylum in early 1915. This generally agrees with other indirect evidence, but no documentation is to be had, and no newspaper articles mention her commitment or its circumstances.

record of a divorce from Burns.[716] Chrestine can be found on the asylum's rolls in the 1920 census, and she died there of "General Paralysis of [the] Insane," a consequence of syphilis, on September 26, 1928.[717] She was 46.[718]

She was buried, without fanfare, in the asylum cemetery the following day.

[719]

Headstone, Chrestine Hendricks Steele Mitchell Cavanagh Burns, Southern Idaho Insane Asylum (now Idaho State Hospital South) Cemetery, Blackfoot, Idaho.

---

716 Although no divorce of Chrestine is found in the records, Burns remarried around 1919, to his brother's widow. The 'divorce' must have been an informal one, since Chrestine was still listed as married in the 1920 census. Burns didn't remain married to his second wife for very long. Edith Bartlett Whitecrow Burns died in 1921 of "a hemorrhage of the lungs," according to her obituary (The Idaho Republican, April 28, 1921, Newspapers.com). The story passed down in the Burns family, however, was that John Burns was responsible for her death (message on Ancestry.com from Trena Kinkaid to Charles Caldemeyer), so the hemorrhage may have come from a beating. At the time, the family was living on the Fort Hall Reservation.

717 U.S. census, 1920, Christina Burns, Southern Idaho Insane Asylum, Blackfoot, Bingham County, Idaho, Ancestry.com.

718 Certificate of Death, State of Idaho Department of Public Welfare, Bureau of Vital Statistics, State File #62966, Mrs. Christine Burns, September 26, 1928, Ancestry.com.

719 Find a Grave Memorial 154157805, Christina Burns, State Hospital South Cemetery, Blackfoot, Idaho, Findagrave.com. Photo credit: Jean G.

Sophia Price Johnson (1877–1931)

Sophia was among the savviest of the women of Willis, and she was better equipped to handle life, both with and without him, than most of his other wives. Maybe that was why his long-distance efforts to scam her ended in failure. Although it's clear that she believed much of the malarkey about his Virginia farms, in the end she did not fall for it, her only interest lying in getting fair value from the properties for her son.

She was born in Hopkins County, Texas, on October 22, 1876, to Oscar and Mary Elizabeth Price.[720] Her father died in 1886 and her mother's second husband, Francis Wineblood, moved the family to the Creek Nation around 1891.[721] She married Wellington Lott Johnson, a fellow Texan who had also moved to the Territories, in 1894. His death following a medical procedure less than four years later was no doubt traumatic for her, but her response to it was an early sign of the resilience she exhibited throughout her life. As 1/16 Creek, Sophia had an allotment of land, as did all of her children, and since their father was deceased, the properties required the oversight of a court-appointed guardian. Sophia did the job for Clay and Todd until 1902, but in the deferential spirit expected of women in that age she probably turned things over to Willis after their marriage. After he left, all her sons' interests, especially Marcus Wilson's, needed management. In April 1908, six months after Dr. McGuire's departure, the courts went with Sophia's choice for the job, a local banker named Adolph O. Johnson. But she maintained general oversight of all of her children's finances until their maturities, and she eventually assumed the official guardianship of all three estates in 1911.

Her divorce from Willis for abandonment, after three years of playing footsie by mail, was probably an easy case to make to the court. Sophia received her judgment on April 26, 1911, some three weeks after Dr. McGuire's supposed death. She probably wanted to be sure that Willis would never again reappear to take control over Marcus's life and the funds derived from his growing oil revenues. The suit alleged that, "defendant is morally and socially unfit to have the care, custody, and education of said child."[722] Well, no lie.

The Oklahoma oil boom was beginning to pay real dividends for the family by 1907, and it only got more lucrative as time went on. By luck, Marcus Wilson's 161 acres over the rich Glenn Pool Oil Field became valuable, whereas Clay's and Todd's holdings did not.[723] On June 8, 1911, the guardianship papers revealed that Wilson's lands were yielding excellent income.[724] There were several instances when Sophia petitioned the court to increase the family's monthly allowance from Wilson's assets, while investing the bulk of the money in local real estate and government bonds. She was fiercely protective of his estate over the

---

720 Sophia's birth year is recorded variously, from 1874 (the 1900 U.S. census) to 1877 (her death certificate). Most of the material from her direct descendants list 1876 as her correct birth year, so that is the year I have used.
721 Findagrave.com Memorial 38585112, biography of Sophia Price, Findagrave.com.
722 In the District Court of McIntosh County, Oklahoma, Sophia McGuire, Plaintiff, vs. George W. McGuire, Defendant, case #495, Petition for Divorce, p. 1, records request from the District Court of McIntosh County.
723 Muskogee County Democrat, June 22, 1916, Newspapers.com.
724 Guardianship papers of Marcus Wilson McGuire, County Court of McIntosh County, June 8, 1911, Oklahoma, U. S., Wills and Probate Records, 1801–2008, Ancestry.com.

years, even suing her own brother, Oscar B. Price, for $462.35 plus 10% interest in 1915. Oscar, a shady realtor in the Muskogee area, was involved in a number of barely legal or worse schemes in eastern Oklahoma before he relocated to California, and the money he owed the estate probably had to do with some rents on Marcus's properties that were not properly accounted for. There was no indication in the papers as to the resolution of the suit.

Back, (L-R): Owen Price, Laura Wineblood Wyatt (?), Oscar B. Price, Benjamin S. Price
Front, (L-R): Evah Wineblood Parker (?), Mary Elizabeth Clark Wineblood, Francis A. Wineblood, Sophia Price White
This photo, taken about 1915, features some of the descendants of Mary Elizabeth Clark Price Wineblood.

Under her leadership, the McGuire family, absent, of course, Dr. McGuire, lived well. All three boys grew up without worries, at least about resources. Sophia encouraged Marcus Wilson to be industrious, unassuming, and unaffected by wealth in these days, perhaps seeing in the boy some self-centeredness and other underlying similarities to his father. The article that follows, as well as two others quoted in Marcus Wilson's biography in the next chapter, detail her commitment to his character development and indicate that she believed his wealth was a danger to him despite the obvious advantages it yielded. Later events demonstrated how much he missed her influence after she was gone.

---

725 Find a Grave Memorial 29620897, Mary Elizabeth Clark Price Wineblood. Photo posted by Frank Parker on Findagrave.com.

HAS $100,000 INCOME, BUT BOY, 11, PREFERS RUNNING POP STAND

Wilson McGuire, boy millionaire, and his mother, Mrs. McGuire-White.

Oil Lands, Owned Because of Creek Indian Blood, Has Made Wilson McGuire Youngest Millionaire in State of Oklahoma.

MUSKOGEE, Okla., July 28.—Since oil was struck in Oklahoma the state has developed many millionaires, and among those who attained riches, the most wealthy boy probably is Wilson McGuire, of this city. He is descended on his mother's side from Creek Indian blood and, though only 11 years old, has an income of more than $100,000 a year.

In spite of his riches, however, the little millionaire has constructed a lemonade stand on his lawn and has become so adept in making his small profits on drink sales mount up into sizable sums.

Wilson takes considerable more interest in this work than he does in his oil wells, and the property he owns in Muskogee and Checotah. His mother encourages him in his little business and he is rapidly developing many practical ideas. As far as appearance goes it would be difficult to tell that young McGuire or his mother, Mrs. McGuire-White, had any Indian blood. They are fairer than most persons of the white race.

The oil land which has made a millionaire out of the boy came to him through government allotment on account of his Indian blood.

The land lies between Sapulpa and Tulsa and is leased by the Gypsy Oil company. The income is invested in first mortgages on real estate in and around Muskogee. The estate is managed by the county court, and Mrs. McGuire-White is guardian. The young millionaire lives with his mother and his stepfather, W. S. White, in a splendid big home here. [726]

---

[726] Muskogee County Democrat, July 28, 1915, Newspapers.com. This article is one of two about Marcus's industriousness in his youth emphasizing Sophia's attempts to keep her son humble and grounded.

Transcription: Since oil was struck in Oklahoma the state has developed many millionaires, and among those who attained riches, the most wealthy boy probably is Wilson McGuire, of this city. He is descended on his mother's side from Creek Indian blood and, though only 11 years old, has an income of more than $100,000 a year.

In spite of his riches, however, the little millionaire has constructed a lemonade stand on his lawn and has become an adept in making his small profits on drink sales mount up into sizable sums.

Wilson takes considerable more interest in this work than he does in his oil wells, and the property he owns in Muskogee and Checotah. His mother encourages him in his little business and he is rapidly developing many practical ideas. As far as appearance goes it would be difficult to tell that Wilson McGuire or his mother, Mrs. McGuire-White, had any Indian blood. They are fairer than most persons of the white race.

The oil land which has made a millionaire out of the boy came to him through government allotment on account of his Indian blood.

The land lies between Sapulpa and Tulsa and is leased by the Gypsy Oil company. The income is invested in first mortgages on real estate in and around Muskogee. The estate is managed by the county court, and Mrs. McGuire-White is guardian. The young millionaire lives with his mother and his stepfather, W. S. White, in a splendid big home here.

Soon after Willis left in late 1907, Sophia moved her three boys from Checotah to Muskogee, although she soon moved back. But in late 1911, after her divorce of Willis was final, she moved to Muskogee for good. On August 27, 1913, four months after his trunk finally arrived from Chihuahua, she married William Saunders White, a Muskogee businessman, and put D.W. Bethel/George W. McGuire behind her once and for all. In 1918, William Ballintine White's birth completed her family.

Sophia Price Johnson McGuire White with her fourth child, William B. White, circa 1918.

---

727 Photograph shared on Ancestry.com by bldrumm, on October 26, 2011.

The White family lived in Muskogee through the 1910s and 1920s. Clay, Todd, and Marcus all were educated at prestigious schools, and began lucrative careers. Clay and Todd ended up in Los Angeles and became successful there, Clay working as an accountant for Hollywood star Bing Crosby and Todd's law firm serving Crosby's legal needs.[728] Marcus Wilson reached maturity in 1924, and he later became an attorney in Los Angeles, too, working at Todd's firm. All three were regularly surrounded by Hollywood royalty, and Sophia and Billy spent at least one summer in Los Angeles with Marcus.[729] But while her first three children indulged in glamorous lifestyles on the west coast, she preferred a life of quiet comfort in Muskogee with William and young Billy.

She was not destined to live to an old age, however. On August 14, 1931, Sophia died of a cerebral hemorrhage at Baptist Hospital in Muskogee, at age 55. She was buried in Memorial Park Cemetery in her adopted city.

[730]

Headstone, Sophia Price Johnson McGuire White, Memorial Park Cemetery, Muskogee, Oklahoma.

What drove the wives of Willis to attach themselves, and remain devoted, to him? I won't spend much time arguing for the exceptionalism of Willis Bethel, but he must have possessed a degree of uniqueness that commanded their loyalty, even in the face of (or maybe partially

---

[728] Obituary, L. Clayton Johnson, The Los Angeles Times, October 7, 1963; *Todd's Law Firm,* shared on Ancestry.com by fwp735 on May 12, 2015.
[729] Muskogee Daily Phoenix, July 22, 1922, Newspapers.com
[730] Find a Grave Memorial 38585112, Memorial Park Cemetery, Muskogee, Oklahoma, Findagrave.com. Photo credit: Frank Parker.

because of) criticism by their friends and families. As time went on and his desertion became confirmed, many of his wives retained affection for him, rejecting him only reluctantly. We can only assume that none of them ever met anyone who attracted them quite like the joking, storytelling, rule-bending Willis Bethel. Maybe his wild side harmonized with theirs in a way that nobody outside of their relationship could understand. Maybe he epitomized a longtime ideal for them. The outlandish dreams of one's youth are usually deflated by the hard realities of adulthood, but they can still be difficult to silence.

16.

The Downstream Gene Pool

■ **I WAS ALSO A DREAMER WHEN I WAS YOUNG,** and deep questions sometimes occupied my thoughts, often to the point where I irritated those around me. I was close to my father, but he was very different — a man of science who believed that with enough experiment and investigation the various disciplines under that heading could and would, in time, explain everything. I still don't completely buy that, but it's hard to deny the benefits the scientific method has brought us. Many people who came to adulthood in the early twentieth century acquired beliefs similar to the ones my father had, and the impact they have had on our culture has been breathtaking. After countless generations of mysticism, demagoguery, and snake-oil solutions, a system finally emerged that allowed human beings to know practical truths, and so to exercise some control over their lives. My father, a medical doctor, believed in it as firmly as his father, a minister, believed in the power of faith.

I remember once I was speculating about the purpose of life, and he said, in the confident, offhand manner of both the scientist and the true believer (and the father who wants his mouthy, ill-informed son to shut up), "The purpose of life is to perpetuate the species." Dad was a practical man from a practical generation, but behind his Darwinian exterior he was also generous, ethical, honest, kind, responsible, and self-sacrificing. He was absolutely nothing like Willis Bethel, a man he would have detested had he ever known him. But on this one point, the words of one man find expression in the actions of the other. This chapter will explore the lives of David Wilson Bethel's perpetuations of our species, as well as their own subsequent, more ethical, contributions to that same great entity. Aside from Bessie, none of the following people would have existed had Willis Bethel not been a detestable skunk.

Bessie Ota Bethel (1885–1968)

Bessie was born January 7, 1885, while Willis and Jennie were still at Kimball, Ohio.[731]

---

[731] Birth record and corrected birth record, Huron County, Ohio, Bessie Ota Bethel, January 7, 1885, records request from the Huron County Clerk of Courts.

Willis was working for the Nickel Plate, his first full time station agent job away from Belmont County, and he was also the small stop's first postmaster. After he abandoned his family in 1886, Jennie moved her daughter back to Flushing, and that became the only home Bessie ever knew. There is no record of her when she was young other than a small item in the Belmont Chronicle in 1890 which recounted a play at the Methodist Church in Flushing, *The Crowning of the Queen of Fame*, in which the five-year-old Bessie played a statue.[732] Later sources indicate that, like her father, she was outgoing, and that she was funny as heck. She graduated from Flushing High School in 1903.

She was 25 in 1910, and she worked as a bookkeeper/secretary at The Peoples Savings & Loan Bank in Flushing, where she remained until her retirement in 1950.[733] A story in the Flushing News in 1961 recognized her as "one of the first women officers of an Ohio banking institution."[734] She was known for her conscientiousness, honesty, and self-sacrificing nature. An unconfirmed story tells of her refusing a raise one year because, according to her in her role as bookkeeper, it wasn't in the bank's best interest. She was also well known for her sense of humor and timing in delivering a one-liner.[735] The latter characteristic likely came to her genetically, from her father. The honesty and other traits, not so much.

[736]

Bessie Ota Bethel, about 1930.

The Methodist church provided a feeling of family for both Jennie and Bessie. Bessie began teaching Sunday School in 1903, at age 18, and continued until 1960, when she was 75. The students in her adult Bible Study class revered her. In 2001, Dan Smith, a Flushing native and genealogist, wrote, "My dad was in her Sunday School class and was like an adopted son to her."[737]

---

732 *Queen of Fame,* The Belmont Chronicle, December 4, 1890, microfilm from the Ohio History Center, Columbus.
733 U.S. census, 1910, Bessie Bethel, Flushing, Ohio, Ancestry.com.
734 *Veteran Flushing Bible Teacher Is Remembered by 'Her Boys,'* The Ohio Valley News, April 9, 1961, article shared via email, Dan Smith to Charles Caldemeyer, April 17, 2001.
735 *Friendship of Four From 1903 Flushing Class Kept Intact*, *The Flushing Times-Leader*, September 21, 1960, shared by Dan Smith via email, April 17, 2001.
736 Photo shared by Dan Smith via email, April 17, 2001.
737 Email from Dan Smith to Charles Caldemeyer, April 17, 2001.

Before her death, Bessie donated a lot adjacent to the church for the construction of the education wing, which still stands.[738]

The Flushing United Methodist Church, on High Street. The education wing is the low annex to the left.

Bessie became something of a local celebrity later in her life. Two stories in the Flushing newspapers from the 1960s give us a sense of the influence she exerted on both her peers and on the younger World War II generation. The first, from 1960, discussed her lifelong friendship with three of her classmates, all of whom had graduated from Flushing High in 1903. The little stories in the article reveal the strong bonds between the four women, each in their mid-seventies at the time, that are characteristic of rural towns. Entitled *Friendship of Four from 1903 Flushing Class Kept Intact*, a transcription follows:

> Eleven seniors graduated from Flushing High School in 1903. Four of the girls had been the closest possible friends since starting the first grade together in 1892. Their friendship has been retained all these years and is still as strong as it ever was.
>
> Participants in this 68-year old friendship are Mrs. Grace Howell, Miss Bessie Bethel, Miss Elsie Todd and Miss Elsie Fisher, all of whom still reside in Flushing and have continued to see each other regularly.
>
> The four attend the First Methodist Church in Flushing, and have sat in the same pew together for the past 14 years. They meet each year for Thanksgiving dinner, and Mrs. Howell and Miss Bethel have taken several trips together,

---

738 *Veteran Flushing Bible Teacher Is Remembered by 'Her Boys,'* The Ohio Valley News, April 9, 1961, reprinted from the Wheeling Intelligencer, shared by Dan Smith, April 17, 2001.
739 Photo by Charles Caldemeyer, 2013.

including one to Europe.

They are the only members of their class still living. Their class was the last to graduate from the old Flushing school, which was destroyed by fire soon after their graduation.

In discussing their grade school days, they recalled "the day the boys stuffed the chimney." On that historic day, it seems, several of the students wished to go to Holloway to see the new roundhouse, but hopes for the trip were pretty dim, it being a school day.

However, several of the boys overcame that obstacle by stuffing old rags, sweaters and any other bulky objects that were convenient for their purpose into the school chimney. The maneuver sent a stream of smoke pouring into the school room, necessitating the dismissal of school.

Mrs. Howell and Miss Bethel now say they were among those who took advantage of the holiday to go see the Holloway roundhouse. Miss Todd and Miss Fisher now emphatically deny that they visited the new railroad structure on that day.

Miss Bethel was the comedian of the group, they all agree, although in general they are reluctant to try to classify each other according to personality differences.

Miss Todd says they couldn't be more different from each other and that perhaps that explains their long friendship. She adds that there is not one that she feels she could not trust in time of need.

After their graduation from school, Miss Todd and Miss Fisher both became teachers. Both have retired, Miss Todd after 41 years and Miss Fisher after 49. Miss Bethel worked in a bank and loan company for 43 years. Mrs. Howell has gained recognition by being a historian of Flushing, having written about the development of the old Belmont County community for a newspaper.

They say that in their frequent get-togethers they have remained about the same as they ever were, still enjoying each other's company and finding it easy to laugh about the old times and just as easy to find new things to laugh about.

Possibly a typical conversation involves their high school graduation, in the old Flushing music hall, where most important social functions then took place.

The entire class sat on the stage, each in a rocking chair. The decorations were crooked, Miss Bethel recalls. Each member of the class had to give an oration.

"Eleven orations!"

"And the people lived through it," Miss Todd said. "Of course, we had good, comfortable rocking chairs."

On the orations Miss Todd said: "But they weren't as lengthy as you think they were."

"They were lengthier than you think they were," Miss Bethel said, with the timing of a Steve Allen.

Two photographs accompanied the article. One of them, the graduation photo from 1903, provided us with Bessie's image at the end of Chapter 2. The other was of the four friends at the time the article was written:

Transcription: Still friends after 68 years are these four members of the Flushing graduating class of 1903. Looking at the scrapbook held by Mrs. Grace Howell are (L-R) Miss Bessie Bethel, Miss Elsie Todd and Miss Elsie Fisher. The four women still maintain an active friendship.

---

740 *Friendship of Four From 1903 Flushing Class Kept Intact*, The Flushing Times-Leader, September 21, 1960, shared via email by Dan Smith, April 17, 2001.

A second article, from the following year, gives us a glimpse of some of Bessie's longer lasting contributions to the community, as well as a good photograph of the 76-year-old:

---

741 *Veteran Flushing Bible Teacher Is Remembered by 'Her Boys,'* The Ohio Valley News, April 9, 1961, reprinted from the Wheeling Intelligencer, shared by Dan Smith, April 17, 2001.

Transcription: Miss Bessie Bethel smiled and her eyes glistened with a trace of tears as she read the inscription on a beautiful cut glass serving tray.

It read: "Bessie O. Bethel, 1903–1960-plus, Bible Teacher, from 'her boys.'"

The tray told the story in a nutshell of Miss Bethel's long service as a Sunday School teacher in the Flushing Methodist Church. Class members presented her with the tray.

It started back in 1903 when she was just a young woman. The silver-haired grand lady still is going strong and her "boys," the 30 and 40 year olds in her Sunday School class, hope she will be around for many more years.

What has Miss Bethel enjoyed best about teaching adult men in her class?

"There is not a thing I didn't enjoy about it over the years," she laughed.

There was a time during World War II that Miss Bethel almost had no class to teach.

A dozen or so of the men in her class were called to service. Just one was left.

"Don't break up the class . . . keep right on teaching," the soldier boys told Miss Bethel, promising that "We'll be back as soon as we can."

So Miss Bethel conducted a Sunday School class for the lone "boy."

Miss Bethel added happily: "They all came back, too."

There was only one other time that Miss Bethel was away from her boys.

It was while she took a seven-week tour to Europe.

Until her retirement 11 years ago, Miss Bethel served as cashier of the People's Savings and Loan bank in Flushing. She was one of the first women officers of an Ohio banking institution.

The Flushing native presented the lot adjoining the Methodist Church where the church's new educational building now stands. She was born in Sandusky, O. but moved to Flushing as a child.

"I like to consider Flushing my home," she concluded.

Caption: Miss Bessie Bethel, of Flushing, looks over cut glass serving tray members of her Sunday Bible class presented her for her "long, devoted service" dating back to 1903.

Bessie died in 1968, at the age of 83, of a heart attack, while in a nursing home in Morristown, Ohio, about eight miles from Flushing. Her obituary follows. She was buried beside Jennie in Flushing Union Cemetery, next to the Methodist church that gave both of them such strong support and feelings of community. A large headstone, somewhat ironically sporting the prominent surname 'Bethel' on one side, marks the spot.

BETHEL, Miss Bessie O.

Submitted by: Daniel Smith Jr.
Source: The Times-Leader, April 23, 1968

Miss Bessie O. Bethel, 83, Flusing, died Monday at 9:30 a.m. at the Bell Nursing Home Morristown, She was born in Sandusky, Ohio, Jan. 7 1885, a daughter of the late Wilson & Eliza Jane Bethel. She was a member of the Flushing Methodist Church and had taught Sunday School there for over 50 yrs. She had been employed as secretary at the Peoples Saving & Loan, Flushing for 30 yrs. Surviving are 6 cousins, Mrs. Nellie Starr, Edith Howell & Marion Howell, all of Beaver Falls, Pa., Mrs. Bertha Goodman, Warren. John Shallcross, Cleveland & Mrs. Helen Workley, Flushing Friends will be received at the Warren Funeral Home, Flushing, after 3 p.m. Wed. Services will be held Thurs. at 2 p.m. at the Flusing Methodist Church with Rev. James Dyer officiating. Burial will be in the Flushing Union Cemetery.

Transcription: Miss Bessie O. Bethel, 83, Flusing [sic], died Monday at 9:30 a.m. at the Bell Nursing Home Morristown. She was born in Sandusky, Ohio, Jan. 7 1885, a daughter of the late Wilson & Eliza Jane Bethel. She was a member of the Flushing Methodist Church and had taught Sunday School there for over 50 yrs. She had been employed as secretary at the Peoples Saving & Loan, Flushing for 30 yrs. Surviving are 6 cousins, Mrs. Nellie Starr, Edith Howell & Marion Howell, all of Beaver Falls, Pa., Mrs. Bertha Goodman, Warren, John Shallcross, Cleveland & Mrs. Helen Workley, Flushing. Friends will be received at the Warren Funeral Home, Flushing, after 3 p.m. Wed. Services will be held Thurs. at 2 p.m. at the Flusing [sic] Methodist Church with Rev. James Dyer officiating. Burial will be in the Flushing Union Cemetery.

---

742 Obituary, Bessie Ota Bethel, The Flushing Times-Leader, April 23, 1968, shared by Dan Smith, April 17, 2001.

Headstone, Eliza Jane Howell Bethel and Bessie Ota Bethel, Flushing Union Cemetery, Flushing, Ohio.

---

743 Photos by Charles Caldemeyer, 2002.

Durward Frederick Fisher {born Durward Frederick Bethel} (1888–1949)

Durward was a smart, earnest child, and he graduated as salutatorian of his high school class in 1904 at the age of sixteen. After several years in the workforce, he matriculated to Michigan State Agricultural College (now Michigan State University), majoring in Horticulture. Upon graduation in 1912, he was hired by the U.S. Department of Agriculture Bureau of Plant Industry, Office of Fruit Diseases, and the following year he was assigned to the Fruit Disease Field Laboratory in Wenatchee, Washington. During his 17 years in Wenatchee, Durward built an excellent record. He is credited with inventing the practice of wrapping apples in oiled paper to reduce apple scald, and with developing sprays to control apple mildew, perennial canker, and other forms of fruit rot that limited the ability of growers to store large quantities of their crops. He also pioneered shipping methods to increase the salability of fruit from the region.[744] An article in 1923 credited him with giving, "to the Northwest, in fact to the apple industry in general, the greatest impetus that has come in recent years."[745]

Durward Frederick Fisher, about 1904.

---

744 Resume, Durward Frederick Fisher, from Fisher family papers.
745 *Nineteen Cars of Winesaps Average $3.44 Per Box Here*, The Wenatchee Daily World, June 27, 1923, from Fisher family papers.

In 1914, Durward married his college sweetheart, Alida Dearborn, who was in many ways as exceptional as he. From a farm in northern Michigan, Alida also received her Bachelor of Science degree in 1912. While Durward was establishing himself in Wenatchee, she remained behind and received a master's degree from the University of Michigan, a rare accomplishment for a woman of the day. They were married on Alida's family farm near Bellaire, Michigan, on March 31, 1914. Willis did not attend.

The couple settled into family life in Wenatchee, and Alida became the town's first bacteriologist, doing her tests in the kitchen of their home. In 1971, when she passed away over 2000 miles away, the Wenatchee paper printed a tribute article describing her contributions to the community.[746] But children came along soon enough: Durward Frederick, Jr. in 1915, Ida Antoinette in 1917, Evan Dearborn in 1921, and Harry Drew in 1922, and Alida became a full-time mother.

Durward was exempted from service in World War I because of his position with the Department of Agriculture. As his career blossomed, he was found to not only have the scientific, but also the organizational and political skill sets necessary for advancement in the department. He was president of the Rotary Club in Wenatchee, and he served as Master of his Masonic Lodge in 1927. He was a trustee of the small city's Chamber of Commerce and a member of the Executive Council of the Boy Scouts. He also served as president of the Northwestern Association of Horticulturalists, Entomologists, and Plant Pathologists. Durward developed key associations with members of the agricultural community, and he was a lifetime member of the Washington State Horticultural Society.[747]

Durward Frederick Fisher, about 1927.

---

746 *First Bacteriologist of Wenatchee Dead at 80*, probably published in The Wenatchee World, late July/early August 1971, from Fisher family papers.
747 Obituary, Durward Frederick Fisher, Ice and Refrigeration magazine, Published by Nickerson & Collins Co., Chicago and New York, November 1949

By 1930, he was a recognized authority in the field of fruit and vegetable diseases with a long experimentation and publication record, and he was promoted to head of the Fruit and Vegetable Transportation and Storage Division of the Bureau of Plant Industry. The family moved to the Washington, D.C. area, residing in Takoma Park, Maryland. Durward's work continued to flourish in this environment. His biography states, "He combined a broad understanding of the industry problems, a scientific attitude toward their solution and administrative ability of high order. He maintained effective and cordial contacts with transportation officials, shippers, and organizations of growers."[748] He was a fellow of the American Association for the Advancement of Science and was a member of Alpha Zeta national fraternity and Sigma Xi scientific research society. He was also an active member of the Presbyterian Church in Takoma Park, serving for twelve years on the Board of Trustees.[749]

Durward and Alida finished raising their family in their Takoma Park home, but tragedy struck in 1941, when oldest son Fred, who by then was teaching Mechanical Engineering at the Missouri School of Mines and Metallurgy at Rolla (now the Missouri University of Science and Technology), died suddenly of a brain aneurysm, only two weeks after his marriage. Fred's health had always been somewhat fragile. But he was a child who, in Durward's words, "in his attitude and ambitions . . . fulfilled our fondest hopes,"[750] and he was also the one to whom the younger children looked for advice and support. Durward appeared philosophical in his answers to the letters of condolences that poured in, writing to one of his friends, "We are glad that he lived long enough to taste most of the good things of life — and was spared the horrors which conceivably may be ahead for those of us who are left,"[751] no doubt a reference to the last stages of his own mother's life. But the stress on him must have been tremendous.

Ida received both bachelor's and master's degrees, in Home Economics and Nutrition, from the University of Maryland and the University of Illinois, respectively. Her master's thesis was (unsurprisingly) entitled, *A Comparison of Thirty Apple Varieties and Seedlings with Reference to Their Use as Food.*[752] She worked through the 1940s as a nutritionist, first for Eastern States Food Cooperative, then for General Foods, and she was a rising star at their New York City headquarters. Her recipes were published as part of the company's advertisements for Swans Down Flour, and in 1942/43 she testified before a subcommittee of Congress concerning the nutritional shortcomings of newly introduced enriched flour.[753] But in 1947, she abandoned her professional career to marry Dr. Everett Caldemeyer.[754] The couple settled in the Washington D.C. area, where they raised three children.

---

748 Ibid.
749 Ibid.
750 Letter from Durward F. Fisher to Dr. William R. Chedsey, Director, Missouri School of Mines & Metallurgy, February 8, 1941, from Fisher family papers.
751 Letter, Durward Fisher to Charles W. Finlayson, January 13, 1941, from Fisher family papers.
752 *Master's Thesis*, Ida Antoinette Fisher, Graduate School of the University of Illinois, 1940, from Fisher family papers.
753 *Ida Fisher's Recipes*, General Foods advertisement for Swans Down Flour; Ida Fisher obituary, from Fisher family papers.
754 *Marriage license*, Everett Caldemeyer/Ida Fisher, December 31, 1947, from Caldemeyer family papers.

Durward and Alida Fisher with their three living children in the back yard of their home in Takoma Park, Maryland in the 1940's. Seated: Durward and Pat, the dog. Standing (L-R): Evan, Alida, Harry, Ida.

Evan, Durward had written to a friend, was "always making something, and goes the rounds of the garbage cans up and down the alley collecting all kinds of discarded rubbish that he finds use for."[756] He received a degree in Mechanical Engineering from the University of Maryland, and after a stint in the Navy during World War II, he put it to use for the U.S. Department of Defense.[757] He worked his entire professional career at Diamond Laboratories

---
755 Photo from Fisher family papers.
756 Letter from Durward F. Fisher to Harry J. Eustace, March 22, 1930, from Fisher family papers.
757 University of Maryland yearbook, 1944, from Fisher family papers.

near Washington, specializing in developing fuses for explosive devices, and by the time he retired he had at least three patents to his name.[758] He married Marilyn Girton in 1949, and they raised three children in the D.C. suburb of Chevy Chase.

Harry also attended the University of Maryland, majoring in accounting, and he was in the student band and on the boxing team.[759] After service in the Army in Europe and the Pacific, he joined the Business Office at the University of Maryland, and by the mid-1950s had become the university's comptroller. He married Helen Harris in 1948, and they raised three children, living first in Kensington, then near Darnestown, Maryland.

Durward Frederick Fisher never got to meet any of his nine grandchildren. In 1949, at the age of 61, he died suddenly of heart failure. He left behind a legacy of achievement in the community of plant pathology. Many of the processes and solutions he pioneered led to later advancements, and some are still in use. He was laid to rest at Fort Lincoln Cemetery, in Brentwood, Maryland, near Washington, D.C., alongside oldest son Fred. Alida lived until 1971, when she passed away of a stroke at her cottage on the Dearborn family farm in Michigan. She now rests beside her husband.

Durward Frederick Fisher, about 1945.

---

758 Justia.com, http://patents.justia.com/inventor/evan-d-fisher.
759 University of Maryland yearbook, 1943, from Fisher family papers.
760 Photo from Fisher family papers.

Durward F. Fisher, U. S. Research Official At Beltsville, Dies

Durward Frederick Fisher, 61, principal horticulturist in charge of transportation and storage research at the Agriculturer Department's Bureau of Plant Industries, Beltsville, Md., died yesterday at Suburban Hospital after a heart attack.

Mr. Fisher was, according to Dr. Robert M. Salter, bureau chief, "a foremost authority" in his field. Under his supervision, the research department made many improvements in packing practices and designs for containers.

A Washington area resident since 1930, when he took charge of his research unit, Mr. Fisher lived at 204 Cedar avenue, Takoma, Park, Md.

He was a native of Clarence, N. Y. He graduated from Michigan State College in 1912 and joined the bureau the same year. From 1924 to 1930 he was stationed at Wenatchee, Wash.

Mr. Fisher was a member of the American Society for Horticultural Science, Botanical Society of Washington, Alpha Zeta national fraternity, Sigma XI honor society, a counselor for the Society of Refrigeration Engineers and a fellow of the American Society for the Advancement of Science. He was past master of a Wenatchee Masonic lodge.

Surviving are his widow, Mrs. Alida Dearborn Fisher; a daughter, Mrs. Ida Caldemeyer, 1615 Kenyon street N.W., and two sons, Evan D. Fisher, 7300 Flower avenue, Takoma Park, and Harry D. Fisher, 2 Forest Way road, Greenbelt, Md.

Funeral services will be held at 2:30 p.m. tomorrow in the Takoma Park Presbyterian Church. Burial will be in Fort Lincoln Cemetery.[761]

---

[761] Obituary, Durward Frederick Fisher, probably from the Washington Post, September 1949, from Fisher family papers.

Transcription: Durward Frederick Fisher, 61, principal horticulturalist in charge of transportation and storage research at the Agriculturer [sic] Department's Bureau of Plant Industries, Beltsville, Md., died yesterday at Suburban Hospital after a heart attack.

Mr. Fisher was, according to Dr. Robert M. Salter, bureau chief, "a foremost authority" in in field. Under his supervision, the research department made many improvements in packing practices and designs for containers.

A Washington area resident since 1930, when he took charge of his research unit, Mr. Fisher lived at 204 Cedar avenue, Takoma Park, Md.

He was a native of Clarence, N. Y. He graduated from Michigan State College in 1912 and joined the bureau the same year. From 1924 to 1930 he was stationed at Wenatchee, Wash.

Mr. Fisher was a member of the American Society for Horticultural Science, Botanical Society of Washington, Alpha Zeta national fraternity, Sigma XI honor society, a counselor for the Society of Refrigeration Engineers and a fellow of theAmerican Society of the Advancement of Science. He was past master of a Wenatchee Masonic lodge.

Surviving are his widow, Mrs. Alida Dearborn Fisher; a daughter, Mrs. Ida Caldemeyer, 1615 Kenyon street N.W., and two sons, Evan D. Fisher, 7300 Flower avenue, Takoma Park, and Harry D. Fisher, 2 Forest Way road, Greenbelt, Md.

Funeral services will be held at 2:30 p.m. tomorrow in the Takoma Part Presbyterian Church. Burial will be in Fort Lincoln Cemetery.

Headstones, Durward Frederick Fisher and Alida Dearborn Fisher, Fort Lincoln cemetery, Brentwood, Maryland.

---

762 Find a Grave Memorials 175439901 and 175440176, Fort Lincoln Cemetery, Brentwood, Maryland, Findagrave.com. Photo credit: KimonthePatuxent.

Mary Ralston Bethel (1891–1958)

After Matilda's death in 1893, Mary, less than two years old, was for all intents and purposes an orphan. Thompson and Sarah Jane McGinnes took over the responsibilities of raising her, and the strong network of McGinnes and Ralston family ties sustained Mary until adulthood. Without them, she would almost certainly have come to an early end.[763] It's possible that Willis maintained a minimal level of contact with the McGinnes family for a while, since Mary was listed as a 'boarder' in the house in the 1900 census, but it's unknown how much board money, if any, he actually sent.[764] Given his inability/unwillingness to send much support for a child for which he professed some affection (Durward), I have strong doubts that he found much of anything for his third child's support. There is no evidence that Willis had any interest in Mary's well-being.

Thompson McGinnes died in 1899, and the farm went to Sarah Jane. The 1900 census listed her living with her children, William (18) and Jessie (16), and young Mary Ralston Bethel, age eight. But in 1902, Sara Jane passed away at the age of 51, and it's likely that the McGinnes children sold the farm for what they could get and moved to the DuBois area soon after.[765] The strong Ralston presence in Clearfield County provided them with a safety net. Jessie, along with Joseph Ralston's wife Louise, seem to have undertaken the care of young Mary. In 1904, two years after her mother's death, Jessie, then 20, married William Arthur Johnston, a machinist for the railroad. The 1910 census finds them living in DuBois, and Mary R. Bethel, 18, boarded with them. She worked as a "saleslady" at "a dry goods store."[766]

Mary lived in DuBois for most of the 1910's, and directories show that her address changed frequently. In 1915, she lived with her uncle Joseph and Aunt Louise Ralston and their family, but for the most part she was independent. She continued to work as a salesperson/clerk in retail establishments.[767]

We don't know when they met, but Alvin Garman Davis and Mary Ralston Bethel were married in 1917, probably in late summer.[768] He was from Ebensburg, about 60 miles south of DuBois, and he worked as a clerk for the Pennsylvania Railroad. It may well have been that the impending war hurried the nuptials, as it did for many young lovers of their generation. Alvin served as a Sergeant in the Army Engineering Corps from April through November 1918.[769]

---

763 Abandoned and orphaned children who lived on the streets, popularly called guttersnipes, were abundant in nineteenth-century America. Since Willis always listed his home state as New York instead of Ohio, there would have been no way to place Mary with any of her father's relatives, even if they had been willing to accept her.
764 U.S. Census, 1900, Sarah Jane McGinnes family, Scrubgrass Township, Venango County, Pennsylvania, Ancestry.com.
765 Find a Grave Memorial 98328991, Sarah Jane Ralston McGinnes, photo credit: Lynda McGinnis.
766 U.S. Census, 1910, Mary R. Bethel, DuBois, Clearfield County, Pennsylvania, Ancestry.com.
767 DuBois, Pennsylvania, directories, 1911, p. 47; 1913, p. 44; 1915, p. 38; 1917, p.38, Ancestry.com.
768 The 1930 census states that both Alvin and Mary were 25 when they were married. Since Alvin was born July 28, 1892 and Mary was born September 30, 1891, the only time when both were 25 years old was July 28 — September 30, 1917, Ancestry.com.
769 Commonwealth of Pennsylvania Veterans Compensation Application, Alvin Garman Davis, March 3, 1934; Headstone, Alvin Garman Davis, Lloyd Cemetery, Ebensburg, Pennsylvania, Ancestry.com.

He came home to a baby daughter. Charlotte Ralston Davis was born November 16, 1918.[770] Mary had remained in Ebensburg during the war, probably so Alvin's parents could care for her during her pregnancy. Charlotte's middle name was an obvious tribute to the only family group Mary had ever known, and her first name was chosen to honor Alvin's younger sister, who had died at the age of three. Alvin and Mary moved to Greensburg, Pennsylvania, a suburb of Pittsburgh, soon after the war. He continued to clerk for the railroad in their Pittsburgh offices, a position he held for the rest of his working life. On September 28, 1920, the couple had another daughter, Phyllis Louise.[771] Phyllis was a given name that is found in Alvin's family, and the middle name of Louise was probably chosen to honor Mary's Aunt Louise who, if not a mother figure to Mary, had at least been a close confidant.

High school yearbook photos from 1936 and 1938, respectively, reveal that Charlotte and Phyllis were pretty, well-adjusted, and active in school events. It makes one wonder about the accuracy of the description of their grandmother, Matilda Ralston Bethel, that Ben Perry had given to Nettie in 1894.

[772]

Greensburg High School yearbook, 1936.

Phyllis Louise Davis [773]

---

770 U.S. Social Security Applications and Claims Index, Charlotte Ralston Davis Lett; Marriage license, Charlotte Ralston Davis/Godfrey Samuel Lett, Ancestry.com.
771 U.S. Social Security Applications and Claims Index, Phyllis Louise Davis Glanz, Ancestry.com.
772 U.S. School Yearbooks, 1900–1999, Greensburg High School, Greensburg, Pennsylvania, Ancestry.com
773 Ibid.

PHYLLIS LOUISE DAVIS
Phyllis . . . has blond hair . . . and gray-green eyes . . . that make her as "pretty as a picture" . . . Playing badminton . . . and dancing . . . are her favorite diversions . . . She will be another of Miss Conley's secretaries-in-the-making next year. [774]

Greensburg High School yearbook, 1938.

Both young women worked in offices immediately following high school, living at the family home.[775] Sometime between 1938 and 1942, Phyllis became a flight attendant.[776] On February 9, 1943, the following item appeared in the Pittsburgh Post-Gazette:

[777]

Transcription: Mrs. Alvin Davis and her daughter, Miss Charlotte Davis, entertained at a tea recently in their home in Harrison avenue, Greensburg, to announce the engagement of Miss Phyllis Louise Davis, to Ensign Edward Frederick Glanz, United States Naval Reserve.

Miss Davis is a daughter of Mr. and Mrs. Alvin G. Davis.

Her fiancé, who is the son of Mrs. Edward Glanz and the late Mr. Glanz of Lakewood avenue, Detroit, is a graduate of the University of Michigan. Ensign Glanz is now in active service with the United States Navy, located in Dutch Harbor, Alaska.

No wedding plans were announced.

It must have been open season on the Davis girls, because four days later Charlotte married Godfrey Samuel Lett, a Canadian immigrant who lived in Pittsburgh and worked as a clerk for

---

774 Ibid.
775 U.S. Census, Alvin Davis family, Greensburg, Westmoreland County, Pennsylvania, 1940, Ancestry.com.
776 Greensburg, Pennsylvania, directory, 1942, Phyllis L. Davis, Ancestry.com.
777 The Pittsburgh Post-Gazette, February 9, 1943, Newspapers.com.

U.S. Steel.⁷⁷⁸ Godfrey also served in the war, as a private in the army, and afterward the Letts moved to Charlotte, North Carolina, where he became a salesman for his former company. Godfrey worked his way up the management chain, and by 1956 he was in management at an Engineering firm.⁷⁷⁹ The couple had two children, a daughter and a son.⁷⁸⁰ Godfrey died in 1969, and Charlotte stayed in the city until her own death in 2007.⁷⁸¹ Her obituary said she was, "an avid Bridge player, [who] loved helping at the Loaves and Fishes Soup Kitchen and was an active member of St. Peter's Episcopal Church."⁷⁸² Unfortunately, my letter to her asking for more information about her family was mailed two days after her death.

Phyllis and Edward Frederick Glanz's engagement must have been solemnized into marriage during the war on one of his leaves, inasmuch as their first child, a daughter, was born in December 1944. Edward became a prominent mechanical engineer after his military service. The Glanz family settled in the fashionable Detroit suburb of Grosse Point, where they raised three children. Phyllis died in Sarasota, Florida on January 17, 1989, but we don't know whether she was still married to Edward at that time.⁷⁸³ We know that Edward remarried, but he died in 1997.⁷⁸⁴

Mary Bethel Davis passed away in 1958 at the age of 66. The cause of death was listed as G.A.S., probably meaning Group A Streptococcus, with Diabetes Mellitus and some kidney and digestive issues as contributory ailments.⁷⁸⁵ After his retirement from the railroad, Alvin moved from Greensburg back to Ebensburg, where he lived until his death in 1985. He and Mary were buried together among Alvin's relatives in Lloyd Cemetery in Ebensburg.

Headstones, Alvin and Mary Ralston Bethel Davis, Lloyd Cemetery, Ebensburg, Pennsylvania.

---

778 U.S. Census, Godfrey S. Lett, Pittsburgh, Pennsylvania, 1940; Marriage license, Godfrey Lett/Charlotte Davis, February 13, 1943, Ancestry.com.
779 Directory, Charlotte, North Carolina, Godfrey Lett, 1956, p. 428, Ancestry.com.
780 email correspondence, Jim Sterrett and Charles Caldemeyer, 2007; Mecklenburg County, North Carolina, birth index, records request from Mecklenburg County Register of Deeds.
781 Social Security Death Index, Charlotte Ralston Davis Lett, Ancestry.com.
782 Obituary, Charlotte Davis Lett, The Charlotte Observer, January 23, 2007, GenealogyBank.com.
783 Florida Death Index, Phyllis Louis Glanz, 1989, Ancestry.com.
784 Obituary, Edward Frederick Glanz, The Detroit Free Press, July 20, 1997, Newspapers.com.
785 Death Certificate, Mary Ralston Bethel Davis, records request from the Pennsylvania Department of Health.
786 Find a Grave Memorials 74404354 and 74562967, Alvin Garman and Mary Bethel Davis, Lloyd Cemetery, Ebensburg, Pennsylvania, Findagrave.com. Photo credit: Tricia.

Elsie Ruth Bethel (1892–1964)

Elsie's birth, out of wedlock as it was, must have come as a surprise to the Rietmans, but there is no indication that they allowed it to cloud her future. In fact, it seems that the family united behind Minnie, and helped her raise her daughter as best they could. There may have been a conversation about propriety, but there was no bastardy suit. The unpublished marriage allowed the Rietmans to keep Minnie's single mother status a secret for over a year, until the birth was quietly legitimized. This was quite a contrast to the way some illegitimate children of the age were treated. The reader will recall the unfortunate case of poor Archibald Ivoy Bethel from Chapter 5.

None of the trauma of such treatment is evident in Elsie's life. After high school, she began working as a stenographer while remaining at the family home at 3020 Columbia Avenue.[787] She lived there until 1918, when she married Herbert James Schmidt.[788] He was a first-generation American, the son of Austrian immigrants, and he anglicized his last name to Smith about the time of their marriage. American involvement in World War I may have had something to do with the change, and although he registered for the draft, he claimed exemption because his income was the only means of support for his mother, and there is no indication that he was called.[789] Herbert worked as an inspector and grader, then as a salesman, for the Mowbray-Robinson Lumber Company almost continuously until his death in 1958 at the age of 69. Herbert and Elsie had some sporadic residences in Kentucky, probably because that was where Mowbray-Robinson operations centered, but by 1922 the family had returned to Cincinnati, and they largely remained there until Herbert's passing.[790]

Herbert and Elsie had one adopted daughter, Alta Marie, born in 1922. She married George Varelmann Witt, also a Cincinnati native, after his service in the Merchant Marines in World War II.[791] The Witts settled in Tampa in the 1950s, and that fact probably provided Elsie with an incentive to relocate there after Herbert died in 1958. Elsie passed away in Tampa on March 2, 1964, at the age of 71. She was buried in the Rietman plot at Spring Grove Cemetery in Cincinnati with her husband, mother, grandparents, and other family members.[792]

---

787 Cincinnati directory, 1912, Elsie R. Bethel, Ancestry.com.
788 Marriage license, Herbert James Smith/Elsie Ruth Bethel, January 19, 1918, Ancestry.com.
789 World War I Draft Registration Card, Herbert James Schmidt, Ancestry.com.
790 *U.S. Census*, 1920, 1930, 1940, Herbert J. Smith; Cincinnati, Ohio directories, 1953, p. 1040; 1956, p. 565, 578; 1958, p. 1243; 1959, p. 1212, all Ancestry.com.
791 U.S. Department of Veterans Affairs BIRLS Death File, George Varelmann Witt: Cincinnati, Ohio, directory, 1947, George and Alta Marie Witt, p. 1403, both Ancestry.com. This record shows that George and Alta Marie were married by 1947 and living at the home at Markbreit Avenue.
792 Burial record, Elsie Bethel Smith, Spring Grove Cemetery, Cincinnati, Ohio, Ancestry.com.

SMITH

Elsie R. (nee Bethel), beloved wife of the late Herbert J. Smith, devoted mother of Mrs. George C. Witt, daughter of Mrs. Minnie Bethel, sister of Clarence Bethel; also survived by three grandchildren; Monday, March 2, 1964, at Tampa, Fla.; formerly of Cincinnati, Ohio. Funeral services Friday, March 6, from the Riedlinger-Lemen Funeral Home, 1309 California Ave., Bond Hill, 10 A. M. Friends may call Thursday, 6 to 9 P. M. [793]

Transcription: Elsie R. (nee Bethel), beloved wife of the late Herbert J. Smith, devoted mother of Mrs. George C. Witt, daughter of Mrs. Minnie Bethel, sister of Clarence Bethel; also survived by three grandchildren; Monday, March 2, 1964, at Tampa, Fla.; formerly of Cincinnati, Ohio. Funeral services Friday, March 6, from the Riedlinger-Lemen Funeral Home, 1309 California Ave., Bond Hill, 10 A. M. Friends may call Thursday, 6 to 9 P. M.

Headstone, Elsie Ruth Bethel Smith, Rietman plot, Spring Grove Cemetery, Cincinnati, Ohio.

George and Alta Marie raised three children, but the couple divorced in 1984.[795] Their two daughters both relocated to Wichita, Kansas, and Alta Marie joined them there. She died in 1993 at the age of 70 and was buried at the Resurrection Cemetery and Mausoleum near Wichita.[796]

---
793 Elsie Ruth Bethel Smith Obituary, The Cincinnati Enquirer, March 4, 1964.
794 Photo by Charles Caldemeyer, 2016.
795 Florida Divorce Index, 1927–2001, Ancestry.com.
796 Find a Grave Memorial 10415485, Alta Smith Witt, Findagrave.com.

Clarence Aubrey Bethel (1895–1970)

Clarence is found in numerous directories and other records throughout his life. This allows us to track him closely, and we also have some contributions from his descendants. He began his working life young — he is listed in the Cincinnati directory as early as 1909, when at the age of 14 he worked as a stock boy at a hardware store.[797] His income was probably a welcome supplement to the family group effort.

By 1915, he was an electrotyper in a printing shop, which may have been his first exposure to the field of chemistry, which would later come into greater prominence.[798] In 1917, we have records of him living in two different locations. The Cincinnati directory lists him simply as a clerk, living at the family's home address of 3020 Columbia Avenue.[799] His draft registration card, however, lists his home as Dayton, and his occupation as tire adjustor for the Fish Rubber Company.[800] When World War I broke out, Clarence enlisted in the Ohio National Guard, and saw action, being deployed as a Private First Class from June 1918 until the war's end in November. He was a Wagoner with the 147th Ambulance Company, 112th Sanitary Train, part of the 37th Division of the American Expeditionary Forces. His job was to transport wounded soldiers to field hospitals, and to maintain vehicles, wagons, and the horses that pulled them. It was dangerous work, as was any occupation outside the trenches. His grandson has reported that Clarence never talked about his time in the army. He was honorably discharged on April 12, 1919.[801]

Clarence returned to Cincinnati, and in the 1920 census he was again living at the family home on Columbia Avenue. Minnie and her mother, along with Minnie's sister Ella and her husband, Jacob Pinger, also resided in the house.[802] Clarence moved with the family to the house on Markbreit Avenue around 1922. He worked as a salesman for a tire company, probably still Fish Rubber, throughout this time, and this may also have been a period when he attended college.[803]

On July 12, 1924, Clarence Aubrey Bethel married Luella A. Feely, the daughter of a Cincinnati fireman. Luella had worked as a stenographer, a tailoress, and a clerk in the years preceding her marriage. Like Clarence, she seems to have been a willing worker, taking any job that might improve her position, and improvising as needed.[804] In 1926, the couple wel-

---

797 U.S. Census, 1910, Cincinnati, Ohio, Clarence A. Bethel; Cincinnati, Ohio, directory, 1910, Clarence A. Bethel, Ancestry.com.
798 Cincinnati, Ohio, directory, 1915, Clarence A. Bethel, Ancestry.com.
799 Cincinnati, Ohio, directory, 1917, Clarence A. Bethel, Ancestry.com.
800 World War I Draft Registration Card, Clarence A. Bethel, Ancestry.com.
801 Ohio Soldiers in World War I, Ancestry.com. Interestingly, Clarence is listed directly beneath Charles William Bethel, whom the reader will remember was the product of Willis's father William's incestuous rape of his daughter, Clara. Thus, Charles was both Clarence's uncle (via William) and his cousin (via Clara).
802 U.S. Census, 1920, Cincinnati, Ohio, Elizabeth, Minnie, and Clarence Bethel, Jacob and Ella Pinger, Ancestry.com.
803 Cincinnati directories, 1921, p. 199; 1923, p. 142, Clarence A. Bethel, Ancestry.com.
804 U.S. Census, 1920, Cincinnati, Ohio, Luella Feely; Cincinnati directories, 1917, p. 615; 1918, p. 616; 1923, p. 461; Luella A. Feely, all Ancestry.com.

comed Elizabeth, and in 1934 a son came into the family.[805]

Clarence had a background in chemistry which he seems to have pursued through higher education, but he only worked in that capacity during World War II. It seems that his greatest interest was in human chemistry, and he gravitated toward sales and mid-level management jobs. This direction took the family, or at least Clarence, on the road throughout the late 1920s and the 1930s. In 1928, he was in the South Bend, Indiana, directory, working as a salesman.[806] The following year, we find him about 100 miles away in Battle Creek, Michigan, working as the Manager of a Sears Roebuck store.[807] By the 1930 census, the family lived just south of Battle Creek, in the Michigan town of Three Rivers, at the same job.[808] Those were the beginnings of difficult times in the American Midwest, and he may have had encountered increasingly limited options for income as the Great Depression spread. Even though he had to move around for his employment, he and Luella retained strong ties to family in Cincinnati, probably returning there often.

The 1940 census recorded a family's current location, of course, but it also asked where they had resided in 1935, and that year the Bethels were in Thomasville, Georgia. It may have been the Works Project Administration that took them there — in 1940, Clarence was working as a Senior Clerk in the Hamilton County (Cincinnati) Tax Office, through the auspices of the W. P. A. If the family had been in Georgia in 1935, they returned to Cincinnati for good the following year. The 1936 Cincinnati directory lists Clarence as an insurance agent, and all records of his and Luella's residence after 1935 are in Cincinnati.[809] They stayed in the family house at 2723 Markbreit Avenue that year while Minnie lived with Herbert and Elsie Smith. Strangely, Clarence and Luella are listed by themselves, without children, although Bettie was 14 and her brother was six. This was likely due to an oversight by the census taker.[810]

By 1942, when he registered for the "old man's draft," Clarence and his family lived at 1142 Halpin Avenue. His draft registration recorded his workplace as the Wright Aeronautical Corporation in nearby Lockland, and the Cincinnati directory listed him as a chemist. It seems likely that he remained in this capacity through World War II, when there was strong demand for more technical skills, and sales jobs were less abundant. Clarence and Luella remained in the house on Halpin Avenue until the early 1950s, when they moved to 3422 Burch Avenue.[811] He was back into sales. Clarence worked the rest of his career selling sandpaper and other items for Dayton Abrasive Products.

Luella Feely Bethel passed away tragically in 1967. The Burch Avenue home caught on fire, and she suffered fatal burns as she and her husband were trying to save some household items. Clarence was also badly burned, and dazed, and "was found wandering in the

---

805 Bethel-Feely Family Tree, courtesy Thomas Trapp.
806 South Bend, Indiana, directory, 1928, p. 132, Clarence A. Bethel, Ancestry.com.
807 Battle Creek, Michigan, directory, 1929, p. 120, Clarence A. Bethel, Ancestry.com.
808 U.S. Census, 1930, Three Rivers, Michigan, Clarence and Luella Bethel, Ancestry.com.
809 Cincinnati, Ohio, directory, 1936, p. 206, Clarence A. Bethel, Ancestry.com.
810 U.S. census, 1940, Cincinnati, Ohio, Clarence and Luella Bethel, Ancestry.com. This census is the source for the information that Clarence had four years of college education.
811 Cincinnati, Ohio, directory, 1953, p. 100, Clarence A. Bethel, Ancestry.com.

street."[812] Three years later, on July 11, 1970, he died of complications from a concussion at the age of 75.[813] He lived a life of genial approval of his responsibilities, with enthusiasm and without complaint. His grandson wrote, "Clarence (we called him Dad) was as good a man as I have ever known, so the seed of David W. didn't hurt him."[814] Clarence and Luella were buried in the Gate of Heaven Cemetery in Montgomery, Ohio, near Cincinnati. They were, in the words of their grandson, "the perfect grandparents."[815]

Clarence and Luella's daughter Bettie married Eugene Frank Trapp in the mid-1940s. The couple had two children, but they divorced in 1966.[816] She later married Forrest Romine, who predeceased her. After her retirement, Bettie was a volunteer for the Fine Arts Fund, a Cincinnati non-profit organization, and served as district chair of the group for the Hyde Park neighborhood in 2009.[817] She passed away, "peacefully in her sleep" on December 30, 2014, at the age of 88.[818]

Clarence and Luella's son is still alive as of this writing.

[819]

Clarence Aubrey Bethel (far left) at the wedding of his grandson, 1968.

---

812 *Hyde Park Woman, 67, Dies in Fire*, The Cincinnati Enquirer, June 18, 1967, Newspapers.com.
813 Email from Thomas Trapp to Charles Caldemeyer, January 19, 2017.
814 Email from Thomas Trapp to Charles Caldemeyer, October 24, 2016.
815 Email from Thomas Trapp to Charles Caldemeyer, January 19, 2017.
816 Suits Filed: Court of Common Pleas, The Cincinnati Enquirer, February 16, 1966, Newspapers.com.
817 *Fine Arts Fund Volunteers*, The Cincinnati Enquirer, January 1, 2009, Newspapers.com.
818 Obituary, Bettie Bethel Romine, The Cincinnati Enquirer, January 4, 2015, Newspapers.com.
819 Photo courtesy Thomas Trapp.

> **BETHEL**
> Clarence A., beloved husband of the late Luella Feely Bethel, father of Mrs. Betty Trapp and Richard Bethel, grandfather of Michael and Tommy Trapp; Saturday, July 11, 1970; residence, 3422 Burch Ave. Service at George H. Rohde & Son Funeral Home, Linwood and Delta Aves.; Tuesday, July 14 at 10:30 A. M. No visitation.

[820]

Transcription: Clarence A., beloved husband of the late Luella Feely Bethel, father of Mrs. Betty Trapp and Richard Bethel, grandfather of Michael and Tommy Trapp; Saturday, July 11, 1970; residence 3422 Burch Ave. Service at George H. Rohde & Son Funeral Home, Linwood and Delta Aves.; Tuesday, July 14 at 10:30 A. M. No visitation.

[821]

Headstone, Clarence Aubrey Bethel, Gate of Heaven Cemetery, Montgomery, Ohio.

---
820 Obituary, Clarence Aubrey Bethel, The Cincinnati Enquirer, July 12, 1970, Newspapers.com.
821 Find a Grave Memorial 86966063, Clarence A. Bethel, Findagrave.com. Photo credit Mike Smith.

Raymond Harry Bethel (1897–1958)

Raymond's obituary gave his place of birth as Detroit, but I have been unable to confirm it, and no birth record is available. The Jerome Frasier farm was about eighty miles from the city, a long way in 1897, so if he was born in Detroit it's likely that Annie stayed with other of her mother's relatives. Whatever the circumstances of his birth, we know that Raymond spent his early childhood years in Los Angeles with the Guardian Angels, until Annie reclaimed him for the divorce proceedings in 1902.

Raymond's granddaughter, Carole Frances Bethel, wrote that her grandfather had been raised by "a maiden aunt," although she did not know her name.[822] But there is only one possibility — Bessie Dalton Reed. We know that Bessie was in Long Beach in 1902, but she was back in Los Angeles in 1904 and 1905, still working as a stenographer.[823] Like her siblings, she seems to have moved around a lot when she was in her twenties. She may have worked for Macy & Co. in nearby Elsinore from 1905–1906.[824] She resurfaced in Long Beach in 1907, this time as a clerk for Fisher & Co., selling curios to tourists on the beach.[825] That was also the year that Raymond was committed to another orphanage, The Boys and Girls Aid Society Home in South Pasadena. This time the records say he was a full orphan, meaning that both parents were dead, but some of the information in the record looks suspicious, and it may have been garbled.[826] It seems likely that Annie had exited the scene by then, either by departure or decease. It's also possible that Raymond was placed in another orphanage in between 1902 and 1907, pulled out, and then placed with the Aid Society Home, since the only public records from orphanages came along every ten years with the census. But the likeliest scenario is that Annie either died or abandoned her son in Long Beach sometime around June 1902, and her single sister raised the boy as best she could until 1907, when he became too much of a burden on her own life and marital aspirations. My best guess is that Annie died. But Bessie, clearly the responsible sister, probably showed Raymond the kindness and caring that his mother did not. Annie seems to have regarded Raymond as a burden, a reminder of her worst decision ever.

The 1910 census finds the 32-year-old Bessie living in Los Angeles again, this time with her brother Guy, his wife Lora, and their three-year-old son Gordon. But soon afterward they all moved to the booming area around Bakersfield, north of Los Angeles in Kern County, where oil was being pumped from the ground in volume. Guy worked as a foreman in the

---

822 Letter, Carole Frances Bethel to Charles Caldemeyer, August 5, 2009.
823 Los Angeles, California, directories, 1904, 1905, Bessie D. Reed, from microfilm supplied by the Family History Center, Provo, Utah.
824 The Riverside Independent Enterprise, July 31, 1906, GenealogyBank.com.
825 Long Beach, California, directory, 1907, p. 162, Ancestry.com.
826 Records request from Five Acres Orphanage, Altadena, California. The record says he was committed on October 1, 1907, the eleventh anniversary of Willis and Annie's wedding, discharged on July 7, 1911, his fourteenth birthday, and that Willis and Annie were married in Chicago, not Perris. Willis is said to have died in 1898 in Chicago and Annie in Long Beach, although the latter date is unrecorded. All of this indicates that the answers to some questions may have been put in the wrong boxes or misread when transcribed later. Orphanage records of the time were sketchy — the staff had plenty to do, and errors such as this were probably common.

oilfields. Bessie married Everett Stiles, who also worked in the fields as a carpenter and driller, in 1911.[827] They lived in the town of Wasco, just northwest of Bakersfield, and Stiles soon became known as one of the best builders in the area.[828] About four months before their wedding, if the orphanage records can be believed, Raymond Harry Bethel was discharged, meaning that a relative, almost certainly his Aunt Bessie, took responsibility for him. He was fourteen.

[829]

Bessie Dalton Reed and Everett Stiles, about 1892 and 1905, respectively. We don't have a photo of Annie, so this one of her older sister, who raised Raymond in his mother's absence, will have to do. This picture of Bessie was probably taken about three years before Raymond's birth, and about 17 years before her marriage to Everett in 1911. Everett likely served as a much-needed father figure for Raymond Harry Bethel during his teenage years.

Ray attended high school in Wasco, completing two years and playing centerfield for the baseball team, before joining the workforce.[830] In early 1917, when he was 19, we find him working for the Kern Trading and Oil Company, a subsidiary of the Southern Pacific Railroad, as a yardman.[831]

---

827 Bakersfield Californian, November 29, 1911, Newspapers.com.
828 Bakersfield Californian Supplement Issue, April 1914, NewspaperArchive.com.
829 Photos originally published on Ancestry.com by ladylittle, July 13, 2007 and July 7, 1907.
830 Bakersfield Morning Echo, December 6, 1914, NewspaperArchive.com; U.S. Census, 1940, Santa Cruz, Santa Cruz County, California, Raymond Harry Bethel, Ancestry.com. This census indicates that Raymond completed tenth grade.
831 California, Railroad Employment Records, Southern Pacific Subsidiaries, Kern Trading and Oil Company, January–April 1917, Ray Bethel, Ancestry.com.

Everett and Bessie had started their own family in 1913 with the birth of a son, followed by twin daughters in 1915 and another one in 1917. It was about this time that they moved on from Wasco, following Bessie's three brothers to a new home in Arizona.[832] Youngest brother George had died of tuberculosis in 1916, but John and his wife were there to welcome their sister's family, and Guy had also moved there following his divorce in 1914.[833] The relocation of the Reeds to Arizona thus included everyone but Annie, further evidence that she was long gone, and not just hiding in the shadows. Ray was probably offered a place to stay if he joined them, but other forces seem to have kept him in Kern County.

He joined the Army in 1916 and was stationed at least part of the time in San Diego, at some point becoming a proficient deep-sea diver.[834] On April 22, 1918, he married Emma Margaret Krossa.[835] She was the daughter of Eastern European immigrants, born in Nebraska as the family made their way across the country. Her parents and siblings all resided in Kern County.[836] Following the war, Raymond went back to Emma, and to working in the oil fields.[837] On March 19, 1920, Raymond Howard Bethel (he went by Howard) was born, and in 1924 another son came along.[838]

We find records of the family in Kern County in the 1920s and early 1930s, as Raymond built his reputation as a rig builder.[839] True to the spirit of the Reeds, he seems to have looked to the present and had little interest in his heritage. The 1920 census listed his birthplace as Michigan, but also lists it as the state of both parents' birth. By 1930, he claimed to have been born in Nevada, while his father and mother are listed as born in the 'United States,' which was what the census taker wrote down when the respondent answered, "I don't know" to the question. Raymond probably didn't know and didn't care. They hadn't been around, he had made it through childhood fine, anyway, and it just didn't matter.

In 1932, the family relocated to Santa Cruz, and for a while he continued to work as a rig builder.[840] By 1934 he was a carpenter on the Santa Cruz Municipal Wharf, and the following year he was a foreman there.[841] By 1939, he was foreman for the city Water Department, a job he remained in for as long as we have professional records of him.[842] He made the papers

---

832 U.S. Census, 1920, 1930, Everett and Bessie Stiles family, Gila County, Arizona, Ancestry.com.
833 Death Certificate, George Bernice Reed, February 17, 1917, Gila County, Arizona; U.S. Census, 1920, 1930, John W. Reed, Ancestry.com. John Reed may be found on the same page as Everett and Bessie in both the 1920 and 1930 Censuses; World War I Draft Registration Card, Guy Bertram Reed, Cochise County, Arizona, Ancestry.com. Guy lived in Arizona, but about 200 miles south of John and Bessie, probably following mining opportunities. Bakersfield Morning Echo, May 8, 1914, NewspaperArchive.com. Guy's wife Lora had divorced him in California in 1914 and was awarded custody of their son.
834 U.S. National Cemetery Interment Control Form, Raymond Harry Bethel, 1958, Ancestry.com; Headstone, Raymond Harry Bethel, Golden Gate National Cemetery, San Mateo County, California, Find A Grave Memorial 73778895, Findagrave.com; Bakersfield Californian, April 22, 1918, NewspaperArchive.com; The Santa Cruz Sentinel, June 20, 1943, Newspapers.com; Letter from Carole Frances Bethel to Charles Caldemeyer, September 3, 2009, p. 1.
835 Bakersfield Californian, April 22, 1918, NewspaperArchive.com.
836 U.S. Census, 1920, John Krossa family, Kern County, California, Ancestry.com.
837 U.S. Census, 1920, Raymond and Emma Bethel, Kern County, California, Ancestry.com.
838 California Birth Index, Raymond Howard Bethel, March 19. 1920; U.S. Census, 1930, Raymond, Emma, R. Howard, and Harry W. Bethel, Kern County, California, Ancestry.com.
839 California Voter Registrations, 1920–1922, 1930, Raymond and Emma Bethel, Kern County, Ancestry.com.
840 Santa Cruz, California, directory, 1932, Raymond and Emma Bethel, Ancestry.com.
841 Santa Cruz, California, directories, 1934, 1935, Raymond and Emma Bethel, Ancestry.com.
842 Santa Cruz, California, directories, 1939, 1948, Raymond and Emma Bethel, Ancestry.com.

often for his projects, and he was an active and respected member of his community.

Transcription: Shown here on the truck which will take Santa Cruz' 3300-pound donation of aluminum to the San Jose scrap metal depot today to be weighed in the national defense drive, are, left to right, Grant Scofield, Drive Chairman Ray Bethel and George Wightman, one of the many boys who assisted in the drive.

Ray was one of the few people to serve in both World War I and World War II. He enlisted in the Navy in early 1942, at the age of 44, and rose to the rank of Chief Carpenter. During the war, he was a deep-sea diver, receiving numerous commendations (as detailed in the articles below) and he was wounded while diving and also suffered the bends, an incident that

---

843 Santa Cruz Sentinel, July 30, 1941, Newspapers.com.

made him, in the words of his granddaughter Carole, "a little balmy."[844] Much of the last two years of his life were spent in Oak Knoll Naval Hospital in Oakland, fighting the effects of his injuries.[845] He died on September 18, 1958, at the age of 61, and was buried with military honors in the Golden Gate National Cemetery in San Bruno, California. He was, in Carole's words, as "nice a man as I can remember."[846] Emma died in 1971 and was laid to rest beside her husband.

[847]

Transcription: U.S. Naval Convalescent Hospital, Sun Valley, Idaho – Outstanding service for his country . . .that's the record of Warrant Carpenter Raymond H. Bethel, U. S. N. R. (whose wife lives at 226 Parkway, Santa Cruz, Calif.), pictured above at the Sun Valley naval hospital following his award of the Purple Heart for injuries received while doing salvage work at Palermo.

Mr. Bethel is the recipient of eight commendations for various services. He enlisted in the navy in 1916 taking part in the Mexican border affair. From 1917 to 1921 he was assigned to duty with the Coast & Geodetic Service. From 1921 to 1940, as a civilian he worked as a deepsea diver and hydraulic engineer. He was listed as one of the best divers in the world and was asked to join the service. He then was assigned to salvage Glen 49 under Commodore Charles Ellsberg, helping to clean up the harbor at Messeur, Iran, lifting dry docks and cruisers. He was at Arsew, Algeria, and at Bizerte where he underwent 92 bombing raids. He accompanied the invasion of Sicily after which he returned to Bizerte for underwater work, and thence to Salerno and Palermo where he was injured.

---

844 Letter, Carole Frances Bethel to Charles Caldemeyer, September 3, 2009, p. 1.
845 Ibid.
846 Ibid, p. 2.
847 Santa Cruz Sentinel, August 2, 1944, Newspapers.com.

He was commended by Admiral Hatch at Monguen, French Morocco, for clearing wreckage of Nathaniel Green [sic]; by Admiral R. L. Connley for work in Arzew on sub nets; by Admiral Hewitt for invasion of Sicily; twice by Commander George H. Patterson for work in Tunis harbor opening locks; twice by Captain Rupert Zimmerli for work at Gela and Lacata, Sicily; and by Secretary of Navy Knox for outstanding work changing propellers underwater, thus saving ships from going to dry dock.

Last Thanksgiving day, Salvage Glen 49 was given the Presidential Unit Citation by Roosevelt, Churchill and Montgomery for combined salvage in the Mediterranean area.

And he has the Legion of Merit given for work at Oran in raising a dry dock that had been sunk with a sub in it. Following his injuries at Palermo, Mr. Bethel was hospitalized and returned to the States and he is now convalescing at Sun Valley famous peacetime resort, which the navy is now utilizing in its effort to restore strength and health to its men returning from war.

Bethel, foreman of the water department here until his enlistment in the navy in May, 1941, had lived in Santa Cruz with his family since 1931. The Bethels came here from Taft, Calif. Bethel was born 47 years ago in Detroit, Mich.

He was home in February and the early part of March of this year visiting his wife and two sons – Harry, now working and expecting to re-enter San Jose State college this fall, and Howard R., awaiting a call into the navy. Mrs. Bethel says her husband has written her that he doesn't know whether he will be sent across again.

Bethel was active in the American Legion and the Masons.

Ray Bethel Suffers Stroke

Ray Bethel, 58, of Laurel Glen road, a former city employe for 21 years, was taken to the Oak Knoll hospital yesterday "in serious condition" suffering from a stroke.

Bethel, a deep sea diver for the U. S. Navy in World War II, suffered the "bends" while in the service. This condition is believed to have caused the stroke. Bethel began working for the city in 1931, and retired because of ill health in 1952. His son, Howard, is a construction foreman for the street department.[848]

Transcription: Ray Bethel, 58, of Laurel Glen road, a former city employe for 21 years, was taken to the Oak Knoll hospital yesterday "in serious condition" suffering from a stroke.

---

848 Santa Cruz Sentinel, January 11, 1957, Newspapers.com.

Bethel, a deep sea diver for the U.S. Navy in World War II, suffered the "bends" while in the service. This condition is believed to have cause the stroke. Bethel began working for the city in 1931, and retired because of ill health in 1952. His son, Howard, is a construction foreman for the street department.

Raymond Bethel Services Set

Raymond H. Bethel, 60, a native of Detroit, Mich., and a resident of Santa Cruz since 1931, died yesterday in a navy hospital in Oakland after a long illness. He came to southern California as a boy and moved in 1914 to Taft where he worked in the oil fields. He served in World Wars I and II, in the latter of which he was injured while diving.

After moving to Santa Cruz, he worked for the city, serving on the wharf crew first and then as a foreman in the water department. He retired from city employment about five years ago. He lived at 1003 Laurel Glen road.

He is survived by his widow, Emma Margaret Bethel of Santa Cruz, two sons, Howard Bethel of Santa Cruz and Harry Bethel of Berkeley, and two grandchildren.

He was a member of Maricopa Lodge 434, F&AM, in Maricopa and Santa Cruz Post 64, American Legion.

Funeral services will be conducted Monday at 10:30 a.m. in White's chapel with interment following in the Golden Gate national cemetery in San Bruno at 1:15 p.m.

[849]

Transcription: Raymond H. Bethel, 60, a native of Detroit, Mich., and a resident of Santa Cruz since 1931, died yesterday in a navy hospital in Oakland after a long illness. He came to southern California as a boy and moved in 1914 to Taft where he worked in the oil fields. He served in World Wars I and II, in the latter of which he was injured while diving.

---

849 Obituary, Raymond Harry Bethel, Santa Cruz Sentinel, September 19, 1958, Newspapers.com.

After moving to Santa Cruz, he worked for the city, serving on the wharf crew first and then as a foreman in the water department. He retired from city employment about five years ago. He lived at 1003 Laurel Glen road.

He is survived by his widow, Emma Margaret Bethel of Santa Cruz, two sons, Howard Bethel of Santa Cruz and Harry Bethel of Berkeley, and two grandchildren.

He was a member of Maricopa Lodge 434 F&AM, in Maricopa, and Santa Cruz Post 64, American Legion. Funeral services will be conducted Monday at 10:30 a.m. in White's chapel with interment following in the Golden Gate national cemetery in San Bruno at 1:15 p.m.

Headstone, Raymond Harry Bethel, Golden Gate National Cemetery, San Bruno, California. Raymond's birth year is listed as 1898, but it was a long-standing error in recording. His actual birth year was 1897.

---

850 Find A Grave Memorial 73778895, Findagrave.com. Photo credit Tom Brocher.

Raymond Howard Bethel, Ray and Emma's son, about 2005.

Raymond Howard Bethel married Frances Pauline Stanley around 1941 and followed his father in working for the Santa Cruz city government, first for the Street Department and finally, also like his father, on the City Wharf as Harbormaster.[852] He and Pauline had two children, a daughter, Carole Frances, and a son, Lee Ray. Howard also ran a fishing boat and was a decorated leader of the Sea Scouts. By 1981, he and Frances had retired to Paradise, California. Frances passed away in 2010, and Howard in 2011, at the age of 91.[853]

Raymond and Emma's second son is still alive as of this writing.

---

851 Photo courtesy Carole Frances Bethel.
852 Santa Cruz, California, directories, 1948, 1950, 1960, Howard R. and Frances Bethel, Ancestry.com.
853 Letter, Carole Frances Bethel to Charles Caldemeyer, September 3, 2009, p. 2; *Social Security Death Index, 1935–2014*, Ancestry.com.

Herbert Benjamin Steele (1899–1942)

Herbert probably didn't have much more contact with his birth mother than he did with his father while growing up. Willis disappeared from his life when he was still an infant, and Chrestine probably passed him off to John and Mathilda Tyberg as soon as she could. Both biological parents were stubbornly self-centered, but Herbert, raised in a loving household that valued hard work, grew up to be an honest man. As a child, he recovered from rheumatic fever, scarlet fever, and diphtheria.[854] It's safe to say that he would have fared far worse without the Tybergs to care for him.

The family improved their stability, and probably their finances, by moving to North Dakota. It was during the general rush to the state in 1906, as Minnesota newspapers bemoaned the population drain.[855] The Tybergs are found in Williams County, near the village of Alamo, in the 1910 census. Herbert, age 10, was listed as Bennie Cavanagh, evidence that Chrestine retained at least some contact with her only son (she divorced the absent James Cavanagh in Pocatello the following year). As her lifestyle increasingly led her away from the steady workaday reality of the Tybergs, and finally to the asylum in 1915, there was probably less and less contact. We don't know if Herbert knew that she died in 1928, although he listed her as deceased on his work records from 1942, so he was certainly informed of her death at some point.[856] The death of Mathilda Tyberg in the mid-1920s was likely a more sorrowful event in Herbert's life than was Chrestine's.

By 1914, J.P. Tyberg, his stepson Godtfred Hendricks, and son Henry Tyberg each had 160-acre parcels they owned and farmed.[857] Herbert, now in his teenage years, likely helped out on his step-grandfather's farm, since John Petter Tyberg was getting old.[858] We know that he left school to work in that year, after completing the ninth grade.[859] The land is semi-arid rolling plains, mostly suited to growing grains.

Herbert enlisted in the Army on May 31, 1918, at the age of 18. He served in the Coastal Artillery Corps, stationed first in North Carolina, then overseas from September 18, 1918, until May 8, 1919. He was discharged on May 20.[860] He listed as his emergency contact his uncle Henry Tyberg, who at only seven years older, and having grown up in the same household, was likely more of an older brother and close friend.

Thanks to Herbert's employment by the Civilian Conservation Corps in the 1930s, and

---

854 Individual Record, U.S. Civilian Conservation Corps, Herbert Benjamin Steele, application, p. 26, March 31, 1939, records request from the National Archives, St. Louis.
855 The Norman County Index, April 5, 1906, p. 4; April 12, 1906, p. 4, microfilm from the Minnesota Historical Society, St. Paul.
856 U.S. War Department Personnel records, Herbert Benjamin Steele employment history, Station Hospital, Fort Lewis, Washington, records request from the National Archives, St. Louis.
857 Land ownership map, Township 159, Range 99 W., of the 5th P.M., Rock Island Township, Williams County, North Dakota, HistoricMapworks.com.
858 The 1910 U.S. census reported that J.P. Tyberg was 66 that year, Ancestry.com.
859 Individual Record, U.S. Civilian Conservation Corps, Herbert Benjamin Steele, application, p. 26, March 31, 1939, records request from NA.
860 North Dakota Military Men, 1917–1918, Herbert Benjamin Steele, Ancestry.com.

later by the War Department, we have a fairly complete work and residence history from his World War I days until his death. After his discharge, there were some overlaps in his record as the young man searched for his vocation. His work history from 1941 lists experience as a laborer, farmer, machinist, apprentice carpenter, car repairer, night watchman, fireman and, finally, as a mess cook, in Minnesota, North Dakota, and Washington. His records tell us that he was fluent in Scandinavian as well as English.[861]

The 1920 census, taken in February, found him engaged in farming on his own account in McHenry County in partnership with a young German immigrant named William Habeck, but he was also doing other jobs.[862] That venture may have gone belly-up, or Herbert may have abandoned the project to his colleague, because in March 1920, he was back near Alamo, working on his uncle Godtfred Hendricks' farm.[863] He continued to go back and forth between farm labor and carpentry in Williams County until 1923, when he reenlisted in the Army. He was stationed at West Point, where he worked in the machine shop. He served until January 1925, when he was again honorably discharged, having been promoted to Corporal in the interim.[864] It's possible that his family needed his presence back in North Dakota, or maybe other forces drew him back to the upper Midwest.

John Petter Tyberg had died by 1925, and in the North Dakota census of that year Henry Tyberg lived with the 72-year-old Mathilda, who would also pass away before long. Oldest brother Godtfred Hendricks had died in 1920, and John Albert Tyberg moved to Forsyth, Montana around 1917, where, according to his World War I draft registration, he worked as a blacksmith.[865] We lose all touch with Herbert's other Tyberg uncle after this record. What became of him is unknown.

Within two months of leaving the service, on March 13, 1925, Herbert married Myrtle Oline Berg, also from a Scandinavian immigrant farming family in Stearns County, Minnesota. His relationship with her indicates that he maintained at least some connection to the state of his childhood. Born in 1902, Myrtle's family story was a tragic one. She lost her mother in 1910 and her father in 1917. The 1920 census finds the 17-year-old living with her older brother Melvin and two sisters, Ruth and Bertha, trying to make a go of the family farm. Melvin must have been trying to keep the family together — he had seen both of their parents die, and two older brothers had also died young — but he, too, died in 1924, and with that event the Berg family unit dissolved. Ruth, Bertha, and youngest sister Mabel all were married about the same time as Myrtle.[866]

---

861 U.S. War Department Personnel records, Herbert Benjamin Steele employment history, Station Hospital, Fort Lewis, Washington, pp. 12-20, 49; Individual Record, U.S. Civilian Conservation Corps, Herbert Benjamin Steele, application, p. 24, March 31, 1939, both records requests from NA.
862 1920 U.S. census, Herbert Steele, Cottonwood Lake Township, McHenry County, North Dakota, Ancestry.com.
863 Godtfred Hendricks would die on unknown causes later that year, in May 1920, Find a Grave Memorial 19580602, Findagrave.com.
864 U.S. War Department Personnel records, Herbert Benjamin Steele employment history, Station Hospital, Fort Lewis, Washington, records request from NA.
865 World War I draft registration card, John A. Tyberg, Forsyth, Rosebud County, Montana, June 5, 1917, Ancestry.com.
866 Minnesota census, 1895 and 1905, family of Peter O. Berg, Stearns County, Minnesota; U.S. census, 1910 and 1920, family of Peter O. Berg, Stearns County, Minnesota, all Ancestry.com; Obituary, Myrtle Oline Berg Steele Fedor, Minneapolis Star-Tribune, August 12, 1962; Obituary, Mabel Berg Fredrick, August 10, 1993, both Newspapers.com.

Things began well for the young couple. They farmed the Williams County acreage, possibly initially in partnership with Herbert's uncle. But Henry soon began a career as a traveling salesman of farm implements. At some point he moved permanently to Saskatchewan, Canada, where he lived for the remainder of his days. On his immigration forms, he listed Herbert as his nearest relation, and it's likely that by that time Herbert was his only close relative.[867]

Beatrice Eileen Steele was born on December 14, 1926, at the farm near Alamo. For about five years, until July 1930, Herbert farmed for himself and his young family, and the 1930 census finds two other men of Norwegian descent, a farm laborer and a carpenter, lodging with the family. But he lost the farm, likely early in the Great Depression, and in October 1930 he went to work as a coal miner. Over the next few years, he moved back and forth between Alamo and Winona, Minnesota, working as a farm laborer. Winona, about 120 miles southeast of Minneapolis, is nowhere near the Tyberg's and the Berg's home bases in the northwestern part of the state, and it seems likely that Herbert was just following work wherever he could get it. According to his Civilian Conservation Corps records, he was unemployed from 1931 until 1934, and the jobs listed on his War Department records for that period may have been temporary in nature.[868] It was certainly a difficult time for many Americans, and many marriages, including Herbert's and Myrtle's, did not survive it. We know that they divorced about this time, although I have been unable to find a divorce record, either in North Dakota or Minnesota.[869]

Myrtle moved Beatrice back to her old haunts in Stearns County, and she married George Fedor, Jr., a Czechoslovakian immigrant who worked as a railroad section hand, sometime before 1935. They had another daughter, Audreye, in late 1938. It seems likely that George Fedor took over parental responsibilities for Beatrice, since Herbert listed himself without dependents on his Civilian Conservation Corps records in 1936.[870] The family remained in Stearns County until around 1946, when they moved to Minneapolis. Beatrice, by that time married and with a young family of her own, resided there. Myrtle remained an important part of Beatrice's life. Her daughter writes, "My mother was devastated when she passed, I can remember that day very well even today." Myrtle died in 1962 at the age of 59.[871]

Herbert maintained sporadic contact with Beatrice through the 1930s and early 1940s.[872] In his 1941 application to the War Department, he claimed Stearns County as his voting

---

867 Canadian Immigration Service, Reports of Admissions and Rejections, Henry Tyberg, April 30, 1928 and March 31, 1929, Ancestry.com.
868 Individual Record, U.S. Civilian Conservation Corps, Herbert Benjamin Steele, application, p. 28, July 19, 1934, records request from NA.
869 Individual Record, U.S. Civilian Conservation Corps, Herbert Benjamin Steele, p. 9; U.S. War Department Personnel records, Herbert Benjamin Steele employment history, Station Hospital, Fort Lewis, Washington, p. 5, both via records requests from NA.
870 Individual Record, U.S. Civilian Conservation Corps, Herbert Benjamin Steele, application, p. 24, July 2, 1936, records request from NA
871 Email, Gwen McDermond Johnson to Charles Caldemeyer, October 10, 2019; Obituary, Myrtle Berg Steele Fedor, Minneapolis Star Tribune, August 12, 1962, Newspapers.com.
872 Beatrice was listed as his emergency contact in his War Department Personnel file from 1942, although his other records, with both the War Department and the Civilian Conservation Corps, list Henry Tyberg in that role, records request from the NA.

residence, although the following year he listed it as Williams County, North Dakota.[873] In most of his government records, he listed Henry Tyberg as his contact, although in 1942 he listed Beatrice, who by that time was 16.[874] The records indicate that he was without roots, moving around the northwestern states from job to job, and that he found stability in work provided by the U.S. government. In October 1934, he was employed at Mandan, North Dakota for a six-month period as a night guard for the Veterans Civilian Conservation Corps, a New Deal program for vets designed to counter the effects of the Great Depression and improve conservation in rural areas. In June 1935, he was hired by the Federal Transient Bureau, another New Deal program to house and feed the homeless, in Helena, Montana. He was a cook and kitchen steward, evidently a skill set he had been developing for years, and at which he became proficient. His evaluations remark about the quality of both his work and his humanity. "A very good man, would recommend him to anyone," and "Excellent cook and mess steward — Excellent character," are examples from his records.[875] He seems to have possessed Willis's charming, easy-going personality traits to go along with the strong work ethic instilled by the Tybergs.

His record was not completely spotless. On October 9, 1936, he sustained a fractured jaw, "accidentally incurred when enrollee was struck on the jaw by a policeman in Spokane, Wash . . . when enrollee was intoxicated."[876] His jaw was wired shut five days later, and he was, presumably, unable to eat solid food for a time. For a cook, this must have been particularly difficult. There is no indication in the records of any disciplinary action for the incident, no mention of the incident in the Spokane newspaper, and no charges were filed, so it seems likely that the injury was truly accidental.

By late 1941, Herbert was employed by the War Medical Department as the chief cook and kitchen steward at the station hospital at Fort Lewis, Washington, near Seattle. His responsibilities included supervision and instruction of junior cooks and mess attendants.[877] On May 22, 1942, he appeared to have finally fully recovered from the effects of the Great Depression and the loss of his family when he married Ida Gertrude Cone.[878] He was simultaneously applying to the War Department to upgrade his job status from temporary to probational. Unfortunately, his new life of happiness ended almost immediately. He failed the physical that went with the application, and the War Department disapproved it on August 11.[879] On August 18, he was admitted to the Veterans Administration hospital in Portland, Oregon, with subacute bacterial endocarditis, an infection of the heart valves. He remained

---

873 U.S. War Department Personnel records, Herbert Benjamin Steele employment history, Station Hospital, Fort Lewis, Washington, p. 5, 48, records request from NA.
874 Ibid., p. 6.
875 Individual Record, Herbert Benjamin Steele, Civilian Conservation Corps, 1934–1941, p. 14, 27; records request from the NA.
876 Ibid.
877 U.S. War Department Personnel records, Herbert Benjamin Steele employment history, Station Hospital, Fort Lewis, Washington, p. 46, records request from NA.
878 Marriage certificate, Herbert Steele and Gertrude Cone, Olympia, Thurston County, Washington, May 22, 1942, Ancestry.com.
879 U.S. War Department Personnel records, Herbert Benjamin Steele employment history, Station Hospital, Fort Lewis, Washington, p. 50, records request from NA.

in the hospital for 68 days, but treatment was unsuccessful, and he finally succumbed to his disease on October 25, 1942, his 43rd birthday. His remains were buried at Forest Memorial Gardens Cemetery in Olympia, Washington.[880]

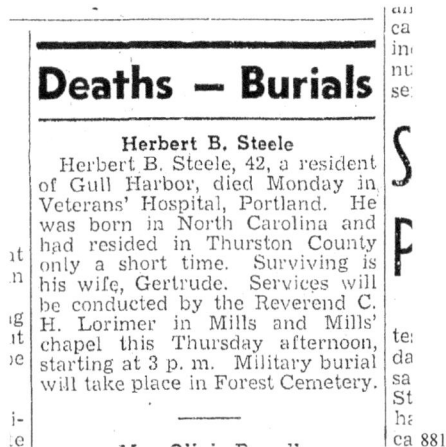

Transcription: Herbert B. Steele, 42, a resident of Gull Harbor, died Monday in Veterans' Hospital, Portland. He was born in North Carolina and had resided in Thurston County only a short time. Surviving is his wife, Gertrude. Services will be conducted by the Reverend C. H. Lorimer in Mills and Mills' chapel this Thursday afternoon, starting at 3 p. m. Military burial will take place in Forest Cemetery.

Beatrice Eileen Steele married William McDermond, who worked as a railway switchman, in the early 1940s. The couple lived in Minneapolis and had ten children, nine of whom were girls, although two, a baby boy and a baby girl, died young.[882] William and Beatrice divorced in 1971, and she married Alan Lennartson in 1978. They divorced in 1984.[883] Beatrice passed away in 1989 at the age of 62.[884]

---

[880] Death certificate, Herbert Benjamin Steele, Veterans Administration Facility, Portland, Oregon, October 25, 1942, records request from the Oregon State Board of Health, Division of Vital Statistics.

[881] Obituary, Herbert B. Steele, the Morning Olympian, October 28, 1942. I cannot find the website that was the source of this obituary, some 1½ years after I first saved it to my computer. The notations appear to be from GenealogyBank.com, and a source directory (Washington Online Historical Newspapers — google.com) says this paper, of this date range, should be found on the GenealogyBank website, but it is not there as of this writing. Quotations from this obituary, along with a source reference for the newspaper, may be found at Findagrave.com, Memorial 139413805.

[882] William and Beatrice's marriage record is unavailable, but records for most of their children's births may be found on Ancestry.com. His occupation is also found there, in the 1946, 1948, and 1950 Minneapolis directories.

[883] Minnesota Marriage Index, 1958–2001; Minnesota Divorce Index, 1970–1995, Ancestry.com.

[884] Death Certificate, Beatrice Eileen Steele McDermond Lennartson, records request from the Minnesota Historical Society, St. Paul.

Marcus Wilson McGuire (1903–1971)

Unlike some of Willis's other progeny, we have a good bit of documentation of Marcus Wilson's childhood, especially after 1907, although some parts of his eventful life remain mysterious. As 1/32 Creek with oil-producing properties and an absent father, both the McIntosh and Muskogee County courts watched his estate like a hawk to make sure that unscrupulous adults (like dear old dad, maybe?) didn't bilk him. These records, of which there are thousands of pages of non-chronological material, are online on Ancestry.com, and they are rich in information, just as the Oklahoma Territory was in oil, as long as you dig. Most of it was related to the court's approval of the plans of his guardian (Adolph O. Johnson from 1908 to 1911 and Sophia after that) for investment and disposition of his funds, but they also include some information which adds to this narrative.[885] The wealth of his estate led newspapers in the area to do stories about the boy millionaire. It's probably fair to say that Wilson[886] grew up thinking he was someone special. Willis's genes may have also contributed to those notions.

Under Johnson's guidance, the estate increased dramatically from 1908 to 1911. Not only did the amount paid by the March Oil Company and its successors rise over time, but Johnson also invested most of the proceeds in local properties with rentals or other kinds of income, and he re-invested most of those returns. In June 1911, two months after Dr. McGuire's death at Miñaca, Johnson estimated the returns to the estate at $500 per month (about $14,000 today), and he felt comfortable asking the court to raise the amount withdrawn for Wilson's (and the rest of the family's) support from $35 to $50 per month.[887] The following year, with Sophia now in charge, the returns had jumped to $1300 per month and the support allowance was increased to $175. Citing her son's delicate health and the advice of physicians, as well as his need to commute to school, in 1912 Sophia petitioned the court to allow the family to spend $1,700 to buy their first automobile.[888] Soon thereafter, Wilson, who was almost ten at the time, was driving with his mother and hit a young girl. Evidently, there was no age requirement for motor vehicle operation in Oklahoma at the time. No one was badly injured, but her father sued, and although Wilson insisted that the accident was her fault, Sophia quickly forked over $100 to settle things.[889]

In summer 1915, another newspaper article about his ongoing summer lemonade business[890] referenced his interest in photography: "Uses his own kodak and develops and prints his own work with fairly good results." Like many others in his era, lightweight cameras

---

885 Oklahoma Wills and Probate Records, Ancestry.com. In the County Court in and of the County of Muskogee, Guardianship Records of Marcus Wilson McGuire, case #1644.
886 Like his father, Marcus Wilson McGuire went by his middle name of Wilson in his childhood and young adulthood.
887 Oklahoma Wills and Probate Records, Ancestry.com. In the County Court in and of the County of Muskogee, Guardianship Records of Marcus Wilson McGuire, case #1644, Petition to increase family allowance, June 8, 1911.
888 Ibid., Petition to buy an automobile, June 4, 1912.
889 The Muskogee Daily Phoenix, June 5, 1913, Newspapers.com.
890 Another article about his summer business from the Muskogee County Democrat is reproduced in the section on Sophia in Chapter 15.

held a fascination for him that continued throughout his life. They went on, "He seems to be totally unaware that he is an unusually fortunate individual, and it is his mother's desire that he remain unsophisticated and continue as he is at present — a very manly, genteel boy."[891]

The following year, he was featured in a story about local newspaper carriers.[892] The eastern Oklahoma papers enjoyed producing heart-warming stories about the millionaire kid who had no need to work but did anyway, since it set such a good example for the less fortunate.

MARCUS WILSON McGUIRE.

[893]

Transcription: A tow-headed youngster with eyes of Irish blue, who delivers the Times-Democrat to patrons on the east side, does his work because he has to earn his living by it.

A few weeks ago when he began his route his folks suggested that they would take him to the office each afternoon in their six cylinder touring car, but he protested for the reason that he did not want to appear "stuck up" to the other boys who deliver papers. He not only courts popularity with the people to whom he carries the evening paper, but he likes to stand well with the other boys. He is ambitious, though, and, according to a system by which the boy who works the hardest to receive his papers first and get through his route the quickest, this youngster has been one of the first three from the first week he began his work.

His name is Marcus Wilson McGuire, and he is very wealthy, having been allotted land in the Glenn Pool Oil Field. It is readily seen from his name how he became possessed of his blue eyes, tow head and sunny disposition. Not very long ago one of his playmates received a present of a little runabout, and, kidlike, nothing would do Wilson but that he have one also, and now that he is getting old enough to choose his own pleasures his folks have decided to buy him a car of his own, and quite soon you may see him delivering

---

891 The McIntosh County Democrat, July 29, 1915.
892 The article about Wilson's lemonade stand may be found in the section about his mother, Sophia, in Chapter 15.
893 The Muskogee County Democrat, June 22, 1916, Newspapers.com.

> his papers in a classy little roadster instead of afoot. Although with much reason to be conceited, you would never discern from his appearance that he is one of the richest, if not the richest, Indian boys in Eastern Oklahoma.
> Contrary to so many cases of its kind, his estate has been carefully managed and enhanced through capable efforts of his mother, Mrs. W. S. White, and, though she is indulgent with him in many of his wishes, his whims and desires are of a conservative nature. He likes to deliver the Times-Democrat because it affords him employment and he is happiest when at work.

Well, you can't believe everything you read in the papers, especially the part about his blue eyes and sunny disposition coming from his Irish McGuire ancestry, of which, of course, he had none.

Discounting the newspapers' agendas, it's clear that Wilson had a charming personality, although it was punctuated, even at this early age, by inexplicable mood swings. It must have been that unevenness that Sophia was trying to address two years later, when she asked the court to allow the withdrawal of enough money so Marcus Wilson, who had just turned 15, could attend the Missouri Military Academy, near the isolated town of Mexico. Her petition stated that he "is desirous and anxious to attend a Military School; that your petitioner believes it to be to the best welfare and interest of said ward that he be permitted so to do."[894] It's hard for me to believe that a teenager, especially a wealthy one who was impressing his friends by driving around town in his own roadster, would really want to be sent off to military school. It seems more likely that it was Sophia's idea, supported by her husband, William White, to deal with a growing disciplinary problem. It proved to be a good move. Marcus thrived in the structured environment, and he graduated two years later, in 1920, at the age of sixteen.[895]

If he studied hard at the academy, he also recreated just as eagerly during his summers and holidays back in Muskogee. In 1919, 1920, and 1921, he was listed in the papers as organizing or attending at least eleven large dances with live orchestras and guest lists of fellow young folks mounting into the hundreds. In June 1920, the paper related that Wilson and his next-older half-brother, Todd, hosted a dance at a local hotel. The following June, he hosted a similar event by himself.[896] World War I had just ended, the flu pandemic was dying down, and the Roaring '20s and the Jazz Age were just beginning. It must have felt like a good time to be coming of age.

Wilson involved himself in numerous social activities. He belonged to the newly formed DeMolay organization, and in fall 1920, when he matriculated to the University of Oklahoma at Norman, the Muskogee paper reported that he joined the Pi Kappa Alpha fraternity.[897] The

---

894 Oklahoma Wills and Probate Records, Ancestry.com. In the County Court in and of the County of Muskogee, Guardianship Records of Marcus Wilson McGuire, case #1644, September 5, 1918.
895 The Mexico Weekly Ledger, May 27, 1920, Newspapers.com.
896 The Muskogee Daily Phoenix, June 4, 1919; August 27, 1920; July 11, July 15, and September 13, 1921; The Muskogee Times-Democrat, August 7, 1919, June 5, June 12, and December 28, 1920, June 19 and December 27, 1921, Newspapers.com.
897 The Muskogee Times Democrat, November 13, 1920, Newspapers.com.

following year, the campus newspaper noted that he was a First Lieutenant in the ROTC program, probably a holdover from his military school background.[898] But his time at O. U. ended in December 1921, after only three semesters.[899] We know that he attended Wesleyan University in Connecticut in 1922, but they have no record of his graduation, either, so he must have transferred again.[900] We know that he spent summer 1922 and 1923 in Los Angeles, and that Sophia and little Billy joined him there.[901] This is about the time Sophia's other two sons, Clay and Todd, were establishing their professional careers in the city. It is unknown from what college Wilson got his undergraduate degree, but it may well have been in Los Angeles. A brief mention in the Muskogee paper from summer 1923 reveals that around this time he began to sometimes call himself William McGuire.[902] We don't know why, but it could have been an adulteration of the name of Wilson.

[903]

Freshman photograph, Marcus Wilson McGuire, University of Oklahoma, spring 1921.

By the time he turned 21 in 1924, Willis's son, a millionaire and then some, was on the fast track to success.[904] Possibly in celebration of both his arrival at maturity and his graduation

---

898 The Oklahoma Weekly, December 6, 1921, Newspapers.com.
899 Email from Molly Cushway, Verification Specialist, Academic Records, The University of Oklahoma, to Charles Caldemeyer, February 19, 2021.
900 Email from Vicki Iaccarino, Alumni & Parent Relations, Wesleyan University, to Charles Caldemeyer, November 6, 2020. A story in the Muskogee Times-Democrat from December 20, 1922 stated that he was home from attending Yale. Since this information was simultaneous with Wesleyan's record of his attendance there, it was likely an error on the paper's part, or possibly Wilson fed the paper a confusion.
901 Muskogee Daily Phoenix, August 8, 1922; Muskogee Times Democrat, June 29, 1923, Newspapers.com.
902 Muskogee Times Democrat, June 29, 1923, Newspapers.com.
903 *University of Oklahoma, 1921, U.S., School Yearbooks, 1880–2012*, Ancestry.com.
904 District Court of McIntosh County, Oklahoma, in the matter of the Guardianship of Marcus Wilson McGuire, Adolph O. Johnson, Guardian; also, In the County Court, Muskogee County, Oklahoma, in the matter of the Guardianship of Marcus Wilson McGuire, Sophia McGuire, Guardian, case #1644.

from college, he left in April 1925 on an extended European tour, staying into the summer, and he entered law school at the University of Southern California later that year.[905] He was awarded his degree in June 1927 and was admitted to the California bar in October.[906] Todd was a practicing attorney in Los Angeles at the time, and Wilson appears to have joined his firm.

He met his first wife, Verna Waterman, while he was still in law school. She was born in Montana, the daughter of a successful apple grower and capitalist who had moved his family to Hollywood. Verna was 17, and she was active with the society set. They were married in Tacoma on June 19, 1926, Verna having moved to Washington the previous year.[907] Because of her age, one wonders if her parents, in an attempt to remove her from the attentions of the brash young law student, had sent her away, but if they did it didn't matter. After a road trip on which they stopped to see Sophia in Muskogee, and a honeymoon in Hawaii, the young couple settled into life in Beverly Hills, seemingly with the brightest of prospects.[908] But trouble came along within a couple of years due to Wilson's increasingly erratic behavior.

The documentation is spotty, and at times, contradictory. Verna first filed for divorce in 1928, but the news stories appear to be backwards, and there are no others that clarify things. On February 3, the following item appeared in the Los Angeles Evening Express:

[909]

Transcription: After listening to Verna Maguire tell about her marital life with Marcus W. Maguire, wealthy oil man living in Beverly Hills, Superior Judge Daniel Beecher today granted her a divorce, an automobile, and $150 a month alimony. Maguire was charged with — Writing to several women in Europe. Burning holes in his wife's clothes. Threatening to kill her.

---

905 Passport application, M. Wilson McGuire, March 17, 1925, Ancestry.com.
906 Email from the USC Registrar Office of Grades, Transcripts and Verifications to Charles Caldemeyer, February 6, 2021; The State Bar of California website, members.calbar.ca.gov.
907 Marriage license, M. W. McGuire and Verna Waterman, Tacoma, Pierce County, Washington, June 19, 1926, Ancestry.com.
908 The age of consent for young women in Washington state was 16. No newspapers from either Tacoma or Olympia in the period are available, and the only mention of Verna in the California papers refer to her and her twin sister, Vera, as bridesmaids at the wedding of their older sister Beulah in January 1925. The only newspaper account of the wedding we have is from the McIntosh County Democrat of July 15, 1926, which reported the couple's visit to the Whites in Muskogee. That article was a reprint of a story the Muskogee Phoenix, which is also lost, Newspapers.com.
909 The Los Angeles Evening Express, February 3, 1928, Newspapers.com.

That's pretty serious conduct that deserves a divorce, but the matter was not as final as the paper suggested. Four months later, the case was still undecided, as Marcus must have appealed, and possibly made a discreet payment, or worse.

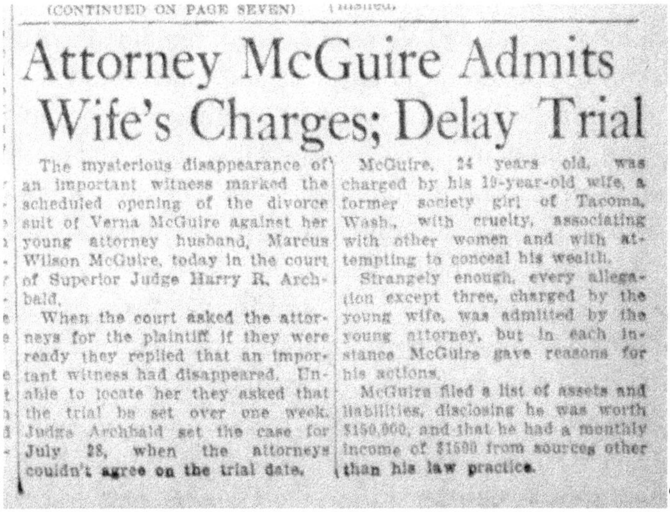
(CONTINUED ON PAGE SEVEN)

Attorney McGuire Admits Wife's Charges; Delay Trial

The mysterious disappearance of an important witness marked the scheduled opening of the divorce suit of Verna McGuire against her young attorney husband, Marcus Wilson McGuire, today in the court of Superior Judge Harry R. Archbald.

When the court asked the attorneys for the plaintiff if they were ready they replied that an important witness had disappeared. Unable to locate her they asked that the trial be set over one week. Judge Archbald set the case for July 28, when the attorneys couldn't agree on the trial date.

McGuire, 24 years old, was charged by his 19-year-old wife, a former society girl of Tacoma, Wash., with cruelty, associating with other women and with attempting to conceal his wealth.

Strangely enough, every allegation except three, charged by the young wife, was admitted by the young attorney, but in each instance McGuire gave reasons for his actions.

McGuire filed a list of assets and liabilities, disclosing he was worth $150,000, and that he had a monthly income of $1500 from sources other than his law practice.

910

Transcription: The mysterious disappearance of an important witness marked the scheduled opening of the divorce suit of Verna McGuire against her young attorney husband, Marcus Wilson McGuire, today in the court of Superior Judge Harry R. Archbald.

When the court asked the attorneys for the plaintiff if they were ready they replied that an important witness had disappeared. Unable to locate her they asked that the trial be set over one week. Judge Archbald set the case for July 28, when the attorneys couldn't agree on the trial date.

McGuire, 24 years old, was charged by his 19-year-old wife, a former society girl of Tacoma, Wash., with cruelty, associating with other women and with attempting to conceal his wealth.

Strangely enough, every allegation except three, charged by the young wife, was admitted by the young attorney, but in each instance McGuire gave reasons for his actions.

McGuire filed a list of assets and liabilities, disclosing he was worth $150,000, and that he had a monthly income of $1500 from sources other than his law practice.

It all sounds really intriguing, but that's the extent of the information we have. Nothing was ever explained about the absent witness, and no report was ever made concerning the trial or its outcome. The young couple must have reconciled, at least for the time being. There were a lot of good shrinks in Beverly Hills. Maybe Verna persuaded her husband to go see one.

Their first child, Marcus Wilson McGuire, Jr., was born on May 29, 1929. Whatever marital relief his arrival provided was short-lived, however. In July 1932 the pregnant Verna again filed for divorce. The cause was 'extreme cruelty,' and court filings listed multiple cases of both physical and emotional abuse. The divorce was granted in early 1933, two

910 Ibid., June 25, 1928.

weeks after the birth of their second son, but Marcus was defiant and obstructionist about the terms, and it was not until 1938, after years of wrangling, that a settlement was reached.[911]

After Verna escaped his grasp, Marcus remained in the Los Angeles area for a few years. He got involved in local politics, managing a campaign in 1932, and he made the papers occasionally for his work as an attorney.[912] His two half-brothers, Clay and Todd, were busy mixing with the Hollywood elite, and Verna seemingly remained closer to them than did her ex-husband.[913] She can be found on the guest lists of Hollywood society in 1933, and she hosted a well-publicized send-off dinner for Todd's wife before the latter left on a trip around the world.[914] In 1939, after enjoying single life for a few years, she married Wilbur Robinson, the president of an oil company, at the home of Eddie Sutherland, a member of Hollywood royalty.[915] Her two sons probably had limited contact with their biological father after 1933, but as we will see, they must have had some.[916]

Increasingly in the late 1920s and early 1930s, if he wasn't using the first name of William, Marcus Wilson McGuire began going by his first name or his initials rather than his middle name, and by the time he remarried in 1936, he was known around town as Marcus W. McGuire. His new bride was Ercell L. Harrington, a 26-year-old Nebraska native who had moved with her birth family to Spokane, then to Los Angeles.[917] Ercell's father, Xavier, had lost his job as a railroad engineer during the Great Depression, and she supported the family by working as a secretary in the law firm where Marcus and Todd practiced. Marcus swept her off her feet with his charm, dashing good looks, and wealth, causing her to break her engagement to another man.[918]

[919]

Ercell Harrington McGuire, 1930's.

---

911 Los Angeles Superior Court documents, case D-107553, Records request from L.A. County Archives and records.
912 The Monrovia News-Post, July 9, 1932, Newspapers.com.
913 Clay Johnson was an accountant for the stars, including Bing Crosby, and Todd was Crosby's attorney.
914 The Los Angeles Times, July 30, 1933, Hollywood Citizen News, February 14, 1933, Newspapers.com.
915 The Sacramento Bee, February 22, 1939, Newspapers.com; 1940 U.S. census, Wilbur Robinson family, Los Angeles, California, 1940, Ancestry.com.
916 Virtual meeting with Damaris Walsh McGuire and Caitlin McGuire Reid, January 16, 2021.
917 California, U. S., Voter Registrations, 1900–1968, Los Angeles County, 1934, Ancestry.com.
918 Virtual meeting with Damaris Walsh McGuire and Caitlin McGuire Reid, January 16, 2021.
919 Photo courtesy Caitlin McGuire Reid.

Verna Waterman McGuire Robinson, 1930's.

The couple must have moved to Oklahoma soon after their vows were exchanged — their only son, Donald Bahnsen McGuire, was born in Tulsa on April 1, 1937. The move may have partially been driven by a desire to escape the southern California lifestyle, but it also allowed him to deal with growing issues over his Oklahoma lands. Marcus Wilson McGuire's inland empire was shrinking in the 1930s, the target of at least five lawsuits over rents, ownership, and oil rights. All but one made him the defendant.[921] One was initiated by his half-brother, Todd, in 1937, to whom the courts awarded a judgement of $1537.36 plus 6% interest and $100 attorney fees.[922]

He was admitted to the Oklahoma Bar on March 11, 1938, but there is no record of him practicing, and he let his membership lapse in 1940.[923] He was evidently unhappy with the legal world, and he began chasing a new career. In the 1940 census, while he was still living in Tulsa with Ercell and Donald, his occupation was listed as 'fiction writer.'[924] We don't know if any stories materialized, or how his aspirations unfolded, but there is no record of

---

920 Photo courtesy Caitlin McGuire Reid.
921 The Indian Journal, December 12, 1929; The Legal Record, January 20, 1933; The Democrat News, September 21, 1933; The Legal Record, April 15, 1935; The McIntosh County Democrat, June 18, 1942; The McIntosh County Democrat, January 30, 1947, all Newspapers.com.
922 The McIntosh County Democrat, February 10, 1938, Newspapers.com.
923 Records request from the Oklahoma Bar Association.
924 1940 U. S census, Marcus McGuire family, Tulsa, Oklahoma, Ancestry.com.

any publication of his work. He must have lived off of the proceeds from his land and oil holdings, although it appears that he increasingly withheld financial support from his family.

Marcus Wilson McGuire, 1930s.

According to the remembrances of his descendants and extended family, he exhibited all the symptoms of bipolar personality disorder, with his charming good humor punctuated by bouts of atrocious behavior.[926] On February 13, 1941, after less than five years of married life, Ercell filed for divorce, alleging "gross neglect of duty and extreme cruelty,"[927] The petition continued,

> That for months past he has not supported his family and that this plaintiff has been forced to, and is earning her own living and supporting their son, Donald; that his cruelty, among other things, has consisted of false accusations and criticisms, all to the great mental pain, humiliation, and suffering of this plaintiff.[928]

---

925 Photo courtesy Caitlin McGuire Reid.
926 Virtual meeting with Damaris Walsh McGuire and Caitlin McGuire Reid, January 16, 2021.
927 State of Oklahoma, County of Tulsa, In the District Court No. D22829, Ercell L. McGuire vs. Marcus Wilson McGuire, records request from the Tulsa County Court; The Tulsa World, February 14, 1941, Newspapers.com.
928 State of Oklahoma, County of Tulsa, In the District Court No. D22829, Ercell L. McGuire vs. Marcus Wilson McGuire, records request from the Tulsa County Court.

After hearing "the evidence of witnesses sworn and examined in open court," and finding "that all the material facts set forth and alleged in plaintiff's petition are true," the court granted her request, finding "that the defendant has been guilty of gross neglect of duty, extreme cruelty, and that by reason of the acts of the defendant and the fault of the defendant, the plaintiff is entitled to an absolute decree of divorce as prayed for." The judgment was rendered on April 2, 1941, one day after Donald's fourth birthday. Along with custody of her son and $25.00 a month in child support until he reached the age of 21, Ercell was given the family home and furniture in Tulsa. Marcus's income-producing properties were not affected by the ruling. He was granted visitation of his son "at reasonable times and under reasonable circumstances."[929]

Marcus Wilson McGuire with his third son, Donald Bahnsen McGuire, about 1942.

Like his father before him in all of his own divorce proceedings, Marcus was a no-show, in fact, he wasn't even in the state at the time. In late March 1941, The Town Talk, a newspaper in Alexandria, Louisiana, ran a long article about a new recreation center for soldiers from nearby Camp Beauregard. It was being run by a "W.P.A. recreational consultant," "an

---

929 State of Oklahoma, County of Tulsa, In the District Court No. D22829, Ercell L. McGuire vs. Marcus Wilson McGuire, records request from the Tulsa County Court.
930 Photo courtesy Caitlin McGuire Reid.

expert of many years [sic] experience in recreation and community organization work," named Marcus W. McGuire.⁹³¹ The paper did not detail his experience, and it's possible that he had done that kind of work professionally before. He had certainly organized many dances in Muskogee, and he had attended numerous parties, hosted by the glamorous set, in Hollywood.

His work with the W.P.A ended in late July 1941, and he must have moved to New Orleans for a time. He was living there when he registered for the World War II draft in February 1942. As in the census two years earlier, his occupation was a self-employed writer. He remained in touch with Ercell during this time, and he designated her as his contact person on the registration card, although at an office, the McBirney Building in Tulsa, which was likely either her work address or that of her lawyer.⁹³² Ercell had been active in the Presbyterian church since her arrival (the Episcopal church of her childhood had refused to marry Marcus and her due to his previous divorce),⁹³³ and now religious education became her livelihood. After establishing her skills as a strong administrator, she was hired as director of education with the Minneapolis Church Federation, an interdenominational group, and she and her son left Oklahoma for good in July 1942.⁹³⁴ Her mother, Edith, who had moved to Tulsa to be with Ercell while the divorce was pending, accompanied her, and she took care of Donald while Ercell pursued her career.⁹³⁵

For his part, Marcus didn't linger long in the Big Easy. The contact address on his draft card was crossed out by some official a year later and replaced with Clay's Los Angeles address. The draft board had at least tried to contact him, possibly because of his military school background and ROTC training while he was at the University of Oklahoma. It was wartime, and everyone with military training was needed. They may have lost interest in his services when informed of some of his doings in Los Angeles.⁹³⁶

According to family lore, Marcus invited Ercell to visit Los Angeles, presumably to try to patch things up with her and to see Donald, soon after she left Tulsa. He paid their train fare from Minneapolis and promised the finest accommodations. When they arrived, Marcus was not to be found. He had tried to book the presidential suite at one of Los Angeles's finest hotels, had been turned down for some reason, and had begun waving a gun around. When Ercell arrived, she was not even allowed to visit him in the asylum where a judge had ordered him to be confined for thirty days.⁹³⁷ These events likely poured cold water on any reconciliation hopes the couple may have entertained.

For the next five years we find numerous news accounts of Ercell's work in the Minneapolis papers, where she was known for conducting programs for both children and adults that emphasized tolerance, diversity, and ecumenicalism. She raised Donald as a single mother

---

931 The Town Talk, March 31, 1941, Newspapers.com.
932 World War II Draft Registration Card, Marcus Wilson McGuire, February 16, 1942, Ancestry.com.
933 Virtual meeting with Damaris Walsh McGuire and Caitlin McGuire Reid, January 16, 2021.
934 The Minneapolis Star, June 27, 1942, Newspapers.com.
935 Virtual meeting with Damaris Walsh McGuire and Caitlin McGuire Reid, January 16, 2021. Edith's husband, Xavier, had been killed in an automobile accident in California in 1941 (Newspapers.com).
936 World War II draft card, Marcus Wilson McGuire, February 16, 1942, Ancestry.com.
937 Virtual meeting with Damaris Walsh McGuire and Caitlin McGuire Reid, January 16, 2021.

until his maturity, although her professional aspirations led her to deposit him at various venues during summer vacations. In 1947, she moved on from Minneapolis "to do graduate work at an eastern college," according to a Minneapolis paper.[938] She ended up in New York City, working for an Episcopal church. This likely represented her reconnection with the church of her childhood, which she had left in 1936. She was remarried, to Frederick Kullberg, in 1957.[939] Ercell remained in social work for the rest of her professional life, moving back and forth between New York City and a cabin in the Catskills. She also lived for a time in France, and with Donald and his family in the Albany area, until her death in 2000.[940]

[941]

Marcus Wilson McGuire, 1940s.

Marcus's brief confinement in California for his mental health issues was his first of which we are aware, but it would not be his last. We lose touch with him from 1942 until 1954, and he may have done some traveling, but it seems likely that he mostly remained in California. It's also possible that he was confined for some or all of that time since his name is totally absent from records during that period. But he reappeared in Tulsa in late 1954. On November 19, the following item appeared in the Tulsa World:

---

938 The Minneapolis Star, August 19, 1947, Newspapers.com.
939 New York Marriage License Index, 1907–2018, license #18895, Ancestry.com.
940 Ibid.
941 Shared on Ancestry.com by Caitlin McGuire Reid, June 10, 2018.

> **'Light-Saver' Pulls Switch On Story, Too**
>
> A 50-year-old Californian was jailed for investigation Thursday night for turning the lights on and off in a downtown department store to "save electricity."
>
> Police said Marcus Wilson McGuire, alias Bill McGuire, denied switching the lights off more than once and said he did that because he "couldn't see any sense in waisting all that electricity."
>
> McGuire was arrested on the 5th floor of the Sears, Roebuck and Co. department store about 6:30 p m. by juvenile Dective Pete Castello who held him until Detectives Murray Smith and John Murray arrived
>
> Ruring questioning at police headquarters. McGuire told conflicting stories about his occupation, including that he is an attorney and that he is the owner of a tourist court on U. S. 66.
>
> He was held for further questioning about three billfolds, two watches and $50 he had in his possession when arrested.
>
> [942]

Transcription: A 50-year-old Californian was jailed for investigation Thursday night for turning the lights on and off in a downtown department store to "save electricity."

Police said Marcus Wilson McGuire, alias Bill McGuire, denied switching the lights off more than once and said he did that because he "couldn't see any sense in waisting [sic] all that electricity."

McGuire was arrested on the 5th floor of the Sears, Roebuck and Co. department store about 6:30 p m. by juvenile Dective [sic] Pete Castello who held him until Detectives Murray Smith and John Murray arrived.

Ruring [sic] questioning at police headquarters, McGuire told conflicting stories about his occupation, including that he is an attorney and that he is the owner of a tourist court on U.S. 66.

He was held for further questioning about three billfolds, two watches and $50 he had in his possession when arrested.

The bizarre incident marked his move back to Oklahoma for good. It also signaled a need for medical attention. He was evidently ordered confined in the Eastern State Hospital, a mental health facility in nearby Vinita, for a year. He was released on November 26, 1955, and he was able to reclaim his former life again, at least for a time.[943] The Oklahoma bar, which had stricken his name in October 1954, admitted him again in June 1956.[944]

The same month, a column in the Tulsa World ran the following unusual item:

---

942 The Tulsa World, November 19, 1954, GenealogyBank.com.

943 In the District Court, State of Oklahoma, in the Matter of the Estate of Marcus Wilson McGuire, Deceased, No. P-71-968, records request from the Tulsa County Court. These documents show an uncollected itemized bill from the hospital from November 26, 1954 until November 26, 1955 that had to be paid before his estate could be settled.

944 It is possible that news of this decision was what triggered his move back to Tulsa. To be stricken meant that he either he had failed to pay his dues or that he had neglected to fulfill his Continuing Legal Education requirements (email, Tracy Sanders of the Oklahoma Bar Association to Charles Caldemeyer, February 22, 2021).

> ★ ★ ★
> THERE is a certain amount of danger in running an item of this kind.
> It can only lead to requests to run many, many more such items. But I have no rule against it yet so here goes:
> Bill McGuire, 610A S. Cincinnati ave., is a newcomer to Tulsa from California. He is eager to get in touch with any members of three social fraternities: Psi Upsilon, Alpha Delta Phi and and Delta Kappa Epsilon.
> I hereby pass a rule against such items in the future.
> ★ ★ ★ [945]

Transcription: There is a certain amount of danger in running an item of this kind. It can only lead to requests to run many, many more such items. But I have no rule against it yet so here goes: Bill McGuire, 610A S. Cincinnati ave., is a newcomer to Tulsa from California. He is eager to get in touch with any members of three social fraternities: Psi Upsilon, Alpha Delta Phi and Delta Kappa Epsilon. I hereby pass a rule against such items in the future.

We know from his descendants that he had a strong affection for fraternity life while in college. He had urged his son Donald to join one, in the process telling how much the experience had meant to him.[946] We don't know why he singled out the three frats mentioned — he was reported to be a member of Pi Kappa Alpha while at Oklahoma University. Marcus also organized a Tulsa chapter of the Phi Delta Phi legal fraternity later in summer 1956.[947] It's unknown how he knew Troy Gordon, the newspaperman who wrote the column in the Tulsa World, but Gordon's tone indicates friendship. The art of charming reporters may have been a skill that came to him from his father.

Notice that he was again going by the name 'Bill McGuire' in these stories. This is the third reference to him that we have under that name or its formal version of William. His oldest son, Marcus Jr., also went by this adulteration of his given name, and he made his social security application under the name "William Wilson McGuire" in 1944.[948] It's unknown if the name William or Bill represented to Marcus Sr. a devil-may-care, rules-don't-apply-to-me persona, in much the same way as the moniker of Willis had for his father.

We have cursory records of him as the attorney of record in two annulment cases and a guardianship case in Tulsa in 1957 and 1958, but it appears that his mental condition

---

945 The Tulsa World, June 13, 1956, GenealogyBank.com. The address in the article confirms that this Bill McGuire was the same man as Marcus Wilson McGuire. Marcus's records from the Oklahoma Bar Association in the 1950's also list 610A S. Cincinnati Ave. as his residence (records request from okbar.org, November 6, 2020)
946 Virtual meeting with Damaris Walsh McGuire and Caitlin McGuire Reid, January 16, 2021.
947 The Tulsa World, July 19, 1956, GenealogyBank.com.
948 Social Security Applications and Claims Index, William Wilson McGuire, January 1944, Ancestry.com.

soon began deteriorating again.[949] In July 1957, he lost ownership of some of his acreage in McIntosh County due to unpaid property taxes.[950] There may have been a defining incident that put him in the custody of the state in summer 1958, or maybe a gradual slide into incapability was observed by those around him. On July 25, notice was published that his mental health would be evaluated in a new civil case, and in August the court declared him incompetent. Warren L. McConnico, a young attorney and possibly an associate, was appointed guardian of his estate, and Marcus was again committed to Eastern State Hospital.[951] There were numerous reports in the Tulsa Daily Legal News concerning aspects of his guardianship and McConnico's filings of petitions to lease his old oil lands, which had been drained by that point, for grazing and other purposes, from 1958 until 1961.[952]

On April 26, 1961, a hearing was scheduled concerning the restoration of his rights. The decision was not reported, but it seems likely that he was released, since McConnico's filings on his behalf all but disappear after that time. We lose all issues of regular Tulsa newspapers in 1960, and all issues of the Tulsa Daily Legal News, which posted court appointments, in 1963, and we have no further coverage of Marcus. He may have remained lucid enough to manage his own affairs during much of the 1960s, or he may have been committed to another institution or otherwise paid his bills at Eastern State Hospital from his oil revenue.[953] We know that he was back into the hospital by at least July 1969.[954]

In November 1970, he was admitted to the Central State Hospital, a similar facility in Norman, Oklahoma, and the following summer he was transferred to the University of Oklahoma Hospital in Oklahoma City for treatment of a lung tumor, which turned out to be inoperable. He died there on July 20, 1971, and he was buried, evidently without a memorial, in Dripping Springs Cemetery in Noble, Oklahoma, just south of Oklahoma City.[955] McConnico was appointed administrator of his estate. Thus, Marcus Wilson McGuire began and ended his life with someone else watching over his assets for him. They had dwindled dramatically from the millions he was worth as a young man, due to years of depletion and poor management. His personal items at his death included only several old cameras and accessories, "all in junk condition," a recorder, a watch, a pocket radio, and an "old 19" black and white portable TV." McConnico sold all of these possessions for a total of $23. After creditor, medical, funeral, and attorney expenses were paid, the entire estate was valued at less than $33,000. He died intestate, and it took some time for McConnico to locate his three

---

949 In the District Court, State of Oklahoma, in the Matter of the Estate of Marcus Wilson McGuire, Deceased, No. P-71-968, bill from Eastern State Hospital, records request from the Tulsa County Court; The Tulsa Daily Legal News, June 6, 1957; November 1, 1957; January 24, 1958, Newspapers.com.
950 The Indian Journal, July 25, 1957, Newspapers.com.
951 In the District Court, State of Oklahoma, in the Matter of the Estate of Marcus Wilson McGuire, Deceased, No. P-71-968, bill from E. S. H., records request from the Tulsa County Court.
952 Tulsa Daily Legal News, 1958–1961, search Marcus McGuire, Newspapers.com.
953 In the District Court, State of Oklahoma, in the Matter of the Estate of Marcus Wilson McGuire, Deceased, No. P-71-968, bill from E. S. H., records request from the Tulsa County Court. The bills from E.S.H. in these documents cease in May 1959 and re-emerge in July 1969.
954 In the District Court, State of Oklahoma, in the Matter of the Estate of Marcus Wilson McGuire, Deceased, No. P-71-968, bill from E. S. H., records request from the Tulsa County Court.
955 Death certificate, Marcus W. McGuire, State File #13449, Oklahoma City, records request from the Oklahoma Department of Health, Vital Records.

sons, all of whom lived in other parts of the country. When the courts were finished with their business, the proceeds of the estate were divided among them.[956]

Marcus Wilson McGuire, Jr. was raised by Verna and her second husband, Wilbur Robinson, and was listed as Marcus Robinson in the 1940 census.[957] As mentioned earlier, by 1944 he went by the name of William, and he spent most of his life in southern California, although he also visited his half-brother Donald in New York from time to time.[958] He worked in sales with industrial equipment manufacturing firms, including the Utility Fan Corporation.[959] He was married at least three times, and each union produced children, five in all.[960] Marcus Jr. retired to the Phoenix area, and he died in Yuma, Arizona, in 2001.

Marcus Wilson McGuire Sr.'s third son, Donald McGuire, was whisked away from Tulsa at the age of four. Ercell raised him with the help of her mother, and she enrolled him at several boarding schools in Minnesota and, later, in the New York City area. Donald attended Columbia University, majoring in history, and he was on the crew team. In 1958, at age 21, he was married in Vermont. He began his teaching career in 1966, working at several schools in New York, enjoying "a lifelong love affair" with the profession. Donald earned many awards, including one from the National Endowment for the Humanities Japanese Studies Program and two summer fellowships from Gilder Lehrman Institute of American History. He and his wife raised a son and two daughters in New York City and a cabin in the Catskills before moving to Albany in 1999. In that year, Donald was diagnosed with A.L.S., which progressed rapidly, and he passed away in 2000.[961]

Marcus Wilson McGuire's second son, via Verna Waterman, is still alive as of this writing.

Most of David Wilson Bethel's descendants seem to have fallen as far from his tree as it was possible to fall. While we can see resemblances in appearance in many of them, and their stories indicate some inherited characteristics, his children and grandchildren lived mostly honest and productive lives. This is certainly a tribute to the women who raised them, but it also begs another question: did Willis Bethel do his kids a favor by abandoning them? While this thought challenges traditional thinking about what a child needs, in his case it seems possible that the most important thing he gave them, aside from the seed that made them, was his own absence.

---

956 In the District Court, State of Oklahoma, in the Matter of the Estate of Marcus Wilson McGuire, Deceased, No. P-71-968, records request from the Tulsa County Court.
957 1940 U.S. census, Wilbur Robinson family, Los Angeles, California, Ancestry.com.
958 Virtual meeting with Damaris Walsh McGuire and Caitlin McGuire Reid, January 16, 2021. He was listed as William Wilson McGuire in 1944 (U.S. Social Security Applications and Claims Index, 1936–2007, Ancestry.com)
959 Directory, Santa Ana, California, 1960, Marcus W. McGuire, Ancestry.com; *Recold Corp. Acquires Assets of Utility Fan,* The Los Angeles Times, November 17, 1961, Newspapers.com.
960 Emily McGuire-Wallace family tree, Ancestry.com.
961 Obituary, Donald Bahnsen McGuire, The Albany Times Union, October 18, 2000, GenealogyBank.com.

Epilogue:
Still on the Trail of the Railroad Skunk

■ **BY THIS POINT ANY REASONABLY ATTENTIVE READER WILL HAVE ASKED,** "What the heck was wrong with this guy?" There are many questions about Willis Bethel's life, such as where he went after 1911, what name he used, how and where he was employed until his death, how, where, and when he died, what other women, if any, he married, and how many more children he fathered. But the most puzzling is still the one posed in the introduction: how could he possibly have thought that the decisions he made would lead to positive outcomes? What drove him to always have a secret lie? And if his deceptions were so important to him, and they seem to have been central to his life, why could he not sustain them? Instead of accumulating his way to some degree of prosperity, he always had to start over. Life was a joyride for Willis Bethel, and when he wrecked one car he just dusted himself off and looked around for another one. His actions cost him his career and all but the most superficial attachments to society, family, and friends. By 1911, Willis's demons had taken from him all the things that most people consider central to their lives.

So, what were those demons? We really need a psychologist for that one, but it's fair to say that Willis's overriding purpose in life was deceit, to "never let any one suspect" that he had a secret. Just as some people aren't happy unless they are always in charge or always in debt, he had to have a con going at all times. His joking face masked a volcanic inner anger at all, an abusive hidden agenda, and his wives were the ones who paid the greatest price. Marriage and procreation became his instruments of abuse. He ensnared his victims with charm and promises, he captured them in a marriage contract he knew would be difficult for them to escape, he encumbered them with dependent children, then he waltzed off to a new place to find a new mark. Like a Venus flytrap, Willis Bethel was a predator. His was a cunning set of ploys, but when one views the timing and simultaneity of his conquests, along with his manipulation of events, this conclusion is not difficult to reach.[962]

---

962 On some level, Willis seems to have been itching to reveal his frauds to the world, while at the same time he worked to maintain them. It was not until he began adopting aliases that he was able to sustain his deceptions. Maturity and experience at conning probably helped, but it may also have been that using an alias fulfilled some of his need to deceive and curbed the tendency to sabotage his own schemes (so characteristic of his previous stops) until the time was right.

I believe that my grandfather, Durward Frederick Fisher, also arrived at this assessment of his biological father. I think it was for this reason, not shame over bigamy or the stain of illegitimacy, that he wrote his father out of the family tree and encouraged his children to do likewise. Durward continued to have contact with Willis after Nettie had ended all communication in September 1897. The 1920 photographs are good evidence, but Willis's letters to Durward from the summer of 1897, most of which the boy replied to, also point to a budding correspondence. As Durward matured into the upright man of character he became, he would have seen Willis's actions as unforgivable. We can only speculate about the conversations William Samuel Bethel had with Willis in his youth about how women were simply objects to be toyed with and manipulated, but if Willis had tried to have similar conversations with Durward, it's easy to imagine that son would have rejected father wholesale. Durward regarded Willis as a dark presence.

After he was married, of course, Durward wanted to insulate his family from any negative influence from his father. His wife, Alida, certainly disapproved of Willis in the strongest terms possible.[963] So why did the young parents agree to his visit of March 28, 1920? I believe the most likely scenario is that Willis told his son that he was dying (whether or not he truly was is a different question), and he begged to be allowed to see his grandchildren. Durward was a man who felt all of his responsibilities deeply, and while the welfare of his family would certainly have come first, he also would have felt a filial obligation to the man who sired him. Hence, the brief visit, its equally cursory documentation, and the uncomfortable looks on the faces of Alida and Fred, the oldest grandchild who was compelled to hold the ogre's hand in the photographs. Kids pick up on things.

It's interesting to me that Durward's repudiation of Willis seems to have been harsher than Nettie's. She kept his correspondence and mementoes. Durward did not — all we have from him is that one pair of barely-labeled photographs. Yet Durward was an amateur photographer who documented his family's doings diligently, and we are in possession of hundreds of his photos, and much of his correspondence, which he carbon-copied and filed, has also come down to us. Alida and he possessed a strong sense of family history and felt a keen obligation to pass along the past, except where David Willis Bethel was concerned.

Nettie, on the other hand, seems to have regarded Willis as a lovable skunk. She kept his 27 letters and the other material (letters from other sources, rail passes, medical school passes, etc.) that he left behind. But why did Durward, and after him Alida, pass any of this material down to us? If Durward's policy was to airbrush his sire out of the picture, why keep anything that might indicate he was ever there? While we can't say with any certainty, the evidence suggests an internal family conflict. Nettie may have wanted future generations to know something of the man she loved but could not have, or maybe she just wanted them to know why the father of her son was not in the family picture. Maybe Durward and Alida saved these items out of respect for her and what she had endured.

---

963 Ida Fisher Caldemeyer related that Durward told Alida about Willis prior to their marriage. It would be interesting to know the details of that conversation. Durward wanted to be sure that the truth about his heritage was not a deal-breaker for his future wife, and this impressed Alida. Her response was said to be, "I'm marrying you, not your father."

It's also possible that a full record of all correspondence from Willis to Durward, along with other items, was once in the family's possession, but that it got thrown away over the decades. Alida Dearborn Fisher may have discarded some items after Durward's death in 1949. Ida Fisher Caldemeyer, who also had a strong sense of family history, was unsentimental about saving things related to the Railroad Skunk. When she and her husband moved from Virginia to Florida in 1976, she condensed the contents of three old trunks down to one, and it's possible that many answers to our questions went into the trash then. Her brother Evan was also known to discard documents that he thought injured the family name. They would have justified it by saying that they were just fulfilling their parents' intentions.

We don't how or where Willis Bethel died. Did Durward? Did he attend to his father's affairs after death? Or did Willis Bethel have another wife or wives, married after 1911, and other children, who looked after him as he declined, and arranged for his burial somewhere? Did he abandon them, too, and die alone? I think the last option is the most likely, but no evidence supports this conclusion. Genetic testing might someday let us know for sure, or maybe a reader of this history will recognize an ancestor in Willis, but until that time these questions will remain unanswered. As I wrote earlier, there is still plenty of story for future generations to uncover.

As we have seen, Durward was a successful plant pathologist with the Department of Agriculture whose work on the causes of fruit and vegetable diseases pioneered modern preservation methods. One of his cousins, Daniel Fisher (the son of Nettie's brother George) was a medical doctor who remained in the Clarence area all his life. Although Daniel was eight years younger, Durward and he were close, and they held each other in high esteem. Both had successfully negotiated their paths from the farm to careers as white collar, science-based, professionals. In a letter to Harry Fisher in 1971, Daniel wrote, "I guess you know that I was always very fond of your father . . . He was a great inspiration to me in my early days, and seemed more like an older brother than a cousin."[964] Even though their fields were very different, both men's work required them to diagnose the causes of ailments. We retain some of the letters that they exchanged from the 1920s until Durward's death in 1949.

One of these letters, from Daniel to Durward in 1928, concerned Nettie's declining health. Reading between the lines, it also might shine an indirect light on Willis's death, if we allow ourselves to speculate wildly (which, of course, we do). Daniel wrote that his Aunt Net's symptoms dated back "a few years," so probably to about 1924 or 1925. She had been under the care of a number of medical specialists, notably eye doctors. It seems that her problems were such as to defy a positive diagnosis, and Daniel did not list them, except to call them "vague" and "unexplained." Nettie's own letters from this period are poorly written, both in terms of grammar and handwriting, and she occasionally referenced her difficulty in seeing clearly.[965] She was looking for a treatment that "would help her be like other folks." At some point in the diagnostic process, doctors theorized that they might be dealing with a case of

---

964 Letter, Daniel Fisher to Harry Fisher, April 8, 1971, from Fisher family papers.
965 Letter, Joannetta Fisher to Durward and Alida Fisher, January 14, 1927, from Fisher family papers.

syphilis. Huh? Syphilis? Nettie had been happily married to John Helwig, a pious man who did not have syphilis, for over two decades when this was suggested. The doctors gave her a Wasserman test, which was negative, and even treated her with arsenic, standard procedure for "antiluetic therapy."[966]

Daniel ended by saying that he didn't believe that Nettie ever had syphilis. But why would the medical community gravitate toward that diagnosis? One explanation is that syphilitics do exhibit 'vague, unexplained symptoms,' and it was a relatively common diagnosis in the era when no cause could be attached to effect. Maybe the doctors were just following the evidence and exhausting all avenues. But it's possible that the doctors were made aware that Nettie's first husband, as her niece wrote, "ran around with other women."[967] Maybe word had gotten back to Durward and Nettie that David Willis Bethel had died of the disease. One of the symptoms of syphilis is impotence, which might also explain why we have no DNA matches after Marcus Wilson McGuire. Willis was only 43 when Marcus was born, and given his history, it seems likely that he would have attempted to procreate again had he been able.[968]

It's easy to assume that a man who had so many wives also enjoyed sex outside of his marriages and had many opportunities to contract syphilis. One of Willis's known wives, Chrestine Hendricks, is known to have died of syphilis, but there were other avenues, of course, for her to contract it, and none of his other wives was known to have the disease. But it's possible for an infected individual to have sexual partners who remain clear of infection. All in all, however, I remain skeptical that Willis Bethel had syphilis without more evidence, but if you read on you'll see that that does not stop me from using the possibility for dramatic effect.

Syphilis can cause insanity and depression. It can even cause the infected person to take his or her own life.[969] And since it would be such an appropriate end to the man, and since I don't have a good ending for this book anyway, well . . . why not?

―――――◇―――――

Oco, a little hamlet in Belmont County, Ohio, is about four miles from Flushing and five from Rock Hill. It's also less than a mile from Bruce, also called Bannock. It's usually not a newsworthy place, but on February 28, 1925, the town made some local gossip. The following item appeared in the Flushing News on March 5:

---

966 Letter, Daniel Fisher to Durward Fisher, August 6, 1928, from Fisher family papers.
967 Letter, Eva Katherine Wiley and Anna Fisher Schurr to Alida Fisher, October 4, 1949, from Fisher family papers.
968 There are, of course, many other possible reasons for our lack of results, the most likely one being descendants who are happy with not knowing their genealogy and haven't yet been tested.
969 Journal of the American Medical Association, July 18, 1903, p. 187

> **Man Killed At Oco Is Still Unknown**
>
> *The Body Will Be In Griffith's Morgue Saturday and Will Be Buried Here*
>
> Coroner Clyde Hardesty was in Flushing Monday trying to identify the man, who was killed Saturday morning at Oco, but was unable to do so. The back of the man's head was mashed, his face bruised and both legs cut off. When found he had only one cent in his pockets and no papers, that might have helped in identification.
>
> He wore a suit of blue material with a white pin stripe and had grey hair and a grey mustache. He should be easily identified as his features are not disfigured.
>
> The body will be held at the Griffith morgue here until Saturday for identification and then buried in Flushing, if the victim remains unknown.[970]

Transcription: Man Killed at Oco Is Still Unknown

The Body Will Be In Griffith's Morgue Saturday and Will Be Buried Here.

Coroner Clyde Hardesty was in Flushing Monday trying to identify the man, who was killed Saturday morning at Oco, but was unable to do so. The back of the man's head was mashed, his face bruised and both legs cut off. When found he had only one cent in his pockets and no papers, that might have helped in identification.

He wore a suit of blue material with a white pin stripe and had grey hair and a grey mustache. He should be easily identified as his features are not disfigured.

The body will be held at the Griffith morgue here until Saturday for identification and then buried in Flushing, if the victim remains unknown.

A man who knew he was dying of syphilis and was half insane from the ravages of the disease, without family and out of money, might want to visit one last time the childhood home he had left for good some 42 years earlier. He might want to walk past the first station he

---

[970] The Flushing News, March 5, 1925, microfilm from the Ohio History Center, Columbus.

had captained, and to breathe his last on the very tracks by which he'd left, taken out of this world by a goliath machine much like the one that had taken him away from his hometown so many decades before. As the monster approached, he might turn his body in such a way that his face would stand a chance of not being mutilated by the awful collision that was to follow. Of course, such a man would have had experience on the railroads that might tell him how to arrange himself in such a manner. The subject might have even come up in conversations with other men in the yard over the years.

Cyril Hollingsworth walked slowly up High Street toward Griffith's Funeral Home. In his mid-50s, Cyril farmed eighty acres between Holloway and Rock Hill with his son, Travis, and his cousin Averill. He had come to town this Saturday morning to look at a wagon that Bill Ramsey was trying to sell, but from what Cyril could see, Bill wanted just a little too much. It was a warm day for early March, and since he was caught up on his early season chores, he decided to go over to the funeral home to see the mystery man everyone was talking about.

Stepping inside Griffith's was always a sobering experience for Cyril, who had had the misfortune of attending several viewings there, most recently his mother's. As he crossed the threshold, he felt he was leaving the living world behind, as if, now in death's antechamber, he was visiting a place he was not yet welcome. Outside, the sun was shining, and the sounds of wheels, motors, and backfires, and the occasional screaming child, snorting horse, and chirping bird, enlivened the tiny hilltop town. But once the heavy door closed behind him, the atmosphere was echoless, thick, quiet. The body was arrayed in a plain casket, spot-lighted in the otherwise darkened room, looking about as good as it could under the circumstances. If that body had been gone over by a train, Griffith had done a pretty good job cleaning it up, Cyril thought. Only the face and front of the shoulders were visible, but aside from some bruising, the features were not disturbed, just as the paper had said.

Cyril didn't recognize the man, but then again, there was something familiar about him. He looked to be about mid-sixties in age, with a Roman nose, a roundish head, and regular features. As he stood there, letting his eyes adjust to the light, he realized that Griffith was standing there, too. Cyril ignored how creepy the sudden appearance was, taking for granted that any good mortician would be about halfway between the human and spirit worlds, anyway.

"Bill," he said, by way of greeting. "Bet you don't get too many like this."

Bill Griffith grinned. "Not too many. Half the town come through so far. Last hour had an old gal come in here, take one look, and faint right away. Gave the Mrs. quite a scare."

"Who was that?"

"Mrs. Jennie Bethel. Come by with her daughter. It took Miss Bessie and the Mrs. quite a few minutes to get her to come back around."

"So, did she know him?" asked Cyril.

"Said she did not," said the undertaker, with emphasis on the last word. "Most likely the warm weather and the dark that made her woozy, she said." He lowered his voice, "But that old shrew is gettin' up in years, and I bet she just don't like lookin' at dead folks, knowin' what's comin' soon enough." Bill Griffith gave a little chortle of superiority because, clearly, that was something that did not bother him.

But the comment reminded Cyril how stuffy the parlor was, and he congratulated Bill on his cleanup work, wished him good luck, and took his leave. Out on High Street, with the sun still pushing an early spring through the sharp clatter of town noise, he decided to head down to Irwin's Garage and take a look at Frank Huffey's new Pierce-Arrow, which was also the talk of the town that spring. A number of local boys of all ages were hanging around there, wasting some Saturday time, and they could see him as walked down.

"Mr. Hollingsworth," Addison Brokaw greeted Cyril, who nodded a greeting back. The group of men stopped talking, and everyone grunted their hellos. It was Bob Reeder who broke the ensuing silence, saying, "Too nice a day to look at dead bodies," to a round of chuckles.

Cyril grinned. "Something familiar about that face, though," he ventured. Old John Kirk and Huffey, who were sitting at the counter drinking coffee, exchanged looks. Old John winked at Frank, and turning back to Cyril, said, "Say, where'd you go to grammar school at, Cyril?"

Cyril grinned again because it was a trick question. Old John's uncle Kersey had owned the farm where that one-room schoolhouse had sat, just across from the toll house. Some of Cyril's earliest memories were of John waving to him from the fields as he ran up to the door at first bell. "Any teacher learn you better'n the rest?" asked John.

Cyril had always liked John, his rough-hewn neighbor with a good heart, who was nine years older and who had helped him out of several scrapes in his younger days. The question had a little edge to it, like there was a point John Kirk was trying to make, so he actually started thinking about his old teachers. He remembered Miss Whitcomb, a grim little woman with a sour expression on her face and a hair-trigger on her birch switch. On the other hand, there was this joking fellow, a little looser than the rest, who . . . all of a sudden, some things started to piece together. He looked back at Old John, who was laughing at his expression, "Narr . . ." Cyril made some kind of non-English noise, and the whole group broke out laughing.

When he had recovered a little, he joined in, sheepishly. "Well, ain't that a bite on the backside," Cyril, known for keeping it clean when he talked, marveled profanely.

John Kirk went on, "Yep! I thought that might be ol' Wilson when I went through there yesterday, but Voorhies Bethel come by here earlier and said that's him for sure. Bill Sam Bethel's first boy finally come home, and a different breed of cat he was, too."

One of the younger men in the room, Howard Pickering, got a puzzled look on his face, and asked, "Izzat right? William Samuel Bethel? That Voorhies Bethel that come by and that old boy up at Griffith's, they was both Bill Sam Bethel's boys?" A number of the group nodded, and Howard said, "My uncle Ed always said he wanted to kill Bill Sam Bethel, but he never would say why." Lou Carter and Tom Schaeffer leaned in and, in low voices despite all the years that had passed, began to educate Howard as to why his uncle had the opinions he did. It was a subject that still raised the ire of some of the local men who had grown up with Clara. None of them had done anything about it at the time, nor could they have, and it only amplified their hatred now, so many years after the fact.

Cyril remembered Clara, but he had a slightly different take. It had been hard for her, he knew, but it was God's will, and there were now three fine men in the area because of the horrible things Bill Sam Bethel had done, and his judgment day had come and gone, resolved by a higher authority. He didn't join in the narration, though, because he had something else on his mind, and he leaned back against the fender of an old Model T and half listened as Lou and Tom took Howard through the whole disgusting story. He bit his lip, thinking things through. He heard Schaeffer growl, ". . . Elmer shoulda done it sooner . . ."

Like most of the men there, Cyril was a God-fearing man who went to church regularly. Unlike some of them, he really believed it, and he was known around town as an upright man who liked to go by the book. So, some of those present seemed to sense what was on his mind as he looked around the room now with a question on his face. Finally, he drew in a deep breath at their not-quite-hostile stares, and asked quietly, "I take it y'all ain't inclined to tell Clyde that's Wilson Bethel up there?" Clyde Hardesty was the Belmont County coroner, who was in town to document the unidentified man's death, and to identify him, if possible.

That stopped all the talk in the room just as cold as Willis was up the hill. Everyone looked at John Kirk, and he rendered a verdict as decisive as any judge. "Hell, no!" he thundered, and finished off the pronouncement with a little laugh. "Why, they'd just stick poor ol' Jennie with the bill. Now, my cousin can be a bit ornery, that's a fact, but she's still a pious woman. Don't you think she's gone through enough, him givin' her a young-un like that and then bein' gone all them years and never sendin' any money? You want that cute little firecracker up at the bank to pay for her daddy's funeral when she ain't even seen his face since she was too young to know it?"

Howard Pickering jumped in again, "Wait a sec," he said. "Bessie Bethel's his daughter? That fella up at Griffith's?" A round of emphatic nods, some of which were telling Howard to put a cap on the questions, greeted him.

John Kirk went on, "Cyril, I know you like to always do right, and I like that about you, but <u>not</u> tellin' Clyde is what's right. Wilson Bethel picked his road a long time back, and it didn't have nothin' to do with us or our'n. It's come full circle on him now, just like it did for his daddy. Voorhies said it best — 'just plant him plain and let it go.'"

Cyril looked down, blinking, thinking. A slow, bemused smile spread onto his face, and a slow set of nods came right behind it. The sense of what John was saying made Cyril think that this was one of those times to put the book away. "Plant him plain and let it go," he said dryly, half to himself. He felt a sudden pang of sadness at the whole situation, at the strange depredations of both father and son and how much pain they had caused, and he said a silent little prayer, too. He sighed and grinned, and looked up. "That coffee any good, John?"

Old John Kirk was sitting right next to the pot. "No, but it don't smell no worse than ol' Wilson does," he said to a round of laughs. "You want a cup?"

"I believe I do, thanks."

Unknown Man Buried Sunday Afternoon

Thought To Have Been Former Bellaire Man, But That Man Appeared and Protested

The dead man found at Oco a little over a week ago and whose body was held at the Griffith morgue until Sunday, went to his grave without having been identified. Several papers in nearby towns printed stories to the effect that the unknown victim was Edward Chatman, a herb peddler, formerly of Bellaire. Saturday Chatman went into a drug store in Bridgeport and registered a protest at being thought dead.

The dead man was buried Sunday afternoon at two o'clock. The funeral was held in the morgue and Rev. W. H. Carlisle conducted the services. Interment was made in the Old cemetery. If relatives of the deceased could have been found, they could not have given him any more proper burial, than the kindhearted Flushing people did.

[971] The Flushing News, March 12, 1925, microfilm from OHC.

Death certificate, John Doe, February 28, 1925.

972 Death Certificate, Unknown, Wheeling Township, Belmont County, Ohio, February 27, 1925, microfilm from OHC.

Bibliography

BOOKS:

Beezley, William H., *Insurgent Governor: Abraham Gonzalez and the Mexican Revolution in Chihuahua,* University of Nebraska Press, Lincoln, 1973.

Benedict, John Downing. *Muskogee and Northeastern Oklahoma*: including the counties of Muskogee, McIntosh, Wagoner, Cherokee, Sequoyah, Adair, Delaware, Mayes, Rogers, Washington, Nowata, Craig, and Ottawa. Chicago: S.J. Clarke Pub. Co., 1922.

Bingham County Centennial Book Committee, *Bingham County History, Commemorating the County's 100th Birthday,* written and compiled by the people of Bingham County, Blackfoot, Idaho, 1985.

Bryant, Keith L., Jr. *History of the Atchison, Topeka & Santa Fe Railway*, Lincoln and London, University of Nebraska Press, 1974.

Caldwell, J. A., *A History of Belmont and Jefferson Counties*, 1880.

Canfield, Kaylene, compiler, *News Clippings from Cokeville and Diamondville, Wyoming, 1878–1913,* 2020.

Dary, David, *Frontier Medicine: From the Atlantic to the Pacific, 1492–1941,* Alfred A. Knopf, New York, 2008.

Dorin, Patrick, *The Chesapeake and Ohio Railway,* Superior Publishing Company, Burbank, California, 1981.

Fifield, James Clark, editor and preparer, *The American Bar: Contemporary Lawyers of the United States and Canada.* Basic Books, Inc., by the James C. Fifield Company, Minneapolis, Minnesota, 1918.

Foster, Harry L., *A Gringo in Manana-Land,* Dodd, Mead and Company, New York, 1924.

Hampton, Taylor, *The Nickel Plate Road: The History of a Great Railroad,* The World Publishing Company, Cleveland, 1947.

Heaton, John W., *The Shoshone-Bannocks: Culture and Commerce at Fort Hall, 1870–1940,* University Press of Kansas, Lawrence, 2005.

Heimburger, Donald J. *Wabash,* House Publishing Company, River Forest, Illinois, 1984.

Hidy, Ralph W., Hidy, Muriel E., Scott, Roy V., and Hofsommer, Don L., *The Great Northern Railway, a History*, Harvard Business School Press, Boston, Massachusetts, 1988.

Hill, Luther B., *A History of the State of Oklahoma*, the Lewis Publishing Company, Chicago, 1909–1910.

Holbrook, Stewart H., *The Golden Age of Quackery*, New York, The MacMillan Company, 1959.

Horan, James D., *The Pinkertons: The Detective Dynasty that Made History*, Crown Publishers, 1969.

Hunter, Andrew Frederick, *A History of Simcoe County, vol. II: The Pioneers,* Published by the County Council, Warwick Brothers & Rutter, Limited, Printers, Toronto, Wentworth Press, 2016.

Jacobs, Janet Liebman, *Victimized Daughters: Incest and the Development of the Female Self,* Routledge, New York and London, 1994.

Knight, Alan, *The Mexican Revolution, vol. I: Porfirians, Liberals and Peasants*, Cambridge University Press, 1986.

Laughlin, Emma E., *Place Names of Belmont County*, Barnesville, Ohio, 1941.

Lewis, Oscar, *The Town that Died Laughing: The Story of Austin, Nevada, Rambunctious Early-Day Mining Camp, and of Its Renowned Newspaper, the Reese River Reveille,* University of Nevada Press, Reno, 1986.

Licht, Walter, *Working for the Railroad: The Organization of Work in the Nineteenth Century*, Princeton, New Jersey, Princeton University Press, 1983.

Ludmerer, Kenneth M., *Learning to Heal: The Development of American Medical Education*, Baltimore and London, The Johns Hopkins University Press, 1985.

Luecke, John C. *The Northern Pacific in Minnesota*, Grenadier Publications, St. Paul, Minnesota, 2005.

Martinez, Oscar J., *Fragments of the Mexican Revolution: Personal Accounts from the Border,* University of New Mexico Press, Albuquerque, 1983

McCutcheon, Marc, *Everyday Life in the 1800's,* Writer's Digest Books, Cincinnati, 1993

Meyer, Michael C., *Mexican Rebel: Pascual Orozco and the Mexican Revolution, 1910–1915*, University of Nebraska Press, Lincoln, Nebraska, 1967.

Nash, Jay Robert, *Hustlers & Con Men,* M. Evans and Company, New York, 1976.

Otis, D. S., *The Dawes Act and the Allotment of Indian Lands,* University of Oklahoma Press, Norman, 1973.

Paher, Stanley W., *Nevada Ghost Towns and Mining Camps,* Nevada Publications, Las Vegas, 1970.

Reed, Robert C., *Train Wrecks: A Pictorial History of Accidents on the Main Line,* Schiffer Publishing, Atglen, Pennsylvania, 1996.

Rennick, Robert M., *Kentucky Place Names,* The University Press of Kentucky, Lexington, 1984.

Richards, James Adair, *An Illustrated History of Bath County, Kentucky, with Historical & Biographical Sketches and Notes & Anecdotes of Many Years*, Yuma, Arizona, Southwest Printers, 1961.

Romig, Walter, *Michigan Place Names*: *The History of the Founding and the Naming of More Than Five Thousand Past and Present Michigan Communities,* Detroit, Wayne State University Press, 1986.

Russell, Diana E. H., *The Secret Trauma: Incest in the Lives of Girls and Women*, New York, Basic Books, Inc., 1986.

Sacco, Lynn, *Unspeakable: Father-Daughter Incest in American History*, Baltimore, The Johns Hopkins University Press, 2009.

Standage, Tom, *The Victorian Internet: The Remarkable Story of the Telegraph and the Nineteenth Century's On-Line Pioneers*, Kindle edition, Bloomsbury, New York, 1998.

Stephenson, Charles, and Asher, Robert, *Life & Labor: Dimensions of American Working-Class History*, State University of New York Press, 1986.

Stover, John E., *History of the Illinois Central Railroad,* Macmillan Publishing Company, New York, 1975.

Sulzer, Elmer G., *Ghost Railroads of Kentucky,* Indiana University Press, Bloomington and Indianapolis, 1967.

Tapp, Hamilton, and Klotter, James C., *Kentucky: Decades of Discord, 1865–1900*, Frankfort, Kentucky, The Kentucky Historical Society, 1977.

Tompkins, Colonel Frank, *Chasing Villa: The Story Behind the Story of Pershing's Expedition into Mexico,* Stackpole Books, Lanham, Maryland, Boulder, New York, London, 1934.

Turner, John B., and Semling, C. Knut, *History of Clay and Norman Counties, Minnesota, Volume 2,* B. F. Bowen & Co., Indianapolis, 1918.

Van Hoy, Teresa, *A Social History of Mexico's Railroads: Peons, Prisoners, and Priests,* Rowman and Littlefield, Lanham, Maryland, 2008.

Wasserman, Mark, *Capitalists, Caciques, and Revolution: The Native Elite and Foreign Enterprise in Chihuahua, Mexico, 1854–1911,* The University of North Carolina Press, Chapel Hill and London, 1984.

Yenne, Bill, *Atlas of North American Railroads,* MBI Publishing Company, St. Paul, 2005.

Multiple authors, *A Centennial History of Belmont County and Representative Citizens*, 1801–1901, published 1903.

Multiple authors, *History and Directory of Riverside County, 1893–1894,* Riverside, California, A. A. Bynon & Son, 1893.

Multiple authors, *Spanning the Century: The History of Ulen, Minnesota, 1886–1986,* Published by the Ulen Union, 1985.

Multiple authors, *History of the Upper Ohio Valley, Volume II: with Family History and Biographical Sketches. A Statement of Its Resources, Industrial Growth and Commercial Advantages,* Brant & Fuller, Madison, Wisconsin, 1890

Multiple authors, *Portrait and Biographical Album of Clinton and Shiawassee Counties, Michigan, 1891,* Chapman Brothers, Chicago, 1891 (courtesy Internet Archive).

SPECIALTY PUBLICATIONS, GENEALOGICAL PUBLICATIONS, AND ARTICLES:

Busbey, T. A., editor and compiler, *The Biographical Directory of the Railway Officials of America,* edition of 1893, published biennially by The Railway Age and Northwestern Railroader.

Davern, Marguerite, compiler. *Yesterday's Schools*, Belmont County O.R.T.A., 1990's.

Dodge, Richard V., *Perris and its Railroad*, printed in *Dispatcher*, November 15, 1959, Issue 29.

Fisher, Daniel C. and Fisher, Irene A., authors and compilers, *A History of the Family and Descendants of Frederick and Catherine Speith Fisher, 1825 — 1978,* unpublished genealogy distributed to interested relatives.

Garde, Carol and Jim, *The Early Bethells and their Descendants, 1635–1994*, Heart of Lakes Publishing, Interlaken, NY, 1995

Hanson, Joan Search and Kenneth L., *Marriages from Venango County Sources, 1795–1885 (All), 1886–1921 (Outside the County),* Closson Press, Apollo, Pennsylvania, 1994

Hanson, Joan Search and Kenneth L., *Venango County, Pennsylvania Death Book Summary & Index (1893–1905),* Closson Press, Apollo, Pennsylvania, 1995

Holmes, Elmer Wallace, *The History of Perris Valley (Part 2)*, Los Angeles, California, Historic Record Company, 1912 (history.raus-place.com)

Keller, Ed, *Cicero J. Hamlin *Village Farm* Among Trotting's Greatest*, from *Harness Horse*, included in *Pictorial and Historical Review, East Aurora and Vicinity, 1940*

Kelly, Howard A., and Burrage, Walter L., *Dictionary of American Medical Biography*, Milford

House, Boston, 1971.

Mason, F. H., *The Twelfth Ohio Cavalry: A Record of Its Organization and Services in the War of the Rebellion.*

Mexico Northwestern Railway Company, *The Road to Wealth*, pamphlet published by the company, 1909.

Northern Pacific Railroad Company, *Transportation Rules, Northern Pacific System of Railroads, in Effect Sept. 1883, Revised May 1886,* published by the company.

Powell, Esther Weygandt, *Tombstone Inscriptions and Family Records of Belmont County, Ohio*, Closson Press, 1969.

Priebe, J. Henry Jr., *Beginnings — The Village of Buffalo*, The Buffalonian, 1997.

Schwartzberg, Beverly. *"Lots of Them Did That": Desertion, Bigamy, and Marital Fluidity in Late-Nineteenth-Century America*, Project Muse, Journal of Social History 37.3 (2004): 573-600 (muse.jhu.edu/article/53055).

Venango County Historical Society, *Venango County, Pennsylvania Cemetery Records and Early Church Histories, Volume 3 — Scrubgrass Township,* Closson Press, Apollo, Pennsylvania, 1995

Focal Forensics Facial Comparison Report, Report Ref: FMAP_20180716_ZG, 10259 Julian CT. Westminster, CO 80031. Examiner: Zac Giammarrusco

A History of the Town of Clarence, pamphlet published by the Buffalo and Erie County Historical Society, 1971.

U.S. Railway Post Office Catalog, published by the Mobile Post Office Society, April 2016, digital version.

GENEALOGICAL WEBSITES:

Ancestry.com. This website, along with its affiliates, Fold3.com and FamilySearch.org, has provided the bulk of the historical records that underlay this research, including but not limited to:
- U.S. census records and voter lists
- Birth, marriage, and death records, including wills and probate records
- U.S. directories, yearbook records, and member lists
- Border crossing, immigration, and consular records
- Public family trees
- Military records

Archives.com. This website is also an Ancestry.com affiliate and has some contemporary records as well as historical ones.

Findagrave.com. The premier website for interment information. Gives cemetery locations, and may provide family information, biographical information, and/or photos of headstones and cemetery plots.

GenDisasters . . . Genealogy in Tragedy, Disasters, Fires, Floods | Events That Touched Our Ancestors' Lives (gendisasters.com)

Legacy.com — U.S. obituaries, mostly recent.

Online Searchable Death Records and Indexes (deathindexes.com).

Online Historical Directories (sites.google.com/site/onlinedirectorysite/)

HISTORICAL NEWSPAPERS WEBSITES:

Historical Newspapers & Indexes on The Internet - USA (researchguides.net) This website provides a listing of Newspaper websites by state and is a useful starting point for research in a particular region.

Newspapers.com. This website has a great number of U.S. newspapers. It is affiliated with Ancestry.com, but direct membership provides access to the full range of papers.

Genealogybank.com — Historical Newspapers, many of which are not available on Newspapers.com.

NewspaperArchives.com — Historical Newspapers.

Chronicling America (chroniclingamerica.loc.gov) — Historical Newspapers assembled by the Library of Congress through the National Endowment for the Humanities.

Google.com/newspapers

Paper of Record (hypernet.ca). This website has many papers from outside the U. S., including Canada and Mexico.

Ohio's Digitized Newspapers (ohiohistory.org)

California Digital Newspaper Collection (cdnc.ucr.edu)

Montana Newspapers (montananewspapers.org)

Digitized Montana Newspapers Online (mhs.mt.gov)

Idaho State Archives (history.idaho.gov/collections/). This website contains ordering information through Interlibrary loan for historic Idaho newspapers on microfilm, as well as a collection of digitized newspapers, which may be viewed online.

Digital Archives of the Marshall Public Library, Pocatello, Idaho (marshallidaho.advantage-preservation.com). Historical newspapers from Pocatello.

University of Illinois Library Newspaper Database (library.illinois.edu)

Colorado Historic Newspapers Collection (coloradohistoricnewspapers.org)

Tulsa City/County Library (tulsalibrary.org)

State Library of Pennsylvania (statelibrary.pa.gov)

NATIONAL, STATE, COUNTY, AND LOCAL RECORDS:

National Archives at St. Louis (archives.gov/st-louis/of)

Belmont County Historical Society (ohiolha.org/member_organization/Belmont-county-historical-society/)

Kentucky Digital Library (kdl.kyvl.org)

University of Kentucky Libraries (nkaa.uky.edu)

Kentucky Historic Institutions (kyhi.org/ksh-admissions-data/)

University of Louisville Libraries, Kornhauser Health Sciences Library (digital.library.louisville.edu)

The Gateway to Oklahoma History, Oklahoma Historical Society (okhistory.org). Has digitized Oklahoma newspapers, brief histories of regions, people, and corporations, and many other useful references.

Oklahoma Department of Libraries (Libraries.OK.gov)

Oklahoma Genealogy Trails, Biographies of Oklahoma (genealogytrails.com)

The Historical Society of Long Beach, California (hslb.org)

The Long Beach Public Library (longbeach.gov/library)
Bedford County Virginia History and Genealogy (genealogytrails.com/vir/Bedford/)
The Historical Society of North Dakota (nd.gov)
Sadieville City History (cityofsadieville.com)
Norman County Minnesota Genweb (usgenwebsites.org/MNNorman/)
Gary, Minnesota history (garymnhistory.wordpress.com)
The Portal to Texas History at the University of North Texas, Denton (texashistory.unt.edu)
Dyer County Historical Society, Dyer County, Tennessee, (dyerhistory.com)
Caldwell County, Kentucky, Genealogy Center (kykinfolk.org/Caldwell/)
Augusta Township History (augustatownship.org/history/). Summarized history of Augusta Township, Washtenaw County, Michigan.
Wyoming Tales and Trails (archive.org)
The Perris Valley Historical Museum (perrisvalleyhistoricalmuseum.com)
University of Texas at El Paso Library (utep.edu/library)

CLERKS OF COURT:

Nottoway County, Virginia Clerk of Circuit Court (nottoway.org)
Bedford County, Virginia, court and land records (courts.state.va.us)
The Randolph County, North Carolina, Register of Deeds (randrod.com)
The Tulsa County Court Clerk, Tulsa, Oklahoma (courtclerk.tulsacounty.org)
Los Angeles County Registrar-Recorder/County Clerk (lavote.net)
The Superior Court of California, County of Los Angeles (lacourt.org)
Polk County District Court, Crookston, Minnesota (mncourts.gov)
Norman County District Court, Ada, Minnesota (mncourts.gov)
Huron County, Ohio Clerk of Court (huroncountyclerk.com)
Belmont County, Ohio Courts (belmontcountycourts.com)

RAILROAD HISTORY WEBSITES:

Locating Railroad Employee Records (genealogytoday.com/guide/railroad-employees.html)
Researching Old Railroad Records (thoughtco.com/researching-old-railroads-and-railway-records-1422753)
The Great Search — Finding Railroad Employment Records (freepages.rootsweb.com/~sponholz/genealogy/railroad.html)
Cyndi's List — Railroads (cyndi'slist.com/railroads)
Library of Congress, Railroad Maps, 1828–1900 (loc.gov/collections/railroad-maps-1828-to-1900/)
Abandoned Rails (abandonedrails.com). This website has maps and brief histories of many of the railroad lines that are no longer in use.
Abandoned (abandonedonline.net). Also has documentation and histories of abandoned facilities, including railroads.
Rails West (railswest.com).
The Iron Road (usgennet.org/usa/ne/topic/railroads/job.html)
Ohio Railroad Stations Past and Present (west2k.com/ohio.htm)

Preserving the History of the Nickel Plate Road (nkphts.org)

Minnesota Railroads: Map, History, and Abandoned Lines (American-rails.com/mn.html)

Operating Divisions of the Northern Pacific (research.nprha.org/Miscelanous%20Documents/NP%20Division%20Points.htm). Lists the various divisions of the company, and the headquarters of each, as they changed over time.

Northern Pacific Railway: Map, Pictures, History, Logo, Roster (American-rails.com/np.html#Top)

Chicago & North Western Historical Society — Genealogy (cnwhs.org/archives_genealogy.htm)

Durand Union Station / Michigan Railroad History Museum (durandstation.org)

The Cleveland and Marietta Railroad/Pennsylvania Railroad | The Guernsey County Historical Society (guernseycountyhistory.com/tag/the-cleveland-and-marietta-railroadpensylvania-railroad/)

Railway Employee Records for Colorado | Denver Public Library History (denverlibrary.org/research-tool/railway-employee-records-colorado-volume-iii)

Southern California Railway Museum (socalrailway.org). Formerly called the Orange Empire Railroad Museum, this collection of equipment and memorabilia is housed in the station at Perris.

WVNC Rails (wvncrails.org). This website has information about many of the railroads that operated in West Virginia and North Carolina during the late nineteenth century.

TRRA Home (terminalrailroad.com)

The Railroad Police (therailroadpolice.com/new-page)

RESEARCH AIDS WEBSITES:

Day of the Week Calculator (searchforancestors.com/utility/dayofweek.html)

The Inflation Calculator (westegg.com/inflation/)

Popular Baby Names by Decade (ssa.gov/OACT/babynames/decades/)

The Meaning and History of First Names (behindthename.com)

Historic Map Works (historicmapworks.com)

JSTOR.org. "A digital library for the intellectually curious," this website is a repository for many academic books, journals, papers, etc.,

Justia.com. This website is a repository for legal documents of all kinds.

Whitepages.com. Has contact information and more about living people, useful in tracking descendants.

MISCELLANEOUS HISTORICAL WEBSITES:

ASARCO Company History (company-histories.com/ASARCO-INCORPORATED-Company-History.html).

Contagion: Historical Views of Diseases and Epidemics, Harvard University Library (library.harvard.edu/collections/contagion-historical-views-diseases-and-epidemics).

Google Books (play.google.com/books). Contains many publications, most no longer in print, including mining journals and several years of *The Railway Age Gazette.* Other publications found here that informed this project were:

Ohio Legal News, volume IV, October 17, 1896 — October 9, 1897

Powell, Fred Wilbur, *The Railroads of Mexico,* The Stratford Co., Boston, 1921.

Special Mexican Claims Commission Report to the Secretary of State, with Decisions Showing the Reasons for the Allowance or Disallowance of the Claims, United States Government Printing Office, Washington, 1940

Wallace's Monthly: An Illustrated Magazine Devoted to Domesticated Animal Nature, Vol. XVIII, No. 1, Published by the American Trotting Register Association, Chicago, March 1892

Busbey, T. Addison, editor and compiler, *The Biographical Directory of the Railway Officials of America*, editions of 1901 and 1906, the Railway Age, Chicago, Publisher

Furlong, Thomas, *Fifty Years a Detective,* C. E. Barnett, St. Louis, 1912

Fyfe, Hamilton, *The Real Mexico: A Study on the Spot,* McBride, Nast & Company, New York, 1914

Powell, Fred Wilbur, *The Railroads of Mexico,* The Stratford Co,. Boston, 1921

Smalley, E. V., compiler, *Northern Pacific Railroad Book of Reference,* published by the Northern Pacific Railroad, 1883

History of Private Investigations (asginvestigations.com/private-investigator/history-of-private-investigations/).

How School Was Different in the 1800s (mentalfloss.com/article/58705/11-ways-school-was-different-1800s).

Internet Archive (archive.org).

Karen V. Wasylowski: Swearing and Cussing — nineteenth-century style (karenvwasylowski.blogspot.com/2100/02/swearing-and-cussing-19th-century-style.html).

Last Arrow Ceremony (jaredfarmer.net/curios/last-arrow-ceremony/).

List of Defunct Medical Schools in the United States (en.wikipedia.org/wiki/List_of_defunct_medical_schools_in_the_United_States).

Shoshoni Language Project (shoshoniproject.utah.edu).

RECORDS REPOSITORIES:

Research for this project took me to the following physical repositories of records and documents:

The Ohio History Center, Columbus (ohiohistory.org). This museum/library has a large collection of Ohio newspapers on microfilm, as well as regional histories, directories, maps, and other materials. Abbreviated OHC.

The Ohio Genealogical Society, Bellville, Ohio (ogs.org). Contains much of the same material, with a focus on helping genealogists. Abbreviated OGS

The Belmont County, Ohio, Clerk of Courts (belmontcountycoc.org). Old books of bound court records which may be photographed.

Victoria Read Public Library, Flushing, Ohio (bcdlibrary.org/About/Victoria-read.asp). Local histories and chance encounters with other genealogists looking for the same people.

The Buffalo and Erie County Public Library, Central Library, Buffalo, New York (buffalolib.org). Microfilmed newspapers and documentation of the late nineteenth-century in western New York.

The Bath County, Kentucky, Clerk of Circuit Courts, Owingsville (kycourts.gov/Pages/Agency404.aspx?oldUrl=https%3a%2f%2fkycourts.gov%2fCounties%2fBath%2fdefault.htm). A basement room filled with old bound court records, which the kind clerk allowed me to page through and photograph.

The Bath County Memorial Library, Owingsville, Kentucky (bathlibrary.org). This library has a genealogy area which contains good documentation of local history, including copies of family genealogies, photographs, and books.

The Kentucky Historical Society, Frankfort (history.ky.gov). Holdings include "archival records such as manuscripts, photographs, maps, atlases; oral history interviews; and microfilm."

Kansas Historical Society and Museum of History, Topeka (kshs.org/). This museum and archive houses the remaining records of the Atchison, Topeka & Santa Fe Railroad.

The Newberry Library, Chicago (newberry.org). This facility houses the remaining records of the Illinois Central Railroad.

The Gale Family Library at the Minnesota Historical Society, St. Paul (mnhs.org). This library/museum complex houses most of the remaining records of both the Northern Pacific and the Great Northern Railroads, as well as other regional railroads. There are also comprehensive regional histories and an exhaustive collection of Minnesota newspapers on microfilm. Abbreviated MNHS.

The Family History Library, Salt Lake City (templesquare.com/explore/family-history-library/). Billed as "the largest genealogical library in the world," this facility contains many helpful materials, including microfilm, records, genealogies, books, maps, and photographs.

The California State Library, Sacramento (library.ca.gov). "Our vaults house thousands of rare books, maps, newspapers, and periodicals in addition to a huge collection of one-of-a-kind photographs, letters, and ephemeral items such as posters, pamphlets, and sheet music." Abbreviated CSL.

California State Railroad Museum (californiarailroad.museum). This museum also houses a library which contains some documentation of the railroads of California.

The Library of Virginia, Richmond (lva.virginia.gov). This large complex houses a good collection of newspapers, both in print and on microfilm, which can only be viewed at the facility, after obtaining a library card.

Nettie Lee Benson Latin American Studies Collection, The University of Texas, Austin (web-prod.lib.utexas.edu/about/locations/benson). Some of the surviving records of the Mexico Northwestern Railway, especially those related to the Mexican Revolution, are housed here.

Appendix I:

Maps

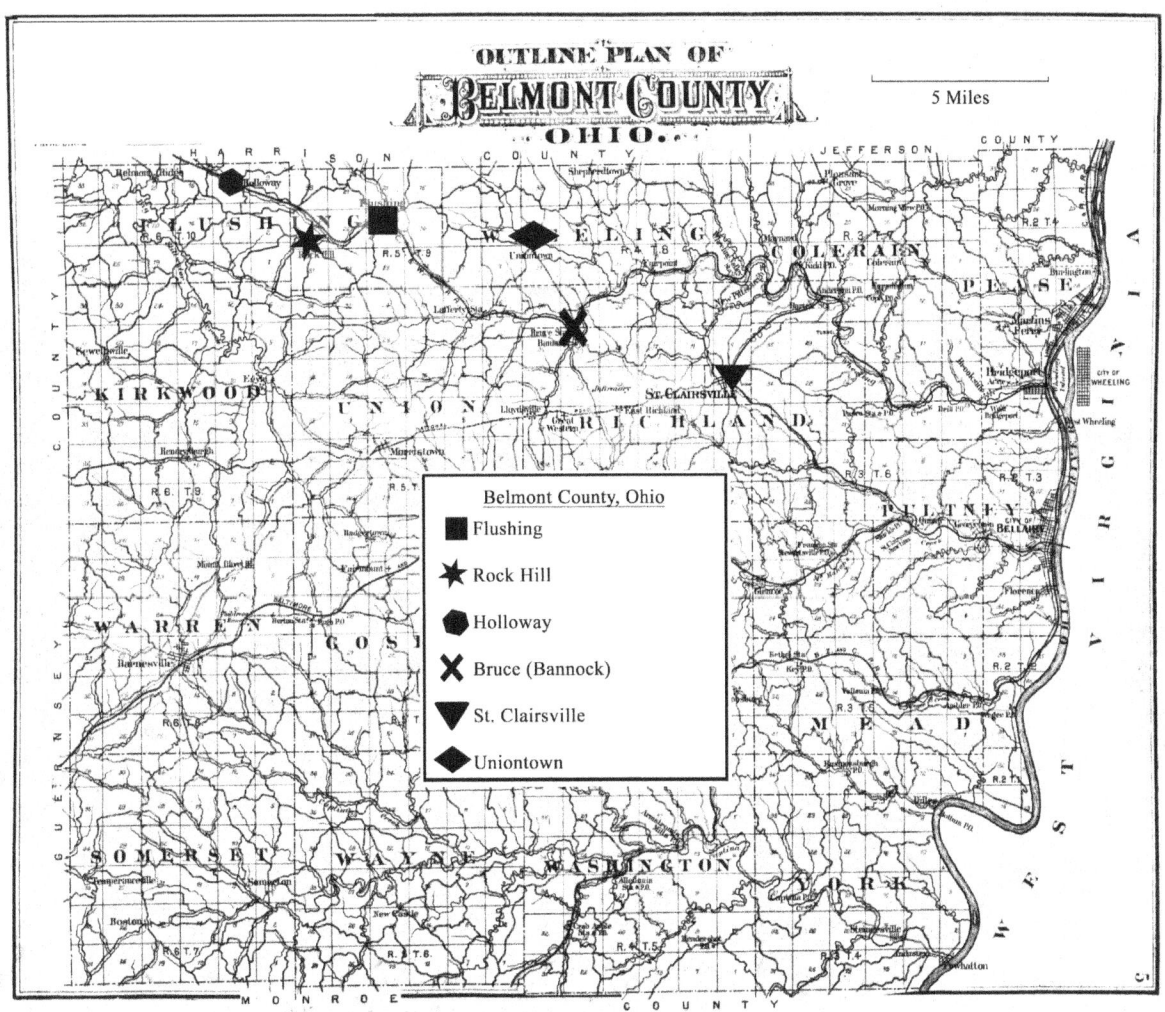

Belmont County, Ohio, 1888, with towns mentioned in the text.

D.W. Bethel's Migrations

The maps on the following pages show D.W. Bethel's movements from 1860 until 1911, as far as we can ascertain from the information available in 2021.

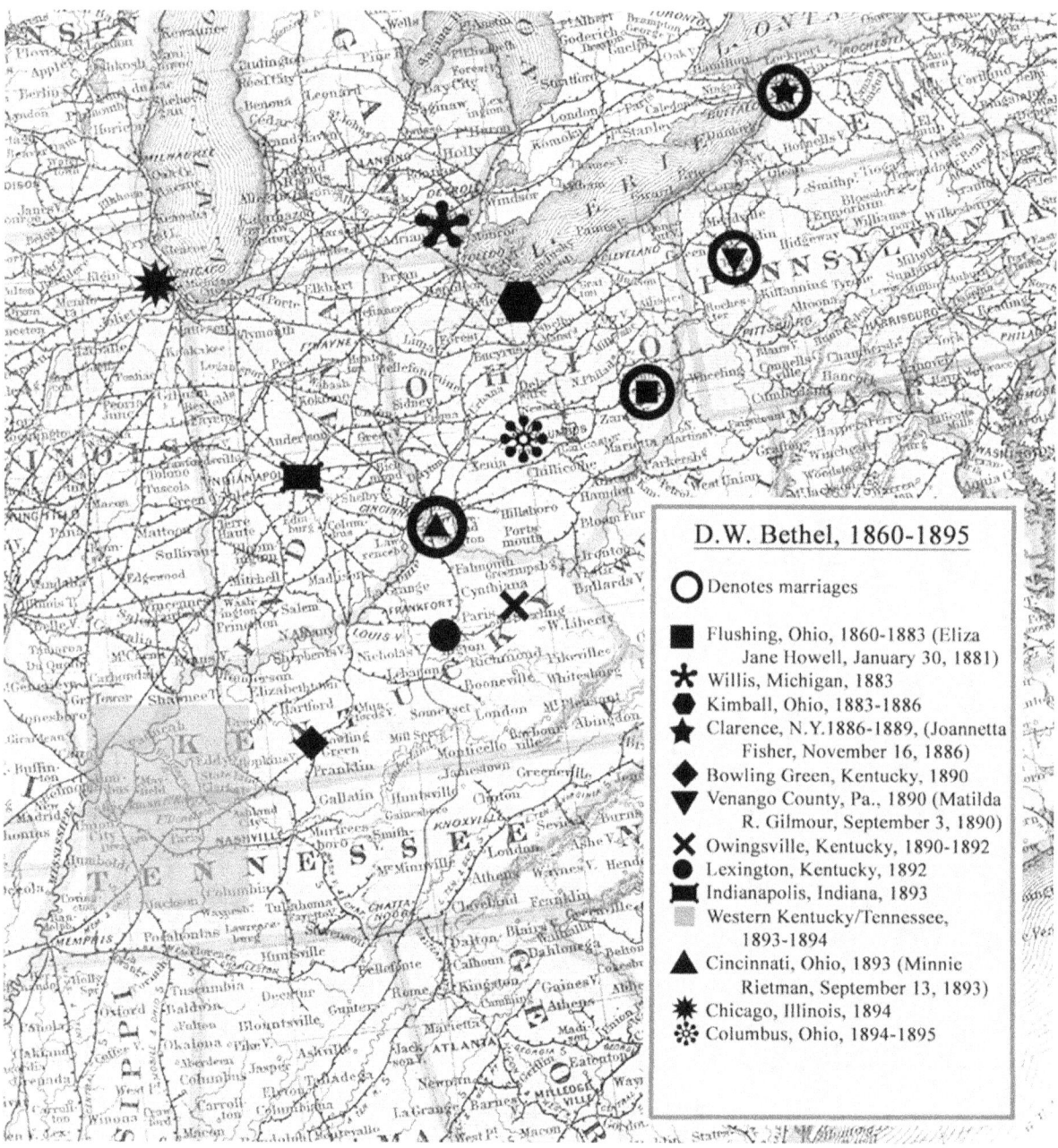

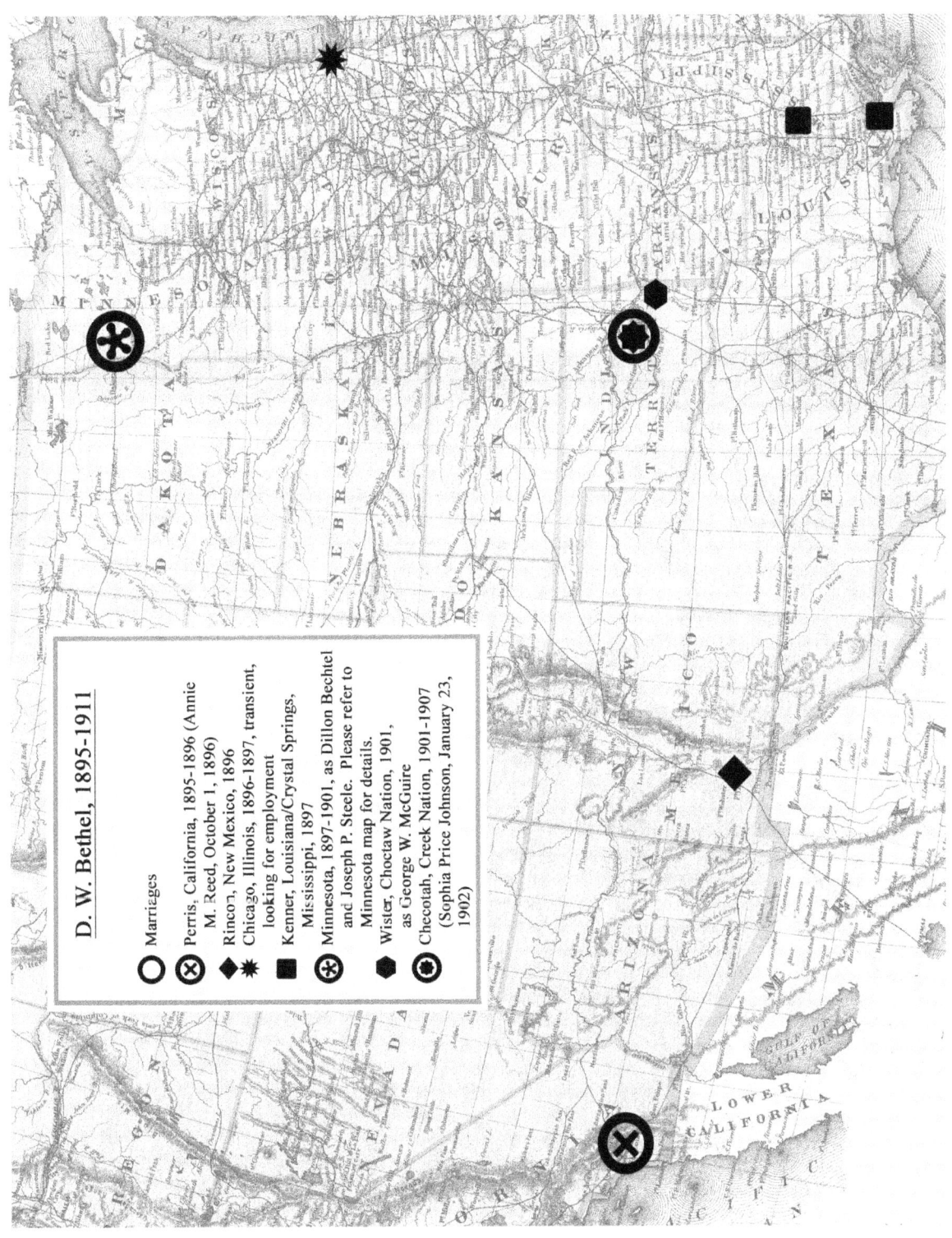

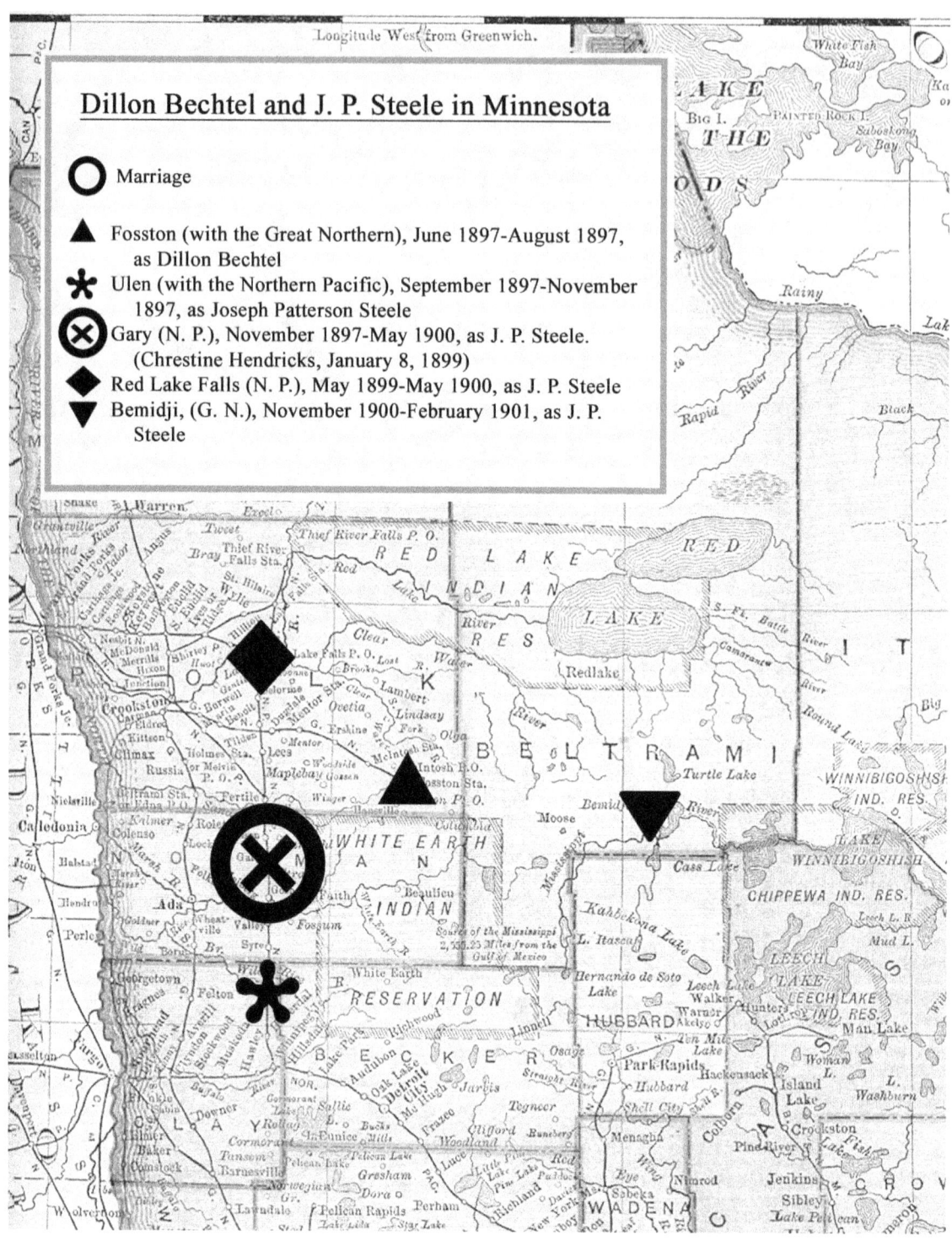

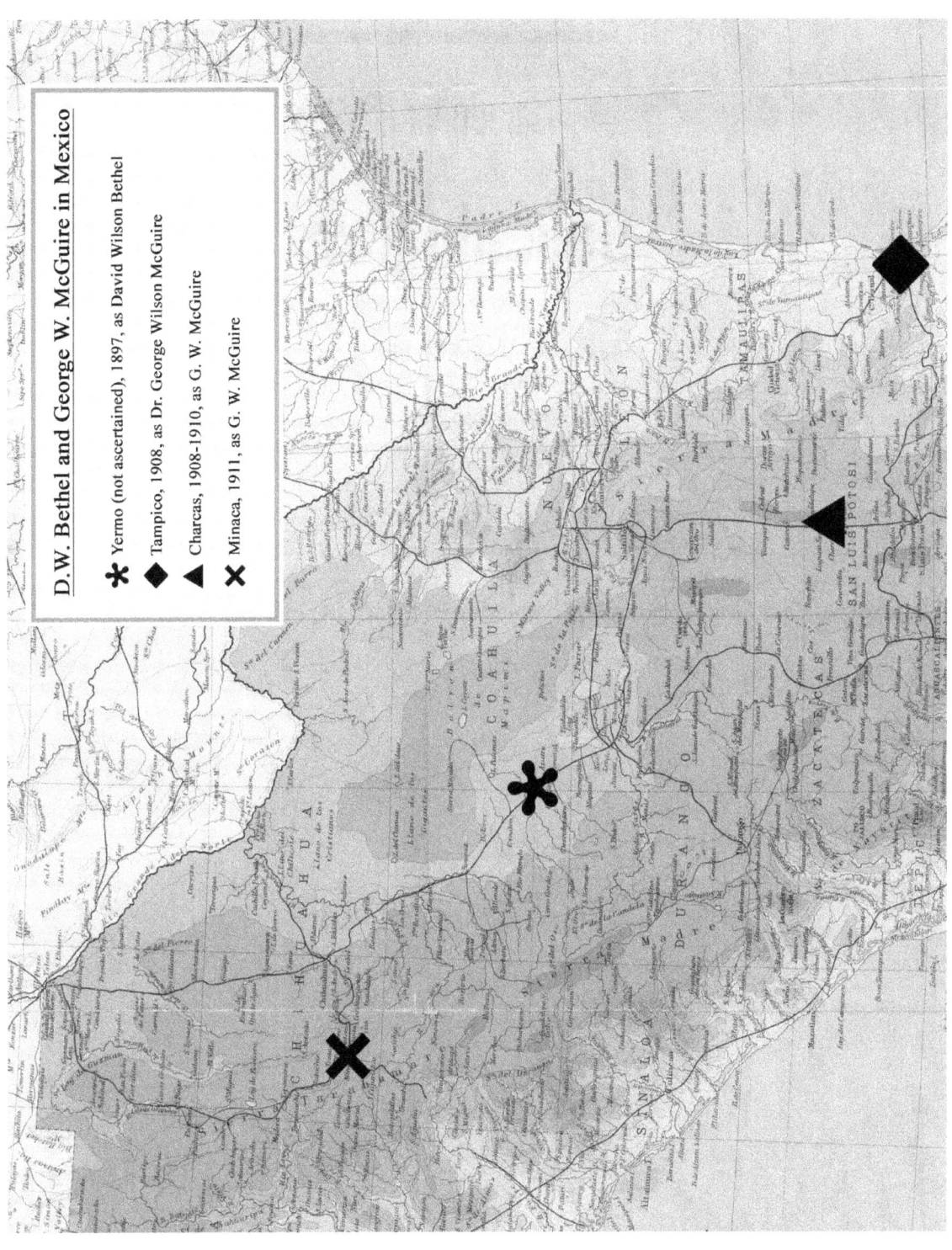

Appendix II:

Genealogies

■ ON THE FOLLOWING PAGES ARE PARTIAL GENEALOGIES for Henry Bethel, David Wilson Bethel, Clara Lucinda Bethel, Eliza Jane Howell, Joannetta Henrietta Fisher, Matilda Ralston, Minnie Rietman, Annie M. Reed, Chrestine Hendricks, and Sophia Price, including many of their relatives who are mentioned in the story. They are meant to be references for the reader of this book and are purposely incomplete to limit confusion. Most of these branches contain many more members than are indicated here. Please note that if one descendant of a family is listed then all of their siblings are also listed (even if they were not mentioned in the story), in order to give a complete picture of that particular family. Other than that, I have tried to illustrate the relationships mentioned in the story with as little clutter as possible.

Selected Descendants of Henry Bethel

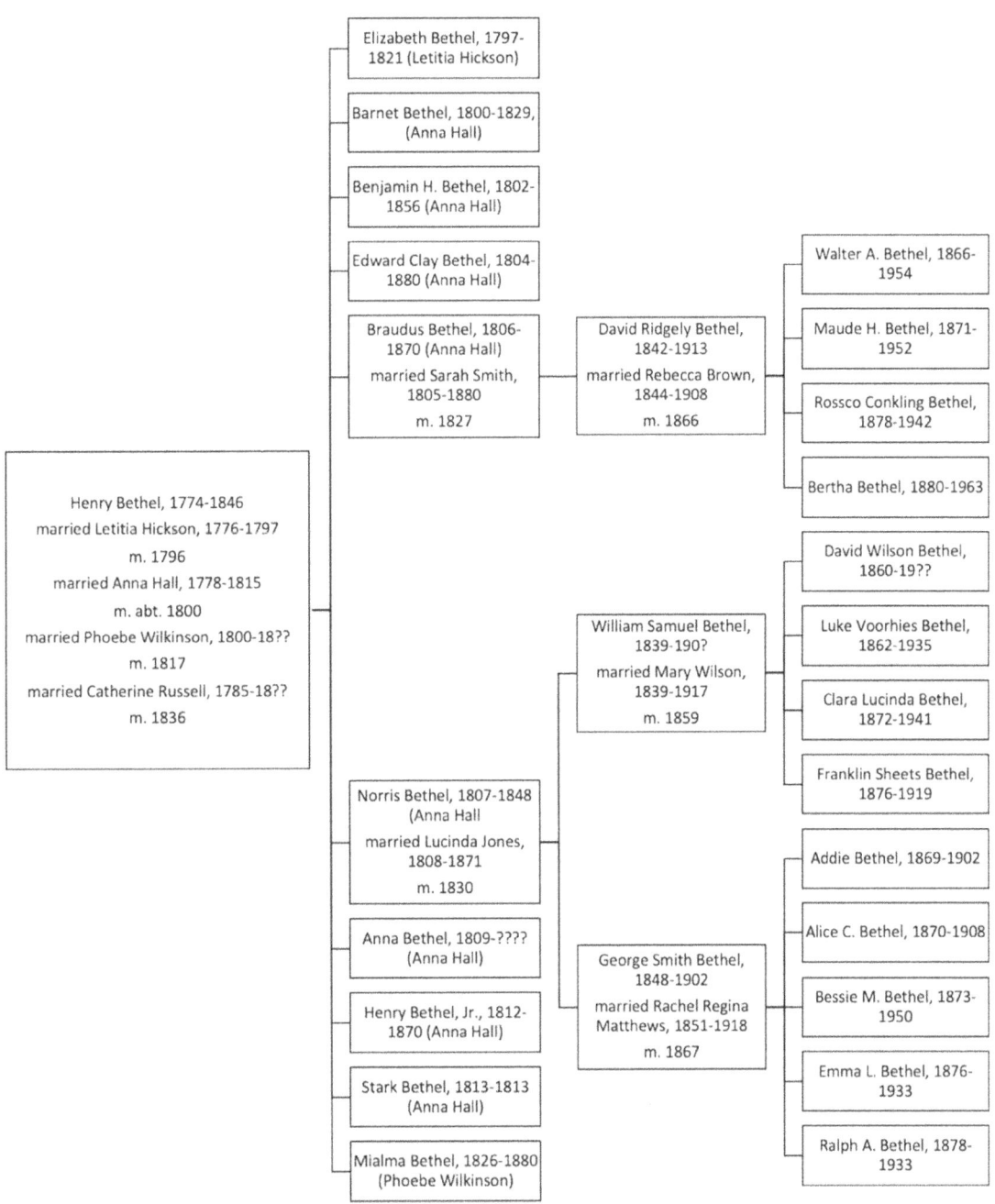

Wives and Descendants of David Wilson Bethel

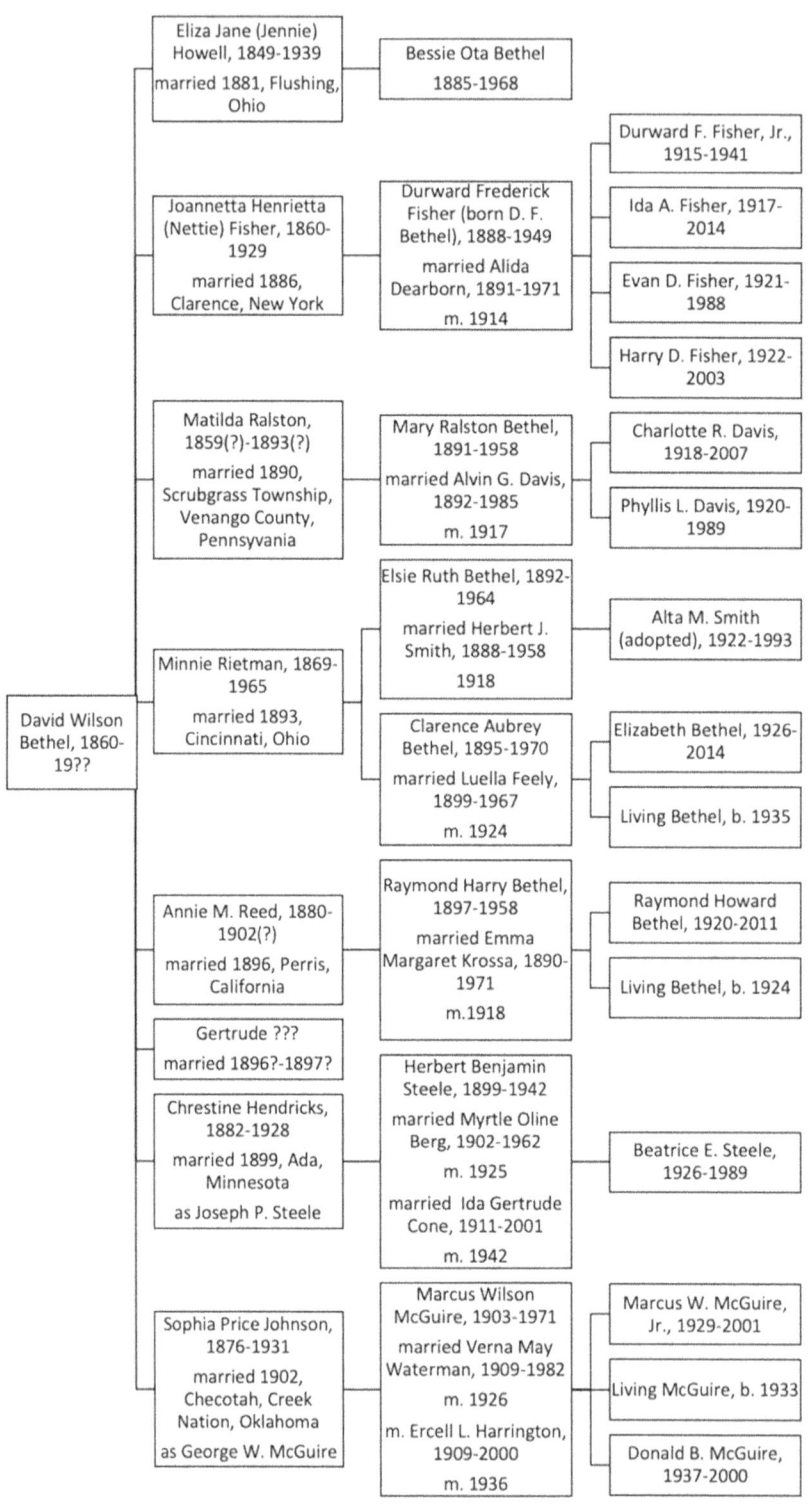

Genealogy of Clara Lucinda Bethel

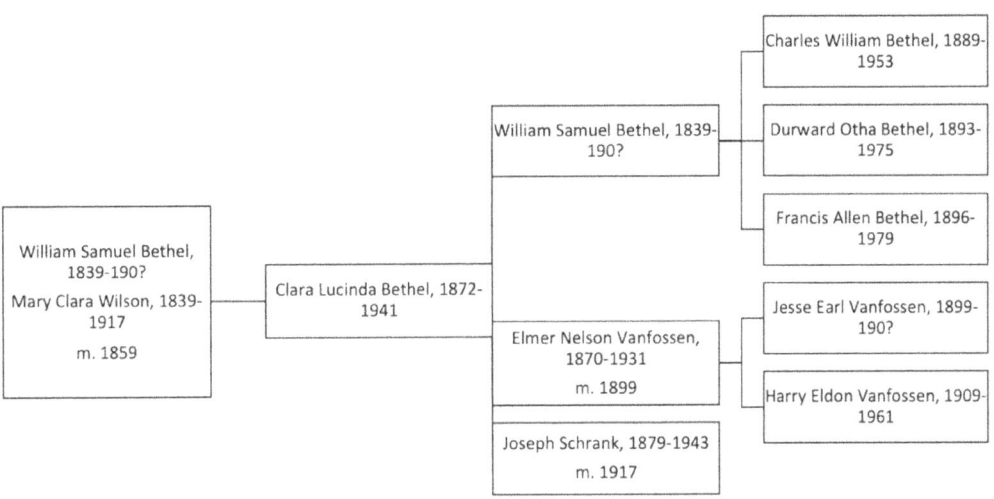

Selected Descendants of Hiram Howell, Flushing Township, Belmont County, Ohio

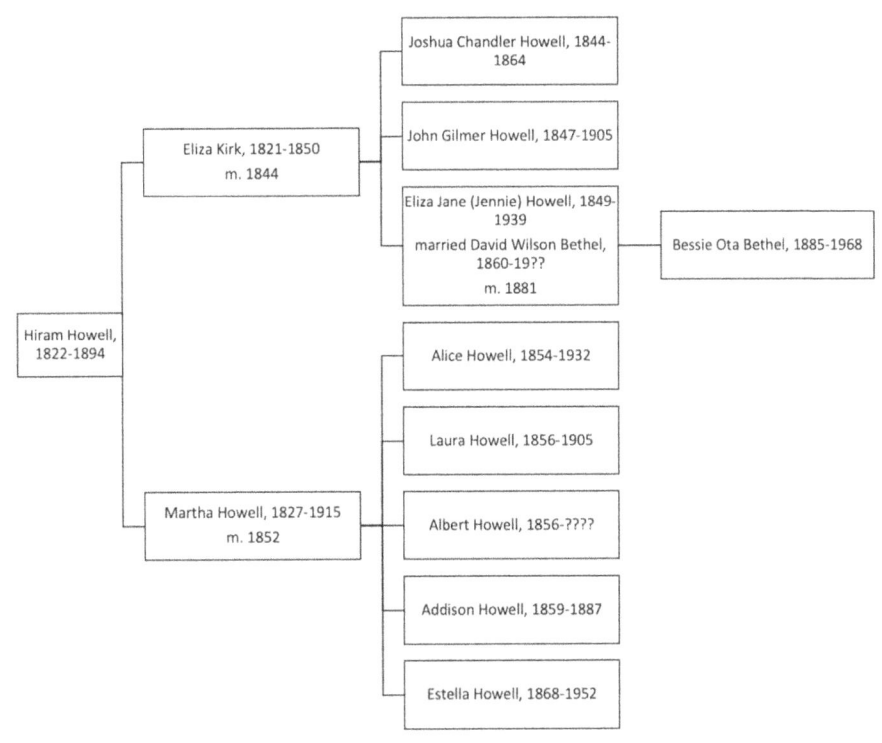

Selected Descendants of Frederick Fisher and Eva Catherine Spieth Fisher, Clarence, New York

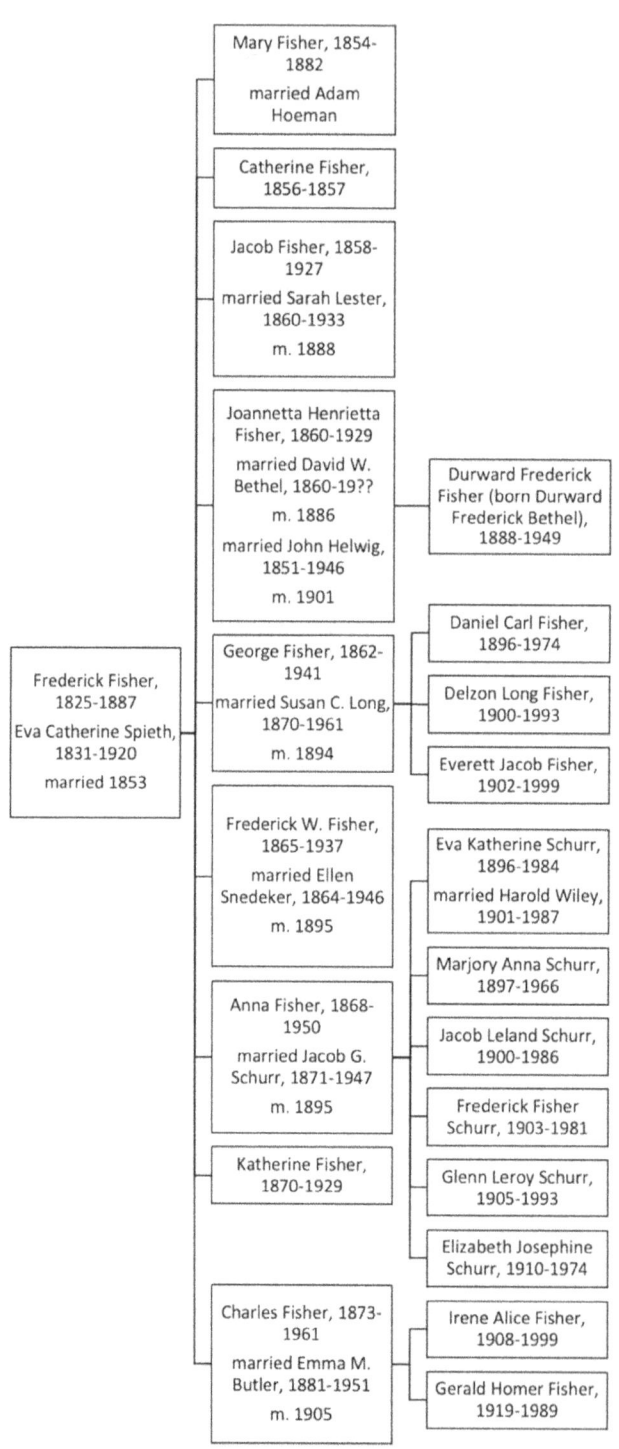

Selected Descendants of William Ralston and Mary Patrick Ralston in Pennsylvania

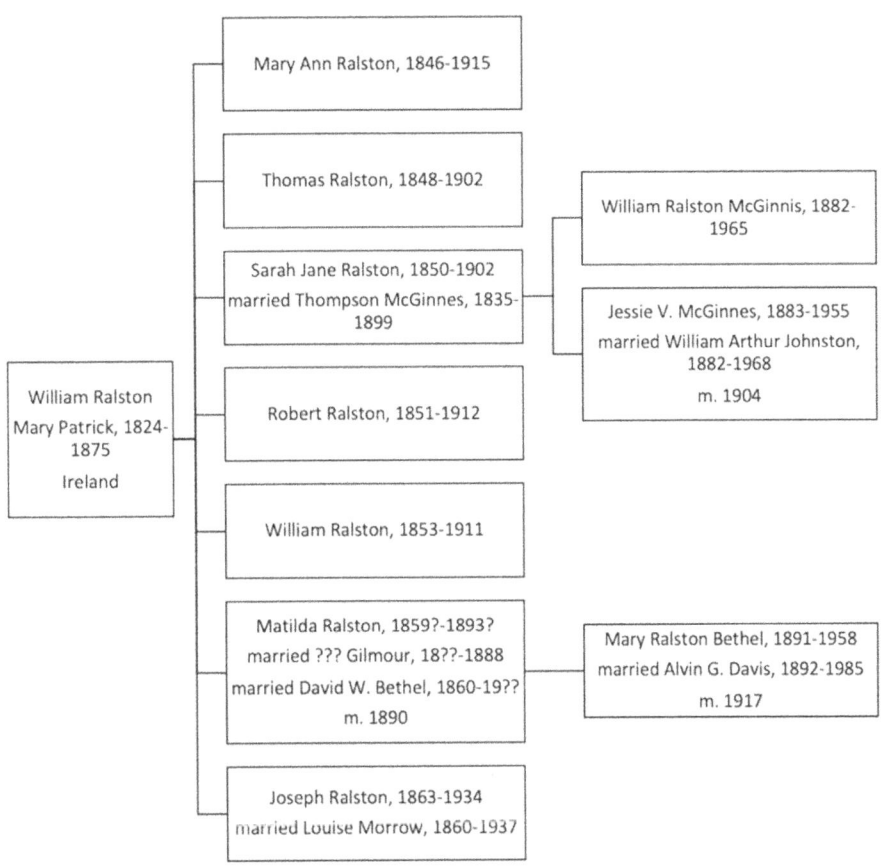

Selected Descendants of George Rietman and Elizabeth Lanfersieck Rietman, Cincinnati, Ohio

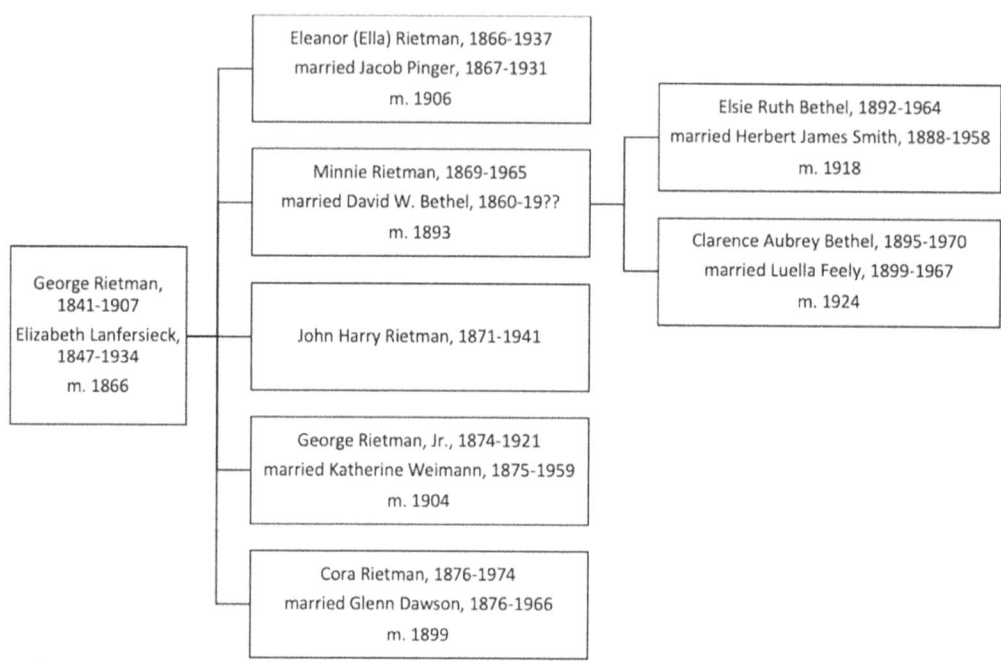

Selected Descendants of William Henry Reed and Martha Frasier Reed, Perris, California

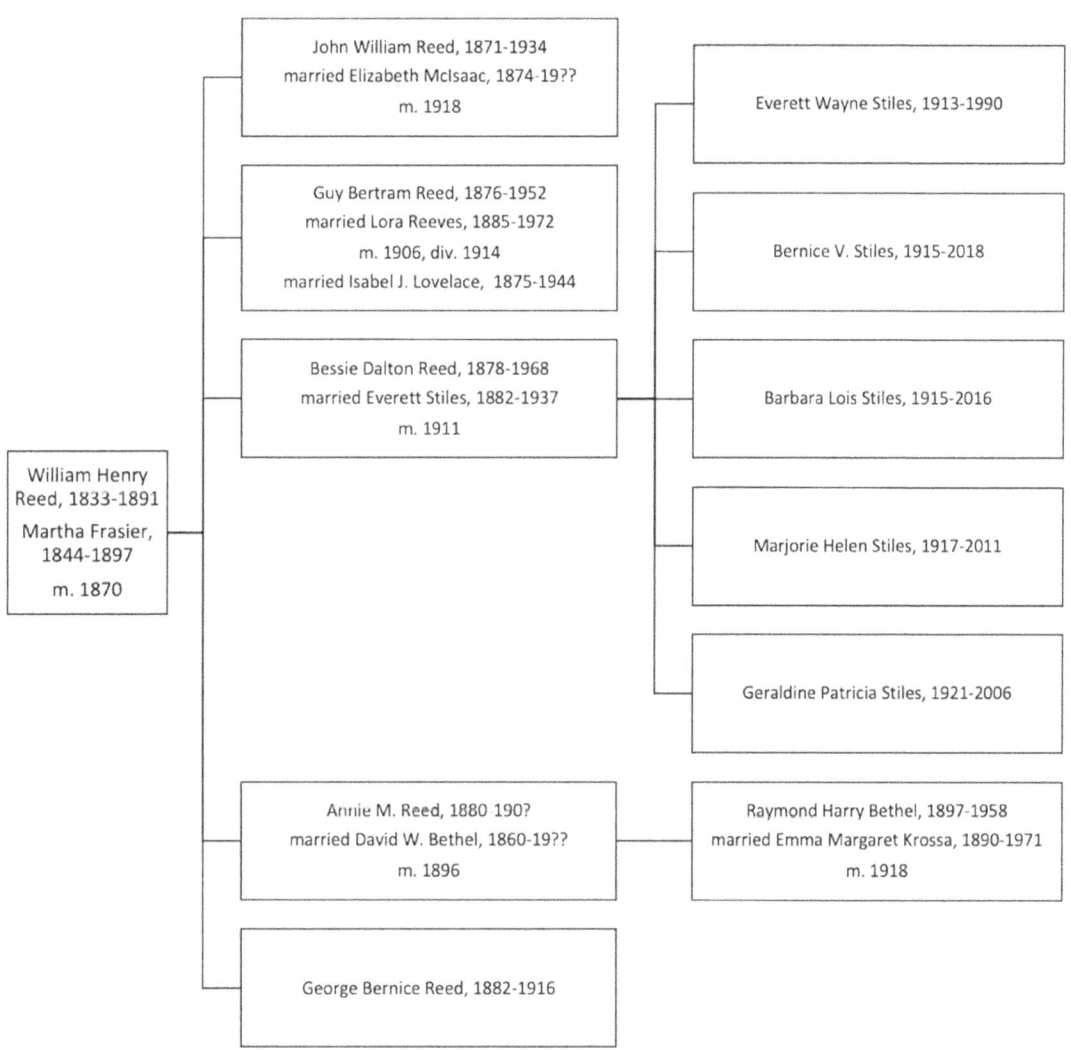

The Hendricks/Tyberg Family, Minnesota and North Dakota

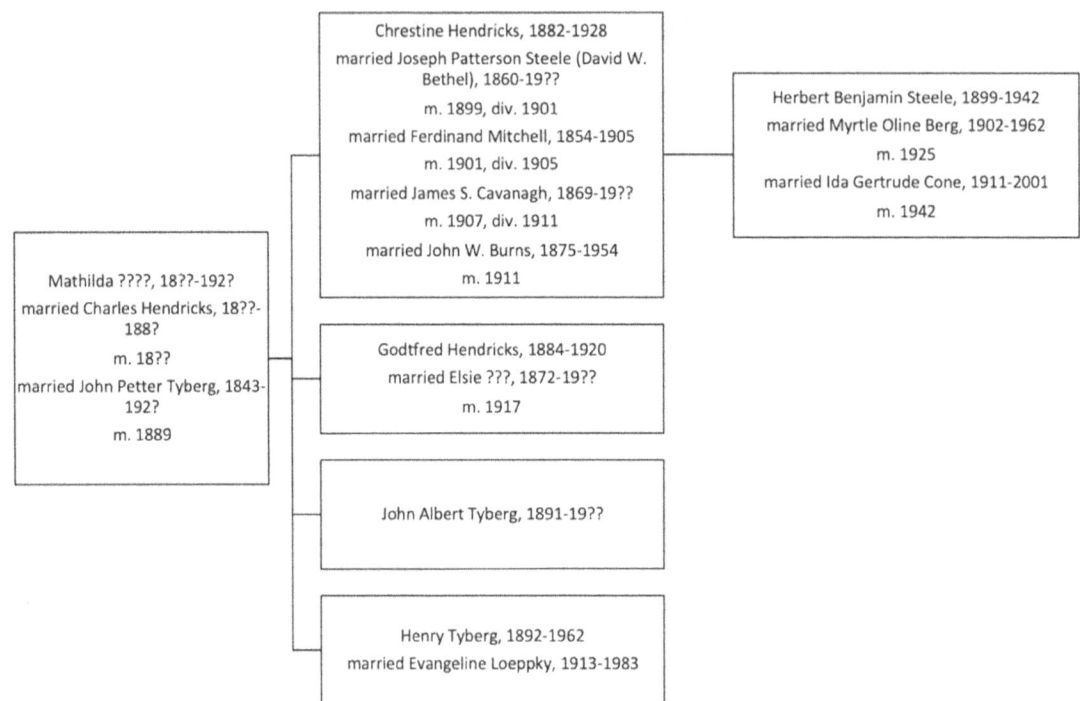

Selected Descendants of Mary Elizabeth Clark Price Wineblood, Creek Nation, Oklahoma Territory

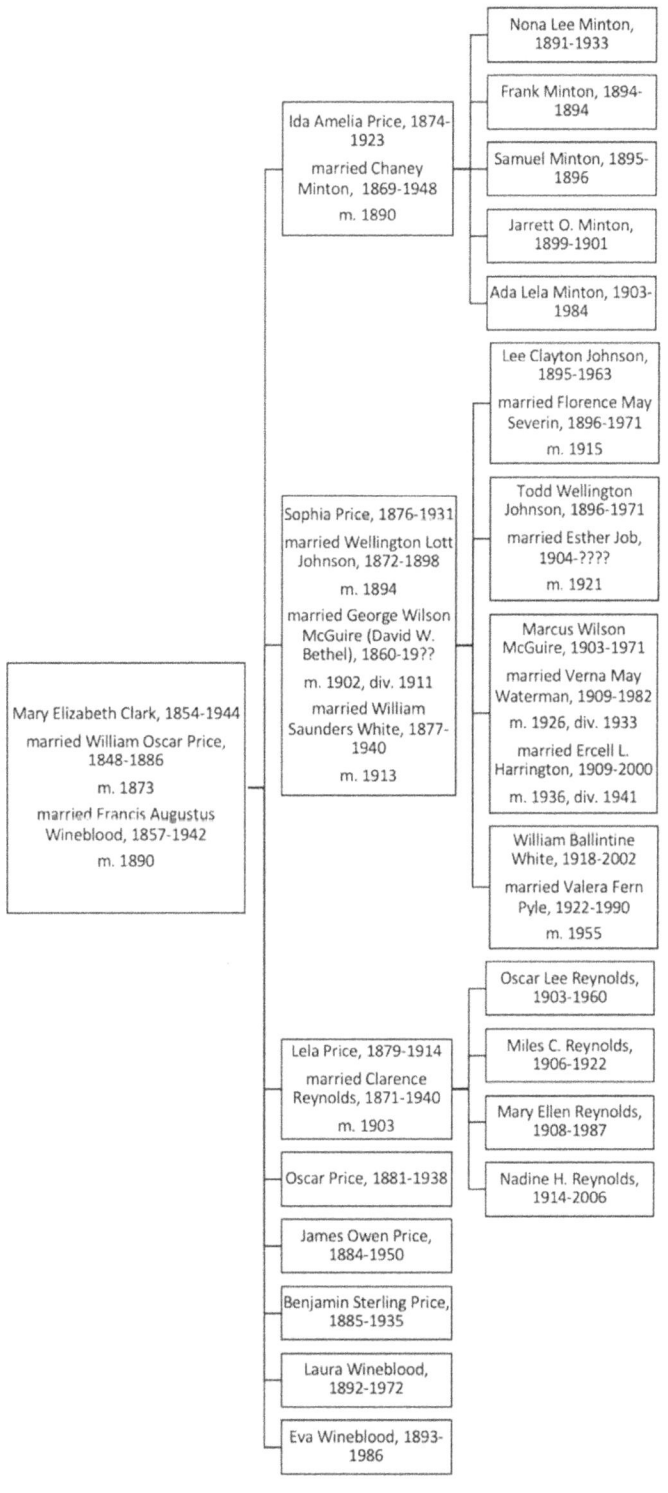

Appendix III:

Marriage Licenses

■ BELOW THE READER WILL FIND THE KNOWN MARRIAGE LICENSES of David Wilson Bethel, including the ones for his marriages under the aliases Joseph P. Steele and George W. McGuire.

D. Wilson Bethel and Jennie E. Howell, Flushing, Ohio, January 29, 1881.

RECORD OF MARRIAGES
In the Town of Clarence, Erie Co., N. Y.

1. Full Name of Groom, David Willison Bethel
2. Place of Residence, Clarence Erie Co N.Y.
3. Age next Birthday, 27 years.
5. Occupation, Rail Road Agent
6. Place of Birth, Sadieville Ken.
7. Father's Name, William S. Beethel
8. Mother's Maiden Name, Mary Williamson
9. No. of Groom's Marriage, First
10. Full Name of Bride, Joannetta Fisher
    Maiden Name if a Widow,
11. Place of Residence, Clarence Erie Co N.Y.
12. Age next Birthday, 27 years.
14. Place of Birth, Newstead Erie Co. N.Y.
15. Father's Name, Frederick Fisher
16. Mother's Maiden Name, Catharine Sherth
17. No. of Bride's Marriage, First

Married by C.E. Swift Pastor M.E. Church at Clarence Erie Co. N.Y.
Witnesses, A.J. Miller & Fred. Fisher Recorded Dec. 7, 1886
Date of Marriage, Nov. 16 1886 Andrew Metz Town Clerk

N. B.—At Nos. 4 and 13, if other than the white race, specify it. At Nos. 9 and 17 state whether first, second, third, &c marriage of each. The names of Bride and Groom should be written out in full for the "given" and family names.

David Willison Bethel and Joannetta Fisher, Clarence, New York, November 16, 1886.

David W. Bethel and Matilda R. Gilmour, Scrubgrass Township, Venango County, Pennsylvania, September 3, 1890.

THE STATE OF OHIO, } ss. Don't Publish *[illegible]* **139.**
HAMILTON COUNTY.

Personally appeared before me, the undersigned, JUDGE OF THE PROBATE COURT, within and for the County of Hamilton David W. Bethel who being duly sworn, deposeth and saith, that he is more than twenty-one years of age, and has no lawful wife living. And that Minnie Rietman is more than eighteen years of age, and has no lawful husband living; that she is a resident of the County of Hamilton aforesaid; and the said David W. Bethel further says, that said Minnie Rietman and affiant are not of nearer relation to each other than that of second cousin, and that he knows of no legal objection to the Marriage contemplated between them. And further this deponent saith not.

Sworn to and subscribed before me this 13" day of Sept 1893

D.W. Bethel

Howard Ferris
PROBATE JUDGE.

By *Chas T Dumont* Deputy Clerk.

MARRIAGE RETURN.

MARRIED, on the 13 day of Sept 1893 David W. Bethel and Minnie Rietman by me a Minister of the Gospel

Alonzo M Dawson

David W. Bethel and Minnie Rietman, Cincinnati, Ohio, September 13, 1893.

David W. Bethel and Annie M. Reed, Perris, California, October 1, 1896.

APPLICATION FOR AND MARRIAGE LICENSE RECORD.

STATE OF MINNESOTA, } ss.
COUNTY OF NORMAN.

I, _J.P. Steele_, of the County of _Norman_, State of _Minnesota_, desiring to procure a license to be joined in marriage unto _Christine J. Hendricks_ of the County of Norman, State of Minnesota, do declare upon oath as follows:

That I am of the full age of twenty-one years.

That the said _Christine_ is of the full age of eighteen years and a resident of the County of Norman, of the State of Minnesota.

That I have no living wife.

That said _Christine J. Hendricks_ has no living husband.

That we are not nearer of kin than first cousins.

That there is no legal impediment to said contemplated marriage.

Signed: _J.P. Steele_

Subscribed and sworn to before me, this _7th_ day of _January_ 189_9_.

_____ Clerk of District Court.

STATE OF MINNESOTA, } ss.
COUNTY OF NORMAN.

IN DISTRICT COURT.

To any Person Lawfully Authorized to Solemnize Marriages within said State:

KNOW YE, That license is hereby granted to join together as husband and wife _J.P. Steele_ of the County of _Norman_ and State of _Minnesota_ and _Christine J. Hendricks_ of the County of Norman and State of Minnesota, being satisfied by the _oath_ of said _J.P. Steele_ that there is no legal impediment thereto.

THEREFORE, This shall be your sufficient authority for solemnizing the marriage of said parties, and making return thereof as provided by law.

IN TESTIMONY WHEREOF, I have hereunto set my hand and affixed the seal of said District Court, at Ada, in said County, this _seventh_ day of _January_ 189_9_.

_____ Clerk.
By _____ Deputy.

STATE OF MINNESOTA, } ss.
COUNTY OF NORMAN.

I HEREBY CERTIFY, That on the _8th_ day of _January_ in the year of our Lord one thousand eight hundred and ninety _nine_ at _Ada_ in said County, I, the undersigned, a _minister_ did join in the holy bonds of matrimony, according to the laws of this State, _J.P. Steele_ of the County of _Norman_ and State of _Minnesota_ and _Christine Hendricks_ of the County of Norman and State of Minnesota, in presence of

Belle Franklin
Kate F. Whitcomb
} WITNESSES. W. A. Whitcomb

A copy of my credentials of ordination is recorded in the Clerk's Office of the District Court for the County of _____, State of Minnesota.

J.P. Steele and Christine J. Hendricks, Ada, Minnesota, January 8, 1899.

George W. McGuire and Sophia P. Johnson, Checotah, Indian Territory, January 23, 1902.

Appendix IV:
Handwriting Samples

■ IT IS CLEAR FROM DNA MATCHES AND ALL AVAILABLE RECORDS that David Wilson Bethel was, in fact, the same person as the individuals known as Joseph Patterson Steele and George Wilson McGuire, and we have handwriting samples of all three personages that link them, as well. Willis wrote almost all of his 27 letters to Nettie in longhand, and we also have his signatures from rail passes and assorted notes. Samples of his handwriting as Joseph P. Steele are limited to his Northern Pacific application form and the signature from his marriage license. George W. McGuire's registration with American consulate at San Luis Potosí, Mexico, in 1909, his signatures on his other two consular registrations, as well as some official documents he wrote in the course of his medical practice in Checotah, Oklahoma, contain good samples of his handwriting. These items are included below.

Most of us write the same way all the time, and Willis's script might be generally described as a loosely flowing scrawl. But unusual variations in his formation of some letters are striking, and those peculiarities also cross between personages. I will leave an analysis of his writing to those with more training, but to my untrained eye there are several notable characteristics. Most obvious are the use of two different kinds of capital 'W' in the signatures of both Bethel and McGuire (sometimes in the same document — see the consular registration from 1909) and the use of both upper and lower case 'e.' When a word ended with the letters "re," Willis would either use a script r with a lower-case e or a printed lower-case r with an upper-case E. These characteristics can be clearly seen in the signatures of George W. McGuire, and they are present throughout the letters of D.W. Bethel. Similar tendencies are also found in the limited handwriting samples of the J.P. Steele alias that are in our possession.

Signatures

Signatures, 1882 - 1897

[signature: David W Bethel]
Med. license; April 29, 1892

[signature: D W Bethel]
Trip Pass; Dec. 18, 1882

[signature: D W Bethel]
Marriage lic. #4; Sept. 13, 1893

[signature: D.W. Bethel]
Trip Pass; April 30, 1883

[signature: D W Bethel]
Letter; Jan. 7, 1896

[signature: D. W. Bethel]
Trip Pass; August 8, 1885

[signature: D W Bethel]
Imploring letter; May 25, 1896

[signature: D W Bethel]
Trip Pass; April 19, 1887

[signature: D W Bethel]
Last letter; Sept. 22, 1897

[signature: Joseph Patterson Steele / J P Steele]

Application to Northern Pacific, September 10, 1897

...d marriage.

Signed: *[signature: J P Steele]*

.... day of ...January........ 189 9

Marriage license application, January 7, 1899

348 | The Railroad Skunk

David Wilson Bethel's application to the Northern Pacific Railroad as Joseph Patterson Steele.

Birth certificate, Marcus McGuire, August 9, 1903

Birth certificate, Ada Minton, March 9, 1905

Registration of American citizen in Mexico, August 11, 1908

Registration of American citizen in Mexico, August 28, 1909

Registration of American citizen in Mexico, March 24, 1911

Birth certificates of Ada Minton and Oscar Lee Reynolds. Both mothers were Sophia's sisters, Ida and Lelia Price.

---

973 Photo courtesy Caitlin McGuire Reid.

Birth certificate of Marcus Wilson McGuire, August 9, 1903.

George W. McGuire's registrations as an American citizen in Mexico in 1909. His registrations from 1908 and 1911 were each filled out by a member of the consular staff, and the only samples of McGuire's handwriting on the documents were his signatures, which are included with McGuire's other signatures above. On this document, most of the handwriting appears to be Willis's.

Below are scans, followed by transcriptions, of five of the 27 letters Willis wrote to Nettie Fisher between 1894 and 1897.

TOLEDO & OHIO CENTRAL RAILWAY CO.

OFFICE OF SUPERINTENDENT.
WESTERN DIVISION.

H. C. FERRIS, Superintendent.

Columbus, ~~Kenton,~~ Ohio, Nov 15 1894

Mrs Nettie Fisher
Clarence N.Y.

Dear Nettie I have looked & looked for a letter from you & had a suit picked out or rather the goods for Durwood? What is the trouble? Why can't I hear from you. Or did you write to me at Hammond Ill.? I wrote you nearly two weeks ago, as the time I told you I was expecting an appointment here as Train Disp.r & I got it. I will write you more fully soon if I can hear from you. My address is 172 north High Street Care M.D. Jones Chief Train Disp.r Columbus Ohio. Love to Durwood & yourself both,

Very Hastily & Sincerely yours
Willis

Letter #4, November 15, 1894, from Columbus, Ohio.

354 | The Railroad Skunk

Envelope addressed to:
Master Durward F. Bethel
Clarence, NY
Erie Co.

Postmark: Columbus Nov. ?

Stationery of Toledo & Ohio Central Railway Co.

Columbus, Ohio, Nov. 15, 1894

Mrs. Nettie Fisher
Clarence, NY

Dear Nettie: I have looked & looked for a letter from you & had a suit picked out or rather the goods for Durward? What is the trouble? Why can't I hear from you. Or did you write to me at Hammond, Ill.? I wrote you nearly two weeks ago. At the time I told you I was expecting an appointment here as Train Disp'r & I got it. I will write you more fully soon if I ever hear from you. My address is 172 North High Street care M. D. Jones Chief Train Disp'r. Columbus Ohio. Love to Durward & yourself both.

Very Hastily & Sincerely Yours,
Willis

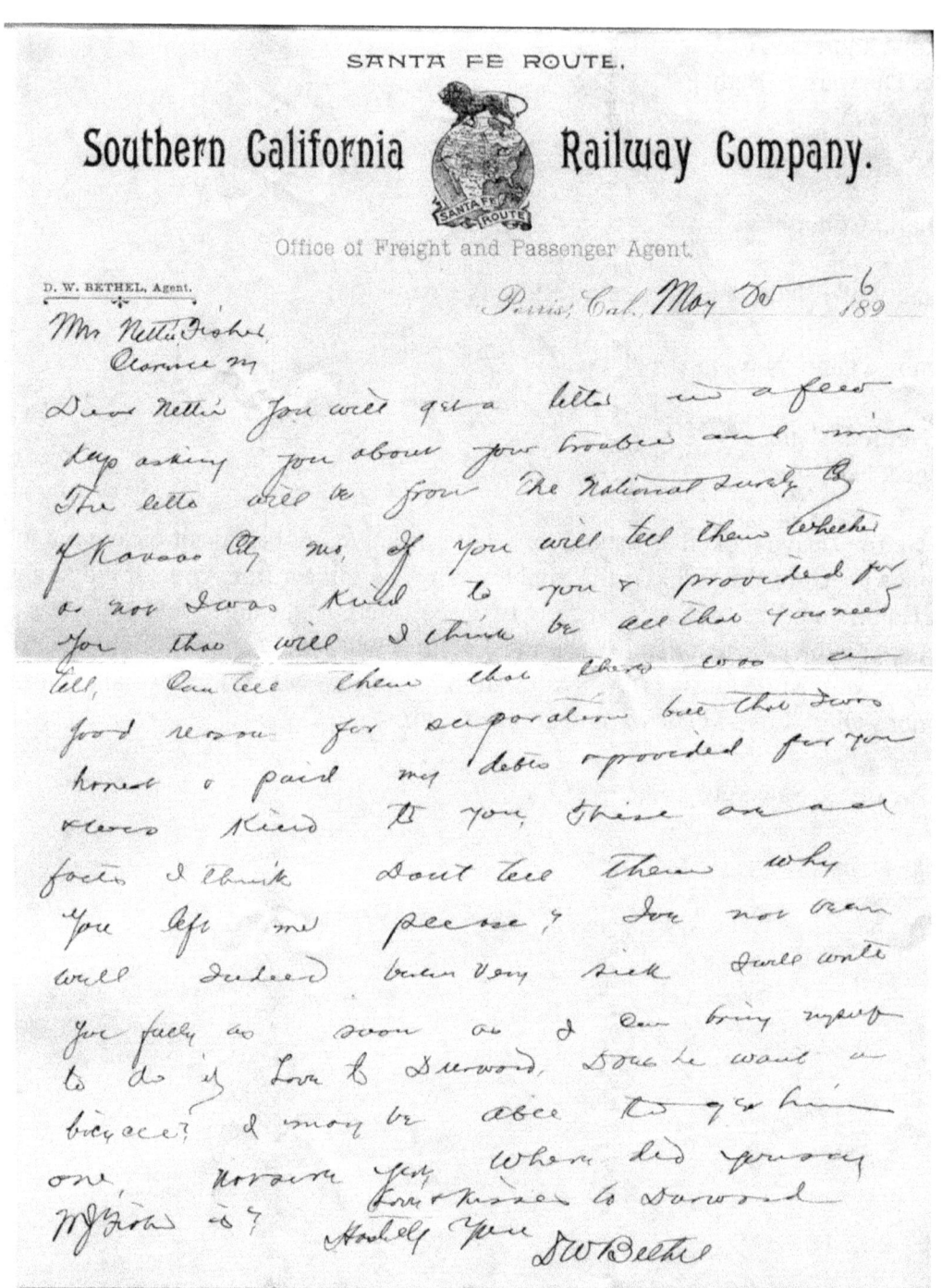

Letter #11, dated May 25, 1896, probably from Pocatello, Idaho.
Although seemingly written from Perris, California, the envelope for this letter is postmarked Cheyenne, Wyoming. Willis probably mailed it from a temporary job at Pocatello, Idaho while the A.T.S.F. investigated his bonding issues.

Railroad envelope
Addressed to:
Mrs. Nettie Fisher
Clarence, New York,
Erie Co.

Postmark: Cheyenne, May 24, 1896
Destination postmarks Crittenden and Clarence, NY, May 28, 1896

Memorandum Stationery of the Southern California Railway Company
Santa Fe Route
D.W. Bethel, Agent
Perris, Cal., May 25, 1896

Mrs. Nettie Fisher
Clarence, NY

Dear Nettie:

You will get a letter in a few days asking you about your trouble and mine. The letter will be from The National Surety Co. of Kansas City, Mo. If you will tell them whether or not I was kind to you & provided for you that will I think be all that you need tell. Can tell them that there was a good reason for separation but that I was honest & paid my debts & provided for you & was kind to you. These are all facts I think. Don't tell them why you left me please? I've not been well. Indeed been very sick. I will write you freely as soon as I can bring myself to do it. Love to Durward. Does he want a bicycle? I may be able to get him one. Not sure yet. Where did you say MJ Fisher is?

Love & kisses to Durward
Hastily yours,
DW Bethel

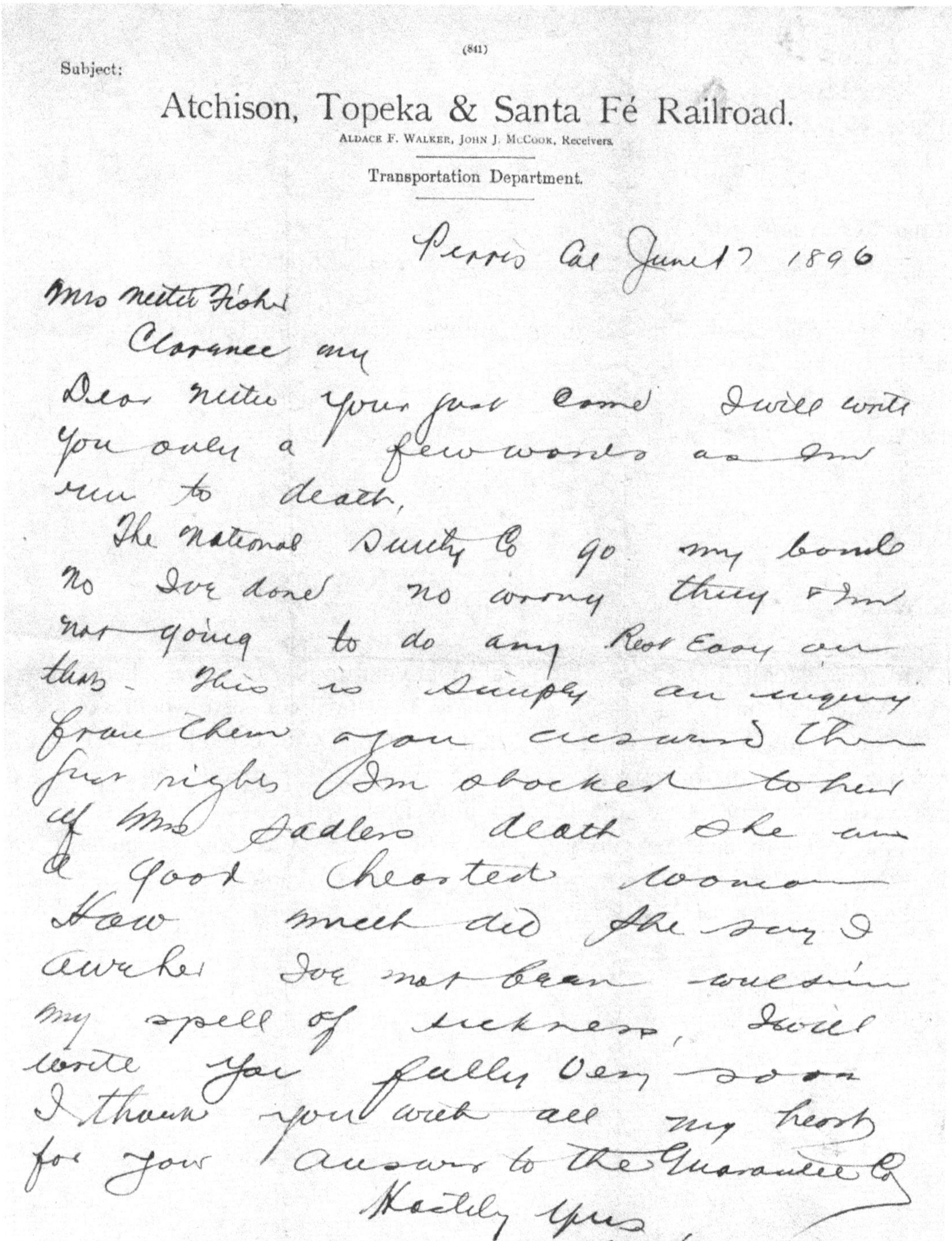

Subject:

(841)

Atchison, Topeka & Santa Fé Railroad.
ALDACE F. WALKER, JOHN J. McCOOK, Receivers.

Transportation Department.

Perris Cal June 17 1896

Mrs Nettie Fish,

Clarence my Dear Nettie your just come I will write you only a few words as Im run to death.

The National Surety Co go my bond no Ive done no wrong they + Im not going to do any Rest Easy on this — This is simply an inquiry from them — you assured them fur rights — Im shocked to hear of Mrs Sadlers death she was a good hearted woman — How much did She say I owe her Ive not been well in my spell of sickness, I will write you fully very soon I thank you with all my heart for your answer to the Guarantee Co

Hastily yours
Willis

Letter #12, June 17, 1896, probably from Rincon, New Mexico.
Again, the location of Perris is likely erroneous. The postmark on the envelope is unreadable, but the location ends with a Q, probably designating Albuquerque, making it likely that he was working for the A.T.S.F. at Rincon, New Mexico at this time.

Envelope of the Atchison, Topeka, & Santa Fe Railroad
Addressed to:
Mrs. Nettie Fisher
Clarence, New York,
Erie Co.

Postmark: illegible
Destination postmark Clarence, NY, June 20, 1896

Memorandum stationery of the Atchison, Topeka, & Santa Fe Railroad
Transportation Department

Perris, Cal., June 17, 1896

Mrs. Nettie Fisher
Clarence, NY

Dear Nettie:

Yours just came. I will write you only few words as I'm run to death.

The National Surety Co. go my bond. No I've done no wrong thing & I'm not going to do any. Rest easy on that. This is simply an inquiry from them and you answered them just right. I'm shocked to hear of Mrs. Sadler's death. She was a good hearted woman. How much did she say I owe her? I've not been well since my spell of sickness. I will write you fully very soon. I thank you with all my heart for your answer to the Guarantee Co.

Hastily yours,
Willis

AMERICAN EXPRESS COMPANY,

Kenner La   State of May 16   1897

Mrs Nettie Fisher
    Clarence Mo,

My Own Dear Nettie Yours of 9th Came to hand yesterday I will write you now and you will get it Tuesday Eve I think Your letter found me quite well & still at work though I guess I will loose out because they want bond and "The National Surety Co" will hardly grant it — I went to see them in Kans City but is fraid they wont grant it. This looks pretty hard when a man has Always handled all the money honestly Ever entrusted to him. I never in my life misapplied a cent & to be bobbed about this way hurts. At Perris I was making my $100.00 to 110.00 a month. & that went up on this account Then I went over in New Mex & was getting $70.00 there & for the same reason lost that after 3 or 4 months service Rail Road Co said they never had a better man in their service but could not use unless I could give bond with the National Surety Co. Lost they come here expecting to secure a place where no bond would be required or get to give in another Co, but I find I'm handicapped & disappointed. Goodness what a trial it is - I have no money. Every cent I got I put into the California property. Luckily I've got that safely & will paid for. If I have to tramp I will do it but have the property paid out.

I shall be very glad indeed to get a letter from Durwood. I will try to answer it promptly. If he is growing up thin he is but following me. I was very thin. Could nearly see through me until I was 33 or 34 then I began & grew fleshy all at once. I now weigh 210 that is 10 pounds more than I weighed when you left our home. What feelings come over me that Dec 31st when I come home & found you gone your things too & all without a single word of warning. I've tried to put a charitable construction on your conduct in that trouble, but it will still

AMERICAN EXPRESS COMPANY,

(333 Jan., 1896.)

_____ State of _____ 18

hong to me like an ugly night mare. I've always thought that you with your Christian religion might have waited until I come home or in case you could not do that have sent for me where we could have talked the matter over in our own home without being molested & threatened with the battering ram. I can never forget the long weary tramp nor the months that passed with so little sleep, of the desperation that finally seized me & finally such actions as I was driven to through desperation. Death however ended that unhappy act. It is well that it did. Hence I am now where I was when we separated except that I've seen nearly all the U.S. & Mexico.

I thank you sincerely for the promise that you will see me. I believe if you & I could see each other & talk it all over that you could scarcely refrain from loving me, if that be desirable at all

Of course in buying the ranch in California I had one thought above all Else. namely, to secure a place for Durwood that he might have a home for himself some time. I thought too that if you should change your mind that you too might live to come then. You could at least if you out lived me for I have Carried $5000.00 Insurance in favor of Durwood. Of Course when I once more get Settled &steady work. I shall want Durwood to Come &stay with me all he can, I shall try to make it so pleasant for him that he will always want to spend what time he can spare away from you with me Im sorry you are going out to clean house, I dont think you ever would have done this had you not left me as you did Surely no man living could have thought more of you or provided for you more ungrudgingly than I did - I done all I Could. more I was not unkind to you. Hence I have some source of Consolation left me

AMERICAN EXPRESS COMPANY,

State of _____ 18__

No I never have seen Carpenter neither do I want to. If I ever do I am going to kill him in cold blood right where I meet him Ever since you left me on his account I have carried a large revolver & always loaded purposely to kill him Once I started to Buffalo when you told me he was prowling on William St with the full determination of killing him I got as far as Marietta Ohio & told Dillon Pickering where & what I was going for He persuaded me to not go further that day, He kept me visiting him there until my leave of absence had expired & I had to go back to my work but do you think I will not get her left some time? I took him in my house & kept him & then to have him step between the object & I loved better than life Had it not been for his act you never would have gone away

I will not try to think of you except as you used to look. I am the same look just the same only I am smooth faced always now, wear no beard of any kind. I looked at & repeatedly kissed your photo at Jacobs Sibly owife felt so sorry for me that they gave me your photo, I had none you know & you always refused to send me one. The one I had of Durward got burned in the Hotel Fire in Perris when I lost Every thing I had in the way of mementos & keepsakes. So I got none of him.

I think mrs Lapp & Long took a peculiar time of year to go to Calif surely they didnt want to see Calif at her best. Are they back yet?

No I could not come now to see you if you wanted me to. Yesterday we had pay day. I drew $75.50 when I paid all I owed I had 40¢ left I got 30¢ worth of postage stamps & have 10¢ left If I get to work this month out there I will have a little money for

AMERICAN EXPRESS COMPANY,

(333 Jan., 1896.)

_____ State of _____ 18___

I owe nothing now & have my board all paid up to yesterday. We are having plenty of vegetables of all kinds tomatoes peaches berries etc etc. Cabbages too but I dont love cabbage any more now than I formerly did when you cooked for me.

If I do well I will hold you to your promise to see me prior to cold weather. Surely I will get a place I can keep some time. Who is living on your old place? It seems Mrs Whipple didnt remember you in her will as she said she would. Instead of living with me in your own house you chose to live with her as her servant & the letter that her brother had the impudence to write to me demanding money for you. Surely I wish the whole gang in hell — I dont think I ever felt so bitter over my fate as I do tonight. I see other men who are no smarter than I going to Church with their wives on their arms where am I— Dropped out for a weak little pusillanimous pulmonic fool, (I refer to Confuter.)

Had a good long letter from Nick Yesterday If its in my pocket I'll send it with this? When will Kate be back? What wages does she get teaching? Does Durwood go to school to Miss Rutterbough? How tall is Durwood? What room is your bed room? Does he like me or does he not? The first time I ever saw you was in that house the next time at the front gate. I never can forget the impression you made on me, I knew then you would be in some way in my life I loved you at first sight madly & have always from that minute Since. Kiss Durwood for me tell him how I want to see him & be with him & have him with me.

Lovingly yours Always
Willis

Letter #16, May 16, 1897, from Kenner, Louisiana.

Envelope of the Illinois Central Railroad Company
Postmark May 16, 1897
Addressed to Mrs. Nettie Fisher, Clarence, Erie Co., New York

Stationery of the American Express Company
Kenner, La., May 16, 1897

Mrs. Nettie Fisher
Clarence, NY

My own Dear Nettie:

Yours of 9th came to hand yesterday. I will write you now and you will get it Tuesday Eve I think. Your letter found me quite well & still at work though I guess I will loose out because they want bond and "The National Surety Co." will hardly grant it. I went to see them in Kansas City but fraid they won't grant it. This looks pretty hard when a man has always handled all the money honestly ever entrusted to him. I never in my life misapplied a cent & to be bobbed about this way hurts. At Perris I was making my $100 to $110 a month & that went up on this account. Then I went over in New Mex. & was getting $70 there & for the same reason lost that after 3 or 4 months service. Rail Road Co. said they never had a better man in their service but could not use unless I could give bond with The National Surety Co. Lost that. Came here expecting to secure a place where no bond would be required or get to give in another Co. but I find I'm handicapped & disappointed. Goodness what a trial it is — I have no money. Every cent I got I put into the California property. Luckily I've got that safely & well paid for. If I have to tramp I will do it but have the property paid out.

I shall be very glad indeed to get a letter from Durward. I will try to answer it promptly. If he is growing up thin he is but following me. I was very thin. Could nearly see through me until I was 23 or 24 then I begun & grew fleshy all at once. I now weigh 210 that is 10 pounds more than I weighed when you left our home. What feelings came over me that Dec. 31st when I came home & found you gone your things too & all without a single word of warning. I've tried to put a charitable construction on your conduct in that trouble but it will still hang to me like an ugly night mare. I've always thought that you with your Christian religion might have waited until I came home or in case you could not do that have sent for me where we could have talked the matter over in our own home without being molested & threatened with the battering ram. I can never forget the long weary tramp nor the months that passed with so little sleep, of the desperation that finally seized me & finally such actions as I was driven to through desperation. Death however ended that unhappy act. It is well that it did. Hence I am now where I was when we separated except that I've seen nearly all the U.S. & Mexico.

I thank you sincerely for the promise that you will see me. I believe if you & I could see each other & talk it all over that you could scarcely refrain from loving me if that be desirable at all. Of course in buying the ranch in California I had one thought above all else. Namely, to secure a place for Durward that he might have a home for himself some time. I thought too that if you should change your mind that you too might like to come there. You could at least if you out lived me for I have carried $5,000 insurance in favor of Durward. Of course when I once more get settled & steady work I shall want Durward to come & stay with me all he can. I shall try to make it so pleasant for him that he will always want to spend what time he can spare away from you with me. I'm sorry you are going out to clean house. I don't think you ever would have done this had you not left me as you did. Surely no man living could have thought more of you or provided for you more ungrudgingly than I did. I done all I could. More I was not unkind to you. Hence I have some source of consolation left me.

No I never have seen Carpenter neither do I want to. If I ever do I am going to kill him in cold blood right where I meet him. Ever since you left me on his account I have carried a large revolver & always loaded purposely to kill him. Once I started to Buffalo when you told me he was practicing on William St. with the full determination of killing him. I got as far as Marietta, Ohio & told Dillon Pickering where & what I was going for. He persuaded me to not go further that day. He kept me visiting him there until my leave of absence had expired & I had to go back to my work but do you think I will not get his life some time? I took him in my house & kept him & then to have him step between the object & I, I loved better than life. Had it not been for his acct. you never would have gone away.

I will not try to think of you except as you used to look. I am the same look just the same only I am smooth faced always now. Wear no beard of any kind. I looked at & repeatedly kissed your photo at Seib's. Seib & wife felt so sorry for me that they gave me your photo. I had none you know & you always refused to send me one. The one I had of Durward got burned in the Hotel Fire in Perris where I lost every thing I had in the way of mementoes & keepsakes, so I've got none of him.

I think Mrs. Lapp & Long took a peculiar time of year to go to Calif. Surely they didn't want to see Calif. at her best. Are they back yet?

No I could not come now to see you if you wanted me to. Yesterday we had pay day. I drew $25.50 when I paid all I owed I had 40 (cents) left. I got 30 (cents) worth of postage stamps & have 10 (cents) left. If I get to work this month out then I will have a little money for I owe nothing now & have my board all paid up to yesterday. We are having plenty of vegetables of all kinds, tomatoes, peaches, berries, etc. etc. Cabbage too but I don't love cabbage any more now than I formerly did when you cooked for me.

If I do well I will hold you to your promise to see me prior to cold weather. Surely I will get a place I can keep some time. Who is living on your old place? It seems Mrs. Whipple didn't remember you in her will as she said she would. Instead of living with me in your own house you chose to live with her as her servant & the letter that her brother had the impudence to write to me demanding money for you. Surely I wish the whole gang in hell. I don't think I ever felt so bitter over my fate as I do tonight. I see other men who are no smarter than I going to church with their wives on their arms. Where am I — dropped out for a weak little pusillanimous pulmonic fool. (I refer to Carpenter).

Had a good long letter from Seib yesterday. If it's in my pocket I'll send it with this? When will Kate be back? What wages does she get teaching? Does Durward go to school to Miss Rittersbaugh? How tall is Durward? What room is your bed room? Does he like me or does he not? The first time I ever saw you was in that house. The next time at the front gate. I never can forget the impression you made on me. I knew then you would be in some way in my life. I loved you at first sight madly & have always from that minute since. Kiss Durward for me. Tell him how I want to see him & be with him & have him with me.

Lovingly yours always,
Willis

FORM 200.
Northern Pacific Railway Company.

Ulen Minn Sept 8" 1897

Mrs Nettie Fisher
Clarence NY

Dear Nettie, Seems Stranger you dont write & answer my letters. I wrote you before I left Fosston & asked you to tell me some matters about Durward so far not a word from you. If you dont want to write might let him write at least If you dont care to write to me now he surely can?

I asked you to write me at Stephen Minn as I was to go there from Fosston but not a word.

I suppose Durward is in school again? How is he getting along? After Vacation I wrote you some time ago & asked you for Frank Carpenters address I hope you will do me the favor to send it to me

Did Kate secure an appointment

Northern Pacific Railway Company.

FORM 200.

in the Buffalo Schools? How does she look since she has grown up? I suppose Rent is quite a good looking girl. She was a prepossessing looking little girl —

I don't know a thing to write you now. Had hoped to have seen you before this but such a torn down letter as you wrote me makes me feel very differently. hence I don't think I shall see you. I think you will regret writing me such a letter at some time. no sense in writing any such a letter. I never gave you any occasion to write one like that — and now you will know I never was ill or cross to you so you accuse me. Has Thompson gone home? Love to Durward

Sincerely yours
D. W. Beebe

Letter # 27, September 22, 1897, from Ulen, Minnesota.
This was Willis's final letter to Nettie. He was going by the alias Joseph Patterson Steele at this time.

Envelope of the Northern Pacific Railway Company, Ry. B.
Postmark: illegible
Addressed to Mrs. Nettie Fisher, Clarence, Erie Co., New York

Stationery of the Northern Pacific Railway Company
Ulen, Minn., Sept. 22, 1897

Mrs. Nettie Fisher
Clarence, NY

Dear Nettie — Seems strange you don't write & answer my letter. I wrote you before I left Fosston & asked you to tell me some matters about Durward. So far not a word from you. If you don't want to write might let him write at least. If you don't care to write me now he surely can?

I asked you to write me at Stephen Minn. as I was to go there from Fosston but not a word.

I suppose Durward is in school again? How is he getting along? After vacation.

I wrote you some time ago & asked for Frank Carpenter's address. I hope you will do me the favor to send it to me.

Did Kate secure an appointment in the Buffalo schools? How does she look since she has grown up? I suppose Bert is quite a good looking girl. She was a prepossessing looking little girl.

I don't know a thing to write you now. Had hoped to have seen you before this but such a torn down letter as you wrote me makes me feel very differently hence I don't think I shall see you. I think you will regret writing me such a letter at some time. No sense in writing any such a letter. I never gave you any occasion to write one like that — and more you will know I never was ill & cross to you as you accuse me. Has Thompson gone home? Love to Durward

Sincerely yours,
D.W. Bethel

About the Author

A college professor for twenty-four years, Charles Caldemeyer was trained in the visual arts. His paintings, which have been exhibited widely across the country, employ implied narratives to explore the interactions of cultural and personal histories. He has also published two essays about the artistic process.

An avid and lifelong reader of history, Caldemeyer has pursued the genealogical research of some of the more interesting characters in his family tree since his retirement from academic life. His goal is to develop accounts of common persons, the folks unnoticed by historians, whose stories nevertheless illuminate their eras.

Caldemeyer lives in northern Michigan on the remains of an old family farm. When he is not researching or writing, he spends his time painting, woodworking, swimming, kayaking, and snowshoeing on frozen lakes. *The Railroad Skunk* is his first book.

www.ingramcontent.com/pod-product-compliance
Lightning Source LLC
Chambersburg PA
CBHW081342070526
44578CB00005B/698